Contributions to Economics

The series *Contributions to Economics* provides an outlet for innovative research in all areas of economics. Books published in the series are primarily monographs and multiple author works that present new research results on a clearly defined topic, but contributed volumes and conference proceedings are also considered. All books are published in print and ebook and disseminated and promoted globally. The series and the volumes published in it are indexed by Scopus and ISI (selected volumes).

Nezameddin Faghih • Ali Hussein Samadi
Editors

Institutional Inertia

Theory and Evidence

Springer

Editors
Nezameddin Faghih
UNESCO Chair Professor Emeritus
Cambridge, MA, USA

Ali Hussein Samadi
Department of Economics
Shiraz University
Shiraz, Iran

ISSN 1431-1933 ISSN 2197-7178 (electronic)
Contributions to Economics
ISBN 978-3-031-51174-5 ISBN 978-3-031-51175-2 (eBook)
https://doi.org/10.1007/978-3-031-51175-2

This Springer imprint is published by the registered company Springer Nature Switzerland AG
The registered company address is: Gewerbestrasse 11, 6330 Cham, Switzerland

This book is dedicated to Hakim Abul-Qasem Ferdowsi Tusi (940–1019/1025), Jalalaldin Maulawi Rumi (1207–1273), Abdurahman Ibn Khaldun (1332–1406), and Douglass Cecil North (1920–2015) for their great historical insights, understanding, and teachings of the concepts of mental inertia, cognitive inertia, institutions, institutional change, and institutional inertia.

Acknowledgments

The editors would like to express their sincere gratitude to Lorraine Klimowich for her great efforts in the publication process of this book. They would also like to wholeheartedly thank all chapter authors and reviewers who have devoted their time, effort, and generosity as without their generous support completing this volume would not have been possible: Omid Adibi, Saeideh Alizadeh, Vahid Ashrafi, Adeleke Oladapo Banwo, Mohammad Bagher Beheshti, Ali Dini-Torkamaani, Saleh Ghavidel-Doostkouei, Narges Haji-Molla Darvish, Zahra Karimi, Bahman Khodapanah, Ehsan Moradi, Hossein Mousavi, Mostafa Nasr-Isfahani, Mohammad Niknami, Hamid Padash, Kameliia Petrova, Saeed Rasekhi, Fatemeh Rezazadeh, Ayhab F. Saad.

Contents

Contributors

Sajjad Afroozeh Department of Economics, Shiraz University, Shiraz, Iran

Masoumeh Alipourian Department of Economics, Shiraz University, Shiraz, Iran

Ares Albirru Amsal Faculty of Economics and Business, Universitas Andalas, West Sumatra, Indonesia

Dian Yuni Anggraini Faculty of Economics and Business, Universitas Andalas, West Sumatra, Indonesia

Adeleke Oladapo Banwo Doctoral Supervision, KMU Akademie & Management AG, Linz, Austria

Faculty of Management Studies, Islamic University In Uganda, Mbale, Uganda

Saleh Ghavidel Doostkouei Department of Economics, Firuzkuh Branch, Islamic Azad University, Firuzkuh, Iran

Nezameddin Faghih UNESCO Chair Professor Emeritus, Cambridge, MA, USA

Donard Games Faculty of Economics and Business, Universitas Andalas, West Sumatra, Indonesia

Rayna Kartika Faculty of Economics and Business, Universitas Andalas, West Sumatra, Indonesia

Zahra Kheiridoust Alzahra University, Tehran, Iran

Mahdi Jamshidi Khosh Independent Scholar, Tehran, Iran

Mahmood Mahmoodzadeh Department of Economics, Firuzkuh Branch, Islamic Azad University, Firuzkuh, Iran

Mir Hossein Mousavi Department of Economics, Faculty of Social Sciences and Economics, Alzahra University, Tehran, Iran

Josiah Chukwuma Ngonadi School of Finance and Economics, Jiangsu University, Zhenjiang, China

Henry Omache School of Business, Uganda Christian University, Mukono, Uganda

Mojtaba Panahi Department of Economics, Shiraz University, Shiraz, Iran

Kameliia Petrova Department of Economics and Finance, SUNY Plattsburgh, Plattsburgh, NY, USA

Alireza Raanaei Department of Economics, Shiraz University, Shiraz, Iran

Saeed Rasekhi University of Mazandaran, Babolsar, Iran

Fatemeh Rezazadeh Faculty of Management and Accounting, Allameh Tabataba'i University, Tehran, Iran

Mina Rezazadeh Industrial Engineering, Faculty of Engineering, Islamic Azad University Shiraz Branch, Shiraz, Iran

Sima Rezazadeh Faculty of Management and Accounting, Islamic Azad University Shiraz Branch, Shiraz, Iran

Agnitra RoyChoudhury Department of Economics, Auburn University at Montgomery, Montgomery, AL, USA

Ali Hussein Samadi Department of Economics, Shiraz University, Shiraz, Iran

Dessy Kurnia Sari Faculty of Economics and Business, Universitas Andalas, West Sumatra, Indonesia

Ali Reza Seifi Independent Scholar, Tehran, Iran

An Introduction to Institutional Inertia-Theory and Evidence

Nezameddin Faghih and Ali Hussein Samadi

In this city of phenomena, He is the prince;
in the realms He is the Ruler.

If He breaks His own instrument,
He mends that which has become broken.

Beyond change are the king's everlasting:
their spirits are circling with the Cupbearer perpetually

Every law that He has cancelled—
He has taken away grass and brought roses in exchange

Night cancels the business of day:
behold an inertia (inanimateness) that enlightens the intellect!

Again, night is cancelled by the light of day,
so that the inertia is consumed by that fire-kindling one.

Although that sleep and rest are darkness,
is not the Water of Life within the darkness?

Did not minds become refreshed in that darkness?
Did not a pause become the source of the voice?

Know that even so are all the changing conditions of the world—
famine and drought and peace and war—from probation

N. Faghih (✉)
UNESCO Chair Professor Emeritus, Cambridge, MA, USA

A. H. Samadi
Department of Economics, Shiraz, Iran
e-mail: asamadi@rose.shirazu.ac.ir

N. Faghih, A. H. Samadi (eds.), *Institutional Inertia*, Contributions to Economics,
https://doi.org/10.1007/978-3-031-51175-2_1

After that scattering I came to myself again
and saw that Sinai and Moses were unchanged,

The justice is the same justice, and the learning is the same learning too;
but those generations and peoples have been changed

The country is preserved from that
by the king's having force and authority to inflict punishment

It is ever changing, like a picture:
the spirit beholds in clairvoyance a world anew and anew

He continually turns you from one state to another,
manifesting opposite by means of opposite in the change

All changes have arisen from the hours:
he that is freed from the hours is freed from change

In this world of search and seeking
every set of people have been tied in the stable peculiar to them,

And over each stable a trainer has been appointed;
save by permission no recalcitrant comes.

If, from vain desire, he should break away from the stable
and intrude into the stable of others,
At once the nimble and goodly stablemen
seize the corner of his halter and drag.

O cunning one, if you behold not your keepers,
behold your choice involuntary.

He became hard rock and changed not from that disposition;
he became sand from which no produce grows

You take children to school by force,
because they are blind to the benefits;

When he becomes aware, he runs to school:
his soul expands at going.

A child goes to school in sore distress
because he has seen nothing of the wages for his work;

When he puts in his purse a single coin (dang)earned by his handiwork,
then he goes without sleep at night, like the thief.

Endeavour that the wages for obedience may arrive:
then you will envy the obedient

The water in this channel has been changed many times:
the reflection of the moon and of the stars remains unaltered.
The pleasure of changing his chest stupefies him anew:
he does not perceive that he is inside the chest

The form of want leads to earn;
the form of strength of arm leads to seize by force

(*Rumi. 1207–1273*i, P.88, 243; ii, P. 93, 108; iii, P. 131, 163; iv, P. 236, 150, 230; vi, 117, 152, 197).

In the literature of economic growth and development, this question has always been raised that "why are some countries poorer (or richer) than other countries?". Although many people have answered this question throughout history, it is still an active field of research.

In this regard and as a criterion for evaluating the cause of poverty and wealth of nations, sustainable growth is always taken into consideration. Sustainable growth requires inclusive growth, and inclusive growth requires economic growth. So economic growth should lead to inclusive growth, and inclusive growth should lead to sustainable growth.

Inclusive growth is a type of economic growth that leads to an increase in the standard of living of a wide range of people. In this growth, all the important factors of human well-being are taken into consideration and the benefits of economic growth are intended to be distributed among a wide range of people and among all sectors. Therefore, high economic growth (increasing the size of the cake) does not necessarily mean inclusive growth (distribution of this cake and the benefits resulting from its enlargement in a fair way among all sections of the society). So economic growth only deals with the size of the cake, but inclusive growth with the size and how the cake is divided among a wide range of people. Inclusive growth is related to economic (such as reducing poverty and inequality, etc.) and social (such as broad participation of people in the growth process, etc.) consequences of economic growth. Inclusive growth is a long-term perspective and requires inclusive political and economic institutions (Acemoglu et al., 2003; Acemoglu & Robinson, 2012; OECD, 2016; Cerra et al., 2022). Acemoglu and Robinson (2012) in *Why nations fail: the origin of power, prosperity and poverty* show that man-made political and economic institutions are vital in this regard.

According to Acemoglu et al. (2005), inclusive institutions refer to those rules of the game in society that provide the possibility of free activity for all citizens. These institutions also provide motivation and permission to enter into productive activities for all capable and interested people. But exploitative institutions are institutions that take away this possibility from people by creating obstacles (legal and illegal) and provide it for few and special people. These rules of the game (inclusive and exploitative institutions) can be in the field of politics and economics.

The problem of economic growth itself can be divided into three sub-problems of its causes, forms and effects. The causes of economic growth are of two categories:

1. *Proximate causes*, such as the accumulation of physical and human capital, endogenous technical change, etc.
2. *Ultimate causes*, such as luck, geography, culture, social capital, and generally political, legal, social, cultural, and economic institutions- including property

rights, market, etc. (Heitger, 2004, p. 381; Acemoglu et al., 2005; Acemoglu, 2006, pp. 83–94; and Rodrik et al., 2004, pp. 131–136).

It is clear from the above that economic growth, the wealth, and poverty of nations are influenced by how political and economic institutions are formed. This issue has been answered in detail in the book *Why Nations Fail* (Acemoglu & Robinson, 2012). Nonetheless, the more important issue is to deal with the cause of change or stability of institutions.

Many articles and books have been written in the field of institutions and institutional changes. There are many *theories* and *forms* for institutional changes. Many aspects and concepts of institutions, institutional change, and *theories of institutional change*, are discussed in North (1989, 1990, 1991), Samadi and Alipourian (2021), and Faghih and Samadi (2021). But in general, there are four important *forms of institutional change* (Frericks, 2017): *displacement, layering, drift*, and *conversion*. The first is to remove the existing rules and replace them with new rules; the second is to introduce new rules alongside the existing rules; the third one refers to the effect of existing rules along with changing their environment, and the last one refers to changing existing rules through changing the shape of existing institutions. Layering is possible and appropriate when the institutional challengers do not have the ability to change the basic rules.

The reason for the persistence and stability of institutions is another issue that Acemoglu and Robinson (2012) and some other scholars have paid attention to. However, less attention has been paid to this issue and in particular to the discussion of institutional inertia. The main purpose of this edited book has been to fill such a gap. In this book, institutional inertia is introduced as the main and fundamental cause of countries becoming poorer or richer.

Institutions (economic, socio-cultural, political and legal) and institutional development appear to be a shared journey of humanity throughout history; the conceptual antecedents go back to Plato, Adam Smith, Immanuel Kant and Friedrich Hegel. Nevertheless, in parallel to Douglass North's description of the concept of institution, especially in contemporary era of globalization, dynamics of institutional change are analogous to the dynamics of change in rules of the games, consisting of changes in formal written rules as well as changes in typically unwritten codes of conduct that underlie and supplement changes in formal rules, i.e., changes in the humanly devised constraints that shape dynamics of human interaction. Nevertheless, there is a resistance to any change and a tendency to do nothing or to remain unchanged; that is *inertia*, i.e., a property by which everything continues in its existing state of rest or uniform motion in a straight-line path, unless that state is changed by an external force; "the power required to overcome friction and the inertia of the moving parts". Thus, Inertia refers **to resistance to change**—in particular, resistance to changes in motion. Inertia may manifest in physical objects or in the minds of people. We learn the principle of inertia early on in life. We all know that it takes a force to get something moving, to change its direction, or to stop it.

Inertia comes from the Latin word, *iners*, meaning inert, idle, and sluggish. In general, inertia is the power of resisting, and the principle of inertia is one of the fundamental principles that are used to describe the motion and dynamicity, and how they are affected by the applied forces on them. In fact, inertia is the resistance to any change or speed and direction of change. An aspect of this property is the tendency to keep moving in a straight-line path at a constant speed, when no force or forces act upon them. Consequently, in common usage, the term "inertia" may refer to an amount of resistance to change in speed, direction or for simpler terms, resistance to a change in motion dynamicity.

Inertia is a concept borrowed from physics, engineering, and applied mathematics. According to Newton's first law, when an object resists a change in speed or direction, it is said that there is inertia. In other words, inertia refers to the tendency of an object to maintain its previous state. In physical systems this is a default. Of course, inertia does not mean *statis* or *no-change* (Graneau & Graneau, 2006). This term has a wider meaning in economic and social systems. Because path dependency in physical objects does not remain after changing; while this is an inherent feature of complex economic and social systems (Kelly & Amburgey, 1991).

In addition to physics, which considers the concept of inertia about the body's tendency to maintain its previous state of rest or motion (linear and angular) and the body's resistance to change in speed or direction, this concept is also considered in many other fields of science, engineering, economics, management, psychology, and social sciences. Some examples are: thermal inertia, i.e., resistance to temperature change; Sylvester's inertia law which is a theorem in algebra of matrices; climate inertia, i.e., the Earth system's slowness to changes in greenhouse gas levels; ecological inertia, i.e., a living system's ability to resist external changes; cognitive inertia, i.e., an individual's beliefs resistance to change; psychological inertia, i.e., lack of motivation to act; psychical inertia, i.e., psyche's resistance to change and development; sleep inertia, i.e., a temporary resistance in the form of decline and disorientation in mood and performance after waking up; social inertia, i.e., psychological—sociological resistance to change; corporate inertia, i.e., unwillingness to consider corporate change and dynamics; organizational inertia, i.e., external and internal resistance to change and organizational adaptation; cultural inertia, i.e., the resistance to cultural change, where, within the framework of cultural inertia, the dominant group is stable and resists cultural change despite the tendency of subordinate groups to cultural changes; political inertia, i.e., the resistance of powerful groups with some special interests in the status quo to change, which can occur at the national or international level; institutional inertia, i.e., the tendency of institutions to resist changes (Potter et al., 2021; Browne, 2013; Rizcallah, 2015; Khurmi & Gupta, 2005; Forrester, 1971; Denzau & North, 1994; Graneau & Graneau, 2006; Gallagher & Crisafi, 2009; Johnson-Laird, 2004; Jones et al., 2011; Wrenn, 2006; Craik, 1967; Rosenbaum, 2022; Loasby, 2001; Lewis, 2005; Price, 1977; Ostrowski, 1959; Tassi & Muzet, 2000; Tebaldi & Friedlingstein, 2013; Boyle & Fairchild, 1997; Stralberg et al., 2020; Hodgkinson, 1997; Mattila, 2003; Walters, 2019; Gao et al., 2020; Parkin, 1981; Stewart, 1963; Guhl, 1968; Ramasco & Morris, 2006; Brook, 2013; Kon, 1989; Abdi et al., 2022; Yamoah et al., 2022; Zárate et al., 2012; Zantvoort,

2017; Aveyard, 2016; CDC – NIOSH, 2023; UIA, 2023; Britannica, 2023; Rosenbaum, 2022).

Institutional inertia refers to the inability of institutions to provide a timely response to the created problems; tendency of institutions to resist changes; stickiness of institutions or how they resist changes; or inability of institutions to changes in national and international environments. There are several reasons that lead to institutional inertia. Some of these reasons are: sunk costs, uncertainty, political conflicts, political cleavages, path dependence (technical, institutional, discursive and cognitive), departure of path, power, legitimacy, the existence of powerful distributional coalitions, etc. These reasons are explained in detail in the third chapter of this book.

However, for enabling rules, the actors' necessary perceptions of why and for what purpose a set of rules exist and are used can be best understood using the concept of a mental model. Mental states are considered as a cognitive structure that forms the basis of reasoning and decision making. A mental model is a description of the thought process and the internal representation of the external world, which includes selected concepts and relationships between them to represent the real world, cognition, reasoning, decision-making, shaping behavior and setting (algorithmic) approaches to solving problems and performing tasks. Nevertheless, in general, mental models are subjective representations of objective realities and mental (subjective) representations of social (subjective) realities (power structures, institutions, etc.), and the latter models are the product of social communication, interaction, and agreement. (Forrester, 1971; Denzau & North, 1994; Gallagher & Crisafi, 2009; Johnson-Laird, 2004; Jones et al., 2011; Wrenn, 2006; Craik, 1967; UIA, 2023; Britannica, 2023; Rosenbaum, 2022).

The existence of institutional inertia (both positive and negative aspects) can have negative and positive effects in many fields. Some of these areas are: trade, energy transition, natural resource management, cheap housing market design, climate change, control of corruption, financial development, financial crises, governance, healthcare policy, industrial development, innovation policies, investment, legislation, macroeconomic policies, poverty alleviation, savings, social support, technology adaption, control of corruption, etc.

The institutional system of any country determines whether the country's institutional structure is producer-friendly or rent-seeker friendly. The structure of rent-seeker friendly (producer-friendly), leads to the creation of predatory (inclusive) institutions. In this structure, a distributive (inclusive) Coalitions is formed and can lead to the creation of institutional inertia with a negative (positive) aspect. Such a factor will be a big obstacle on the way of economic growth and therefore inclusive growth, and sustainable growth. It is very important to pay attention to institutions, institutional changes and institutional inertia in this aspect.

The purpose of this contributed volume is to explore the meaning of inertia, and institutional inertia, identifying the types, causes and effects of institutional inertia, through a wealth of insights by outstanding experts in the field of institutions and institutional Inertia. This book seeks to bridge an important research gap by questioning the types of institutional inertia that improve economic performance and impact on the effectiveness of the state, and to study the role of institutional inertia in the dynamics of institutional change and capture its development over time and path dependence, to trace and understand the different evolutionary paths of societies. Thus, this edited volume explores the concepts, types, causes, and effects of institutional inertia. Ways to overcome institutional inertia is another important issue that is not considered in this book and is left for future research.

The book is divided into five parts and contains fourteen chapters (including this introductory chapter).

Chapter "An Introduction to Institutional Inertia-Theory and Evidence" is an introduction to the book, to introduce the book and the main idea of this edited volume, that institutional inertia is an important and fundamental factor in explaining the cause of poverty and wealth of nations. However, this is a factor that has received less attention in the recent literature on institutional economics. Therefore, the introductory chapter states that the objectives of this book are to explore the meaning of inertia and to identify the types, causes, significance, and effects of institutional inertia. Thus, this book presents the concept of inertia from two positive and negative aspects and explains the concept and types of institutional inertia. Then the effects and causes of institutional inertia are also explained. It is also noted that this book appears to be the first such attempt on institutional inertia and differs from the existing literature in several ways: (i) unlike the existing literature, it has a comprehensive look at the definition of inertia, institutional inertia, types of institutional inertia, its roots and effects; (ii); it has a special look at the roots of cognitive inertia and introduces it as the main source of institutional inertia; (iii) it presents a comprehensive view of organizational inertia; (iv) it comprehensively discusses the impact of institutional inertia in the fields of trade, energy transition, climate change, innovation and entrepreneurship. Hence, this edited volume on *Institutional Inertia* embraces a wide spectrum of topics such as inertia (resistance and endurance); the origin of development, critical juncture, and institutional inertia; inertia in informal institutions (concepts, and effects); the roots of cognitive inertia (an introduction to institutional changes); cognitive inertia as a fundamental cause of institutional inertia; overview of institutional-organization inertia nexus; internal empowerment dynamics of organizational inertia management; trade and institutional inertia; transition to sustainable energy and institutional inertia; legitimacy, institutional inertia, and climate change; early entrepreneurship entry and institutional rigidities in emerging market economies (evidence from the Global Entrepreneurship Monitor); inertia, innovation failures, and learning from innovation failures (some insights from MSEs in an emerging market economy). Then the book proceeds in five parts consisting of thirteen chapters.

Part I presents concepts, types, causes, and effects of institutional inertia in Chapters "Inertia: Resistance and Endurance", "An Introduction to Institutional Inertia: Concepts, Types and Causes", "The Origin of Development, Critical Juncture, and Institutional Inertia", and "Inertia in Informal Institutions: Concepts and Effects"..

Chapter "Inertia: Resistance and Endurance" studies the concept of inertia, resistance and endurance. In fact, inertia is known as a fundamental and effective phenomenon in nature, humans and human (social) institutions. This phenomenon is woven into their warp and weft. In this chapter, inertia and its place in physical and non-physical structures is studied by examining the history of this concept and phenomenon as a mental model. There are two main viewpoints on inertia, i.e., Newton's point of view about inertia (as a virtual force and a resistance factor to changes in motion), and Mach and Graneau's point of view about inertia (as a real force and a preservative factor for the structure of bodies and universe). By reviewing the literature and taking this subject into contemplation, it is concluded that inertia consists of positive and negative aspects: the positive aspect works as a structure preservative and stabilizing force (Endurance Force), and the negative aspect works as a resistant force to structure change and dynamic state (Resistance Force). These two aspects of inertia have a fundamental and vital role in institutions' structure, dynamics, and preservation. Furthermore, topics such as angular momentum and moment of inertia, wide applications of inertia, the origin of inertia, inertia as a mental model, cognitive inertia, inertia in society, phylogenetic inertia and ecological pressure in institutional evolution, and entropic inertia in institutional evolution are also studied. Finally, the institutional renewal time function is introduced and proposed, and the result of the balance between inertia and overcoming it, that is, the evolution of structural preservation, is also considered, emphasizing future research on the application of institutional renewal time function to different institutions and economies, and especially comparative studies on economies at different levels of development for a deeper understanding of institutional inertia.

Chapter "An Introduction to Institutional Inertia: Concepts, Types and Causes" is an introduction to institutional inertia, concepts, types, and causes. Institutional resistance to change (or institutional inertia) is one of the important issues in institutional economics. In this chapter, the concept of inertia, types of inertia in human sciences and the causes of institutional inertia are explained. Also, types of inertia at the level of individuals, inertia at the level of social and political structures, and inertia at the level of knowledge development, concepts and ideas are explained. Due to the importance of institutional inertia and the fact that this type of inertia includes a large number of other types of inertia (such as organizational inertia, psychological inertia, and socio-political inertia), sixteen major and fundamental factors causing institutional inertia have also been introduced and explained. These factors are divided into four categories: economic, socio-political, historical, and psychological factors and are briefly explained. Another contribution of this chapter is providing evidence of the compatibility of institutional changes and institutional continuity.

Chapter "The Origin of Development, Critical Juncture, and Institutional Inertia" investigates the origin of development, critical juncture, and institutional inertia. Different from proposing many theories, it is difficult to identify the primary cause of nations' backwardness. Scientists seek the main cause of nations' backwardness. They seek a response to the questions of what causes nations' rise and fall and why some countries are underdeveloped while others are developed. Historical-critical juncture is a point in a nation's history where a development turnaround occurs. This chapter identifies three coordinates for the historical-critical juncture. First, the historical-critical juncture is not a multifactor but a single factor. In other words, the cause of development is not a set of correlated factors. This chapter cautions researchers not to consider development's cause as a set of factors. Second, many historical-critical junctures created by humans in nations' history are not historical determinism. For this reason, the historical quasi-experimental method rejects historical determinism hypotheses, such as geography and culture. Third, to find the cause of development, we must philosophize on the causation. Philosophizing the causes/effects brings us closer to the original cause. This chapter eliminates many causes, such as the difference between geography, culture, and institution, from the list of development causes and also argues that a critical juncture causes institutional inertia.

Chapter "Inertia in Informal Institutions: Concepts and Effects" investigates inertia in informal institutions, that is, the culture and values of a society. The limited cognitive capacity of the human mind and the complex relationships between different institutions are the reasons identified for the inertia of informal institutions. Humans' limited cognitive capacity forms beliefs, on the one hand, and human habits, on the other. Concerning institutions and organizations, beliefs and habits cause institutional inertia. The limited human cognitive capacity, accompanied by issues such as human interest and the "free rider problem", forms the inertia of informal institutions in another way. Furthermore, since we are not always faced with the inertia of informal institutions and sometimes sudden changes may occur in informal institutions, we address in this chapter the speed and direction of changes in informal institutions. Of course, culture should be dynamic and able to change along with technological and economic developments, protecting society's cultural endowment, identity, and special values to avoid cultural revolution and decay. Furthermore, this chapter addresses viewpoints that ignore inertia in informal institutions.

Part II considers cognitive inertia, in Chapters "The Roots of Cognitive Inertia: An Introduction to Institutional Changes" and "Cognitive Inertia as a Fundamental Cause of Institutional Inertia".

Chapter "The Roots of Cognitive Inertia: An Introduction to Institutional Changes" explores the roots of cognitive inertia in institutional changes by analyzing the concept of cognitive inertia, investigating the roots of its formation, and then examining the role of cognitive inertia in creating institutional changes. Cognitive inertia means the tendency to perpetuate beliefs after they are formed. The findings of this chapter show that cognitive biases play an effective role in the emergence of cognitive inertia. Among the most important identified biases that have a greater impact on the formation and escalation of cognitive inertia, this chapter identifies the following: *status-quo bias*, *confirmation bias*, *commitment escalation bias*, *belief bias*, *conservatism bias*, and *self-attribution bias*. Also, the results of this chapter show that one of the most important reasons for not forming institutional changes in a society can be attributed to the problem of cognitive inertia. Institutional economist, Douglas North argues that there is a close relationship between mental models, belief systems, and institutions. He believes that institutions are derived from belief systems. He also believes that the difference between rich and poor countries comes from the difference in their beliefs. Therefore, the lack of change in the belief system can lead to the lack of institutional changes.

Chapter "Cognitive Inertia as a Fundamental Cause of Institutional Inertia" considers cognitive inertia as a fundamental cause of institutional inertia. Various reasons have been stated to explain the formation of institutional inertia. The best factor to explain this phenomenon is the factor that plays a unique role in the formation and development of institutions. Based on this, cognitive factors can be considered the basic factors of creating institutions at the fundamental level. However, in the institutional economics literature, less attention has been paid to these factors. According to the relationship between the institutions and cognitive factors, it may be argued that cognitive inertia is the cause of the formation of institutional inertia. Therefore, cognitive factors can be seen as the most important formation of institutions. The main idea of this chapter is based on the synthesis of institutional economics and behavioral economics. Therefore, in this chapter, the question of how cognitive inertia leads to institutional inertia is studied.

Part III examines organizational inertia, in Chapters "Overview of Institutional–Organizational Inertia Nexus" and "Internal Empowerment Dynamics of Organizational Inertia Management".

Chapter "Overview of Institutional–Organizational Inertia Nexus" provides an overview of institutional–organizational inertia nexus. This chapter provides insights on institutional-organizational inertia nexus using multiple dimensions of age dynamics, organizational age dynamics, the sphere of Inertia (myopia-hubris perception), level of motivation, rate of reaction, organizational politics, action-inaction dynamics, board of directors, corporate governance framework and communication-information nexus. Dimensions of inertia are topical and multifaceted and the attendant problems are contextual due to their multidisciplinary nature. Using extant literature of studies conducted in different contexts, it is evident that the dimensions of institutional-organizational inertia would continue due to increasing rates of disruptive changes, human cognition, and contextual push and pull factors. Understanding the factors that cause resistance to change and acceptance of change requires a contextual insight into the perceptual benefits and threats it poses to organizations and society. Furthermore, the institutional-organizational nexus connotes the critical impact of institutions and environmental forces on organizational actors. Scholarly evidence suggests the need to appreciate the evolving nature of this structural domain, and the role of organizational actors and decision-makers. The findings and recommendations are premised on the need to adopt a holistic approach to investigate inertia.

Chapter "Internal Empowerment Dynamics of Organizational Inertia Manage ment" explores internal empowerment dynamics of organizational inertia management. Due to the rapid progress of science and technology and the complexity of the organizational environment, organizational survival and dynamism require continuous innovation and changes. The inability to foresee and predict the future or the failure to respond to internal and external demands for change and adaption is the primary characteristic of organizations of this century. Organizations must either be able to adapt to the rapid and sometimes sudden changes in their surroundings or disband. A proper understanding of organizational inertia can help managers to deal with the resistance to change in the organization appropriately and prevent the failure of the change process. Organizations facing environmental and internal changes need to create capabilities in organizational resources. Hence, resources empower an organization to react appropriately to issues and changes and take the organization out of inertia. Organizational inertia has been mainly investigated exclusively. However, despite the great importance and impact of identifying how the path of organizational resource empowerment is formed in line with organizational stress management, less attention has been paid to this category. Therefore, this chapter aims to explain and interpret how to manage organizational inertia through organizational resource empowerment. In this regard, the present study used a descriptive-analytical approach to review available literature using the library studies method. These research findings indicate that organizational inertia management and taking advantage of stopping or limiting inertia in organizational relationships requires a particular focus on the quadruple empowerment strategies, including manager, employee, organizational context, and employment relationships. Notably, desired realization of these strategies leads to determining the path of relationship formation in the positive, dynamic, cooperative, and humanistic integrated organizational space through a creative integrated organizational plan consistent with social identity.

Part IV deals with trade, energy and environments, in Chapters "Trade and Institutional Inertia", "The Transition to Sustainable Energy and Institutional Inertia", and "Legitimacy, Institutional Inertia, and Climate Change".

Chapter "Trade and Institutional Inertia" focuses on Trade and Institutional Inertia. The importance of institutions and their relationship with macroeconomic variables has attracted the attention of many researchers. The existing literature indicates a significant relationship between institutions and the economic environment, which is strengthened by trade openness. Also, the economic literature shows that the phenomenon of inertia is ambiguous and like a double-edged sword. It also seems that the existence of inertia, especially for developing countries, leads to suboptimal macroeconomic and foreign trade performance. By understanding these conditions, this chapter examines the relationship between foreign trade and institutional inertia. To answer this question while reviewing the literature, a simple theoretical model based on Gartner (1993) has been used. The findings show that there is a significant relationship between foreign trade and institutional inertia. Accordingly, although institutional change and foreign trade can move independently of each other, if they move together and this issue is addressed by policymakers, it can lead to a stronger relationship between institutions and economic performance.

Chapter "The Transition to Sustainable Energy and Institutional Inertia" studies the transition to sustainable energy and institutional inertia.

The increase in energy consumption, especially fossil fuels, and its environmental effects, has shown the necessity of transitioning to sustainable energy more than ever. However, in the transition to sustainable energy, laws, regulations, infrastructure, supply chains and interest groups with political power support the existing energy systems against any changes. As a result, the establishment of energy systems with clean and renewable technologies will be difficult. In this chapter, the approaches of new institutionalists about the transition to sustainable energy have been explained, especially, the literature of socio-technical transition (STT). In the STT approach, innovation is very important for sustainable change, so governance becomes important in empowering sustainable innovations and creating deep changes in energy systems. Also, in order to understand why different countries are transitioning to sustainable energy at different speeds and paths, the institutional inertia resulting from the resistance of existing energy systems and the role of path dependence in this regard have been analyzed. In the end, by providing evidence of the impact of path dependence on institutional inertia and the successful experience of some countries in the energy transition through the use of renewable energies, we have shown that although the transition is difficult, it is possible.

Chapter "Legitimacy, Institutional Inertia, and Climate Change" considers Legitimacy, Institutional Inertia, and Climate Change. The increasing impact of climate change on the environment has led to more efforts, programs and global actions to control these changes. In the meantime, some obstacles hinder the effectiveness of environmental measures and policies. Part of these obstacles is related to institutional inertia. In this chapter, the effects of legitimacy, as one of the mechanisms that create institutional inertia, on environmental performance have been investigated. The legitimacy of the state is an issue that has received less attention in climate change discussions. In this chapter, using a regression model, the effect of government legitimacy on environmental performance has been investigated based on the data of 171 countries. The results show that there is a direct relationship between state legitimacy and environmental performance. The results also showed that, if the state legitimacy is low or it is facing a crisis of legitimacy, this issue creates institutional inertia in the field of environmental policy. In turn, this issue will worsen the environmental performance.

Part V focuses on innovation and entrepreneurship, in Chapters "Early Entrepreneurship Entry and Institutional Rigidities in Emerging Market Economies: Evidence from the Global Entrepreneurship Monitor" and "Inertia, Innovation Failures, and Learning from Innovation Failures: Some Insights from MSEs in an Emerging Market Economy".

Chapter "Early Entrepreneurship Entry and Institutional Rigidities in Emerging Market Economies: Evidence from the Global Entrepreneurship Monitor" explores early entrepreneurship entry and institutional rigidities in emerging market economies with evidence from the Global Entrepreneurship Monitor (GEM). Variation in the effectiveness of local economic institutions is one of the most important reasons behind different levels of economic development in countries around the world. This chapter investigates how different types of institutional rigidities affect early entrepreneurship entry in emerging market economies. Emerging economies are characterized with low to moderate GDP per capita, high GDP growth rates, dynamic consumer markets, increased competition levels, underdeveloped financial markets, predominance of state-owned enterprises, policies for active reduction of trade barriers, and an increased integration into the global economy. The empirical analysis is based on a multilevel logit model and nascent entrepreneurship entry data from GEM for 20 emerging economies from 2000 to 2017. The institutional rigidity indices used in the study are from the Economic Freedom of the World data set. This chapter focuses on state ownership of assets, property rights protection, tariffs, capital and people movement control, credit market regulations, administrative requirements, bureaucracy costs, bribes and favoritism. The results indicate that better functioning capital markets and relaxed trade barriers have a positive effect on nascent entrepreneurs. The effect of administrative requirements and bureaucracy on the propensity to become a nascent entrepreneur is insignificant. This could be explained with entrepreneurs easily moving to the informal sector to avoid dealing with regulations. Higher prevalence of state ownership positively affects the propensity to become a nascent entrepreneur. Lastly, the chapter provides a brief discussion on policies that can improve nascent entrepreneurial activities within a nation.

Chapter "Inertia, Innovation Failures, and Learning from Innovation Failures: Some Insights from MSEs in an Emerging Market Economy" studies inertia, innovation failures, and learning from innovation failures with some insights from MSEs in an emerging market economy. It is widely accepted that inertia may inhibit small businesses' innovation and growth. However, little is known as to why some small businesses experience inertia and how this relates to innovation failures and learning from such failures. The objective of this study is to examine inertia, innovation failures, and learning from innovation failures through the lens of micro and small enterprises. Micro and small business enterprises have been seen as informal ways of doing business without a formal institutionalization. As an emerging market economy, Indonesia sets an exemplary context that may enrich the understanding of institutional inertia. This study uses a qualitative approach by interviewing 25 small business owners in West Sumatra, Indonesia. The data are analyzed by using thematic analysis. It is found that most interviewees failed to learn from their failures because of their incapability to institutionalize business strategies. Nevertheless, some patterns emerged, and they present clues leading to innovation failures and lessons to be learned, which in turn, reduce inertia. The present study provides some propositions that capture the essence of the issue, which can be used for future research.

It is hoped that this book will appeal to a wide range of academics, researchers and global audiences, provide creative discussions, satisfy scholarly and intellectual interests in institutional inertia, and hence add insight for better understanding and serve as a useful reference work.

It should also be noted that the information, opinions, views, facts, conclusions, comments, findings, positions, and strategies expressed by the authors and chapter contributors are theirs own and do not necessarily reflect the views, opinions, positions or strategies of the editors of this contributed volume and does not constitute endorsement or approval by the editors. The chapter authors and contributors are responsible for the citation of sources and accuracy of their bibliography and references. The editors of this contributed volume cannot be held responsible for any errors or consequences arising from the use of information contained in the chapters or for any defects, lacks, or possible violations of the rights of third parties. While the editors make every effort to ensure that no inaccurate or misleading opinions, statements or data appear in this volume, responsibility for the data, their use, opinions, and interpretations appearing in each and every chapter rests solely with the contributors and the corresponding authors. The editors accept no liability whatsoever for the consequences of any such misleading or inaccurate data, information, opinion, or statements.

References

Abdi, E., Safari Gerayli, M., & Rezaei Pitenoei, Y. (2022). Corporate inertia and information asymmetry: Evidence from Iran. *Iranian Journal of Accounting, Auditing and Finance*. https://doi.org/10.22067/IJAAF.2022.76181.1130

Acemoglu, D. (2006). *Introduction to economic growth*, MIT, (chapters 4, and 18).

Acemoglu, D., & Robinson, J. (2012). *Why nations fail: The origins of power, prosperity and poverty* (1st ed., p. 529). Crown.

Acemoglu, D., Johnson, S., Robinson, J., & Thaicharoen, Y. (2003). Institutional causes, macroeconomic symptoms: Volatility, crises and growth. *Journal of Monetary Economic, 50*, 49–123.

Acemoglu, D., Johnson, S., & Robinson, J. (2005). Chapter 6: Institution as the fundamental cause of long-run growth. In P. Aghion & S. Durlauf (Eds.), *Handbook of economic growth*. Elsevier.

Aveyard, S. C. (2016). Political inertia. In *No solution* (pp. 197–219). Manchester University Press.

Boyle, T. P., & Fairchild, J. F. (1997). The role of mesocosm studies in ecological risk analysis. *Ecological Applications, 7*(4), 1099–1102.

Britannica. (2023). https://www.britannica.com/

Brook, S. (2013). Social inertia and the field of creative labor. *Journal of Sociology, 49*(2–3), 309–324.

Browne, M. (2013). *Schaum's outline of physics for engineering and science*. McGraw-Hill Education.

CDC – NIOSH. (2023). https://www.cdc.gov/niosh/work-hour-training-for-nurses/longhours/mod7/03.html#:~:text=Sleep%20inertia%20is%20a%20temporary,reasoning%2C%20remembering%2C%20and%20learning

Cerra, V., Eichengreen, B., El-Ganainy, A., & Schindler, M. (Eds.). (2022). *How to achieve inclusive growth*. Oxford University Press.

Craik, K. J. W. (1967). *The nature of explanation*. Cambridge University Press.

Denzau, A. T., & North, D. C. (1994). Shared mental models: Ideologies and institutions. *Kyklos, 47*(1), 3–31.

Faghih, N., & Samadi, A. H. (Eds.). (2021). Dynamics of institutional change in emerging market economies: Theories, concepts and mechanisms. *Springer Nature*. https://doi.org/10.1007/978-3-030-61342-6, Series ISSN:1431-1933, https://www.springer.com/gp/book/9783030613419

Forrester, J. W. (1971). Counterintuitive behavior of social systems. *Theory and Decision, 2*(2), 109–140.

Frericks, P. (2017). "Machinery" or "spirit" of the welfare state: Institutional change as institutional inertia. *International Journal of Sociology and Social Policy, 37*(5/6), 341–352. https://doi.org/10.1108/IJSSP-07-2016-0090

Gallagher, S., & Crisafi, A. (2009). Mental institutions. *Topoi, 28*(1), 45–51. https://doi.org/10.1007/s11245-008-9045-0

Gao, K., Yang, Y., Sun, L., & Qu, X. (2020). Revealing psychological inertia in mode shift behavior and its quantitative influences on commuting trips. *Transportation Research Part F: Traffic Psychology and Behaviour, 71*, 272–287.

Gartner, M. (1993). *Macroeconomics under flexible exchange rates*. Harvester Wheatsheaf.
Graneau, P., & Graneau, N. (2006). *In the grip of the distant universe: The science of inertia*. World Scientific.
Guhl, A. M. (1968). Social inertia and social stability in chickens. *Animal Behavior, 16*(2–3), 219–232.
Heitger, B. (2004). Property rights and the wealth of nations: A cross-country study. *Cato Journal, 23*, 381–402.
Hodgkinson, G. P. (1997). Cognitive inertia in a turbulent market: The case of UK residential estate agents. *Journal of Management Studies, 34*(6), 921–945.
Johnson-Laird, P. N. (2004). The history of mental models. In K. I. Manktelow & M. C. Chung (Eds.), *Psychology of reasoning: Theoretical and historical perspectives* (pp. 179–212). Psychology Press.
Jones, N. A., Ross, H., Lynam, T., Perez, P., & Leitch, A. (2011). Mental models: An interdisciplinary synthesis of theory and methods. *Ecology and Society, 16*(1). https://doi.org/10.5751/ES-03802-160146
Kelly, D., & Amburgey, T. L. (1991). Organizational inertia and momentum: A dynamic model of strategic change. *Academy of Management Journal, 34*(3), 591–612.
Khurmi, R. S., & Gupta, J. K. (2005). *A textbook of machine design*. S. Chand publishing.
Kon, I. (1989). The psychology of social inertia. *Soviet Review, 30*(2), 59–76.
Lewis, P. A. (2005). Structure, agency and causality in post-revival Austrian economics: Tensions and resolutions. *Review of Political Economy, 17*(2), 291–316. https://doi.org/10.1080/09538250500067320
Loasby, B. J. (2001). Time, knowledge and evolutionary dynamics: Why connections matter. *Journal of Evolutionary Economics, 11*(4), 393–412.
Mattila, A. S. (2003). The impact of cognitive inertia on postconsumption evaluation processes. *Journal of the Academy of Marketing Science, 31*, 287–299.
North, D. (1989). Institutions and economic growth: A historical introduction. *World Development, 17*(9), 1319–1332.
North, D. C. (1990). *Institutions, institutional change and economic performance*. Cambridge University Press.
North, D. C. (1991). Institutions. *Journal of Economic Perspectives, 5*(1), 97–112.
OECD. (2016). *The governance of inclusive growth*. OECD Publishing. https://doi.org/10.1787/9789264257993-en
Ostrowski, A. M. (1959). A quantitative formulation of Sylvester's law of inertia. *Proceedings of the National Academy of Sciences, 45*(5), 740–744.
Parkin, A. (1981). Repetition, mourning and working through. *The International Journal of Psycho-Analysis, 62*, 271–281.
Potter, M. C., Nelson, E. W., Best, C. L., & McLean, W. G. (2021). *Schaum's outline of engineering mechanics: Dynamics*. McGraw-Hill Education.
Price, J. C. (1977). Thermal inertia mapping: A new view of the earth. *Journal of Geophysical Research, 82*(18), 2582–2590.
Ramasco, J. J., & Morris, S. A. (2006). Social inertia in collaboration networks. *Physical Review E, 73*(1), 016122.
Rizcallah, J. A. (2015). Moment of inertia by differentiation. *The Physics Teacher, 53*(8), 482–484.
Rodrik, D., Subramanian, A., & Trebbi, F. (2004). Institutions rule: The primacy of institutions over geography and integration in economic development. *Journal of Economic Growth, 9*, 131–165.
Rosenbaum, E. (2022). Mental models and institutional inertia. *Journal of Institutional Economics, 18*, 361–378. https://doi.org/10.1017/S174413742100059X
Rumi. (1207–1273i). The Mathnawí of Jalaluddín Rumi, Translation and Commentary, Nicholson, Reynold A, Volume I, 1926. Messrs Luzac & Co. LTD.
Rumi. (1207–1273ii). The Mathnawí of Jalaluddín Rumi, Translation and Commentary, Nicholson, Reynold A, Volume II, 1926. Messrs Luzac & Co. LTD.

Rumi. (1207–1273iii). The Mathnawí of Jalaluddín Rumi, Translation and Commentary, Nicholson, Reynold A, Volume III, 1926. Messrs Luzac & Co. LTD.
Rumi. (1207–1273iv). The Mathnawí of Jalaluddín Rumi, Translation and Commentary, Nicholson, Reynold A, Volume IV, 1926. Messrs Luzac & Co. LTD.
Rumi. (1207–1273vi). The Mathnawí of Jalaluddín Rumi, Translation and Commentary, Nicholson, Reynold A, Volume VI, 1926. Messrs Luzac & Co. LTD.
Samadi, A. H., & Alipourian, M. (2021). Institutions and institutional change: Concepts and theories. In N. Faghih & A. H. Samadi (Eds.), *Dynamics of institutional change in emerging market economies* (pp. 107–132). Springer.
Stewart, W. A. (1963). An inquiry into the concept of working through. *Journal of the American Psychoanalytic Association, 11*(3), 474–499.
Stralberg, D., Arseneault, D., Baltzer, J. L., Barber, Q. E., Bayne, E. M., Boulanger, Y., et al. (2020). Climate-change refugia in boreal North America: What, where, and for how long? *Frontiers in Ecology and the Environment, 18*(5), 261–270.
Tassi, P., & Muzet, A. (2000). Sleep inertia. *Sleep Medicine Reviews, 4*(4), 341–353.
Tebaldi, C., & Friedlingstein, P. (2013). Delayed detection of climate mitigation benefits due to climate inertia and variability. *Proceedings of the National Academy of Sciences, 110*(43), 17229–17234.
UIA Encyclopedia of World Problems & Human Potential. (2023). http://encyclopedia.uia.org/en
Walters, G. D. (2019). Psychological inertia revisited: Replicating and extending the differential effect of proactive and reactive criminal thinking on crime continuity. *Deviant Behavior, 40*(2), 156–170.
Wrenn, M. V. (2006). Agency and mental models in heterodox economics'. *Journal of Economic Issues, 40*(2), 483–491. CrossRefGoogle Scholar
Yamoah, F. A., Sivarajah, U., Mahroof, K., & Peña, I. G. (2022). Demystifying corporate inertia towards transition to circular economy: A management frame of reference. *International Journal of Production Economics, 244*, 108388.
Zantvoort, B. (2017). Political inertia and social acceleration. *Philosophy & Social Criticism, 43*(7), 707–723.
Zárate, M. A., Shaw, M., Marquez, J. A., & Biagas, D., Jr. (2012). Cultural inertia: The effects of cultural change on intergroup relations and the self-concept. *Journal of Experimental Social Psychology, 48*(3), 634–645.

Part I
Concepts, Types, Causes, and Effects

Inertia: Resistance and Endurance

Nezameddin Faghih, Mahdi Jamshidi Khosh, and Ali Reza Seifi

1 Introduction: State of Rest, Motion, and Inertia

Is this open book in front of you in its state of rest, motionless, and unchanged? At first sight and on a familiar and usual scale, it seems so, but with an accurate observation (experimental) on a small and unusual scale, there is chaos in its warp and wept. The atoms of this book are constantly moving (Holton et al., 1971, 1981). Moreover, on a macro and extraterrestrial scale, the book that is supposed to be still and motionless at this moment, is moving with you and Planet Earth while orbiting the sun at an average speed of 29.6 Km/s! Therefore, it is obvious that motion and state of rest are relative concepts and they become meaningful about different opinions and reference systems (Earth, Sun, etc.). Also, with a more accurate observation and taking this subject into contemplation, it can be concluded that the physical world and nature are based on motion,

Questioning the state of rest, motions and the reason for their existence has caught the attention of human minds from a very long time ago. According to the paradigm and the thinking manner of each era, different answers have been found and discussed that are more or less recorded in the history of thoughts. This chapter will briefly review these answers:

Aristotle believed that the universe is made of four elements of Earth, Water, Air, and Fire which are ordered based on their gravity in nested spheres, i.e., Earth sphere is placed in the center, then Water is placed in the surrounding area to the previous sphere, after that is the placement of Fire sphere, and air sphere surrounds the other spheres. And the reason behind the motion of every moving body is its attraction and flow toward its original place, e.g., if a body that is made of Earth is placed in the Air

N. Faghih (✉)
UNESCO Chair Professor Emeritus, Cambridge, MA, USA

M. J. Khosh · A. R. Seifi
Independent Scholar, Tehran, Iran

N. Faghih, A. H. Samadi (eds.), *Institutional Inertia*, Contributions to Economics,
https://doi.org/10.1007/978-3-031-51175-2_2

sphere, it moves toward the Earth sphere. Contrarily if the body is made of Air and is placed in the Earth sphere, it moves toward the Air sphere (upper parts). This attitude prevailed almost to the end of the Middle Ages (Holton et al., 1971, 1981).

Like the rings of a chain and relying on each other, Kepler, Galilei, and Newton were the scientists who studied motions based on observation, experience, experiment, fundamental framework, and formulation while criticizing Aristotle's motions paradigm. These scientists are now known as the founders of modern physics and even modern science. The result of their work is published in Newton's book "The Mathematical Principles of Natural Philosophy[1]" (Newton, 1833) under the title of Newton's Dynamic Law as below:

From the effect (that is, force) of other bodies on a specific body, their state of rest or motion changes, and the amount of this change (i.e., acceleration) is inversely dependent on that specific body's intrinsic and fundamental characteristics which are maintaining the current state and resisting to a change of state. Kepler has called this state "inertia", this word comes from a Latin word meaning idle and sluggish. The greater the inertia, the less the change or acceleration; the less the inertia, the greater the change or acceleration. This phenomenon is expressed briefly in the language of mathematics with the following equation (Newton's Second Law):

$$F = m.a \tag{1}$$

Where, F is force, a is acceleration and m is the mass of an object, or in other words, it is the inertia size of an object.

In the absence of the effect of other objects on this specific object, or when these effects (forces) cancel each other out, and the resultant of forces is zero (in absolute space), the object remains in its current state: if the object is in its state of rest, it continues to stay on that state, and if the object is moving uniformly in a straight path, it remains in that state, that is, Newton's First Law, Law of Inertia (Landsberg, 1972).

2 Newton's First Law (Law of Inertia)

After Johannes Kepler (1571–1630), a German astronomer, noticed a characteristic known as "*inertia*" in bodies, it was Galileo Galilei's turn (1564–1642) to achieve deeper findings about inertia force in bodies through his experiments and observations (Graney, 2012, 2015; Zuber, 1998).

Galileo Galilei discovered the principle of inertia through an experiment using two inclined planes placed against each other. He rolled a ball down one of those inclined planes, after going down, the ball would run up on the opposite inclined plane. This smart experiment showed that the smoother the second inclined plane,

[1]Philosophiæ Naturalis Principia Mathematica

the closer the ball would get to its original height, then he reasoned that any differences between the ball's initial and final height were due to friction or any other resistant opposing forces. The smaller these resistant opposing forces, the longer the ball continues to move—property of inertia (Parrish & Beaubien, 2000; Graney, 2015).

In 1624, Galilei wrote a letter to Francesco Ingoli (1578–1649) and explained the Principle of Inertia, stating that, if natural bodies are supposed to derive their natural motion from nature itself, then this motion can be cyclic, and it is not possible for nature to tend to its integral parts to move in a straight path. . . . The parts of the universe are in their best composition and arrangement, and they are all set in a place where they should be. . . . It can be said that nature and God have completely adjusted their structure. . . . The parts of the world are adjusted in the best way; the linear motion would be an extra and unnatural *action* and it can only be performed when something changes the mentioned body from its natural state by force.

Finally, Isaac Newton (1643–1727) introduced his First Law of motion which is also known as the Inertia Law, by examining the theories of previous scientists and his observations. This law states that a body at rest remains at rest, and a body in motion remains in motion at a constant velocity and in a straight line unless acted on by an unbalanced external force. If there is no external force (something like friction), the object continues to be as it was, i.e., it remains at rest or in motion.

René Descartes (1596–1650) talks about Inertia in his book, "Principles of Philosophy" (Descartes, 1984, 2012), stating that the first law of nature is to remain in the same state as long as it can; therefore, when a body is in motion, it continues to remain in motion (Parrish & Beaubien, 2000).

In 1786 Immanuel Kant (1724–1804) wrote that all changes in the objects have an external cause (everything remains in its state of rest or motion in a straight path, unless it is influenced by an external force). This mechanical law is known as the Law of Inertia (Kant, 1786; Butts, 1986).

All objects have inertia: if you are sitting in a moving car and suddenly the driver stops the car, you will lean, bend, or even be thrown forward depending on the speed and intensity of the brake. If you have not fastened your seat belt, your head may hit the windshield. In terms of effective forces, no forces have been applied to you in the forward direction, but when the driver stops the car, a force is applied to the vehicle to reduce its speed. Therefore, you will continue to be in motion.

In another situation, if you are sitting in a car and the driver suddenly drives faster, you will feel that you are being pulled and squeezed into your seat. In terms of effective forces, to accelerate a car, by stepping on the gas, a force is applied to the car but not you, therefore you stayed behind for a moment while the seat moves with the car, thus you will feel being pushed backward. Every body (including your own body in above mentioned example) behaves based on Newton's First Law, and its tendency to resist motion is called inertia. Newton's First Law is also known as Inertia Law (Stollberg & Hill, 1965, 1966; Stollberg et al., 1965).

3 Momentum and Newton's Second Law

Now imagine a train pulling into a station and blowing its whistle to stop. The driver never pulls the brakes at the moment that she/he wants to stop, but he does it well and in advance, so that a train weighing hundreds or even thousands of tons may have enough time to stop at the desired location.

Because of a fact that is known as "momentum", a train cannot stop exactly at the moment of pulling the brakes by driver:

$$P = m.v \tag{2}$$

Equation (2) calculates momentum, where P is the momentum, m is mass and v is velocity. When an object with a certain amount of mass is in motion, momentum is produced. The greater the mass and the greater the velocity, the greater the momentum of the object. If you go out for a running session, the force you need to stop is far less than the force the train needs to stop, because you are lighter and you move slower. Doubling the velocity or mass of an object doubles the amount of momentum (Parrish & Beaubien, 2000).

However, in Newton's Second Law, the relationship between force and acceleration indicates that mass is considered when inertia is formed. When a force is applied to an object, that object accelerates in the direction of the applied force, and increasing the applied force will increase the acceleration. If the applied force on the object remains constant, the mass increase will decrease the acceleration. Also, the greater the mass, the greater the inertia. In comparison to lighter objects, for heavier objects, more force is needed to accelerate or decelerate the movement (Potter et al., 2021; Browne, 2013; Rizcallah, 2015; Khurmi & Gupta, 2005).

Thus, Newton's Second Law of motion states that the acceleration of an object is the result of two things: the applied forces, and their mass. This can be compared to the first law, which states that if the applied forces cancel each other, an object will remain at its current velocity. Accordingly, acceleration is the result of applied forces (Potter et al., 2021; Browne, 2013; Rizcallah, 2015; Khurmi & Gupta, 2005).

4 Angular Momentum and Moment of Inertia

The rotational analogue of linear momentum, that is, rotational momentum, is usually referred to as angular momentum. In this case, the equivalent of Eq. (2) will be as follows:

$$L = I.\omega \tag{3}$$

Linear momentum and angular momentum have the same form and are examples of the parallels between linear and rotational motion. In Eq. 2, linear momentum

(P) is proportional to m and v, i.e., mass and linear velocity. In Eq. (3), angular momentum (L) is proportional to I and ω, i.e., angular mass—known as moment of inertia (I)—and angular velocity (ω). The greater the moment of inertia or the greater the angular velocity, the greater the angular momentum of the body. For instance, doubling the angular velocity or moment of inertia of a body doubles the amount of angular momentum (Potter et al., 2021; Browne, 2013; Rizcallah, 2015; Khurmi & Gupta, 2005).

As already noted, any object resists changes in translational velocity, and this tendency to remain at rest or in motion is known as inertia. It is easy to imagine how difficult it is to stop the movement of a very heavy object. Since inertia depends on the mass of an object, it can be interpreted as a measure of inertia. It can also be seen that a rotating object (or at rest) exhibits a similar type of resistance to changes in rotational velocity, known as the moment of inertia, and this is not only related to the mass but also to the distance between the axis of rotation and the center of mass (Potter et al., 2021; Browne, 2013; Rizcallah, 2015; Khurmi & Gupta, 2005).

The moment of inertia of an object depends on the distribution of matter (shape), its mass and the distance of the mass from the axis of rotation. It is usually denoted by the letter I (or J). It should also be noted that the moment of inertia should not be confused with the quadratic moment, which is mostly used in the calculation of bending and resistance of materials. That is, the quadratic moment only considers the geometry, but not the mass. The moment of inertia can be used, for example and among other applications, to dimension a motor to know if the motor is able to handle the inertia of the object it is supposed to move and if it can start and stop it (Potter et al., 2021; Browne, 2013; Rizcallah, 2015; Khurmi & Gupta, 2005).

Thus, moment of inertia quantifies an object's resistance to rotation, just as mass represents an object's resistance to linear motion. The farther the object is from the axis of rotation, the greater the resistance to movement. In fact, it is necessary to establish an angular velocity ω at all points of the system. Linear velocity is proportional to angular velocity times radius r; that is:

$$v = r.\omega \tag{4}$$

where, v is linear velocity, r is radius of rotation, and ω is angular velocity (the rotational analogue of linear velocity). Linear velocity is a measure of the time rate of change of displacement, as a body moves in a straight line. Angular velocity is the time rate of change of angular displacement of a rotating object (or particle) around a central axis (or point), i.e., relative to the origin (Potter et al., 2021; Browne, 2013; Rizcallah, 2015; Khurmi & Gupta, 2005).

The linear velocity to be given to an element depends on its distance from the axis of rotation. The greater the distance, the greater the velocity, the more energy is required to move the system. A solid mass element (a mass point) m_i, placed at a distance r_i from the axis of rotation, has a moment of inertia:

$$I_i = m_i\, r_i^2 \tag{5}$$

Therefore, for a mass composed of mass elements (mass points) and rotating around an axis of rotation, it is necessary to add all the elements of the mass to know the moment of inertia of the whole solid.

$$I = \sum_i m_i {r_i}^2 \tag{6}$$

The moment of inertia of an object is equal to the sum of the moments of inertia of its masses. For instance, for a bar made up of several metal cubes, the moment of inertia of the bar is equal to the sum of the moments of inertia of each of the cubes (passing through the same axis). It should also be noted that each object has several moments of inertia, each of which corresponds to a specific axis of rotation. The number of different moments of inertia and their magnitude depends on the way the mass of the body is distributed. For example, in the case of a solid sphere, all axes of rotation passing through the center of the sphere have the same moment of inertia. The basic rule here is that the greater the moment of inertia, the greater the mass farther from the axis of rotation. However, the moment of inertia of rotation corresponds to the inertial mass of translation (Potter et al., 2021; Browne, 2013; Rizcallah, 2015; Khurmi & Gupta, 2005).

5 The Origin of Inertia

Generally, there are two views about the origin of inertial force: first, inertia is a virtual force and second, inertia is a real force. Interestingly, Newton considered inertia as a virtual and hypothetical concept to justify his observations, experiences, and formulation of laws. However, this story is related to Albert Einstein (1879–1955) and his Theory of Relativity (first Special Relativity and then General Relativity), which questioned Newton's absolute space and established the foundations of relativity. Therefore, this concept takes on a different color and becomes more complicated (Sciama, 1953).

Undoubtedly, the correct understanding of this concept requires a detailed and technical examination of this theory, but to shorten it, firstly, in special relativity, the absoluteness of space and time is challenged, and space, time, and motion are considered as relative phenomena (and related to each other) and become dependent. Secondly, in general relativity, gravity, which is related and proportional to mass and inertia, is defined in Newtonian physics as the force exerted by an object on its surroundings. It pulls other objects towards it like an invisible rubber band and conforms to the shape of space, i.e., every object bends its surrounding space due to its mass (inertia size), which causes a change in the position and movement of other objects and their rolling in bending. Because in special relativity, space and time should be made one in four-dimensional "space-time", it should be said that objects can cause bending in the "space-time" around them! (Al-Khalili, 2019). Thus, with Einstein and relativity, inertia and mass are connected with space and time. But in contrast, other scientists like Ernst Mach (1838–1916)—and later developed by Graneau & Graneau (2006); Berman (2008)—have considered inertia as a real force.

First, Ernest Mach used a cosmological model and considered the inertial force as the result of constant stars' effects. After that Peter and Neal Graneau developed Mach's theory and stated that Inertia is the force that holds the universe together. Without this force, things will fall apart and matter would not have the required and necessary forces to form its current state and composition. It is also what keeps us safe from catastrophic events and resistant to change: If it was possible to stop inertia at the push of a button, then the universe would collapse into a pile of matter in an instant (Graneau & Graneau, 2006; Berman, 2008).

To understand that there is a real force involved, D'Alembert's principle (Bates & Nester, 2011) can be examined; that is,

$$F_a + F_i = 0 \tag{7}$$

where F_a is an applied force on a body and F_i is the inertial force.

This equation indicates that the sum of applied and inertial forces on every object is equal to zero. Consequently, by considering Newton's Second Law, from Eq. (1), that is: $F_a = m.\ a$, it is seen that: $F_i = -m.\ a$; the negative sign indicates the opposite direction of the inertial force to the applied force. Therefore, not only the inertia force has the dimensions of a force, but we have a clear and specific formula for its function. Thus, there is no reason not to consider inertia as a real force. If the applied force is real, then the opposite force cannot be imaginary or unreal (Graneau & Graneau, 2006).

6 Wide Applications of Inertia

Undoubtedly, the principle of inertia as one of the most important laws of physics throughout history and its increasing understanding has played an important role in the comprehensive development of physics and engineering. A closer look at the gravitational coupling of matter and spacetime that leads to inertia may provide researchers with more useful information (Shu et al., 2020).

Inertia, as a concept borrowed from physics that expresses resistance to change and refers to the desire to maintain the previous state, has wide applications in many other academic fields. In addition to physics, which considers the concept of inertia about the body's tendency to maintain its previous state of rest or motion (linear and angular) and the body's resistance to change in speed or direction, this concept is also considered in many other fields of science, engineering, economics, management, psychology, and social sciences. Some examples are as follows:

Thermal inertia: resistance to temperature change.
Sylvester's inertia: a theorem in algebra of matrices.
Climate inertia: the Earth system's slowness to changes in greenhouse gas levels.
Ecological inertia: a living system's ability to resist external changes.
Cognitive inertia: an individual's beliefs resistance to change.
Psychological inertia: lack of motivation to act.
Psychical inertia: psyche's resistance to change and development.
Sleep inertia: a temporary resistance in the form of decline and disorientation in mood and performance after waking up.
Social inertia: psychological—sociological resistance to change.
Corporate inertia: unwillingness to consider corporate change and dynamics.
Organizational inertia: external and internal resistance to change and organizational adaptation.
Cultural inertia: the resistance to cultural change, where, within the framework of cultural inertia, the dominant group is stable and resists cultural change despite the tendency of subordinate groups to cultural changes.
Political inertia: the resistance of powerful groups with some special interests in the status quo to change, which can occur at the national or international level.
Institutional inertia: the tendency of institutions to resist changes.

(Potter et al., 2021; Browne, 2013; Rizcallah, 2015; Khurmi & Gupta, 2005; Forrester, 1971; Denzau & North, 1994; Graneau & Graneau, 2006; Gallagher & Crisafi, 2009; Johnson-Laird, 2004; Jones et al., 2011; Wrenn, 2006; Craik, 1967; Loasby, 2001; Price, 1977; Ostrowski, 1959; Tassi & Muzet, 2000; Tebaldi & Friedlingstein, 2013; Boyle & Fairchild, 1997; Stralberg et al., 2020; Hodgkinson, 1997; Mattila, 2003; Walters, 2019; Gao et al., 2020; Parkin, 1981; Stewart, 1963; Guhl, 1968; Ramasco & Morris, 2006; Brook, 2013; Kon, 1989; Abdi et al., 2022; Yamoah et al., 2022; Zárate et al., 2012; Lewis, 2005; Zantvoort, 2017; Aveyard, 2016; CDC – NIOSH, 2023; UIA, 2023; Britannica, 2023; Rosenbaum, 2022).

7 Inertia as a Mental Model

A mental model is a description of the thought process and the internal representation of the external world, which includes selected concepts and relationships between them to represent the real world, cognition, reasoning, decision-making, shaping behavior and setting (algorithmic) approaches to solving problems and performing tasks. Nevertheless, in general, mental models are mental (subjective) representations of objective realities and mental (subjective) representations of social (subjective) realities (power structures, institutions, etc.), and the latter model is the product of social communication, interaction, and agreement. Especially for enabling rules, the actors' necessary perceptions of why and for what purpose a set of rules exist and are used can be best understood using the concept of a mental model. Mental states are considered as a cognitive structure that forms the basis of reasoning and decision making (Forrester, 1971; Denzau & North, 1994; Gallagher, 2013; Gallagher & Crisafi, 2009; Johnson-Laird, 2004; Jones et al., 2011; Wrenn, 2006; Craik, 1967; UIA, 2023; Britannica, 2023; Rosenbaum, 2022).

Structures of mental representation mean that different elements are arranged by relations such as dependencies or assumed causes. Such causes and dependencies can be social or physical. Thus, the facts provided by mental models include not only reports of objects and events, but also assumed causal relationships between events and objects, including the assumed effects of one's own and others' actions in a particular context. Mental models are like physicists' diagrams or architects' models because their structure resembles the structure of the situation they represent. Despite being subjective (mental), mental models are not specific and idiosyncratic, but have common interpretations and meanings, and also filter information (Denzau & North, 1994; Loasby, 2001; Lewis, 2005; Rosenbaum, 2022).

However, as far as institutional inertia is concerned, it is argued that many institutions are sustained because of mental models and are recreated through social interactions reshaped by such models. Therefore, the resulting institutional inertia is both a precondition for the functioning of institutions and also a factor that prevents, delays or slows down efforts to achieve institutional changes. It suggests that in doing so, only a deeper and better understanding of social reality can provide a basis for further development of institutional theory (Lewis, 2005; Lawson, 1994, 2003, 2012a, b, 2016a, b; Rosenbaum, 2022).

Many socially reproduced institutions, as enabling structures, need to be procreated through intentional actions that are not only mentally represented, but these mental models must somehow be considered as important bearers of the institutions, such as the principle of rationality. For institutions, the concept of a complementary mental model is necessary, in particular, for enabling rules (Denzau & North, 1994; Jones et al., 2011; Lewis, 2005; Rosenbaum, 2022).

It is argued that institutions as socially accepted enabling rules are not only self-reinforcing, but often supplemented and complemented by complex and culturally transmitted mental models. Both characteristics prevent rapid changes and are manifested in institutional inertia. This means that agents receive positive feedback from the application of such rules and change presupposes or requires learning processes that can be time-consuming and slow the adoption of new rules and reforms or changes in existing institutions. Institutional inertia cannot be seen as entirely negative—quite the opposite. Empowering institutions form the structural backbone of societies (and their unique role) is that they do not need an enforcer and therefore do not raise the question of who does the enforcement. Since these institutions must also be firm and solid in people's mental models (minds), any rapid change undermines their ability to empower and constrain actions. Hence, their stability can be a prerequisite for their transformative reconstruction and social acceptance. If mental models carry many institutions in the way discussed above, that is, in the sense of necessary complements, then institutional change requires changing the corresponding mental models, not just the corresponding rules (formal rules). Such change is expected to be gradual, in the sense that at least not all holders of a particular mental model will change or modify at the same time. Thus, institutions are stable not only because they are useful (the functional argument), but also because they are embedded in mental models, models that are learned and must be replaced by other (or modified) mental models if an institution is to change. Self-enforcing institutions in particular are inherently stable, regardless of the availability of more efficient alternatives. Or in other words, they resist change and thus show inertia. Furthermore, it is not only institutions that appear to resist change, but also the large number of institutional facts that are based on these institutions, probably after some time attaining a quality that approximates them to physical realities. These facts themselves tend to exert a normative force that shapes social interactions over a relatively long period (Rosenbaum, 2022).

However, in moving from a physical position to a non-physical inertia, two aspects of inertia should be considered: the positive aspect, i.e., the sustaining or preservative aspect of inertia as a supporting and stabilizing force of the structure (endurance), and the negative aspect and resistance to change, i.e., the force resisting the change of structure and dynamic state (resistance) that must be overcome. Thus, inertia is a useful model for a better understanding of human beings' elements, including thinking patterns and habits. Naturally, we tend to resist new issues, and this resistance is in contrast to the necessary effort for change. The normal routine of life does not require any kind of effort and there is little mistrust in fixed routines. We need force to create change and force requires effort. This mental model (inertia) puts a lens over our eyes so that we can see concepts of integrity (the positive side) and resistance to change (the negative side).

8 Cognitive Inertia

When we go to the grocery store, we buy things that we've been buying for a long time, and our preferences are formed accordingly, and we rarely spend energy thinking critically about the products that we have been buying dozens of times, even if we have used those products for a longer time. As much as these products are more embedded in our lives, even if we realize that they are unhealthy, we rarely change our decision immediately. The reason for this problem can be better understood in the light of Newton's Second Law.

The force equation applies similarly to our habits: the longer we do something, the more it becomes part of our identity and understanding of the world. Therefore, the effort required to change a habit will be more due to the direct relationship with the time spent on that habit (moment of inertia). Inertia tells us that when we stop doing something, starting again is harder than continuing. Many studies about brain function also show that when we change our focus from one task to another, we need more energy and time to complete our tasks than if we first finish one and then move on to another one. Inertia also explains why we continue our bad habits and why it is difficult to make systematic changes. In many cities, instead of focusing on improving the necessary infrastructure to create sidewalks to facilitate people's movement for walking or cycling, because of habits, the focus is still on the development of automobile infrastructure. We continue to work in jobs we hate and avoid meaningful conversations with people with different opinions, all because it's easier for us to stay on our current path, no matter how stagnant or imperfect it is (Parrish & Beaubien, 2000).

As a perspective, inertia indicates that our beliefs can become habits. Habits are ingrained behaviors, some of them are good, and some are bad. Belief systems have enormous evolutionary inertia, which indicates that belief capacity is one of the critical mechanisms, and this biological connection explains why beliefs are resistant to change. Sometimes the inertia of our beliefs prevents us from progressing, like when they close our eyes to new opportunities. Or when we reject new ideas or information because they don't fit with our thoughts about the world. For instance, the history of invention is the story of abandoning old ideas. From radios and telephones to cars, airplanes, and laptops, many lifestyle-changing inventions were initially dismissed because of being irrelevant or unusable. There are many stories of people who missed opportunities to develop and invest in these new technologies and later regretted their lack of foresight. In contrast, there are dreamers whose beliefs were flexible enough to support them in their struggle against inertia. Therefore, cognitive Inertia can be a good thing. Values with strong inertia can help us resist obstacles and failures. Of course, this does not mean that we should follow them blindly and become reluctant to update them as we grow older (Parrish & Beaubien, 2000).

Strong beliefs can be flexible while remaining strong. If we continuously renew and develop them based on new experiences and information, they can continue to support us against challenges. Most stories of emerging new theories and inventions show both aspects of cognitive inertia. The positive aspect makes scientists and inventors continue their work despite others' rejection and its negative aspect which comes from the environment, prevents them from moving forward for change (Parrish & Beaubien, 2000).

Cognitive Inertia (belief) can prevent fundamental change in the world. But at the same time, this same inertia can help purposeful people to move forward for a change by maintaining their beliefs. Nevertheless, many studies show that cognitive inertia is a phenomenon that describes the inability to react to changes in the environment, adapting the resources and capabilities, and updating the strategic schemes accordingly. Empirical research results show that cognitive inertia can delay action and lead to lower performance. While empirical studies demonstrate the effects of cognitive sluggishness, they provide little insight into the processes and determinants that lead to cognitive sluggishness; for instance, why and under what circumstances top managers are unable to adapt their strategic schemes to the changing environment. In addition, they offer little advice on what skills and methods can be used to prevent or overcome cognitive sluggishness. Cognitive inertia arises when the strategic schemes underlying cognitive processes are characterized by low complexity and strong focus. Additionally, such schemes, in combination with contextual features of strategic decision-making and the working conditions, prevent using more controlled processing methods. In order to avoid cognitive sluggishness, it is therefore necessary to regularly create opportunities in order to consciously switch to such reflexive, controlled processes. This reflection requires a temporary demarcation from everyday processes and suspension of the associated inertia-promoting contextual features. Regular workshops enable this separation and create the framework for the use of specific methods such as collective retrospection or scenario thinking (Frost & Westermayer, 2008; Westermeyer & Frost, 2009).

9 Inertia in Society

Most of the time our consumption patterns are based on our habits rather than our new thoughts. Why do some products stay around us for centuries even when better and cheaper products come on the market? Why do new products come with so much promise but quickly leave the scene? We can use the concept of inertia to provide some responses to these questions.

The longer a product has been used in society, the more difficult it will be to replace that product with a new product, even if the new product has obvious advantages. This is partly why simply proving that something is harmful is not always enough to bring about a change in society's behavior. The inertia of a product, a habit or an idea increases the more it circulates.

There are endless social and untrue myths that have long been part of our understanding of the world, even though there is overwhelming evidence that they are inaccurate. The perspective of inertia helps us understand the dynamics of these social issues and gives us insight into thinking about the things we want to change.

However, a major problem is that society tends to repeat and replicate itself. Illusions and Prejudices tend to keep continuing from one generation to another, and the problems associated with them also continue. The prejudices and illusions of the elders tend to continue in the youth and so does the problem of hostility. This hostility will never end until we teach children to obey and conform to what adults say. Hence, we must develop an inquiring mind that questions what it is told, is aware that it has many biases that need to be examined and discarded, and is willing to take on the task of discovering the truth. But encouraging and respecting dissent is essential if we are not to create a stagnant society inflexibly stuck in a fossilized rut. Today, there is considerable inertia in society and the only approach to change it is to generate a mind that investigates not only scientific questions, but also social, mental, and moral questions; that is, a mind that can be intelligent and smart about the whole of life and not just one aspect of it (Gohil, 2017).

10 Phylogenetic Inertia and Ecological Pressure in Institutional Evolution

Man can be defined as an institution-building animal (Chapin, 1927). Institutions play an essential role in the development process of societies and are important for understanding and studying economic changes. They include a framework and set of behavioral rules that guide social interactions involved in economic, social, and national policy activities. The growth of the actors that make up a society follows the institutions, and by analyzing the current institutions, the future direction of the economy or society can be analyzed and predicted. Hence, many studies have been conducted on institutions to provide insight into the reception and response to institutional change (Bergh & Stagl, 2003; Vega-Redondo, 1993; North, 1990; Moroni, 2010; Aksom, 2022b; Lee et al., 2023).

Institutions (as rules of the game) are not unique and vary by time or region. They exist in many forms and evolve over time. Limited attention has been paid to endogenous changes in institutions. Institutions are usually considered as fixed and constant exogenous factors in economic development, and the focus has been on the external environment affecting institutions and how institutions affect social actors. However, institutions are evolutionary subjects that constantly change with space, time, and endogenous mechanisms (Coriat & Weinstein, 2002; Firsova et al., 2022; Lewis & Steinmo, 2012; Bergh & Stagl, 2003; DiMaggio & Powell, 1983; Meyer & Rowan, 1977; Moroni, 2010; Prieto, 2022; Sui & Liu, 2020; Aksom, 2022b; Lee et al., 2023).

An institution that is endogenously maintained for a long time creates path dependence, tends to stick, and causes institutional resistance to change, a phenomenon known as institutional inertia. The concept of institutional inertia emphasizes the function of endogenous resistance in adopting and changing institutional characteristics (Aksom, 2022b, 2023; Firsova et al., 2022; Munck et al., 2014; Lee et al., 2023).

Factors such as inertia that affect institutional evolution have been qualitatively analyzed by scholars and researchers. However, a quantitative approach has also been proposed that uses algorithms and creates a phylogenetic tree. Two quantitative measures have been proposed based on this tree:

(i) institutional inertia that resists change,
(ii) ecological pressure that causes change.

Both ecological pressure and institutional inertia change the dynamics of institutional evolution to be rapid or gradual, respectively. In particular, inertia causes a paradigm shift from gradualism to equilibrium (from gradualism to punctuated equilibrium) due to its diverse influence on institutional evolution. In the gradualist model, rapid institutional change is suppressed, while it is endogenously strengthened as institutions evolve and the pattern shifts toward a punctuated equilibrium (Lee et al., 2023).

This quantitative approach measures institutional inertia by applying phylogenetic inertia (in biological evolution), a constraint on evolution that is endogenously formed in phylogeny and refers to evolutionary history. To measure phylogenetic inertia, a phylogenetic tree of institution is constructed based on artifact phylogenetic tree algorithm. Then the measured phylogenetic inertia of institution is defined as institutional inertia. In addition, exogenous pressure in the tree is also measured and defined as ecological pressure. Therefore, using the interaction between ecological pressure, which changes institutions, and institutional inertia, which resists change, the dynamics of institutional evolution are empirically studied and identified (Hannan et al., 2004; Shanahan, 2011; Lee et al., 2022; Gould, 1994; Kim et al., 2020; Lee et al., 2023).

11 Entropic Inertia in Institutional Evolution

Some theories of deinstitutionalization consider the question and process of whether and how institutionalized and even highly institutionalized norms, beliefs, and practices may tend to weaken, decay, erode, and disappear over time (Oliver, 1992; Røvik, 1996; Clark & Jennings, 1997; Dacin & Dacin, 2008; Maguire & Hardy, 2009; Kondra & Hurst, 2009; Gilmore & Sillince, 2014; Becker, 2014; Clemente & Roulet, 2015; Patora-Wysocka, 2015; Christiansen & Kroezen, 2016; Chaudhry & Rubery, 2019; Aksom, 2022b, 2023).

However, the theorists of many disciplines usually do not find it easy to understand and adapt the concept of entropy to their fields of science (Ryan, 1980; Corning & Kline, 1998; Kåberger & Månsson, 2001; Gillett, 2006; Volkenstein, 2009; Swendsen, 2011, 2012; Koutsoyiannis & Sargentis, 2021; Aksom, 2022b). Entropy is a very abstract concept and the second law of thermodynamics has a spectrum of different understandings and formulations. The concept of entropy arose from the need to represent and express irreversible processes. When a system evolves into the future, entropy must increase. Ambiguities are due to an idea established in the extensive literature of many scientific disciplines that shows thermodynamic entropy as a result of the second law of thermodynamics in many phenomena and systems, including social organizations, mainly as information uncertainty, disorganization, and disorder. Entropy is a measure of certain probability distributions, a characteristic of the state of matter, and a state function (comparable to temperature or energy). Considering the probabilistic nature of entropy in thermodynamics, it is no longer exclusively a concept of statistical physics and is also recognized as a fundamental property of information and uncertainty. The information perspective leads to the generalization of the concept of entropy and not being limited to thermodynamics. Thus, entropy is not merely a measure of the depreciation of energy, but also a measure of the degree of disorder of a system. It means equilibrium, i.e., a state of inevitable higher probability of a system over time. Therefore, entropy also represents disorder because it is the most probable state. But this disorder is of a different type than the disorganization and disorder of macroscopic systems. Information is the negation of entropy because a decrease in entropy corresponds to an increase in information and vice versa. In fact, entropy corresponds to probability, and increasing entropy, i.e., the law of increasing entropy, is the law of decreasing information, and increasing disorder and uncertainty. It relates to a system that moves over time from a highly improbable, organized, and certain state to the most probable state, which implies loss of information and control, and leads to the organization's inability to function. The highest degree of disorder is related to thermodynamic equilibrium because over time the configuration corresponding to the maximum entropy, which is the most probable configuration, is realized. Maximum entropy is related to the equilibrium state of a system. Hence, a non-equilibrium state of low entropy is characteristic of organized systems (Rowlinson, 1970; Elitzur, 1994; Bratianu & Bejinaru, 2020; Pascal & Pross, 2015; Wicken, 1986; Volkenstein, 2009; Swendsen, 2012; Bratianu, 2019). Eigen, 1971; Ebeling, 1978; Ebeling & Volkenstein, 1990; Collier, 1986; Elitzur, 1994; Corning & Kline, 1998; Brillouin, 1950, 1956, 1961; Volkenstein & Chernavskii, 1978; Volkenstein, 1977; Feistel & Ebeling, 2016; Aksom, 2022b).

The concept of entropy, which originates from thermodynamics (especially statistical thermodynamics), represents a fundamental concept of science, and according to the second law of thermodynamics, it states that the entropy of an isolated system that evolves spontaneously cannot decrease (because it always reaches a state of thermodynamic equilibrium, where entropy is highest). This probabilistic view generalizes and unifies the physical, biological, and socioeconomic phenomena that must obey the second law because they can ultimately be reduced to the processing, storage, and exchange of information. The most common interpretation is related to the view of entropy as a measure of uncertainty, disorder, and lack of information, and this understanding of entropy can be followed in social systems and human organizations as a link between entropy and information. Traditionally, the following features and the relationship between information, entropy, order, uncertainty, and complexity are essential characteristics of entropy in social systems: information quantity of a system measuring its degree of order and organization; entropy of a system measuring its degree of disorder and disorganization; entropy of a system that has a positive relationship with information loss and increasing uncertainty. Furthermore, the higher the entropy level, the more information is not available about the current state of an organization. Maximum entropy is related to the complete state of disorder of a system and thus the minimal or complete loss of information about the true state of the system. Therefore, maximum entropy is a reflection of maximum uncertainty and vice versa. An increase in disorder is associated with both a decrease in information and an increase in entropy. When entropy decreases, useful information increases. Hence, over time, valuable information and entropy change in the opposite direction (Mavrofides et al., 2011; Bawden & Robinson, 2015; Bratianu, 2019; Bratianu & Bejinaru, 2020; Ebeling, 1978; Volkenstein, 2009; Elitzur, 1994; Pross, 2003; Wicken, 1978, 1979, 1980, 1986; Stuart, 1985a, b; Grabow & Andrews, 2019; Wicken, 1986; Haddad, 2017; Bawden & Robinson, 2015; Susskind, 1997; Eigen, 1971; Volkenstein, 2009; Adami, 2016; Schuster, 2016; Haken & Portugali, 2016; Aksom, 2022b).

A common problem is usually in the concept and understanding of disorder, and like many other misunderstandings and misinterpretations of entropy, in institutional theory, entropy has been directly implicated as a factor in decay, disorder, and erosion of institutions. Institutions are sometimes viewed as social systems and, as such, are affected by entropic forces, and thus institutions require maintenance efforts by field members. For instance, institutional work is sometimes justified as a necessary condition for overcoming the entropic tendencies of most institutions, and it is argued that efforts to maintain institutional order are needed to prevent institutional drift and erosion. Such assumptions seem to imply that institutionalization and institutions are not natural states, structures and processes and are doomed to erode, collapse and disappear without purposeful efforts. Nevertheless, institutional continuity appears as the norm and organizational fields seem to tend towards institutionalization via self-organization and self-ordering mechanisms; i.e., a state of institutionalization is a natural tendency and thus in the absence of external disturbances, institutionalization should be expected. However, conscious attempts are also made to establish and maintain order; otherwise, it will lead to a state of disorder. Additionally, it should be noted that a living organism (as an open system in which matter and energy flow) is certainly a system far from equilibrium. Concepts derived from the physics of thermodynamic systems far from equilibrium are therefore necessary, but not sufficient, to approach the whole of an organism in its ecosystem. An organism organizes itself (self-organization) and its environment, and leads to improve both (organism and environment) constantly, transforming in a historical time that generates profound changes in all networks of external interactions (Scott, 2015; Montgomery & Dacin, 2020; Lok & De Rond, 2013:185; Dacin & Dacin, 2008; Dacin et al., 2010; Oliver, 1992; Styer, 2000; Koutsoyiannis & Sargentis, 2021; Styer, 2008; DiMaggio & Powell, 1983; Chollat-Namy & Longo, 2022; Aksom & Tymchenko, 2020; Aksom & Firsova, 2021; Aksom, 2022b, c).

A socioeconomic system can also evolve (similar to physical systems) in the direction of maximum entropy. However, since institutionalization is the cause of maximum uncertainty, entropy does not increase in already institutionalized practices, so entropy is not expected to erode, deinstitutionalize, and destroy highly institutionalized functions and practices. On the contrary, these practices and functions are institutionalized since entropy corrodes and destroys their technical meaning. This is similar to what happens in innovations that always appear as solutions to specific real problems. Innovations are actually informational responses that include factual and relevant information gathered from the environment in order to create certainty or reduce uncertainty. Institutionalization is indeed revealed as a means of inducing and instilling value, providing intrinsic worth to a process or structure that, prior to institutionalization, had merely instrumental utility (Oliver, 1992; Lok & De Rond, 2013; Raynard et al., 2021; Willmer, 1977; Mellemvik et al., 1988; Scott, 1987; Aksom, 2022b).

Moreover, based on the second law of thermodynamics and its probabilistic interpretation, it can be explained why institutional persistence and stability is more likely than institutional decay and change. It should be noted that institutional isomorphism and institutionalization correspond to the most probable state and according to the second law the probability of a particular state increases with its entropy, and systems tend to transform from less stable to more probable and stable state. Also, disorder arises spontaneously and is associated with more probability and more entropy, which is because an ordered state is less likely than a disordered state. Entropy drives systems toward the most probable state, and the full institutionalization of an organizational practice or function is the most stable state for a social system, i.e., with maximum uncertainty (Volkenstein, 2009; Aksom, 2022b).

In summary, by adapting information theory, researchers found institutionalization as reducing valuable information and increasing uncertainty in organizational contexts. It is argued that entropy is not a reason for the erosion or deterioration of institutions, but rather a manifestation of the reduction of valuable information. The system itself moves to the most stable and possible configuration with the highest entropy. Maximum entropy is related to institutionalized functions and practices that are the product of perceptions and beliefs, not information and knowledge. By examining and revealing the characteristics and true nature of institutional entropy, it can be seen that entropy contributes to institutional continuity, change, maintenance, reproduction, isomorphism, persistence, stability, endurance, longevity, even deinstitutionalization (although not easily and merely in case of necessity), and also decision-making under conditions of uncertainty. Entropy does not cause the erosion, decay and deterioration of institutions, but is a reflection and a reason for institutionalization. Furthermore, it is argued that institutions are not subject to entropic tendencies, but the value of information-processing and information capabilities. From this point of view, the manifestation and presence of entropy makes sense and is compatible with the basic principles of institutional theory. The correspondence between entropy, uncertainty, information and institutionalization is best understood when viewed through the lens of Shannon information theory (Shannon, 1948). The information theory perspective provides the best understanding of the concept of entropy and then why institutionalization occurs and why this is a natural and inevitable process of self-organization and self-ordering in organizational contexts (Shannon, 1948; Aksom, 2023, 2022a, b).

Institutional Renewal Time Function

Every moment the world is renewed,
and we are unaware of its being renewed whilst it remains.
Life is ever arriving anew, like the stream,
though in the body it has the semblance of continuity.
From its swiftness it appears continuous,
like the spark which you whirl rapidly with your hand.
If you whirl a firebrand with dexterity,
it appears to the sight as a very long fire.

Rumi (1207–1273).

we know a lot about institutions and their economic performance, but we do not know how institutions change.

Douglas C.North (1990).

Nezameddin Faghih proposes an institutional renewal time function that can be derived based on the ordinary renewal theory (often used for life cycle assessment).

Suppose for an institution, the institutional renewal time t is a random variable with probability density function p(t). Then, based on the theories of the ordinary renewal process, the function g(t), the expected number of renewals until time t, which is defined as the renewal time function, can be derived. In a renewal process, the renewal time (t) of the process is considered as a continuous random variable, following a probability density function p(t), which can be assessed or assumed for a specific renewal process. Nonetheless, for a particular institution or a particular economy, the probability density function p(t) can be estimated by examining the time history and statistical parameters (such as histogram, mean, variance, etc.) of the institution or the institutions of the country under study (Faghih, 1989, 1992, 1998, 1993; Faghih & Faghih, 2007; Choudhury, 1998; Choudhury & Choudhury, 1998; Faghih & Faghih, 2008; Cox, 1962, 1983; Barlow & Proschan, 1964).

However, in the computations of the renewal process and the derivation of renewal theory formulas, the Laplace transform can be used to avoid complicated convolution integrals. The Laplace transform of the probability density function p (t) is usually denoted by P(s):

$$\mathrm{P(s)} = \mathrm{L}\{\mathrm{p(t)}\}, \tag{8}$$

where s and L stand for Laplace transform operator and Laplace transform operation, respectively. Thus, the renewal theory computations arrive at:

$$\mathrm{G(s)} = \mathrm{P(s)/s}\ [1 - \mathrm{s\ P(s)}], \tag{9}$$

where G(s) is the Laplace transform of the renewal time function g(t), that is, the expected number of renewals until time t. Therefore, if the probability density function of the institutional renewal times, p(t), is known, its Laplace transform P (s) can be obtained and substituted into Eq. (9). Then G(s), in inverse Laplace transform, gives the institutional renewal time function g(t), from which the expected number of renewals, E (N_t), up to any time t can be obtained as follows:

$$\mathrm{E}(N_t) = \mathrm{g}(t) = L^{-1}\{\mathrm{G(s)}\} = L^{-1}\{\mathrm{P(s)/s}\ [1 - \mathrm{s\ P(s)}])\}, \tag{10}$$

where L^{-1} stands for inverse Laplace transform operation. It should also be noted that the Laplace transform and the inverse Laplace transform of the functions p (t) and G(s) depend on the mathematical type of the function and it can be obtained analytically (Laplace transform operations—integration, and the remainder theorem, respectively), from Laplace transform tables, or by numerical methods, accordingly (Faghih, 1989, 1992, 1993, 1998; Faghih & Faghih, 2007; Choudhury, 1998; Choudhury & Choudhury, 1998; Faghih & Faghih, 2008; Cox, 1962; Cox, 1983; Barlow & Proschan, 1964; Choukade & Mangalekar, 2019; Datko, 1987; Davies & Martin, 1979; Saucedo & Schiring, 1968; Distefano et al., 1997).

When the expected number of renewals, E (N_t), is obtained from Eq. (10), then it can be assumed to be equal to unity for the first renewal, that is:

$$E\ (N_t) = g(t) = 1 \tag{11}$$

Thus, the institutional renewal time t can be calculated by solving the following equation:

$$g(t) - 1 = 0 \tag{12}$$

where, g(t) is available from Eq. (10).

Finally, for future research, the proposed institutional renewal time function can be applied to different institutions and economies, and especially comparative studies on economies at different levels of development are suggested for a deeper understanding of institutional inertia.

12 The Result of the Balance Between Inertia and Overcoming it: The Evolution of Structural Preservation

The general rule in nature is a complex, non-linear, and dynamic dialectic between stability, change, order, and disorder. Different thinkers in various fields and various ways have formulated and expressed this dialectic (Faghih, 2003, 2005; Farazmand, 2003; Smith & Graetz, 2006; Young & Kiel, 1994; Best, 1991; Bohm & Peat, 1987; Harvey, 1993; Prigogine, 1998; Prigogine & Stengers, 1984; Nicholis & Prigogine, 1977). Following nature, it is worthy and necessary to search for and implement such plans and dialectics in society and human institutions, with the summary that: the thesis of "tradition" can be considered as an inertia that maintains the structure, order, survival, and durability of societies and institutions, and the antithesis of "modernity and innovation" as the necessary changes in the current structure and order by overcoming the inertia of tradition, the result of which is the synthesis of "necessary new order and structure" which is not destructive and apart from the context of tradition, climate, and culture (such as modernism and modernization and in the form of a project), but as Alexander defines it, it will be conducted in a process of "Structure-Preserving Transformation" (Alexander, 2002, 2020a, b), and on the context of tradition, climate, and culture in a gradual process. There are time-places (breakpoints) in the context of this dialectic and creativity, where the change is so fundamental and essential that it occurs in a sense of breaking and metamorphosis (Land & Beth, 1998) like a silkworm that becomes a butterfly.

13 Conclusion

Inertia was studied as a fundamental and effective phenomenon in nature, men, and human institutions, that is woven into their warp and weft in two physical and non-physical structures as a mental model. It was concluded that this phenomenon has two positive and negative aspects: the positive aspect is known as the preserving, maintaining, and stabilizing force of the above structures (endurance force), and the negative aspect is known as the force that resists the change and dynamics of those structures (resistance force) and by considering the key title of this book, the concepts of *"institutional persistence"* and *"institutional resistance"* can be created and they can be usefully used in the dynamics analysis of institutions and organizations. These two aspects of inertia have a fundamental and vital role in institutions' structure, dynamics, and preservation. Furthermore, topics such as angular momentum, moment of inertia, wide applications of inertia, the origin of inertia, inertia as a mental model, cognitive inertia, inertia in society, phylogenetic inertia and ecological pressure in institutional evolution, and entropic inertia in institutional evolution were also studied. Finally, the institutional renewal time function was introduced and proposed, and the result of the balance between inertia and overcoming it, that is, the evolution of structural preservation, was also considered.

This chapter emphasizes future research on the application of institutional renewal time function to different institutions and economies, and especially comparative studies on economies at different levels of development for a deeper understanding of institutional inertia.

References

Abdi, E., Safari Gerayli, M., & Rezaei Pitenoei, Y. (2022). Corporate inertia and information asymmetry: Evidence from Iran. *Iranian Journal of Accounting, Auditing and Finance*. https://doi.org/10.22067/IJAAF.2022.76181.1130

Adami, C. (2016). What is information? *Philosophical Transactions of the Royal Society A: Mathematical, Physical and Engineering Sciences, 374*(2063), 20150230.

Aksom, H. (2022a). Institutional inertia and practice variation. *Journal of Organizational Change Management., 35*(3), 463–487.

Aksom, H. (2022b). Entropy and institutional theory. *International Journal of Organizational Analysis*. https://jyx.jyu.fi/bitstream/handle/123456789/83386/PDF_4.PDF.pdf?sequence=2.

Aksom, H. (2022c). Reconciling conflicting predictions about transience and persistence of management concepts in management fashion theory and new institutionalism. *International Journal of Organizational Analysis, 30*(2), 430–453.

Aksom, H. (2023). Deinstitutionalization revisited. *International Journal of Organizational Analysis*. forthcoming.

Aksom, H., & Firsova, S. (2021). Structural correspondence between organizational theories. *Philosophy of Management, 20*(3), 307–336.

Aksom, H., & Tymchenko, I. (2020). How institutional theories explain and fail to explain organizations. *Journal of Organizational Change Management., 33*(7), 1223–1252.

Alexander, C. (2002). *The nature of order: An essay on the art of building and the nature of the universe, book 2: The process of creating life*. Center for Environmental Structure, Taylor & Francis Publication.
Alexander, C. (2020a). The nature of order: An essay on the art of building and the nature of the universe: The process of creating life. *The Nature of Order*, 1–631.
Alexander, C. (2020b). The nature of order: An essay on the art of building and the nature of the universe: A vision of a living world. *The Nature of Order*, 1–682.
Al-Khalili, J. (2019). *Gravity: A ladybird expert book*. Penguin UK.
Aveyard, S. C. (2016). Political inertia. In *No solution* (pp. 197–219). Manchester University Press.
Barlow, R. E., & Proschan, F. (1964). Comparison of replacement policies, and renewal theory implications. *The Annals of Mathematical Statistics, 35*(2), 577–589.
Bates, L. M., & Nester, J. M. (2011). On D'Alembert's principle. *Communications in Mathematics, 19*(1), 57–72.
Bawden, D., & Robinson, L. (2015). "A few exciting words": Information and entropy revisited. *Journal of the Association for Information Science and Technology, 66*(10), 1965–1987.
Becker, S. D. (2014). When organizations deinstitutionalize control practices: A multiple-case study of budget abandonment. *European Accounting Review, 23*(4), 593–623.
Bergh, J. C. V. D., & Stagl, S. (2003). Coevolution of economic behaviour and institutions: Towards a theory of institutional change. *Journal of Evolutionary Economics, 13*(3), 289–317. https://doi.org/10.1007/s00191-003-0158-8
Berman, M. S. (2008). On the Machian origin of inertia. *Astrophysics and Space Science, 318*, 269–272.
Best, S. (1991). Chaos and entropy: Metaphors in postmodern science and social theory. *Science as Culture, 2*(2), 188–226.
Bohm, D., & Peat, F. (1987). *Science, order and creativity*. Routledge.
Boyle, T. P., & Fairchild, J. F. (1997). The role of mesocosm studies in ecological risk analysis. *Ecological Applications, 7*(4), 1099–1102.
Bratianu, C. (2019). Exploring knowledge entropy in organizations. *Management Dynamics in the Knowledge., 7*(3), 353–366.
Bratianu, C., & Bejinaru, R. (2020). Knowledge dynamics: A thermodynamics approach. *Kybernetes, 49*(1), 6–21.
Brillouin, L. (1950). Thermodynamics and information theory. *American Scientist, 38*(4), 594–599.
Brillouin, L. (1956). *Science and information theory*. Dover.
Brillouin, L. (1961). Thermodynamics, statistics, and information. *American Journal of Physics, 29*(5), 318–328.
Britannica. (2023). https://www.britannica.com/
Brook, S. (2013). Social inertia and the field of creative labor. *Journal of Sociology, 49*(2–3), 309–324.
Browne, M. (2013). *Schaum's outline of physics for engineering and science*. McGraw-Hill Education.
Butts, R. E. (Ed.). (1986). *Kant's Philosophy of Physical Science: Metaphysische Anfangsgründe der Naturwissenschaft 1786–1986* (Vol. 33). Springer Science & Business Media.
CDC – NIOSH. (2023). https://www.cdc.gov/niosh/work-hour-training-for-nurses/longhours/mod7/03.html#:~:text=Sleep%20inertia%20is%20a%20temporary,reasoning%2C%20remembering%2C%20and%20learning
Chapin, F. S. (1927). A new definition of social institutions. *Soc F, 6*, 375.
Chaudhry, S., & Rubery, J. (2019). Why do established practices deinstitutionalize? An actor-centered approach. *British Journal of Management, 30*(3), 538–557.
Chollat-Namy, M., & Longo, G. (2022). Entropy, Negentropy and anti-entropy: The play of tensions to think about the living. *ISTE Openscience*. https://www.di.ens.fr/users/longo/files/CholłatLongo-entropies.pdf
Choudhury, M. A. (1998). *Studies in Islamic science and polity*. Palgrave Macmillan Books.

Choudhury, M. A., & Choudhury, M. A. (1998). A theory of renewal and continuity in Islamic science. In *Studies in Islamic science and polity* (pp. 76–91). Palgrave Macmillan.
Choukade, N. K., & Mangalekar, A. P. (2019). Engineering application of Laplace transform. *International Journal of Research in Informative Science Application & Techniques (IJRISAT), 3*(6–7), 27–36.
Christiansen, L. H., & Kroezen, J. J. (2016). Institutional maintenance through business collective action: The alcohol industry's engagement with the issue of alcohol-related harm. In J. Gehman, M. Lounsbury, & R. Greenwood (Eds.), *How Institutions Matter!* (Research in the Sociology of Organizations) (Vol. 48B, pp. 101–143). Emerald Group Publishing.
Clark, V., & Jennings, P. D. (1997). Talking about the natural environment: A means for deinstitutionalization. *American Behavioral Scientist, 40*(4), 454–464.
Clemente, M., & Roulet, T. J. (2015). Public opinion as a source of deinstitutionalization: A "spiral of silence" approach. *Academy of Management Review, 40*(1), 96–114.
Collier, J. (1986). Entropy in evolution. *Biology and philosophy, 1*(1), 5–24.
Coriat, B., & Weinstein, O. (2002). Organizations, firms and institutions in the generation of innovation. *Research Policy, 31*(2), 273–290.
Corning, P. A., & Kline, S. J. (1998). Thermodynamics, information and life revisited, part I:'To be or entropy'. *Systems Research and Behavioral Science: The Official Journal of the International Federation for Systems Research, 15*(4), 273–295.
Cox, D. R. (1962). *Renewal theory*. Methuen/Wiley.
Cox, D. R. (1983). Point processes and renewal theory: A brief survey. *Electronic systems effectiveness and life cycle costing*, 107–112.
Craik, K. J. W. (1967). *The nature of explanation*. Cambridge University Press.
Dacin, M. T., & Dacin, P. A. (2008). Traditions as institutionalized practice: Implications for deinstitutionalization. In R. Greenwood, C. Oliver, K. Sahlin, & R. Suddaby (Eds.), *The Sage handbook of organizational institutionalism* (pp. 327–351). Sage.
Dacin, M. T., Munir, K., & Tracey, P. (2010). Formal dining at Cambridge colleges: Linking ritual performance and institutional maintenance. *Academy of Management Journal, 53*(6), 1393–1418.
Datko, R. (1987). Laplace transform techniques in control and stabilization problems. In *Operator methods for optimal control problems* (p. 131). CRC Press.
Davies, B., & Martin, B. (1979). Numerical inversion of the Laplace transform: A survey and comparison of methods. *Journal of Computational Physics, 33*(1), 1–32.
Denzau, A. T., & North, D. C. (1994). Shared mental models: Ideologies and institutions. *KYKLOS-BERNE, 47*, 3–3.
Descartes, R. (1984). *Principles of philosophy: Translated, with explanatory notes* (Vol. 24). Springer Science & Business Media.
Descartes, R. (2012). *Principles of philosophy*. Simon and Schuster.
DiMaggio, P. J., & Powell, W. W. (1983). The iron cage revisited: Institutional isomorphism and collective rationality in organizational felds. *American Sociological Review, 48*(2), 147–160. https://doi.org/10.2307/2095101
DiStefano, J. J., Stubberud, A. J., & Williams, I. J. (1997). Schaum's outline of feedback and control systems. *McGraw-Hill Professional.*
Ebeling, V. (1978). *Formation of structures in irreversible processes. Introduction to the theory of dissipative structures*. Mir.
Ebeling, W., & Volkenstein, M. V. (1990). Entropy and the evolution of biological information. *Physica A: Statistical Mechanics and its Applications, 163*(1), 398–402.
Eigen, M. (1971). Self-organization of matter and the evolution of biological macromolecules. *Naturwissenschaften, 58*(10), 465–523.
Elitzur, A. C. (1994). Let there be life: Thermodynamic reflections on biogenesis and evolution. *Journal of Theoretical Biology, 168*(4), 429–459.
Faghih, N. (1989). *Maintenance engineering*. Navid Publications.
Faghih, N. (1992). *Science in the Mathnawí of Maulawi*. Navid Publications.

Faghih, N. (1993). Some scientific doctrines in the Mathnawi of Mawlana JalalalDin Mawlawi Rumi. *Hamdard Islamicus, 16/II*, 79–96.
Faghih, N. (1998). *Statistical quality control*. Samt Publications.
Faghih, N. (2003). *Dynamic systems: Principles and identification*. Samt Publications.
Faghih, N. (2005). *A cryptography of change and development in human systems*. Navid Publications.
Faghih, N., & Faghih, A. (2007). *Rumi and modern scientific views*. Xlibris.
Faghih, Nezameddin & Faghih, Ali (2008). *Nyquist frequency in sequentially sampled data*. https://mpra.ub.uni-muenchen.de/14311/
Farazmand, A. (2003). Chaos and transformation theories: A theoretical analysis with implications for organization theory and public management. *Public Organization Review, 3*, 339–372.
Feistel, R., & Ebeling, W. (2016). Entropy and the self-organization of information and value. *Entropy, 18*(5), 193.
Firsova S, Bilorus T, Olikh L, Salimon O (2022). *International Journal of Organizational Analysis* https://doi.org/10.1108/IJOA-12-2021-3061
Forrester, J. W. (1971). Counterintuitive behavior of social systems. *Theory and Decision, 2*(2), 109–140.
Frost, J., & Westermayer, T. (2008). Reflexive sensemaking to overcome cognitive inertia. *Strategic Competency Management in Business Administration: An Assessment of the Current Situation*, 91–98.
Gallagher, S. (2013). The socially extended mind. *Cognitive Systems Research, 25–26*, 4–12. https://doi.org/10.1016/j.cogsys.2013.03.008
Gallagher, S., & Crisafi, A. (2009). Mental institutions. *Topoi, 28*(1), 45–51. https://doi.org/10.1007/s11245-008-9045-0
Gao, K., Yang, Y., Sun, L., & Qu, X. (2020). Revealing psychological inertia in mode shift behavior and its quantitative influences on commuting trips. *Transportation Research Part F: Traffic Psychology and Behaviour, 71*, 272–287.
Gillett, S. L. (2006). Entropy and its misuse, I. Energy, free and otherwise. *Ecological Economics, 56*(1), 58–70.
Gilmore, S., & Sillince, J. A. A. (2014). Institutional theory and change: The deinstitutionalization of sports science at Club X. *Journal of Organizational Change Management, 27*(2), 314–330.
Gohil, M. D. G. (2017). *Education in 21st century, a challenge, towards excellence*, Dec, 2017. Vol. 9, Issue no. 3. https://hrdc.gujaratuniversity.ac.in/Uploads/EJournalDetail/27/37/33.pdf
Gould, S. J. (1994). Tempo and mode in the macroevolutionary reconstruction of darwinism. *Proceedings of the National Academy of Sciences of the United States of America, 91*(15), 6764–6771. https://doi.org/10.1073/pnas.91.15.6764
Grabow, W. W., & Andrews, G. E. (2019). On the nature and origin of biological information: The curious case of RNA. *Biosystems, 185*, 104031.
Graneau, P., & Graneau, N. (2006). *In the grip of the distant universe: The science of inertia*. World Scientific.
Graney, C. M. (2012). Francesco Ingoli's essay to Galileo: Tycho Brahe and science in the Inquisition's condemnation of the Copernican theory. *arXiv preprint arXiv:1211.4244*.
Graney, C. M. (2015). *Setting aside all authority: Giovanni Battista Riccioli and the science against Copernicus in the age of Galileo*. University of Notre Dame Press.
Guhl, A. M. (1968). Social inertia and social stability in chickens. *Animal Behaviour, 16*(2–3), 219–232.
Haddad, W. M. (2017). Thermodynamics: The unique universal science. *Entropy, 19*(11), 621.
Haken, H., & Portugali, J. (2016). Information and self-organization. *Entropy, 19*(1), 18.
Hannan, M. T., Pólos, L., & Carroll, G. R. (2004). The evolution of inertia. *Ind Corp Change, 13*(1), 213–242. https://doi.org/10.1093/icc/13.1.213
Harvey, D. (1993). The nature of environment: Dialectics of social and environmental change. *Socialist register, 29*.

Hodgkinson, G. P. (1997). Cognitive inertia in a turbulent market: The case of UK residential estate agents. *Journal of Management Studies, 34*(6), 921–945.
Holton, G., Rutherford, F. J., & Watson, F. G. (1971). 2. An introduction to the project physics course: An introduction for teachers (I. Special Issue on Harvard Project Physics Seminar). *Journal of the Physics Education Society of Japan, 19*(3), 182–203.
Holton, G. J., Rutherford, F. J., & Watson, F. G. (1981). *Project physics: Resource book*. Holt, Rinehart and Winston.
Johnson-Laird, P. N. (2004). The history of mental models. In K. I. Manktelow & M. C. Chung (Eds.), *Psychology of reasoning: Theoretical and historical perspectives* (pp. 179–212). Psychology Press.
Jones, N. A., Ross, H., Lynam, T., Perez, P., & Leitch, A. (2011). Mental models: An interdisciplinary synthesis of theory and methods. *Ecology and Society, 16*(1). https://doi.org/10.5751/ES-03802-160146
Kåberger, T., & Månsson, B. (2001). Entropy and economic processes—Physics perspectives. *Ecological Economics, 36*(1), 165–179.
Kant, I. (1786). *Kritik der Urteilskraft und Schriften zur Naturphilosophie* (Vol. 5). Insel-Verlag.
Khurmi, R. S., & Gupta, J. K. (2005). *A textbook of machine design*. S. Chand publishing.
Kim, J., Yoon, J., & Lee, J. D. (2020). Dominant design and evolution of technological trajectories: The case of tank technology, 1915–1998. *Journal of Evolutionary Economics, 1–16*. https://doi.org/10.1007/s00191-020-00697-1
Kon, I. (1989). The psychology of social inertia. *Soviet Review, 30*(2), 59–76.
Kondra, A. Z., & Hurst, D. C. (2009). Institutional processes of organizational culture. *Culture and Organization, 15*(1), 39–58.
Koutsoyiannis, D., & Sargentis, G. F. (2021). Entropy and wealth. *Entropy, 23*(10), 1356.
Land, G. & Beth J. (1998) *Breakpoint and beyond: Mastering the future today*, leadership 2000 Inc publication.
Landsberg, G. S. (Ed.). (1972). *Textbook of elementary physics: Oscillations and waves, optics, structure of atom* (Vol. 3). Mir Publishers.
Lawson, C. (1994). The transformational model of social activity and economic analysis: A reinterpretation of the work of J.R. Commons. *Review of Political Economy Edward Arnold, 6*(2), 186–204. https://doi.org/10.1080/09538259400000009
Lawson, T. (2003). Institutionalism: On the need to firm up notions of social structure and the human subject. *Journal of Economic Issues, 37*(1), 175–207.
Lawson, T. (2012a). Ontology and the study of social reality: Emergence, organisation, community, power, social relations, corporations, artefacts and money. *Cambridge Journal of Economics Narnia, 36*(2), 345–385. https://doi.org/10.1093/cje/ber050
Lawson, T. (2012b). *Reorienting economics*. Taylor and Francis. https://doi.org/10.4324/9780203929964
Lawson, T. (2016a). *Collective practices and norms* (pp. 249–277). Springer. https://doi.org/10.1007/978-3-319-28439-2_11
Lawson, T. (2016b). Comparing conceptions of social ontology: Emergent social entities and/or institutional facts? *Journal for the Theory of Social Behaviour, 46*(4), 359–399. https://doi.org/10.1111/jtsb.12126
Lee, J. D., Jeong, D., Jung, E. Y., Kim, Y., Kim, J., He, Y., & Choi, S. (2022). Mapping the evolutionary pattern of mobile products: A phylogenetic approach. *IEEE Transactions on Engineering Management*. https://doi.org/10.1109/TEM.2022.3214489
Lee, H., Jeong, D., & Lee, J. D. (2023). Drivers of institutional evolution: Phylogenetic inertia and ecological pressure. *Journal of Evolutionary Economics*, 1–30.
Lewis, P. A. (2005). Structure, agency and causality in post-revival Austrian economics: Tensions and resolutions. *Review of Political Economy, 17*(2), 291–316. https://doi.org/10.1080/09538250500067320
Lewis, O. A., & Steinmo, S. (2012). How institutions evolve: Evolutionary theory and institutional change. *Polity, 44*(3), 314–339. https://doi.org/10.1057/pol.2012.10

Loasby, B. J. (2001). *Cognition, imagination and institutions in demand creation* (pp. 13–27). Springer.
Lok, J., & De Rond, M. (2013). On the plasticity of institutions: Containing and restoring practice breakdowns at the Cambridge University Boat Club. *Academy of Management Journal, 56*(1), 185–207.
Maguire, S., & Hardy, C. (2009). Discourse and deinstitutionalization: The decline of DDT. *Academy of Management Journal, 52*(1), 148–178.
Mattila, A. S. (2003). The impact of cognitive inertia on postconsumption evaluation processes. *Journal of the Academy of Marketing Science, 31*, 287–299.
Mavrofides, T., Kameas, A., Papageorgiou, D., & Los, A. (2011). On the entropy of social systems: A revision of the concepts of entropy and energy in the social context. *Systems Research and Behavioral Science, 28*(4), 353–368.
Mellemvik, F., Monsen, N., & Olson, O. (1988). Functions of accounting—A discussion. *Scandinavian Journal of Management, 4*(3–4), 101–119.
Meyer, J. W., & Rowan, B. (1977). Institutionalized organizations: Formal structure as myth and ceremony. *The American Journal of Sociology, 83*(2), 340–363. https://doi.org/10.1086/226550
Montgomery, A. W., & Dacin, M. T. (2020). Water wars in Detroit: Custodianship and the work of institutional renewal. *Academy of Management Journal, 63*(5), 1455–1484.
Moroni, S. (2010). An evolutionary theory of institutions and a dynamic approach to reform. *Planning Theory, 9*(4), 275–297. https://doi.org/10.1177/1473095210368778
Munck, A. F., Rosenschöld, J., Rozema, J. G., & Frye-Levine, L. A. (2014). Institutions and policy processes: the means to the ends of adaptation. *Wiley Interdisciplinary Reviews: Climate Change, 5*(5), 639–648. https://doi.org/10.1002/wcc.29
Newton, I. (1833). *Philosophiae naturalis principia mathematica* (Vol. 1). G. Brookman.
Nicholis, G., & Prigogine, I. (1977). *Self-organization in nonequilibrium systems: From dissipative structures to order through fluctuations*. Wiley-Interscience.
North, D. C. (1990). *Institutions, institutional change and economic performance*. Cambridge University Press.
Oliver, C. (1992). The antecedents of deinstitutionalization. *Organization Studies, 13*(4), 563–588.
Ostrowski, A. M. (1959). A quantitative formulation of Sylvester's law of inertia. *Proceedings of the National Academy of Sciences, 45*(5), 740–744.
Parkin, A. (1981). Repetition, mourning and working through. *The International Journal of Psycho-Analysis, 62*, 271.
Parrish, S., & Beaubien, R. (2000). *The great mental models volume 2: Physics, Chemistry and Biology*. Latticework Publishing.
Pascal, R., & Pross, A. (2015). Stability and its manifestation in the chemical and biological worlds. *Chemical Communications, 51*(90), 16160–16165.
Patora-Wysocka, Z. (2015). Deinstitutionalization of practice–a trigger of organizational change in the internationalization process of companies. *Social Sciences, 89*(3), 84–98.
Potter, M. C., Nelson, E. W., Best, C. L., & McLean, W. G. (2021). *Schaum's outline of engineering mechanics: Dynamics*. McGraw-Hill Education.
Price, J. C. (1977). Thermal inertia mapping: A new view of the earth. *Journal of Geophysical Research, 82*(18), 2582–2590.
Prieto, P. P. (2022). The institutional evolution of central banks. *Journal of Evolutionary Economics, 32*(3), 1049–1070. https://doi.org/10.1007/s00191-021-00759-y
Prigogine, I. (1998). *The end of certainty: Time, chaos, and the new law of nature*. The Free Press.
Prigogine, I., & Stengers, I. (1984). *Order out of chaos*. Bantam.
Pross, A. (2003). The driving force for life's emergence: Kinetic and thermodynamic considerations. *Journal of Theoretical Biology, 220*(3), 393–406.
Ramasco, J. J., & Morris, S. A. (2006). Social inertia in collaboration networks. *Physical Review E, 73*(1), 016122.
Raynard, M., Kodeih, F., & Greenwood, R. (2021). Proudly elitist and undemocratic? The distributed maintenance of contested practices. *Organization Studies, 42*(1), 7–33.

Rizcallah, J. A. (2015). Moment of inertia by differentiation. *The Physics Teacher, 53*(8), 482–484.
Rosenbaum, E. (2022). Mental models and institutional inertia. *Journal of Institutional Economics, 18*(3), 361–378.
Røvik, K. A. (1996). Deinstitutionalization and the logic of fashion. In B. Czarniawska & G. Sevon (Eds.), *Translating organizational change* (pp. 139–172). Walter de Gruyter.
Rowlinson, J. S. (1970). Probability, information and entropy. *Nature, 225*(5239), 1196–1198.
Rumi. (1207–1273). *The Mathnawí of Jalaluddín Rumi* (p. 74), Translation and Commentary, Nicholson, Reynold A, Volume I, 1926. Messrs Luzac & Co. LTD.
Ryan, J. P. (1980). Information—Entropy interfaces and different levels of biological organization. *Journal of Theoretical Biology, 84*(1), 31–48.
Saucedo, R., & Schiring, E. E. (1968). *Introduction to continuous and digital control systems*. Mac-Millan.
Schuster, P. (2016). Increase in complexity and information through molecular evolution. *Entropy, 18*(11), 397.
Sciama, D. W. (1953). On the origin of inertia. *Monthly Notices of the Royal Astronomical Society, 113*(1), 34–42.
Scott, W. R. (1987). The adolescence of institutional theory. *Administrative Science Quarterly, 32*(4), 493–511.
Scott, W. R. (2015). Institutional theory: Contributing to a theoretical research program. In K. G. Smith & M. A. Hitt (Eds.), *Great minds in management: The process of theory development* (pp. 460–484). Oxford University Press.
Shanahan, T. (2011). Phylogenetic inertia and Darwin's higher law. *Studies in History and Philosophy of Biological and Biomedical Sciences, 42*(1), 60–68. https://doi.org/10.1016/j.shpsc.2010.11.013
Shannon, C. E. (1948). A mathematical theory of communication. *Bell System Technical Journal, 27*(3), 379–423. https://doi.org/10.1002/j.1538-7305.1948.tb01338.x
Shu, L., Liu, X., Cui, K., Liu, Z., & Liu, W. (2020). Fluctuation and inertia. *Nuclear Physics B, 950*, 114873.
Smith, A. C., & Graetz, F. (2006). Complexity theory and organizing form dualities. *Management Decision, 44*(7), 851–870.
Stewart, W. A. (1963). An inquiry into the concept of working through. *Journal of the American Psychoanalytic Association, 11*(3), 474–499.
Stollberg, R., & Hill, F. F. (1965). *Physics: Fundamentals and frontiers*. Houghton Mifflin publication.
Stollberg, R., & Hill, F. F. (1966). Book and film reviews: Physics fundamentals and Frontiers. *The Physics Teacher, 4*(2), 88–88.
Stollberg, R., Hill, F. F., & Foland, W. (1965). Physics: Fundamentals and frontiers. *American Journal of Physics, 33*(11), 972–973.
Stralberg, D., Arseneault, D., Baltzer, J. L., Barber, Q. E., Bayne, E. M., Boulanger, Y., & Whitman, E. (2020). Climate-change refugia in boreal North America: What, where, and for how long? *Frontiers in Ecology and the Environment, 18*(5), 261–270.
Stuart, C. I. J. M. (1985a). Bio-informational equivalence. *Journal of theoretical Biology, 113*(4), 611–636.
Stuart, C. I. J. M. (1985b). Physical models of biological information and adaptation. *Journal of Theoretical Biology, 113*(3), 441–454.
Styer, D. F. (2000). Insight into entropy. *American Journal of Physics, 68*(12), 1090–1096.
Styer, D. F. (2008). Entropy and evolution. *American Journal of Physics, 76*(11), 1031–1033.
Sui, J. G., & Liu, Y. (2020). Co-evolution of technology and institutions in emerging industries: Case from elec- tric vehicles in China. *Journal of Industrial Integration and Management, 5*(1), 13–31. https://doi.org/10.1142/s2424862219500143
Susskind, L. (1997). *The black hole war: My battle with Stephen Hawking to make the world safe for quantum mechanics*. Little Brown.

Swendsen, R. H. (2011). How physicists disagree on the meaning of entropy. *American Journal of Physics, 79*(4), 342–348.
Swendsen, R. H. (2012). Choosing a definition of entropy that works. *Foundations of Physics, 42*(4), 582–593.
Tassi, P., & Muzet, A. (2000). Sleep inertia. *Sleep Medicine Reviews, 4*(4), 341–353.
Tebaldi, C., & Friedlingstein, P. (2013). Delayed detection of climate mitigation benefits due to climate inertia and variability. *Proceedings of the National Academy of Sciences, 110*(43), 17229–17234.
UIA Encyclopedia of World Problems & Human Potential. (2023). http://encyclopedia.uia.org/en
Vega-Redondo, F. (1993). Technological change and institutional inertia: A game-theoretic approach. *Journal of Evolutionary Economics, 3*(3), 199–224. https://doi.org/10.1007/BF01200868
Volkenstein, M. V. (1977). The amount and value of information in biology. *Foundations of Physics, 7*(1), 97–109.
Volkenstein, M. V. (2009). *Entropy and information*. Base.
Volkenstein, M. V., & Chernavskii, D. S. (1978). Information and biology. *Journal of Social and Biological Structures, 1*(1), 95–108.
Walters, G. D. (2019). Psychological inertia revisited: Replicating and extending the differential effect of proactive and reactive criminal thinking on crime continuity. *Deviant Behavior, 40*(2), 156–170.
Westermeyer, T., & Frost, J. (2009). Understanding and preventing cognitive inertia–a dual process perspective. *Journal of Competences, Strategy & Management, 3*.
Wicken, J. S. (1978). Information transformations in molecular evolution. *Journal of Theoretical Biology, 72*(1), 191–204.
Wicken, J. S. (1979). The generation of complexity in evolution: A thermodynamic and information-theoretical discussion. *Journal of Theoretical Biology, 77*(3), 349–365.
Wicken, J. S. (1980). A thermodynamic theory of evolution. *Journal of Theoretical Biology, 87*(1), 9–23.
Wicken, J. S. (1986). Information, entropy and evolution: An agenda for dialogue. *Journal of Social and Biological Structures, 9*(3), 275–277.
Willmer, M. (1977). Information theory and organization structure. *Kybernetes, 6*(4), 277–287.
Wrenn, M. V. (2006). Agency and mental models in heterodox economics. *Journal of Economic Issues, 40*(2), 483–491.
Yamoah, F. A., Sivarajah, U., Mahroof, K., & Peña, I. G. (2022). Demystifying corporate inertia towards transition to circular economy: A management frame of reference. *International Journal of Production Economics, 244*, 108388.
Young, T. R., & Kiel, L. D. (1994). Control, prediction, and non-linear dynamics. In *The Red Feather Institute series on non-linear social dynamics* (p. 212). The Red Feather Institute.
Zantvoort, B. (2017). Political inertia and social acceleration. *Philosophy & Social Criticism, 43*(7), 707–723.
Zárate, M. A., Shaw, M., Marquez, J. A., & Biagas, D., Jr. (2012). Cultural inertia: The effects of cultural change on intergroup relations and the self-concept. *Journal of Experimental Social Psychology, 48*(3), 634–645.
Zuber, M. S. (1998). Dialectic, dialogue, and controversy: The case of Galileo. *Science in Context, 11*(2).

An Introduction to Institutional Inertia: Concepts, Types and Causes

Ali Hussein Samadi, Masoomeh Alipourian, Sajjad Afroozeh, Alireza Raanaei, and Mojtaba Panahi

1 Introduction

In the Aristotelian worldview (which dominated throughout the Middle Ages), change was thought to result from random changes in the properties of durable matter, all material beings on earth tended toward their natural place, and since rest took precedence over change, change and movement were things that needed to be explained (Bostock, 2008).

From the sixteenth century onwards, scientific, political and philosophical developments questioned the priority of "*rest*" over "*change*". The Copernican Revolution dispelled the notion that the Earth was at rest at the center of the universe. The development of physics, chemistry, biology, and geology showed that everything, from physical elements, living organisms, to our planet, is subject to constant processes of change, decay, and transformation, and ultimately, even time and space are relative. In politics, a series of political and social revolutions—from the Dutch revolt against the Spanish crown in 1572, to the revolution in England, to the American and French revolutions—disrupted the established social order (Arendt, 2006). In philosophy, the critique of religion and the traditional authority of belief in eternal nature undermined God-given social hierarchy and immutable natural order.

From the nineteenth century onwards, the scientific study of heat and the behavior of gases and fluids completely changed Newton's view. Newtonian physics describes a "*clockwork universe*", a stable universe characterized by eternal physical laws, exemplified by the regular rotation of celestial bodies. But the study of heat, begun by Fourier and Carnot, and continued with technological inventions during the Industrial Revolution, showed that many processes in nature are irreversible. From a thermodynamic point of view, in all natural processes, energy is irreversibly

A. H. Samadi (✉) · M. Alipourian · S. Afroozeh · A. Raanaei · M. Panahi
Department of Economics, Shiraz University, Shiraz, Iran
e-mail: asamadi@rose.shirazu.ac.ir

N. Faghih, A. H. Samadi (eds.), *Institutional Inertia*, Contributions to Economics,
https://doi.org/10.1007/978-3-031-51175-2_3

lost. Therefore, time is not reversible, but has a certain direction, and we face disorder or "entropy" (Atkins, 2010).

Entropy is increasing and tends to a maximum state (Prigogine & Stengers, 1984). Entropy is a measure of the expression of the second law of thermodynamics, where any isolated system (that is, a system that does not exchange any energy with the outside) spontaneously evolves toward thermodynamic equilibrium. That is, a state in which no measurable changes occur and thermal, mechanical, radiation and chemical potentials reach their maximum stability. The second law of thermodynamics states that within any given system, or between systems that are connected, there is a tendency to "level out" differences, so that the system becomes increasingly less capable of producing work. While the total amount of energy is conserved, the distribution of energy in any system tends to become homogeneous (Herbert B. Callen, 1985).

The discovery of the second law of thermodynamics fundamentally undermined the Newtonian picture of a "stable" universe and reinforced the idea that "change" takes precedence and that "stability" must be explained. This was a fundamental step in the transition from the Aristotelian worldview to a modern and dynamic view of nature (Zantvoort, 2015) and caused a fundamental change in our way of thinking about the world. We no longer think of "reality" in terms of a fixed, natural order, but rather in terms of processes of generation and decay. For this reason, the concept of resistance to change or "inertia" plays an important role in explaining the "stability of institutions".

The stability of institutions makes them meaningful, but does not prevent attempts at institutional change and makes institutional change "extremely gradual" (North, 1990). The response of institutions to new challenges, which aim to support changes, is often very slow, leading to specific types of support for existing institutions (which do not correspond to social needs). Therefore, understanding the "sources of institutional stability" (or sources of institutional inertia) is very important for understanding the process of institutional change. In the analysis of how institutions change over time based on the "source of change", four theories of institutional change can be mentioned: collective choice theory, evolutionary theory, equilibrium theory, and deinstitutionalization theory. The first three theories discuss the emergence of new beliefs and practices; While the last theory discusses the weakening and disappearance of beliefs and practices (Samadi & Alipourian, 2021).

In the social, economic, political, and psychological fields, the term *inertia* is often used to describe an irrational or counterproductive resistance to change in individuals or institutions that are considered necessary, desirable, or inevitable. Institutions, ideas, and power structures take root over time and may become ineffective or obsolete, even if they once served a legitimate or useful role. According to Freud (1989), there is an "*inherent inertia* in organic life": the human organism is inherently conservative and changes only when forced to change by external conditions. Similar to individuals, institutions and other social structures are inherently inert: that is, institutions (rather than gradually adapting to changing environmental, technological, or social conditions) last for some time beyond their useful life, but suddenly reach a stage of collapse.

The studies of new institutionalists brought a concept called "*institutional inertia*" from physics to economics. Institutional inertia and resistance to change is a defining feature of institutions, because they have considerable stability and predictability (North, 1990: 89). Despite the fact that the concept of inertia and institutional inertia has entered economic literature decades ago, there is no comprehensive definition of the concept of inertia and institutional inertia. The purpose of this chapter is to cover this gap in the institutional economics literature. To achieve this goal, the concept of inertia in physics must be well understood. This issue is considered in this chapter (Sect. 2) and an attempt has been made to explain it in the simple language of inertia.

Investigating the concept of institutional inertia, the types of institutional inertia and the factors that create it, is another goal pursued in this chapter. In the existing studies, these titles have been mentioned sporadically, but no comprehensive study can be found that has done such a work. This chapter aims to fill such a gap. Accordingly, the concept of institutional inertia is explained in Sect. 3. Since inertia, apart from economics, has entered many sciences such as medicine, psychology, politics, sociology and management; Different types of inertia have been investigated in different sciences. In Sect. 4, types of institutional inertia are explained. In this chapter, types of inertia at the level of individuals, inertia at the level of social and political structures, and inertia at the level of knowledge development, concepts and ideas are explained. By reviewing the literature of new institutionalism, sixteen main factors causing institutional inertia were identified. These factors are divided into four categories: economic factors, socio-political factors, historical factors, and psychological factors and are briefly explained. Among the other contributions of this chapter, we can mention providing evidence of the compatibility of institutional changes and institutional continuity (Sect. 6).

This rest of this chapter is organized as follows. The concept of inertia is mentioned in Sect. 2, and institutional inertia is mentioned in Sect. 3. Types of inertia are explained in Sect. 4. In Sect. 5, the sources of institutional inertia are discussed in detail. In Sect. 6, some evidence of the compatibility of institutional changes and institutional continuity is presented. Section 7 is dedicated to conclusion.

2 The Concept of Inertia

Inertia means stillness, stationary, immobility, and stickiness.[1] Inertia is derived from the Latin word "*iners*" which means idle and sluggish. This concept has gradually entered the literature of management, economics, political, and social science from physics to include a range of characteristics (such as resistance to

[1] To read more about the concept of inertia, refer to Chapter "Inertia: Resistance and Endurance" of this book.

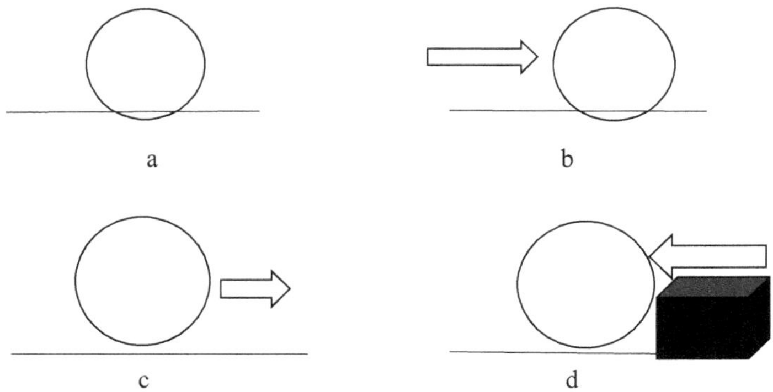

Fig. 1 Newton's first law of motion
Source: authors' own figure

change) related to social systems. Inertia was first proposed by Kepler to explain why a planet needs an external force in the opposite direction to move from a state of inertia or slow motion in a circular motion around the Sun. This issue was used in a different way by Galileo to explain why particles move with acceleration in a fixed path when affected by friction and other external forces. In explaining why an object moves with constant acceleration in a straight line and how an external force deflects it, Newton raised some issues. This definition is known as Newton's famous first law of motion or the *law of inertia*. Newton's first law states:

> When the outcome of the forces acting on the things are zero, if the things are at rest, it will remain stationary forever, and if the things are moving (at a constant speed), it will remain forever with the same speed and in the same direction continues to move.

Newton's first law is shown in Fig. 1 (Earman & Friedman, 1973). In this figure, the object is shown as a circle, and the force applied to the object is shown as an arrow, and the direction of movement is shown with a linear arrow. Also, the surface is shown with a straight line and the obstacle with a black cube. According to Newton's first law or the law of inertia, if no force is applied to an object at rest, that object will remain in the same state (Fig. 1a). If a force is applied to this object, the object will move (Fig. 1b). If no force is applied to the moving object, this object will continue to move with a constant direction and speed (Fig. 1c). This movement will continue until a force is applied to the object (Fig. 1d).

In classical physics, which was based on Aristotelian principles, it was believed that objects on or near the earth; move in a straight line near their natural location, slightly lower or higher. Of course, objects can be moved against their natural location; like throwing stones or arrows. This type of movement was called violent motion. In addition, celestial bodies should not be made of four earthly elements and their movement should be around a circle. In modern physics, this duality was rejected and the same sets of laws were considered valid for the movement of all objects, both terrestrial and celestial. Also, in modern physics, the belief in the necessity of a driving force for any movement was discarded. The basis of modern physics was the law of inertia, which was proposed by Newton among his three laws. Newton's law of inertia comes directly from Descartes' studies (Cohen, 1964).

Inertia is generally defined as the resistance of a physical body against changing the speed or direction of movement (Serway & Beichner, 2000; Tielens & Van Hertem, 2016). In other words, inertia refers to the tendency of an object to maintain its previous state unless forces are applied to it. In physical systems this is a default. Of course, inertia does not mean statis or no-change.

The concept of inertia is also used to talk about resistance to change in people and in political and social structures, and in academic discourse it is used in various fields such as sociology, psychology, organization theory, economics, political science and philosophy. This term has a broader concept in economic and social systems. Because path dependency in physical objects does not remain after changing; while this is an inherent characteristic of complex economic and social systems.

Physical objects do not resist change, they simply continue to move in the absence of forces. But when the concept of inertia is used in society, it has a normative content that does not exist in the physical context. To say that a person, an institution, or a society in general is inert is a value judgment. In other words, when talking about institutional or social inertia, people are not providing an objective analysis of a situation, but talking about what is possible and desirable. In order to better understand this topic, in the next part, we will discuss the concept of institutional inertia and its synonyms from the point of view of institutionalists.

3 Institutional Inertia

Institutions[2] can be defined as a combination of norms, rules, and functions in a specific policy environment. Norms are determined through collective ideas regarding the definition of the policy domain, relevant actors, and appropriate patterns of interaction. Rules are guidelines that support state power and bind actors. Finally, functions are interactive models. This definition shows the actors who are materially seeking self-interest and rationale, they are limited by formal rules and can be placed through this definition in wider political, historical, and cultural contexts (Banchoff, 2002).

In many empirical and theoretical studies on institutions, it is assumed explicitly or implicitly that institutions are stable (Acemoglu, 2006). Institutional inertia is defined by the "stickiness" of institutions or how they resist change (Pierson, 2011). This resistance to change is a defining characteristic of institutions, as they tend

[2] Institutions are the rules of the game in a society or the human-designed constraints that shape human interactions. Institutions reduce uncertainty by providing structure to everyday life." Institutions include both formal rules such as laws and constitutions and informal constraints such as contracts and norms (North, 1990: 3). Fundamentally, institutions are seen as enduring rules that govern human interactions, and are designed by human hands. For further reading, refer to Samadi and Alipourian (2021).

significantly toward stability and predictability (Hoffman & Ventresca, 1999; Munck af Rosenschöld et al., 2014). In some other studies, the failure to transform an ineffective organizational form into an efficient one has been suggested as institutional inertia (Valderrama, 2009). In Sunstein's (2014) study, the decisions of governments are listed due to substantive judgments and institutional constraints. These limitations are presented in the form of three sets of opportunity cost, political cost and decision cost. These limitations can make institutional changes costly and difficult. Thus, for government decision makers, there are degrees of institutional inertia resulting from cost-benefit analysis.

From the point of view of new institutionalists, institutional inertia means resistance to change. Creating change requires a radical break with the past, abandoning past habits and routines, and outdated institutions and transitioning to new institutions and structures. In order to achieve institutional change, institutional inertia (which is inherent in institutions) must be overcome. Once institutional inertia is overcome, new institutions can be established. Of course, institutional inertia will be created again after the establishment of new institutions, and institutions will resist change (Genschel, 1995). Institutions must be relatively stable and durable to create order. This characteristic of institutions leads to their resistance to change (Kingston & Caballero, 2009; North, 1990). In general, institutional inertia refers to:

- Institutions' inability to provide timely answers to the created problems,
- The tendency of institutions to resist changes,
- The stickiness of institutions or how they resist changes and
- Institutions' inability to respond appropriately to changes in the national and international environments.

In the literature of institutional economics, there are other terms and concepts that are either synonymous with inertia or are closely related to it. From the point of view of some institutionalists, "*institutional inertia*" means the stickiness of institutions and their resistance to changes (Munck af Rosenschöld et al., 2014, p. 640). "*Institutional stickiness*" also refers to the situation or states in which institutions should change but do not change or do not have the conditions for change (Haase et al., 2009).

Acemoglu et al. (2021) also mention the strategic stability of institutions and "*institutional stasis*". Institutional strategic stability occurs when institutions remain in place for fear of subsequent, less beneficial changes that follow initial reforms. Institutional stasis is actually the simplest type of *institutional continuity*. Institutional stasis is an unchanging institutional equilibrium; That is, the same institutional arrangements that we start with are repeated over and over again. There are several reasons for institutional stasis, but the most important of them is that power begets power. In other words, power generates more power. That is, the groups that are empowered through current institutions take advantage of these institutions and as a result use their power to maintain them and, in this process, reproduce their power over future institutions. However, Acemoglu et al. (2021) believe that despite the popularity of ideas based on institutional stasis in the literature of economics and political science, most institutions are in a constant state of fluctuation and successive changes, but their path may still be shaped by past institutional choices. Therefore, there is path dependence, which indicates that the initial conditions determine the subsequent paths of institutions and how they react to shocks. In other words, although there are examples of institutional stasis and the thinking of many economists and political scientists is shaped by such dynamics, institutional stasis is rare. Instead, most institutions are in a constant state of flux.

In another approach, the concept of *path-dependent change* is used. In this approach, current institutions determine the future course of institutional change, both because of internal dynamics and because even small differences can cause large divergences in response to shocks. Of course, "*dependency on the traveled path*" should not be confused with *inertia*. North (2010) believes that path dependence is a constraint on the choice set in the present, which is caused by past historical experiences.

From the above discussions, it can be concluded that *institutional rigidity* is synonymous with *institutional inertia*; But it is different from *institutional stasis*. Because the inertia of the institutions is compatible with the fluctuations and changes of the institutions. What is emphasized in institutional inertia is that the institutions do not move towards the desired reforms and there are obstacles on their way. However, institutional inertia does not mean no changes or institutional stasis. Thus, Acemoglu's analysis of institutional stasis is not incompatible with the concept of institutional inertia.

4 Types of Institutional Inertia

"Institution" has a multi-dimensional and multi-level concept. Each branch of the school of institutionalism has provided a definition of the institution according to its intellectual tradition. From the point of view of the old institutionalists, the aspect of structural dominance over individual action is more pronounced (Hodgson, 2000). This is while in the definition of new institutionalism, the activism of individuals is more decisive in the formation of the institution. The purpose of this chapter is not to deal with the different definitions of the institution, and only the multi-layered characteristic of the institution has been paid attention to achieve the goals of this chapter. According to the different definitions of the institution, a three-level classification of the institution can be presented:

- Definitions that emphasize the *structural aspect of the institution*: according to these definitions, the institution as a collective action shape and directs individual action (for more reading, see (Commons, 1931)).
- Definitions that emphasize *the aspect of individual action*: according to these definitions, the institution is derived from individual rules, and what determines the institution at the structural level is the behavioral patterns of the people in the society. (For more reading, see (Acemoglu et al., 2019; North, 1990, 2010)).

- Definitions that pay attention to the mediation of the institution between the person and the structure: this definition, which is less discussed in the literature, considers the institution as an intermediary between the relationship between the individual level and the structure level (for more studies, see (Dubois, 2019)).

This three-level classification is important because in the classification of types of inertia, we face structural and individual inertia. For example, *organizational inertia* is an example of *structural inertia* and *cognitive inertia* is an example of *inertia in individual level*. According to the classification of three levels of the institution, *institutional inertia* can be considered comprehensive of all types of inertia, because institutional inertia includes both structural inertia and individual inertia.

In addition to physical and natural sciences, the term inertia has also been used in sciences related to human behavior (such as: social sciences, economics, political sciences, management, psychology and medicine). In these sciences, inertia is defined as the tendency of individuals to remain in the existing situation and resist change. Of course, this definition is general and in different branches of human sciences, according to the characteristics of that branch, there are specific and distinct definitions of inertia. In fact, we define three types or levels of inertia that include types of inertia in different sciences. These three levels are: inertia in individual level, inertia in social and political structures, and inertia in the development of knowledge and concepts. In the following, these three levels of inertia are examined and the inertias in various human sciences related to each level are also given.

4.1 Inertia in Individuals

It is said that individuals stick to their beliefs and ways of thinking in the face of conflicting evidence, and continue to act as they always have, even when other ways of acting become possible and sometimes have become more suitable. In more severe cases, psychological resistance becomes the subject of psychoanalysis or other forms of psychotherapy that try to change irrational or destructive behaviors and beliefs. Hegel (1977) links inertia to anxiety and states: People resist change because they are more familiar with the status quo and change leads to uncertainty and fear. The roots of this level of inertia can be found in cognitive science and psychology. Therefore, in the following, cognitive inertia and psychological inertia will be investigated. Also, in addition to the inertias that exist in psychology and psychotherapy, there is also a type of inertia in medicine and the treatment of the human body, which is known as *"clinical inertia"*. This type of inertia is also discussed in this section.

4.1.1 Cognitive Inertia

William J. McGuire presented the first theory of cognitive inertia in 1960. This theory was based on emerging theories in social psychology and cognitive psychology (which centered on cognitive consistency, (including Fritz Heider's balance theory and Leon Festinger's cognitive dissonance). McGuire used the term cognitive inertia to explain the initial resistance to change the way an idea is processed after acquiring new information (contrary to the original idea).

Cognitive inertia refers to a particular orientation in how a person thinks about an issue, belief, or strategy to resist change. In the clinical and neuroscience literature, cognitive inertia is often defined as the lack of motivation to engage in the distinctive cognitive processes required to address a problem or issue. Cognitive inertia happens because people do not want to change. This applies to personal behavior, beliefs, relationships and commitments. Once someone believes something, it is usually difficult for her to change his mind.[3]

The basic idea of cognitive inertia is rooted in philosophical epistemology. Early references to reducing cognitive inertia can be found in Plato's Socratic dialogues. Socrates exposes the opposing person's fallacy and forces him to change his mind or face the fact that their thought processes are in conflict (Overholser (2011), Jones and Simmons (2017)).

4.1.2 Psychological Inertia

One of the important types of inertia in human sciences is *psychological inertia*, which is closely related to a concept called "tendency to stay in the existing situation" in psychology. One of the scholars who raised this issue well is David Gal. Gal (2006) shows how psychological insight into the nature of behavior and preferences emphasizes the strong desire of people to remain in the status quo and states that:

- People when do not have a clear preference between the status quo and alternatives (or change), they tend to remain in the status quo.
- Furthermore, the ambiguous and uncertain nature of preferences suggests that people will often have uncertain preferences between alternatives, and hence, the tendency to stay in the status quo is likely to be a strong effect.

Gal also states that people will not act to change the status quo unless they are motivated to do so. And this will eventually lead to psychological inertia.

[3]To read more about the concept, and causes of cognitive inertia, and its effect on institutional change and institutional inertia, refer to Chapters "Cognitive Inertia as a Fundamental Cause of Institutional Inertia" and "Overview of Institutional–Organization Inertia Nexus" of this book.

Therefore, the concept of psychological inertia can be defined as follows: Psychological inertia is the tendency to maintain the status quo (or the default option), unless forced to intervene or reject it by a psychological motivation (Gal, 2006).

Psychological inertia is similar to status quo bias, but it has one fundamental difference. Psychological inertia involves the reluctance to perform any action or activity, while status quo bias involves avoiding any change that is perceived as a disadvantage. Limited research has been done on psychological inertia and its causes. It has been seen that between choosing the default option and other options, people prefer to choose the default option (even if other options are more beneficial to them). For example, psychological inertia may cause people to hold off on a losing investment, despite information telling them otherwise, causing them to suffer more losses.

4.1.3 Clinical Inertia

Clinical inertia was initially defined in 2001 by Phillips. According to this definition, clinical inertia applies only to the management of risk factors, when therapeutic targets are clearly defined and the benefits to reach those targets are well established. Effective therapies should be widely available, and practice guidelines disseminated extensively. Clinical inertia appears whenever the health-care provider does not initiate or intensify therapy appropriately when therapeutic goals are not reached: "recognition of the problem, but failure to act". In fact, the discrepancy between Guidelines and clinical practice is defined in the literature as "clinical inertia" or "therapeutic inertia.

Clinical inertia includes three categories of physician-related factors, patient-related factors, and treatment system-related factors. Therefore, clinical inertia is not an appropriate title for this category because it is well established that clinical inertia is not always related to the physician but often to patient-related factors (like denial of illness, incorrect medication use, or low health literacy) or related factors. It is related to the health system (for example, limited access to health services). According to this, "*therapeutic inertia*" is a more suitable title to describe the lack of success in advancing or reducing the intensity of treatment (Karam et al., 2020).

Phillips et al. (2001) described therapeutic inertia as a situation in which physicians provide patient care despite being aware of the patient's failure to achieve therapeutic goals in the management of chronic diseases (including hypertension, dyslipidemia, and diabetes). They have proposed three factors for therapeutic inertia related to health care providers: overestimating the quality of care, making excuses for refusing to intensify treatment and lack of facilities, time and training necessary to intensify treatment in order to achieve treatment goals.

4.2 *Inertia in Social and Political Structures*

Institutions, laws and ideas develop at a particular moment in time and in response to particular conditions and social problems. Since "institutions tend to isolate themselves from their environment and persist in changing conditions, they can become obsolete" and when the reason for their existence has long disappeared, according to an outdated logic continues to work. Francis Fukuyama (2011) introduces this form of inertia with the concept of political decline and states that: "Conservatism of societies in relation to laws... is the source of political decline. Laws or institutions created in response to one set of environmental conditions become dysfunctional in later circumstances, but cannot be changed because of people's heavy emotional investment in them" and just as inertia in people can be caused by social factors, social inertia is also affected by people in different ways. An example is the desire for security and stability and the anxiety caused by change.

In the relationship between the individual level and the social level of inertia, it should also be noted that one of the reasons for inertia in people is at the border between the individual and the social: People cannot change because they feel they have to conform to a social role. They depend on publicly available concepts and norms that one cannot change on their own. or are subject to what psychologists' call "groupthink".

Among the inertias in the humanities and corresponding to this level of inertia are social and political inertia and organizational inertia, which are examined below.

4.2.1 Social Inertia and Political Inertia

In sociology, *social inertia* is resistance to change or tolerance of stable relationships in societies or social groups. Social inertia is the opposite of social change. The basic concept of social inertia is rooted in the works of Bourdieu. According to Bourdieu, each person in a social space occupies a position that is formed by his social class as well as social relations and social networks. Through the individual's involvement in the social space, he develops a set of behaviors, lifestyles, and habits that often serve to maintain the status quo. Thus, people are encouraged to "accept the social world as it is, to take it for granted, rather than rebel against it, or try to change it" (Bourdieu, 1985). This can explain the persistence of social order over time. Social inertia has also been used to explain how dominant social classes maintain their position and privilege over time (Stiglitz, 2013).

Sociologists have explored how economic and cultural legacy is passed down between generations, which can lead to strong social inertia even in times of social progress. In particular, Bourdieu (1985) found in his studies of Algeria that even in times of rapid economic change, cultural and symbolic factors limit society's flexibility to rapidly adapt to change (Gal, 2006).

Some scholars, including Francis Fukuyama (2011), consider social and political inertia to be complementary to each other. Fukuyama, in his recent work on political order and political decay, argues that political inertia is the result of cognitive and institutional inertia that is ultimately rooted in human nature, and thus inertia is an inherent feature of political systems.

According to Fukuyama, political decay is the result of the inability of political institutions to adapt to changing conditions. Therefore, a special form of institutional inertia, which according to him has two main causes, causes it: the innate human ability to follow rules, which causes institutional and cognitive rigidity. The tendency of people to favor family and close friends, leads to the return of state institutions, "elite capture " of those institutions, and resistance to change by vested interests. According to Fukuyama, inertia is an inherent characteristic of institutions, which is ultimately rooted in human biology, stating that:

> There is something like the law of conservation of institutions. Humans follow animals by nature. They are born to conform to the social norms they see around them, and they imbue these rules with often-transcendent meaning and value. When the environment changes and new challenges arise, there is often a disconnect between existing institutions and current needs. These institutions are supported by entrenched interest groups that oppose any fundamental change (Lee, 2013).

4.2.2 Organizational Inertia

Organizational inertia is the tendency of the organization to remain in the existing situation and resistance against any change and transformation (Godkin & Allcorn, 2008). Organizational inertia is the most important factor that prevents the identification of environmental threats for the organization and slows down the speed of the organization's adaptability to the environment (Tsai et al., 2008). Organizational inertia is a static phenomenon and reflects excessively static conditions in the organization's services, production methods, and policies. In the case of ruling current operations and actions, organizations automatically react based on experiences and show strong internal resistance to changes (Dainton & Zelley, 2022).

Organizational inertia includes several types of inertia, which include[4]:

(a) **Insight Inertia:** It is related to the lack of correct understanding of the changes that occur in the organization's environment and causes the members of the organization not have a correct understanding of the organization and cannot understand the reason for the changes (Liao et al., 2008).

(b) **Action Inertia:** It occurs when management responses to activities and environmental changes are too slow, or information seems insufficient to implement a conscious action. Factors such as *role-constrained learning* (refers to the fact that people have learned the necessary knowledge to perform the task, but cannot exactly act on the basis of the new knowledge obtained), *audience learning* (occurs when people respond to the learned knowledge change their behavior,

[4]To read more about the organizational inertia, refer to Chapters "Internal Empowerment Dynamics of Organizational Inertia Management" and "Trade and Institutional Inertia" of this book.

but they cannot persuade others to change their behavior) and *superstitious learning* (occurs when people do not have a correct understanding of the impact of organizational actions on the environment), cause the formation of this type of inertia (Huang et al., 2013).

(c) **Psychological inertia:** Organizational resistance to changes is often known as psychological inertia. Resistance to change is a psychological phenomenon that expresses people's internal unwillingness to accept change. If people's interest in change is threatened, change will be resisted. Change is threatening; hence, people tend to remain in their previous state. Anxiety and stress caused by the change have a significant effect on creating these resistances in the organization.

In another research, Haag (2014) proposed other aspects for organizational inertia, including structural inertia and economic inertia. According to Hug, structural inertia is related to the organization's structure and processes. This type of inertia occurs when the organization cannot change its processes. Economic inertia is related to saving the costs and costs spent by the organization in changing the processes for new approaches. Usually, organizations resist new systems or new solutions regarding the economy (Haag, 2014).

4.3 Inertia in the Development of Knowledge, Concepts and Ideas

The problem of inertia in the development of knowledge, concepts and ideas can also be investigated in different ways. Most philosophers have investigated this type of inertia. The history of ideas is a complex amalgamation of everyday language and common sense, religious beliefs, political ideologies, philosophical systems, as well as technical and scientific knowledge. It is common to think that systems of knowledge can become obsolete, that ways of thinking can persist and prove themselves against better evidence. Francis Bacon (1960) already formulated the effect of what is now called "*cognitive bias*":

> Human understanding, when it has once accepted an opinion, attracts all other things to support and agree with them. Although more weight and number of examples can be found on the other side, he either ignores and despises them, or rejects them with differences; so that the authority of its previous results remains intact.

Inertia clearly affects people's behavior, and it is also related to social and political factors in various ways. The most famous systematic research on resistance to change in the development of scientific knowledge, taking into account the many complex interactions between different levels, is Thomas Kuhn's Structure of Scientific Revolutions. Kuhn (1996) argues that scientific progress is not continuous and gradual, but that scientists adhere to "paradigms" that lead them to ignore, or unconsciously suppress conflicting evidence**.** Until the body of evidence that contradicts the paradigm becomes so large that a revolution occurs and leads to a new paradigm that can incorporate more evidence.

According to Kuhn's (1996) theory, in times of crisis, when scientists become fully aware of the inadequacy and inefficiency of their paradigm and try to fix the problems and correct it, they face a unified whole. This integrated whole has concepts, laws and principles that are interwoven in a network of metaphysical, theoretical and instrumental beliefs and commitments like the threads of a tangled web and presents a picture of the world that cannot be changed or modified in any part of it, unless this image is rejected and a new image of the world is presented. The scientific revolution is actually the stage in which this change takes place. After the revolution, it seems that "the professional community (scholars) are suddenly transferred to another planet where familiar things are seen in a different light, and unfamiliar things also appear."

5 Sources of Institutional Inertia

By examining the literature of new institutionalists, the main sources and factors that create institutional inertia can be divided into four general categories: economic factors, political-social factors, historical factors, and psychological factors. In Table 1, these factors are categorized separately, in different types, and are briefly explained below.

5.1 *Endogenous Preferences*

In positive economics, preferences are the starting point of the analysis. It is discussed how changes in the rules of institutions lead to different collective outcomes (Gerber & Jackson, 1993). Endogenous preferences are preferences that cannot be considered as given and exogenous, rather, these types of preferences are influenced by an individual's internal reactions to external factors. The important point is that in endogenous preferences, people's preferences change over time. Endogenous preferences play a role in the formation of institutional inertia

Table 1 Sources of institutional inertia

Types	Source (Cause) of institutional inertia
Economic	Endogenous preferences, bounded rationality, uncertainty, sunk costs, free rider problem, lack of information, lack of resources,
Socio-political	Informal constraints, power and legitimacy, distributional coalitions, political conflict, strategic linkages and complementarities Interrelationship between social mobility and institutional preferences, interrelationship between culture and institutions
Historical	Path dependence
Psychological	Mental models

Source: Authors' own table

(Kingston & Caballero, 2009). Historical institutionalists believe that preferences are formed endogenously, while rational choice institutionalists consider preferences as exogenous and fixed (Praça, 2009).

An important potential source of institutional inertia, particularly emphasized in "old" institutional economics, is endogenous preferences. Veblen (1899) and Hayek (1973) saw the evolution of "human habits of thought" (Veblen) or "mind" (Hayek) as an integral part of institutional changes. In Veblen's theory, institutions (considered as shared habits of thought) create the social context in which individual habits (tendencies to act in certain ways) are formed. Institutions influence habits by influencing behavior, and "by influencing habits, institutions can indirectly influence our goals or preferences" (Hodgson, 2004: 187), because the individual preferences and habits of people are aligned with "common mental habits" and potentially strengthen the stability of the institutions themselves. Thus, according to Hodgson (2007: 331), some flexibility of preferences may be necessary to fully explain the evolution and stability of institutions. Institutional stability may be fostered precisely because of the capacity of institutions to be restructured to change preferences. In this view, at the same time as individuals form institutions, institutions form the preferences of individuals.

Bowles (2004, Chap. 11) has investigated the co-evolution of institutions and preferences using evolutionary game theories. Of course, in evolutionary game theory models, players do not have "preferences" as such – they have behaviors (or strategies). In addition, behaviors that produce higher returns are more likely to be repeated. However, Bowles sees the process of reproduction as involving the copying not of behaviors but of "learned norms" that are internalized as part of the individual's preferences and influence their choices in certain types of situations—a process he refers to as "cultural transmission." People are more likely to copy and internalize the norms of players, which makes them behave in a way that leads to success. People are more likely to copy and internalize the norms of players, which makes them behave in a way that leads to success. Bowles links changes in preferences with changes in behavior and states that: "Preferences are endogenous when one's experiences lead to lasting changes in one's behavior in a particular situation" (Bowles, 2004: 378). Therefore, the link between behavior and preferences (which, according to Veblen, is created through "habit"), according to Bowles, is created through "internalized norms".

By analyzing individual's preferences at critical junctures, it is possible to examine all the institutional possibilities ahead. In addition, whether preferences are exogenous or endogenous has another importance in the discussion of institutional inertia. If we consider preferences as exogenous and given, then it is possible to predict how people's preferences will change in case of institutional changes. In fact, institutional changes can be placed in the direction of increasing people's desirability. However, if the exogenous assumption of preferences is a false assumption, and instead preferences are formed exogenously – as shown by Albert and Hahnel (2017) and Bowles (1998) – there is a possibility of inertia formation in two ways: First, preferences are constantly changing and it is not clear how preferences are changing when institutional changes are being formulated. Second, after the implementation of institutional reforms, it is not known whether the changes in preferences are in line with the estimate that the policymaker had before and according to which he applied the institutional changes or not. As a result, the endogeneity of preferences can cause the formation of institutional inertia.

5.2 Bounded Rationality

Bounded rationality refers to the limited capacities of actors in processing important information and using it in decision-making (Cairney, 2019; Jones, 1999; March & Simon, 1958). From the perspective of some institutionalists, bounded rationality plays an important role in creating institutional inertia. Some or all actors may hold incorrect beliefs about the possible effects of a proposed institutional change and, with their bounded rationality, process incomplete information (about the environment and the strategies of other players) in a complex and changing environment. Thus, the way people process information and solve problems may influence the nature of institutional change. For example, people may systematically misperceive opportunities in a new environment. Alternatively, some equilibriums may become more focal than others due to the way people learn (individually and collectively). Institutional changes will not be possible if the actors at the policy-making and decision-making levels cannot properly analyze the situation and interpret the information due to bounded rationality. Also, if the actors do not have a correct understanding of the institutional changes due to bounded rationality, they are completely pessimistic and resist the changes. Because of bounded rationality and the impossibility of making correct decisions and analyzing the future results of changes, it can be one of the causes of institutional inertia.

According to the institutionalist view, bounded rationality can affect not only the speed but also the direction of institutional change, and can be a source of institutional inertia even in the long run. For example, people may simply be unaware of potentially beneficial institutional changes until new institutions are "invented." Advances in social science knowledge constitute a form of learning that can increase the "supply" of new institutions available to political entrepreneurs. For example, in the 1980s, advances in economic theory enabled the design of new rules to create an artificial market for the trading of sulfur dioxide emissions (Williamson, 2000; Ostrom, 2005; Ruttan, 2006; Kingston & Caballero, 2009).

Aoki (2007, 6) considers institutions as "salient and self-sustaining patterns of social interactions" that create "shared knowledge among players about a specific equilibrium path of the game", so that institutional change involves moving to a new equilibrium path. Nevertheless, due to "bounded rationality", each individual agent has an incomplete understanding of this general equilibrium and only observes a shortened and simplified version (or mental model). From this perspective, "institutions" can be thought of not as a set of rules, but as a set of shared perceptions that bind together all the individualized and truncated mental models. Changing the exogenous or endogenous parameters can destroy the existing general equilibrium, so that some agents realize that their strategies are no longer optimal, without necessarily understanding why. Subsequently, agents individually experiment with new strategies as they collectively move toward a new general equilibrium. Finally, their strategies and mental models converge in a new equilibrium, either through a decentralized process (in which case canonical points may play an important role in choosing the equilibrium), or possibly through the leadership of an organization or political entrepreneur.

5.3 *Uncertainty*

Ensuring the occurrence of consequences and predictability is one of the characteristics of stability and inertia. However, in world of bounded rationality, knowledge about institutional alternatives is necessarily incomplete. In addition, the results and consequences of applying changes or policy measures (which are associated with changes) are uncertain and are associated with a kind of uncertainty. It is often difficult to even imagine alternatives to the status quo institutions. But even if models of alternative institutions are available, their effects are much more difficult to predict than those of predetermined institutions are. It is unclear how they will be implemented, when they will be fully operational, and how they will affect the relative positions of different actors. All knowledge about them is second-hand or merely conjectural, while the old institutions – with all their advantages and disadvantages – are known by experience. Consequently, any change from an old institution to a new one involves an element of uncertainty and risk. If the stakes are high and there is risk aversion, actors may stick to their old institutions even if they believe there are better alternatives (Shepsle, 1986: 75).

These uncertainties arise due to the unpredictable nature of the problem ahead and how we perceive it, as well as the challenges of quantifying future investment benefits, which constitute structural inertia beyond costs. Given the uncertainty associated with the introduction of new institutions, perfectly rational people may be reluctant to change, especially in the case of radical institutional change. Finally, a combination of uncertainty with a lack of information about the desired policy along with deficiencies in administrative capacity and financial resources as well as interdependencies between organizations can effectively create institutional inertia (Börzel, 2003; Kingston & Caballero, 2009; Hovi et al., 2009; Powell & DiMaggio, 2012; Munck af Rosenschöld et al., 2014; Campbell, 2021).

5.4 *Sunk Costs*

These types of costs are huge initial start-up costs. Actors must learn rules, codes and customs. They must develop specific skills, competencies, and tools, make specialized personal contacts, and sometimes even build additional physical infrastructure.

Building all these assets takes time, money and effort. Nevertheless, once they are in place, they can potentially be used for a very long time. They represent a durable form of capital. But this capital tends to a certain institution and cannot be transferred easily. The infrastructure built according to the specifications of one institution must be reconstructed to conform to the specifications of another institution. Institutional experience accumulated in one institution is worthless in the context of another. Codes that apply in one institution do not apply elsewhere, etc. The characteristic of institutional capital makes changing institutions costly. The capital that is dependent on an old institution and its yield cannot be transferred to the new institution. The investment for the new institution must start from zero. New resources have to be spent and until the new institution is operational, the transition has its own time and complexity. Given these "complications of transition", it often makes sense to stick with old institutions even after new and potentially better ones become available (Stinchcombe, 1968: 120–123; Scharpf, 1987: 143–142).

According to (Genschel, 1995), the cost of time, money and work to teach rules, guidelines and contracts to actors, create infrastructure, and provide the necessary tools to create a new institution is very high. In addition, institutions are durable after they are created, like a capital, and remain in place for a long time. To build a new institution, you have to start again from scratch. Laws and guidelines should be revised and harmonized. At the time of institutional transition, there is also confusion. For these reasons, sometimes even when there is a possibility of improving the institutions, we stick to the former institutions (Genschel, 1995 cited by Stinchcombe, 1968). Actors have more confidence in the performance of institutions that they know, compared to institutions that they have no knowledge of.

5.5 *Free-Riding Problem*

The issue of free riding can be an obstacle to collective cooperation to change existing laws and institutions. In this case, even if institutional change is important to the individual, he avoids protest, membership in political groups, voting and even studying the effects of institutions (Kingston & Caballero, 2009). Institutional change is a public good. The characteristics of public goods are such that they encourage people to free ride (Brennan, 2009). Occurrence of the free riding problem makes it difficult to provide the material cost of changes or social and political response to create institutional changes and creates institutional inertia. Although political entrepreneurs can solve the problem of free riding with institutional innovations in some cases; but the expected private return should be greater than the private cost of allocating political resources to act on the supply of innovation (Ruttan, 2006).

5.6 *Incomplete Information*

Policy makers and other people whose interests are affected by institutional changes have incomplete information. This incomplete information is distributed asymmetrically among them. On the one hand, policy makers and decision makers have insufficient information about the issues that the society is involved with, in the first place, they fail to recognize the issues correctly, and secondly, after making a decision, they do not have appropriate methods to evaluate the effectiveness of policies (Campbell, 2021). On the other hand, the people of the society do not know much about the decisions and the consequences of the changes. As a result, due to the incomplete information, both the policy makers and the people of the society are not very interested in institutional changes, and they prefer that the inertia continue. It should be said that the incomplete information is one of the causes of uncertainty.

5.7 *Resource Scarcity*

Access to resources – for example money and political influence – is a key and important element. If policy makers and decision makers do not have access to these resources, their institutional change ideas will not be realized, however much innovative or path breaking. Aldrich (1999) has used similar arguments in the realization of entrepreneurs' ideas and the importance of access to resources (Aldrich, 1999). For example, nineteenth century merchants and industrialists in the United States were able to create large corporate organizations because they had the resources to win legal battles to reduce local business regulation, personal responsibility in limit bankruptcy, and remove other institutional and political barriers to the growth of these political organizations (Campbell, 2021).

As Acemoglu, Greif and Campbell state, institutional changes also change the distribution of resources (Acemoglu, 2012, p. 853; Acemoglu et al., 2005, p. 6; Campbell, 2021; Greif & Laitin, 2004). Naturally, with this change in the distribution of resources, a group will benefit and a group will suffer. If the actors realize that the institutional changes increase their access to resources, they will naturally welcome such changes, but if these changes limit the beneficiaries' access to resources, it is obvious that they will show resistance to the changes and institutional inertia is formed. In fact, institutional changes are a process of struggle and bargaining. If decision-makers and policy makers have the necessary resources to implement institutional changes and their effective continuation, then institutional changes will be more revolutionary than evolutionary (Campbell, 2021).

The importance of resources (scarcity and redistribution of resources) can be investigated in two ways:

- The resources needed to implement institutional changes
- Change in access to resources and its redistribution due to institutional changes

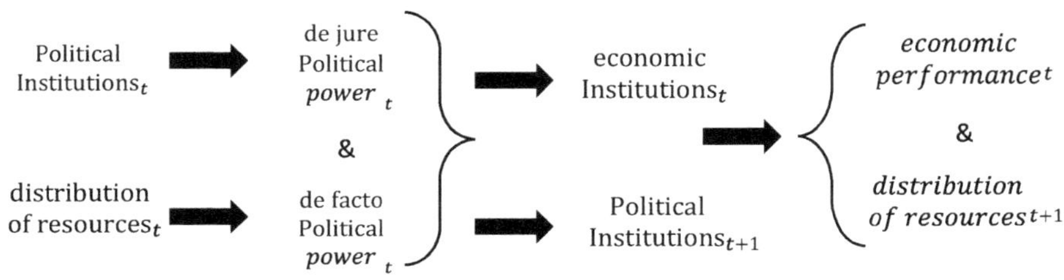

Fig. 2 The role of resource scarcity and resource redistribution in institutional inertia
Source: Acemoglu et al., (2005, 2012) (In Acemoglu (2012), this form is called: "Components of a dynamic framework". According to the objectives of this chapter, we have chosen the title "The role of scarcity and redistribution of resources" for this figure)

Acemoglu and colleagues (Acemoglu, 2012, p. 852; Acemoglu et al., 2005, p. 6) have investigated both cases. As seen in Fig. 2, the distribution of resources and political institutions at time t determine de jure[5] and de facto[6] political power in society.[7] This stage of resource distribution corresponds to the first case where resources are needed to apply institutional changes. Depending on how resources are distributed, we can talk about the possibility or impossibility of institutional changes. In the following, the interaction and interplay of de jure and de facto political power shape economic institutions at time t and also political institutions at time t + 1. Depending on the type of interaction between de jure and de facto political power, political institutions may remain in the same form at time t and here a kind of institutional inertia is formed from the political aspect. Another possibility is that the political institutions at time t + 1 are different from time t. In any case, the economic institutions arising from the conditions of time t with the political institutions at time t + 1 determine the economic performance at time t + 1. It is also the type of political and economic institutions that can transform the distribution of resources at time t + 1. Here exactly the second mode of the discussion of the role of resources in institutional inertia appears. The distribution of resources at time t + 1 may be the same as at time t, and may have changed. Changes in the distribution of resources depend on economic and political institutions. The most important determining factor in the occurrence of this redistribution in resources is the status of interest groups for whom these changes have consequences.

[5]De facto and de jure institutions are not antonyms; they may overlap (Marciano & Ramello, 2018, p. 525).

[6]De jure means a state of affairs that is in accordance with the law, i.e., de jure institutions constitute a subclass of formal institutions and must necessarily be external in nature (Marciano & Ramello, 2018, p. 525).

[7]De facto means a state of affairs that is true in fact but does not have to be officially sanctioned, i.e., de facto institutions may be formal or informal, as well as external or internal, provided that they are operative (Marciano & Ramello, 2018, p. 525).

5.8 *Informal Constraints*

Humans need informal restrictions to implement formal institutions such as a system of laws or codified rules. According to Durkheim (2019), in a contract, not everything is contractual. This means that for the implementation of contracts, rules and norms are needed that are not necessarily codified in the law. Hodgson (2001) emphasizes that formal legal systems are always incomplete and depend on custom and culture to function and play their role. Ruttan (2006: 258) notes that "cultural endowments" can actually facilitate some types of institutional change. He gives the example of Japan, where "traditional patterns of cooperation" that emerged in the distant past have facilitated modern rural development programs.

North (1990) gives informal rules or restrictions a central role in institutional changes. In North's view, formal rules change through a political process as a result of deliberate (and quite rational) actions by organizations and individual entrepreneurs. The motivation to try to change formal rules can come from changes in exogenous or endogenous parameters (including learning). North combines this theory with a theory in which informal rules evolve alongside formal rules and as an extension of formal rules. Informal rules are reproduced through an evolutionary process of cultural transmission and play a key role in institutional change because they change slowly and cannot be deliberately changed. Following the change of the formal rules, the informal rules that "had gradually evolved as an extension of the previous formal rules" are changed, leading to a "restructuring of the general restrictions in both cases and the establishment of a new equilibrium that is far less revolutionary.[8]

According to North (1990), in the long run, informal constraints are the main source of institutional inertia because of their evolutionary character in terms of change, meaning that they change only slowly. The continuation of these informal restrictions, which are extended from previously set formal rules, results in only small changes in the general restrictions resulting from discrete changes in formal rules. In fact, the changes of informal restrictions depend on the type of culture, norms and values of a variable and diverse society. If the culture or values of a society do not have the necessary flexibility, it is not possible to make changes in official rules and institutions.

5.9 *Power and Legitimacy*

The power and relationships in it are also one of the factors that create institutional inertia (Munck af Rosenschöld et al., 2014). Intergenerational conflicts, conflicting interests of different groups, and political and electoral competitions can cause

[8]To read more about the inertia in informal institutions, refer to Chapter "The Roots of Cognitive Inertia: An Introduction to Institutional Changes" of this book.

resistance to institutional changes. Intergenerational conflicts, conflicting interests of different groups, and political and electoral competitions can cause resistance to institutional changes. Also, the established power with tools such as legislation and media can prevent institutional changes. The dominant power is more resistant to changes that affect the distribution of power and resources. The continuation of the interests of the political power and elites and the political conflict between them dictates that the existing conditions remain intact in most cases. Therefore, one of the reasons for the formation of institutional inertia is the interests of those in power and political elites.

The legal system or the system that specifies the dos and don'ts can have dual effects against institutional changes. In the framework of the legal system, some actions may be considered legitimate, and some actions may be rejected because they are not legal. Hence, on the one hand, the legal framework can prevent institutional changes that are outside the scope of the legal system, and on the other hand, the same legal framework can encourage institutional changes in certain directions. Therefore, legal systems and frameworks that value actions can be considered as one of the factors of institutional inertia.

The dominant power by using the resources at its disposal can question the legitimacy and appropriateness of institutional changes and cause institutional inertia (Munck af Rosenschöld et al., 2014). Legitimacy is closely related to power.[9] The power network and political groups are always trying to show their goals, institutions and policies as legitimate and the other side's goals, institutions and policies as illegitimate. The winner of the party's competition to establish the desired institutions is the party that can show its institutions as legitimate in the eyes of the society. In this case, even if these institutions are not the best for the society, by legitimizing them, institutional change is prevented.

In the literature of new institutionalists, the path, direction and speed of policy change are guided by power blocks in the government structure. Activists in these power blocs can characterize the normative dimension of policy-making in the business management and the free market, thereby undermining the potential of minority groups to effect significant policy change. Ignoring these economic drivers, the ability of such a development process to overcome institutional inertia is insufficient (Levy & Egan, 2003; Okereke, 2007; Okereke et al., 2009; Wittneben et al., 2012; Munck af Rosenschöld et al., 2014) and it depends on the legitimacy of institutions in creating standards of acceptable and appropriate actions and maintaining or canceling policies. On the other hand, delegitimization of new ideas can also be a tool for resistance against institutional changes. How legitimacy is used, whether to limit or enhance institutional change depends on the interests of powerful actors. These actors derive legitimacy from institutions that actively interact with broader social systems and are therefore embedded in larger power networks (March & Olsen, 1989; Matthews & Sydneysmith, 2010; Cashmore &

[9]To read more, refer to Chapter "Early Entrepreneurship Entry and Institutional Rigidities in Emerging Market Economies: Evidence from the Global Entrepreneurship Monitor" of this book.

Wejs, 2014; Munck af Rosenschöld et al., 2014). The power network and political groups are always trying to show their goals, institutions and policies as legitimate and the other side's goals, institutions and policies as illegitimate. The winner of the party's competition to establish the desired institutions is the party that can show its institutions as legitimate in the eyes of the society. In this case, even if these institutions are not the best for the society, by legitimizing them, institutional change is prevented.

Levi (1990) emphasizes that formal rules can "empower" certain groups, and disadvantaged groups may try to cause institutional change by "dissatisfaction" with existing institutional arrangements. This dissatisfaction can take the form of an organized collective action, or it can also occur through the decentralized actions of many individuals. The legal system or the system that specifies the dos and don'ts can have dual effects against institutional changes. In the framework of the legal system, some actions may be considered legitimate, and some actions may be rejected because they are not legal. Hence, on the one hand, the legal framework can prevent institutional changes that are outside the scope of the legal system, and on the other hand, the same legal framework can encourage institutional changes in certain directions. Therefore, legal systems and frameworks that value actions can be considered as one of the causes of institutional inertia.

5.10 The Existence of Distributional Coalitions (Interest Groups and Their Bargaining Power)

One of the important elements in the direction of institutional changes is the preferences of interest groups. Existing institutions can influence the organization of interest groups as well as the bargaining power of these groups (as a source of inertia). In addition to the decision-makers and policy-makers who are at work, other political elites are looking for opportunities to use their influence and gain the necessary points. Here, coalitions[10] are formed among these people. If some or all actors trying to change the rules misperceive the effects of potential changes, it may affect the process of political bargaining (through which institutions are formed in collective choice theories). Furthermore, attempts to block institutional change may be made by groups with vested interests in the status quo (for example, based on maximizing returns and reducing costs associated with change). Risk aversion exacerbates these problems (North, 1990; Ostrom, 2005; Kingston & Caballero, 2009).

[10] Olson uses the concept of coalition in the two meanings of "distributive coalition" and "inclusive coalition" (Olson, 2008). Both types of coalitions are trying to gain access to the political environment. A distributive coalition is a special interest group that only represents the interests of a small group of political elites. This group is trying to maintain its position in achieving benefits and privileges arising from the existing institutional relations. In contrast, the inclusive coalition seeks to redistribute benefits and privileges among the society.

Existing institutions can influence the organization of interest groups as well as the bargaining power of these groups (as a source of inertia). If some or all actors trying to change the rules misperceive the effects of potential changes, they may affect the process of political bargaining (through which institutions are formed in collective choice theories). Furthermore, attempts to block institutional change may be made by groups with vested interests in the status quo (for example, based on maximizing returns and reducing costs associated with change). Risk aversion exacerbates these problems (North, 1990; Ostrom, 2005; Kingston & Caballero, 2009).

In general, if there are strong distributive coalitions in a society, it is obvious that institutional changes that are contrary to the preferences of interest groups will not be applied, and therefore, the society will experience institutional inertia. Because institutions can be both stable and in the process of change, powerful coalitions may want to create more organizational measures to slow or prevent change (Acemoglu et al., 2021).

5.11 Political Conflict

Institutions often have a distributional bias that systematically makes it easier for some actors to achieve their goals than others. In this case, the groups whose interests are less considered should equip and mobilize resources to get more shares. This biased potential causes conflict and political conflict instead of the desire for change and new institutions. The beneficiaries of the status quo must be bought in or won over, and the proponents of change must agree on a common plan. Actors must mobilize followers; build coalitions, resolve disputes, and hedge against strategic risk. All of these actions are time-consuming and costly (and not necessarily successful), transaction costs that are avoided unless actors believe that the benefits of a change are relatively significant. These costs provide a measure of stability for institutions that they will never enjoy in a world without transaction costs (Machiavelli, 1965: 33; Shepsle, 1989: 144, Heiner, 1983, Genschel, 1995, Shepsle, 1986). In general, intergenerational conflicts, conflicting interests of different groups, and political and electoral competitions can cause resistance to institutional changes. In addition, the established power with tools such as legislation and media can prevent institutional changes. The dominant power is more resistant to changes that affect the distribution of power and resources. The continuation of the interests of political power and the rulers of power and the political conflict between them in most cases dictates that the existing conditions remain intact.

5.12 Strategic Linkages and Complementarities

The existence of strategic and complementary links between institutions in different fields can cause institutional inertia. Due to the interconnectedness of the institutions, it is not possible to make a fundamental change in a minor area. In addition, if there is a change in one component, the overall balance and order of the system will be disrupted (Kingston & Caballero, 2009; Aoki, 2001). For example, if a government wants to make radical changes in the field of laws and institutions affecting employment, due to its effect on the entire system, other areas resist the change. The reason for this resistance to change is the influence of the labor factor on all other economic areas. If the cost of the worker increases and the relationship between the worker and the employer undergoes a fundamental transformation, the current balance of the system will be disturbed. The relationships between different components of the system are not such that a fundamental change in one area does not affect other areas.

5.13 Path Dependence

History is associated with institutional inertia due to its path-dependent nature of institutional change as a process. Societies have moved according to different paths from a historical past until today, the institutions of each society are susceptible to what behaviors or changes, depends on the path they have taken. A specific path can emerge based on small events in the past that determine specific solutions in favor of this path (North, 1990: 94). If the path traveled was a path in which institutional inertia is fixed, and the desire for dynamism and changes is small, as a result, it will be difficult to implement changes and overcome inertia in that society. In path dependence despite self-reinforcing sequences, inertia involves mechanisms that reproduce a particular institutional pattern over time. In contrast, with reactive sequences, inertia involves mechanisms of action and interaction that give the event chain an "inherent logic" in which one "natural" event leads to another. This inherent logic of path dependence creates institutional inertia (Mahoney, 2000).

By surrounding the power structures, the existing institutions can block the way of institutional changes. Resources, physical and human capital, skills, technologies and organizations in an institutional set can gradually change the set of available and possible institutions and affect the institutional development in the future (Kingston & Caballero, 2009). This problem shows the importance of the past institutional status of the system for creating institutional changes. The capacity and power of a system for institutional change largely depends on its institutional status in the past and what has happened to institutions in the past. For example, previously adopted technological innovations can create significant barriers to institutional change. Investment, technology and knowledge can be factors that create path dependence. Path dependence is as much a social-cognitive issue as it is a technical interconnection issue (Caplan, 2003, 2012). Cognitive limitations in systems may cause decision makers to continue the same old and fixed work (Lamberg & Tikkanen, 2006).

In general, both categories of formal and informal institutions (rules, laws, practices, and procedures) are associated with path dependence. The trend and speed of development paths are determined by a combination of technologies, bureaucracies, and worldviews. The slow response of some institutions to environmental concerns and the transition to sustainable energy, related to the relationship between institutions and existing knowledge and policy networks, the dynamics of social power structures, relationships and everyday practices that maintain institutional arrangements. These relationships, in turn, reveal the role of historical trajectories in maintaining current practices (Hoffman & Ventresca, 1999; Burch, 2011; Munck af Rosenschöld et al., 2014).

Some scholars like Nelson and Winter (1982) and Dosi and Malerba (2002) believe that path dependence is a necessary condition for saving the system and pooling resources. On the other hand, researchers like Child (1972) consider path dependence as a serious threat to save the system. In fact, from a negative point of view, path dependence is seen as inertia, and from a positive point of view, path dependence is simply the dependence of results on the past (and not just current conditions) (Lamberg & Tikkanen, 2006).

5.14 *Mental Models*

As mentioned in the subsection of bounded rationality, actors have a specific and limited capacity to interpret and understand the surrounding environment. This limited and specific capacity is dependent on cognitive processes. People interpret phenomena based on their mental models. Actors use mental models to interpret the results of institutional changes.

Mental models are a cognitive structure[11] that forms the basis of reasoning, decision-making and behaviors (Jones et al., 2011). Mental models are mental representations of objective reality and mental representations of mental and social reality, institutions and power structures (Rosenbaum, 2022). North (1981 and 2010) has pointed out the importance of cognitive rules in explaining human behavior. He says that institutions provide a motivational structure that directs human behavior and structures human interaction. But this motivational structure itself cannot be unrelated to the way of perceiving the world by the mind. Therefore, in fact, on the one hand, institutions form the structure of motivations, which causes the direction of human behavior, and on the other hand, this motivational structure is dependent on human understanding of the environment (North, 1981, 2010).

[11]To read more, refer to Chapter "Overview of Institutional–Organization Inertia Nexus" of this book.

In short, the understanding that a person obtains from phenomena depends on his mental models. Actors understand their surrounding environment based on the mental models governing their cognition. What kind of value judgment each actor has towards the phenomena depends on his mental model. As a result, actors may obtain a fixed understanding of institutions based on mental models. What kind of value judgment each actor has towards the phenomena depends on his mental model. As a result, actors may obtain a fixed understanding of institutions based on mental models. This established understanding provides a framework for judging institutional change. On the one hand, actors based on their mental model have gained a specific understanding of institutional changes, on the other hand, the same established understanding prevents the acceptance of institutional changes, and as a result, actors show resistance to institutional changes.

5.15 Interrelationship Between Social Mobility and Institutional Preferences

Another force that can destabilize institutions or contribute to their stability is the interrelationship between social mobility and institutional preferences. If a person does not have political power in an institutional arrangement, but expects to thrive and benefit from the existing institutional structure, then they may be less inclined to act against it. This is an example of projected social mobility that further stabilizes existing institutions. According to Acemoglu et al. (2018), projected social mobility may destabilize certain regimes, particularly democracy. For example, when the current median voter expects to be in a different social position in the future, he may want to initiate a process of shifting political power toward his future position.

5.16 Interrelationship Between Culture and Institutions

The interrelationship between culture and institutions is another powerful factor can create both institutional change and institutional continuity. On the one hand, when cultural change occurs naturally under the auspices of a particular institution, it may be a force to undermine those institutions. On the other hand, culture may adapt itself to an institutional environment and further strengthen its position in society (Acemoglu et al. (2021)).

A summary of the sources and reasons for creating institutional inertia from the point of view of institutional economists is given in Table 2.

Table 2 Sources of institutional inertia from the point of view of institutionalists

Sources of institutional inertia	The reason for creating institutional inertia and its effective mechanism	Source
Endogenous preferences	By influencing habits, institutions can indirectly affect the goals or preferences of individuals because individual preferences and habits of individuals align with "common mental habits" and potentially strengthen the stability of institutions.	Bowles (2004), Hodgson (2004) and Hodgson (2007)
Bounded rationality	The way people process imperfect information and solve problems with bounded rationality in a complex and changing environment may affect the nature of institutional change, and people systematically misperceive opportunities in a new environment. Or some equilibria may become more focal than others because of how people learn (individually and collectively).	Williamson (2000), Aoki (2007), Ruttan (2006), Ostrom (2005), Kingston and Caballero (2009) and Börzel (2003)
Uncertainty	Risk aversion may cause attempts by groups with special interests to block institutional changes in the status quo. And perfectly rational people would be reluctant to change, especially in the case of radical institutional change, given the uncertainty associated with introducing new institutions.	Shepsle (1986), Börzel (2003), Kingston and Caballero (2009), Hovi et al. (2009), Powell and DiMaggio (2012), Munck af Rosenschöld et al. (2014) and Campbell (2021)
Sunk costs	The characteristic of institutional capital makes changing institutions costly. Investment for the new institution should start from scratch. New resources have to be spent and until the new institution is operational, the transition has its own time and complexity.	Stinchcombe (1968) and Scharpf (1987)
Free-rider problem	Free riding makes it difficult to finance the material cost of changes or social and political response to create institutional changes and causes institutional inertia.	Ruttan (2006), Kingston and Caballero (2009) and Brennan (2009)
Incomplete information	Due to the lack of information, both the policy makers and the people of the society have not much desire for institutional changes, and they prefer that the inertia continue.	Campbell (2021)

(continued)

Table 2 (continued)

Sources of institutional inertia	The reason for creating institutional inertia and its effective mechanism	Source
Resource scarcity	If the actors realize that the institutional changes increase their access to resources, they will naturally welcome such changes, but if these changes limit the beneficiaries' access to resources, it is obvious that they will show resistance to the changes and institutional inertia is formed.	Greif and Laitin (2004), Acemoglu et al. (2005), Acemoglu et al. (2012), Campbell (2021)
Informal constraints	In the long term, informal restrictions change slowly due to their evolutionary characteristics, so they are the main source of institutional inertia.	North (1990), Ruttan (2006) and Kingston and Caballero (2009)
Power and legitimacy	Actors in power blocks can characterize the normative dimension of policymaking, making it difficult to overcome institutional inertia by ignoring the potential of minority groups to effect significant policy change. It depends on the legitimacy of the institutions in creating standards of acceptable and appropriate actions and maintaining or canceling policies.	March and Olsen (1989), Levi (1990), Levy and Egan (2003), Bowles and Naidu (2006), Okereke (2007), Okereke et al. (2009), Matthews and Sydneysmith (2010), Wittneben et al. (2012), Munck af Rosenschöld et al. (2014) and Cashmore and Wejs (2014)
Distributive coalitions) interest groups and their bargaining power(	Actors who try to change the rules have a poor understanding of the effects of the changes, which may affect their political bargaining process through which institutions are formed in collective choice theories.	North (1990), and Kingston and Caballero (2009)
Political conflict	Institutions often have a distributional bias that systematically makes it easier for some actors to achieve their goals than others. Therefore, it causes political conflict instead of the desire for change and new institutions.	Machiavelli (1965) and Shepsle (1989)
Strategic linkages and complementarities	Due to the interconnectedness of institutions, a fundamental change in one area affects other areas, and with a change in one component, the overall balance and order of the system is disrupted, so other areas resist change and cause institutional inertia.	Aoki (2001) and Kingston and Caballero (2009)

(continued)

Table 2 (continued)

Sources of institutional inertia	The reason for creating institutional inertia and its effective mechanism	Source
(Historical) path dependency	A specific path can emerge based on small events in the past that determine specific solutions in favor of this path. Thus, previously adopted technological innovations can create significant barriers to institutional change.	Libecap, (1989), North (1990), Hoffman and Ventresca (1999), Mahoney (2000), Kingston and Caballero (2009), Foxon et al. (2013), Munck af Rosenschöld et al. (2014) and Burch (2011)
Mental models	Actors may obtain a fixed understanding of institutions based on mental models, and this fixed understanding prevents the acceptance of institutional changes. As a result, actors show resistance to institutional changes.	North, (1981, 2010), Jones et al. (2011) and Rosenbaum (2022)
The interaction between social mobility and institutional preferences	If the median voter expects a different social position in the future, he may initiate a process of shifting political power toward his future position.	Acemoglu et al. (2018)
Interaction between culture and institutions	If cultural change occurs naturally under the supervision of a particular institution, it may be a force to undermine those institutions.	Acemoglu et al. (2021)

Source: Authors' own table

6 Consistency of Institutional Continuity and Institutional Change: Evidence

Institutions (as constraints on human behavior and a framework for coordinating expectations) are only meaningful if they are at least somewhat durable. Acemoglu and Robinson (2001), provide evidence that executive constraints can persist, while many aspects of institutions change frequently. Less developed countries oscillate between democracy and dictatorship and often change their constitutions. Likewise, while the current economic problems in Latin America often go back to the colonial era (Engerman & Sokoloff, 1997; Acemoglu et al., 2002), certain institutions that once underpinned the colonial economy (such as encomienda, or slavery) have long since disappeared. These observations contribute to our better understanding of simultaneous change and continuity in institutions.

One of the best examples of the continuation of economic institutions as a result of the continuation of the actual power of political elites is related to the southern United States. In the period before the Civil War, the people of the southern United

States were relatively poor. The rate of urbanization was 9% compared to 30% in the northeast. It had relatively few railways and was technologically stagnant (Wright, 1986). The economy was based on slavery and cotton production, and in many states, it was illegal to teach slaves to read and write. After the civil war, with the abolition of slavery and the freed slaves having the right to vote, a significant change in economic institutions was predicted. But what emerged was a labor-oriented, low-wage, low-educated, and repressive economy that in many ways was remarkably similar to that of the prewar South. Slavery was gone, but Redemption replaced Reconstruction, which meant re-imposing many of the economic practices of the slavery era that forced blacks into low-wage, low-skilled, forced labor relationships on large plantations (Wiener, 1978). And finally, Redemption became Jim Crow, in which extreme forms of social and economic discrimination were accompanied by systematic economic subjugation and complete political disenfranchisement of blacks, despite the Fifteenth Amendment (Woodward, 1955). This desire to influence future institutions is linked to the desire of the political elite of the mid-nineteenth century southern United States to secede from the rest of the United States, and because that was not possible, they fought a great war to have a say in future institutions (Potter, 1976; Weingast, 1998).

This type of institutional continuity is called "institutional stasis" (an unchanging institutional equilibrium). The most important reason is that power begets power. That is, the groups that are empowered by the current institutions take advantage of these institutions and, as a result, use their power to maintain them. Consequently, these groups reproduce their power over future institutions in the process. In the case of the southern United States, large plantation owners were the most powerful group in the prewar period. This group was both relatively cohesive and convinced that the political and economic institutions under slavery were in their favor. They had enough strength and cohesion, and even after the reconstruction, they were able to retain much of their political power (Wiener, 1978).

The view of many social scientists on institutional continuity is shaped by this kind of institutional persistence and that power dynamics are power generators. For example, Engerman and Sokoloff's famous thesis on the institutional problems of Latin America emphasizes how colonial practices create economic inequality, and this economic inequality empowers the wealthier sections of society, leading to institutional persistence (Engerman & Sokoloff, 1997). Examples of this type of institutional stasis exist in Latin America (Guatemala), in the US South before the Civil War, and in North Korea today. For the most part, however, institutional persistence in Latin America was not like this. Even when inequality persisted and had institutional roots, it was not because the same elites held power, nor because the economic system was permanently fixed.

In practice, institutional persistence often takes a much richer and more varied form than institutional stasis, for two reasons. First, institutional stasis does not simply result from the fact that power is the generator of power; Rather, there may be incompatibility between political and economic arrangements. That is, groups empowered under current institutions prefer a different set of institutional arrangements. For example, repressive institutions may impose major economic costs, which even the controlling group with political power may want to avoid. An example of this phenomenon in recent history is the elite-oriented (political) reform movement in the Soviet Union that gathered power in the 3 years between 1989 and 1991. The Communist Party certainly had enough political control and coercive power to keep things going, and there were plenty of people who wanted to do it. But powerful enough constituencies were convinced that the economic costs of this strategy were too high. They decided to pursue a reform process instead. Their plan was to carry out limited reforms and modernize the economy, but to keep the communist regime more or less intact (Roland, 1991).

But the reality of institutional change was more complicated than these. A classic historical example of this type of institutional reform is North and Weingast's theory of the Glorious Revolution as an institutional commitment to repay government debt, which then initiated a process of deeper political change (North & Weingast, 1989). Many Marxist theories of the transition from feudalism to capitalism also fall into this broad category, emphasizing the internal contradictions of the feudal system, especially when cities and early industries flourished. Another example of this logic is the Lizzeri and Persico (2004), s theory of democracy, where elites may decide to expand the franchise because intra-elite competition becomes increasingly costly for them in a limited franchise regime.

Second, even if the politically powerful have no direct economic benefit from initiating institutional change, political threats from non-elites can compel them to do so. This is especially true in non-democratic political systems, where elite control over the political system depends on the inability of the majority to organize and solve its collective action problem. However, changes in actual non-elite power do occasionally occur, and both such changes themselves and their anticipation can become powerful drivers of institutional change. For example, after episodic periods of unrest or revolutionary fervor, major institutional changes may be imposed on elites. As the Russian imperial aristocracy experienced amid the Russo-Japanese War of 1904–1905 and, even more clearly, after the Bolshevik Revolution of 1917 (Service, 2005). Alternatively, elites may find that they must initiate reforms themselves to avoid worse outcomes. Acemoglu and Robinson (2000, 2006) argue that the emergence of democracy in many European countries and some Latin American countries during the 19th and early 20th centuries shows this logic. In their theory, when citizens solve their collective action problem during temporary opportunities, they effectively gain the power to challenge the ruling system. Elites may want to commit to a political system that is responsive to their demands as a way to appease these practices. Democratization is an effective engagement tool of this kind because it distributes political power more evenly in society (Acemoglu & Robinson, 2006).

However, these sources of incompatibility between economic and political considerations do not always lead to institutional change. This is because "Strategic Stability". That is, powerful political groups may resist institutional change because they are concerned about subsequent institutional dynamics. Acemoglu et al. (2012) present a general theory of "slippery slopes" that formalizes this type of strategic stability. An obvious case is the reform process in the Soviet Union. The reformers planned to limit political change while modernizing the economy and improving the allocation of resources in the communist system. But When the reform process was underway, it went much further and faster than the communist reformers wanted or could have predicted (Fischer, 1994; Treisman, 2011). Thus, if preserving the Soviet Union and its political system was a major priority for reformers, they might have reason to avoid early strategic reforms, even if these reforms were useful because they were the first step down a slippery slope. Many autocratic leaders of former Soviet republics, such as Azerbaijan, Belarus, Turkmenistan, or Uzbekistan, have been reluctant to accept deep economic reforms and may have learned from the Russian experience. Similarly, as argued by Acemoglu et al. (2010), many African leaders have refrained from building strong armies despite the need for military power against insurgencies and internal enemies. They saw it as the first step towards a slippery slope where the army would become more powerful and capable of engineering a coup against them.

A more general concept of institutional continuity has been proposed in path dependency studies such as (Pierson, 2000; Mahoney, 2000; and Thelen, 1999). Acemoglu and Robinson (2012) have used the concept of "path-dependent change" to show continuity in institutions. Path-dependent change can result from internal dynamics. That is, small differences can put society on a path to attract very different institutional equilibria. Or, path-dependent change may be exogenous, whereby small differences are amplified by shocks. There are many examples of this type of institutional continuity or institutional inertia concept. Examples include: industrialization opportunities that lead to large divergences among Former European colonies with different institutional structures in the nineteenth century (Acemoglu et al., 2002), the different routes of Guatemala and Costa Rica following advances in transportation technology that led to the coffee boom in both economies (Acemoglu & Robinson, 2019), and divergence between Northern and Southern Italy (Putnam, 1993).

7 Conclusion

"Inertia" is primarily used to refer to physical phenomena that were first described by Kepler, Galileo, and Newton: The tendency of an object to remain in a state of motion or rest, unless forces are applied to it. However, it is also used to talk about the resistance of individuals behavior, social structures and the development of knowledge to change. Resistance to change has been studied in various academic disciplines, such as psychology, economics, political science, international relations, and philosophy. Individuals and organizations perpetuate and maintain themselves through a variety of more or less active processes, resistance to changes in their environment. However, what is useful or legitimate at one point in time may be obsolete and ineffective at another. The analysis of this normative aspect of the concept of inertia was our goal in this chapter.

Habit can cause people to get stuck in outdated, ineffective, or even self-destructive ways of thinking and acting. But under normal conditions it allows them to repeatedly and effectively perform complex sequences of tasks. Similarly, institutions need a certain amount of institutional inertia to provide the stability and legitimacy they need to function effectively (Hannan & Freeman, 1984). Therefore, negative and positive aspects can be considered for institutional inertia.[12] Resistance to change can become a problem when change seems desirable or necessary, but it also adds stability and predictability to individual and social life. This double feature of resistance to change is the result of the transformation of our worldview in the modern era.

In this chapter, after the definition of inertia in the second section, the concept of institutional inertia and its synonyms from the point of view of institutionalists have been examined in the third section. In institutional economics, other terms and concepts such as: institutional rigidity, strategic stability, institutional stasis and path-dependent change have also been used to analyze institutional inertia. From the perspective of Haase et al. (2009), institutional rigidity refers to situations where institutions should change but do not change or do not have the conditions for change. Institutional stasis is a state of unchanging institutional equilibrium, in which institutional arrangements repeat themselves over and over (Acemoglu et al., 2021). Institutions are constantly undergoing successive changes, but their path is related to past institutional choices. Therefore, path dependence is effective in how institutions react to shocks and determine their next paths (Acemoglu et al., 2021). In general, we can say: Since institutional inertia is compatible with institutional changes, institutional rigidity is synonymous with institutional inertia but different from institutional stasis.

Considering the multi-dimensional and multi-level concept of the institution, definitions of the institution based on the structural aspect of the institution, individual action and the mediation of the institution between the individual and the structure have been mentioned. According to the different definitions of the institution, in the fourth section, a three-level classification of types of inertia is presented: inertia in individual behaviors, inertia in social and political structures, and inertia in the development of knowledge and concepts. From the contents of this section, we can conclude: just as inertia in individual behaviors can be caused by social factors, social inertia can also be influenced by people in different ways. Conceptual inertia also affects people's behavior and is related to social and political factors in various ways. Since institutional inertia includes both individual inertia and structural inertia, institutional inertia can be considered comprehensive of all types of inertia.

Identifying sources of institutional inertia is important in understanding the process of institutional changes based on the source of change. Therefore, in the fifth section, by reviewing the literature of new institutional economics, 16 main factors causing institutional inertia were identified. These factors can be divided into four general categories: economic factors, socio-political factors, historical factors

[12] For a more conceptual study of these aspects, refer to the Chapter "Inertia: Resistance and Endurance" of this book – Faghih et al.

and psychological factors. These categories are described in detail in the fifth section of this chapter.

In the sixth section, evidence from some countries and the intellectual structure of social scientists about institutional continuity (institutional stasis) and institutional changes are given. This work has been done in order to better understand the simultaneous change and continuity in institutions, and to point out some concepts synonymous with institutional inertia used by thinkers of new institutional economics. Institutional changes can be caused by incompatibility between political and economic arrangements. This inconsistency, due to the existence of "strategic stability", does not always lead to institutional changes, rather, it is the concern of the powerful politicians about the reactions of the non-elite of the society that forces them to make such changes. Acemoglu and Robinson (2012) used the concept of "path-dependent change" (caused by internal or external dynamics). These researchers have shown that institutions, while they can be continuous, but many of their aspects change frequently.

In this chapter, the general framework of institutional inertia is presented. Investigating issues such as: the relationship of institutional inertia with each of the theories of institutional changes, and the quantifying the concept of institutional inertia, are in front of the researchers, which should be addressed in the future.

References

Abelson, R. P. (1968). Psychological implication. In R. P. Abelson, E. Aronson, W. J. McGuire, T. M. Newcomb, M. J. Rosenberg, & P. H. Tannenbaum (Eds.), *Theories of cognitive consistency: A sourcebook* (pp. 112–139). Rand McNally.

Acemoglu, D., & Robinson, J. A. (2000). Why did the west extend the franchise? Democracy, inequality, and growth in historical perspective. *The Quarterly Journal of Economics, 115*(4), 1167–1199.

Acemoglu, D., & Robinson, J. A. (2001). A theory of political transitions. *American Economic Review, 91*(4), 938–963.

Acemoglu, D., Johnson, S., & Robinson, J. A. (2002). Reversal of fortune: Geography and institutions in the making of the modern world income distribution. *The Quarterly Journal of Economics, 117*(4), 1231–1294.

Acemoglu, D., Johnson, S., & Robinson, J. A. (2005). Institutions as a fundamental cause of long-run growth. *Handbook of Economic Growth, 1*, 385–472.

Acemoglu, D., & Robinson, J. A. (2006). *Economic origins of dictatorship and democracy*. Cambridge University Press.

Acemoglu, D., Ticchi, D., & Vindigni, A. (2010). A theory of military dictatorships. *American Economic Journal: Macroeconomics, 2*(1), 1–42.

Acemoglu, D., & Robinson, J. A. (2012). *Why nations fail: The origins of power, prosperity, and poverty*. Crown Publishers.

Acemoglu, D., Egorov, G., & Sonin, K. (2012). Dynamics and stability of constitutions, coalitions, and clubs. *American Economic Review, 102*(4), 1446–1476.

Acemoglu, D. (2006). A simple model of inefficient institutions. *The Scandinavian Journal of Economics, 108*(4), 515–546.

Acemoglu, D. (2012). Introduction to economic growth. *Journal of Economic Theory, 147*(2), 545–550.

Acemoglu, D., Laibson, D., & List, J. A. (2019). *Economics*. Pearson.
Acemoglu, D., & Robinson, J. A. (2019). *The narrow corridor: States, societies, and the fate of liberty*. Penguin.
Acemoglu, D., Egorov, G., & Sonin, K. (2018). Social mobility and stability of democracy: Reevaluating de Tocqueville. *The Quarterly Journal of Economics, 133*(2), 1041–1105.
Acemoglu, D., Egorov, G., & Sonin, K. (2021). Institutional change and institutional persistence. In *The handbook of historical economics* (pp. 365–389). Elsevier.
Aoki, M. (2001). Toward a compartive insitutional analysis (P. Milgrom, M. Aoki, & A. Greif (Ed.), (CIA). The MIT Press.
Aoki, M. (2007). Endogenizing institutions and institutional changes. *Journal of Institutional Economics, 3*(1), 1–31.
Albert, M., & Hahnel, R. (2017). *Quiet revolution in welfare economics* (Vol. 5008). Princeton University Press.
Aldrich, H. (1999). *Organizations evolving*. Sage.
Arendt, H. (2006). *On revolution*. Penguin Books.
Aristotle, Physics &, D. Bostock (Ed.), (2008). (Robin Waterfield Trans.). Oxford University Press
Atkins, P. (2010). *The Laws of thermodynamics* (p. 52). Oxford University Press.
Bacon, F. (1960). *The new Organon and related writings*. Prentice Hall.
Banchoff, T. (2002). Institutions, inertia and European Union research policy. *JCMS: Journal of Common Market Studies, 40*(1), 1–21.
Börzel, T. A. (2003). *How the European Union interacts with its member states* Institute for Advanced Studies 1–23.
Bostock, D. (2008). *Aristotle, Physics, Robin Waterfield* (p. 229). Oxford University Press.
Bourdieu, P. (1992). *The logic of practice*. Stanford University Press.
Bourdieu, P. (1985). The social space and the genesis of groups. *Social Science Information, 24*(2), 195–220.
Bowles, S. (1998). Endogenous preferences: The cultural consequences of markets and other economic institutions. *Journal of Economic Literature, 36*(1), 75–111.
Bowles, S. (2004). *Microeconomics: Behavior, institutions and evolution*. Princeton University Press.
Bowles, S., & Naidu, S. (2006). *Persistent Institutions*.", working paper,. Santa Fe Institute.
Burch, S. (2011). Sustainable development paths: Investigating the roots of local policy responses to climate change. *Sustainable Development, 19*(3), 176–188.
Brennan, G. (2009). Climate change: A rational choice politics view. *Australian Journal of Agricultural and Resource Economics, 53*(3), 309–326. https://doi.org/10.1111/j.1467-8489.2009.00457
Cairney, P. (2019). *Understanding public policy: Theories and issues*. Bloomsbury Publishing.
Callen, H. B. (1985). *Thermodynamics and an introduction to thermostatistics*. Wiley.
Campbell, J. L. (2021). *Institutional change and globalization in institutional change and globalization*. Princeton University Press.
Caplan, R. (Ed.). (2012). *Exit strategies and state building*. Oxford University Press.
Caplan, B. (2003). The idea trap: the political economy of growth divergence. *European Journal of Political Economy, 19*(2), 183–203.
Cashmore, M., & Wejs, A. (2014). Constructing legitimacy for climate change planning: A study of local government in Denmark. *Global Environmental Change, 24*, 203–212.
Cohen, I. B. (1964). 'Quantum in se est': Newton's concept of inertia in relation to Descartes and Lucretius. *Notes and Records of the Royal Society of London, 19*(2), 131–155.
Commons, J. R. (1931). Institutional economics. *The American Economic Review, 21*, 648–657.
Dainton, M., & Zelley, E. D. (2022). Applying communication theory for professional life: A practical introduction. Sage publications.
Dosi, G., & Malerba, F. (2002). Interpreting industrial dynamics twenty years after Nelson and winter's evolutionary theory of economic change: a preface. *Industrial and Corporate Change, 11*(4), 619–622.

Drake, S. (1999). 1. Galileo and the law of inertia. In T. Levere & N. Swerdlow (Eds.), *Essays on Galileo and the history and philosophy of science: Volume 2* (pp. 121–133). University of Toronto Press. https://doi.org/10.3138/9781487572037-012

Dubois, V. (2019). Institutional order, interaction order and social order: Administering welfare, disciplining the poor. *Social Policies, 6*(3), 507–520.

Durkheim, E. (2019). The division of labor in society. In *Social stratification* (pp. 178–183). Routledge.

Earman, J., & Friedman, M. (1973). The meaning and status of Newton's law of inertia and the nature of gravitational forces. *Philosophy of Science, 40*(3), 329–359.

Engerman, S., & Sokoloff, K. (1997). *Factor endowments, institutions, and differential paths of growth among New World economics* (pp. 260–304). Stanford University Press.

Fenner, C. J., & Piotrowski, C. (2018). Communication theory in leadership research: Which theories predominate. *Psychology & Education: An Interdisciplinary Journal, 55*(2), 10–18.

Fischer, S. (1994). *Russia and the Soviet Union then and now* (pp. 221–258). University of Chicago Press.

Foxon, T. J., Pearson, P. J., Arapostathis, S., Carlsson-Hyslop, A., & Thornton, J. (2013). Branching points for transition pathways: Assessing responses of actors to challenges on pathways to a low carbon future. *Energy Policy, 52*, 146–158.

Freud, S. (1989). Beyond the pleasure principle. In P. Gay (Ed.), *The Freud reader* (pp. 594–626). WW Norton & Co.

Fukuyama, F. (2011). *The origins of political order: From Prehuman Times to the French Revolution*. Farrar, Straus and Giroux.

Gal, D. (2006). *A psychological law of inertia and the illusion of loss aversion*. Cambridge University Press.

Genschel, P. (1995). *The dynamics of inertia: Institutional persistence and institutional change in telecommunications and health care* (MPIFG discussion paper 95/3).

Hegel, G. W. F. (1977). *Phenomenology of spirit* (A.V. Miller Trans.). , Oxford University Press, p. 51.

Gerber, E. R., & Jackson, J. E. (1993). Endogenous preferences and the study of institutions. *American Political Science Review, 87*(3), 639–656.

Godkin, L., & Allcorn, S. (2008). Overcoming organizational inertia: A tripartite model for achieving strategic organizational change. *The Journal of Applied Business and Economics, 8*(1), 82.

Greif, A., & Laitin, D. D. (2004). A theory of endogenous institutional change. *American Political Science Review, 98*(4), 633–652.

Haag, S. (2014). *Organizational inertia as barrier to firms' IT adoption–multidimensional scale development and validation*. Goethe University Frankfurt.

Haase, M., Roedenbeck, M., & Söllner, A. (2009). A sketch of a mechanism-based explanation of cognitive path processes, lock-in of individual mental models and institutional rigidity. In *Methoden in der Betriebswirtschaftslehre* (pp. 21–46). Springer.

Hannan, M., & Freeman, J. (1984). Structural inertia and organizational change. *American Sociological Review, 49*(2), 149–164.

Hayek, F. A. (1973). *Law, legislation and liberty, vol. 1: Rules and order*. University of Chicago Press.

Heiner, R. A. (1983). The origin of predictable behavior. *The American Economic Review, 73*(4), 560–595.

Hodgson, G. M. (2000). What is the essence of institutional economics? *Journal of Economic Issues, 34*(2), 317–329.

Hodgson, G. M. (2001). *How economics forgot history: The problem of historical specificity in social science*. Routledge.

Hodgson, G. M. (2004). *The evolution of institutional economics: Agency, structure and darwinism in American institutionalism*. Routledge.

Hodgson, G. M. (2006). What are institutions? *Journal of Economic Issues, 40*(1), 1–25.

Hodgson, G. M. (2007). The revival of Veblenian institutional economics. *Journal of Economic Issues, 16*(2), 325–340.
Hoffman, A. J., & Ventresca, M. J. (1999). The institutional framing of policy debates: Economics versus the environment. *American Behavioral Scientist, 42*(8), 1368–1392.
Hovi, J., Sprinz, D. F., & Underdal, A. (2009). Implementing long-term climate policy: Time inconsistency, domestic politics, international anarchy. *Global Environmental Politics, 9*(3), 20–39.
Huang, H. C., Lai, M. C., Lin, L. H., & Chen, C. T. (2013). Overcoming organizational inertia to strengthen business model innovation: An open innovation perspective. *Journal of Organizational Change Management., 26*, 977–1002.
Huff, J. O., Huff, A. S., & Thomas, H. (1992). Strategic renewal and the interaction of cumulative stress and inertia. *Strategic Management Journal, 13*(S1), 55–75.
Jones, B. D. (1999). Bounded rationality. *Annual Review of Political Science, 2*(1), 297–321.
Jones, J. G., & Simmons, H. W. (2017). *Persuasion in society*. Routledge.
Jones, N. A., Ross, H., Lynam, T., Perez, P., & Leitch, A. (2011). Mental models: An interdisciplinary synthesis of theory and methods. *Ecology and Society, 16*(1).
Karam, S. L., Dendy, J., Polu, S., & Blonde, L. (2020). Overview of therapeutic inertia in diabetes: Prevalence, causes, and consequences. *Diabetes Spectrum: A Publication of the American Diabetes Association, 33*(1), 8–15.
Kingston, C., & Caballero, G. (2009). Comparing theories of institutional change. *Journal of Institutional Economics, 5*(2), 151–180.
Kuhn, T. S. (1996). *The structure of scientific revolutions*. University of Chicago Press.
Lamberg, J. A., & Tikkanen, H. (2006). Changing sources of competitive advantage: cognition and path dependence in the Finnish retail industry 1945–1995. *Industrial and Corporate Change, 15*(5), 811–846.
Lee, Y. T. (2013). Review of the origins of political order: From Prehuman Times to the French Revolution, by Francis Fukuyama. New York: Farrar, Straus, and Giroux, 2011. *Journal of Cultural Interaction in East Asia, 4*(1), 85–91.
Levi, M. (1990). A logic of institutional change. In K. Schweers & M. Levi (Eds.), *The limits of rationality*. University of Chicago Press.
Levy, D. L., & Egan, D. (2003). A neo-Gramscian approach to corporate political strategy: Conflict and accommodation in the climate change negotiations. *Journal of Management Studies, 40*(4), 803–829.
Libecap, G. D. (1989). *Contracting for property rights*. Cambridge University Press.
Liao, S. H., Fei, W. C., & Liu, C. T. (2008). Relationships between knowledge inertia, organizational learning and organization innovation. *Technovation, 28*(4), 183–195.
Lizzeri, A., & Persico, N. (2004). Why did the elites extend the suffrage? Democracy and the scope of government, with an application to Britain's "age of reform". *The Quarterly Journal of Economics, 119*(2), 707–765.
Machiavelli, N. (1965). *The prince*. Airmont.
Mahoney, J. (2000). Path dependence in historical sociology. *Theory and Society, 29*(4), 507–548.
March, J. G., & Simon, H. A. (1958). *Organizations*. Wiley.
March, J. G., & Olsen, J. P. (1989). *The organizational basis of politics*. The Free Press.
Marciano, A., & Ramello, G. B. (2018). *Encyclopedia of law and economics*. Springer.
Matthews, R., & Sydneysmith, R. (2010). Adaptive capacity as a dynamic institutional process: Conceptual perspectives and their application. In *Adaptive capacity and environmental governance* (pp. 223–242). Springer.
McGuire, W. J. (1960). Cognitive consistency and attitude change. *The Journal of Abnormal and Social Psychology, 60*(3), 345–353.
McGuire, W. J. (2013). An additional future for psychological science. *Perspectives on Psychological Science, 8*(4), 414–423.

Munck af Rosenschöld, J., Rozema, J. G., & Frye-Levine, L. A. (2014). Institutional inertia and climate change: A review of the new institutionalist literature. *Wiley Interdisciplinary Reviews: Climate Change, 5*(5), 639–648. https://doi.org/10.1002/wcc.292

Nelson, R. R., & Winter, S. G. (1982) *An evolutionary theory of economic change*. Harvard University Press, Cambridge, MA.

North, D. C. (1981). *Structure and change in economic history*. Norton.

North, D. C., & Weingast, B. (1989). Constitutions and commitment: The evolution of institutions governing public choice in seventeenth-century England. *Journal of Economic History, 49*(4), 803–832.

North, D. C. (1990). *Institutions, institutional change and economic performance*. Cambridge University Press.

North, D. C. (2010). *Understanding the process of economic change*. Princeton University Press.

Okereke, C. (2007). An exploration of motivations, drivers and barriers to carbon management: The UK FTSE 100. *European Management Journal, 25*(6), 475–486.

Okereke, C., Bulkeley, H., & Schroeder, H. (2009). Conceptualizing climate governance beyond the international regime. *Global environmental politics, 9*(1), 58–78.

Olson, M. (2008). The rise and decline of nations. In *The Rise and Decline of Nations*. Yale University Press.

Ostrom, E. (2005). *Understanding institutional diversity*. Princeton University Press.

Overholser, J. C. (2011). Collaborative empiricism, guided discovery, and the Socratic method: Core processes for effective cognitive therapy. *Clinical Psychology: Science and Practice, 18*, 62–66.

Praça, S. (2009). Preference formation and institutional change. *Brazilian Political Science Review (Online), 4*(SE), 0–0.

Pierson, P. (2000). Increasing returns, path dependence, and the study of politics. *American Political Science Review, 94*, 251–267.

Pierson, P. (2011). *Politics in time*. Princeton University Press.

Phillips, L. S., Branch, W. T., Jr., Cook, C. B., Doyle, J. P., El-Kebbi, I. M., Gallina, D. L., et al. (2001). Clinical inertia. *Annals of Internal Medicine, 135*(9), 825–834.

Polites, G. L., & Karahanna, E. (2012). Shackled to the status quo: The inhibiting effects of incumbent system habit, switching costs, and inertia on new system acceptance. *MIS Quarterly, 36*, 21–42.

Potter, D. (1976). *The impending crisis, 1848–1861*. Harper & Row.

Powell, W. W., & DiMaggio, P. J. (Eds.). (2012). *The new institutionalism in organizational analysis*. University of Chicago press.

Prigogine, I., & Stengers, I. (1984). *Order out of Chaos* (pp. 113–115). Heinemann.

Putnam, R. D. (1993). *Making democracy work: Civic traditions in modern Italy*. Princeton University Press.

Rapp, C. (2012). *Aristotle on the moral*. Psychology or Persuasion.

Reid, A. A. L. (1977). Uncertainty and inertia. *Telecommunications Policy, 1*(3), 207–211.

Roland, G. (1991). The political economy of transition in the Soviet Union. *European Economy, 49*, 197–216.

Rosenbaum, E. (2022). Mental models and institutional inertia. *Journal of Institutional Economics, 18*(3), 361–378.

Ruttan, V. W. (2006). Social science knowledge and induced institutional innovation: An institutional design perspective. *Journal of Institutional Economics, 2*(3), 249–272.

Samadi, A. H., & Alipourian, M. (2021). Institutions and institutional change: Concepts and theories. In *Dynamics of institutional change in emerging market economies* (pp. 107–132). Springer.

Sandri, S., Schade, C., Musshoff, O., & Odening, M. (2010). Holding on for too long? An experimental study on inertia in entrepreneurs' and non-entrepreneurs' disinvestment choices. *Journal of Economic Behavior & Organization, 76*(1), 30–44.

Sautua, S. I. (2017). Does uncertainty cause inertia in decision making? An experimental study of the role of regret aversion and indecisiveness. *Journal of Economic Behavior & Organization, 136*, 1–14.
Scharpf, F. W. (1987). Grenzen der Institutionellen Reform. In T. Ellwein, J. J. Hesse, R. Mayntz, et al. (Eds.), *Jahrbuch zur Staats- und Verwaltungswissenschaft, Band 1* (pp. 111–151). Nomos.
Service, R. (2005). *A history of modern Russia from Nicholas II to Vladimir Putin*. Harvard University Press.
Serway, R., & Beichner, J. J. (2000). *Physics for scientists and engineers* (5th ed.). Holt Rinehart & Winston.
Shepsle, K. A. (1986). Institutional equilibrium and equilibrium institutions. *Political Science: The Science of Politics, 51*, 51.
Shepsle, K. (1989). Studying institutions. Some lessons from the rational choice approach. *Journal of Theoretical Politics, 1*, 131–147.
Stiglitz, J. E. (2013). Equal opportunity, our national myth. *New York Times, 16*.
Stinchcombe, A. L. (1968). *Constructing social theories*. Harcourt, Brace & World.
Steinhilber, S., Wells, P., & Thankappan, S. (2013). 'Socio-technical inertia: Understanding the barriers to electric Vehicles'. *Energy Policy, 60*, 5319.
Sunstein, C. R. (2014). Nudging: a very short guide. *Journal of Consumer Policy, 37*, 583–588.
Swartz, D. L., & Zolberg, V. L. (Eds.). (2006). *After Bourdieu: influence, critique, elaboration*. Springer Science & Business Media.
Thelen, K. (1999). Historical institutionalism in comparative politics. *Annual Review of Political Science, 2*(1), 369–404.
Treisman, D. (2011). *The return: Russia's journey from Gorbachev to Medvedev*. Free Press.
Tielens, P., & Van Hertem, D. (2016). The relevance of inertia in power systems. *Renewable and Sustainable Energy Reviews, 55*(March), 999–1009. https://doi.org/10.1016/j.rser.2015.11.016
Tsai, C. Y., Lin, J. L., & Fang, S. C. (2008, July). The paradox of threat and organizational inertia. In *International conference on business and information* (pp. 07–09).
Valderrama, M. L. (2009). *Institutional inertia* (Vol. 09, p. 1).
Veblen, T. (1899). *The theory of the leisure class: An economic study of institutions*. Macmillan.
Weingast, B. (1998). *Political stability and civil war: Institutions, commitment, and American Democracy* (pp. 148–193). Princeton University Press.
Wiener, J. M. (1978). *Social origins of the new south: Alabama, 1860–1885*. Louisiana State University Press.
Williamson, O. (2000). The new institutional economics: Taking stock, looking ahead. *Journal of Economic Literature, 38*, 595–613.
Wittneben, B. B., Okereke, C., Banerjee, S. B., & Levy, D. L. (2012). Climate change and the emergence of new organizational landscapes. *Organization Studies, 33*(11), 1431–1450.
Woodward, C. V. (1955). *The strange career of Jim Crow*. Oxford University Press.
Wright, G. (1986). *Old south, new south: Revolutions in the southern economy since the civil war* (p. 1986). Basic Books.
Zantvoort, B. (2015). Cosmos and history. *The Journal of Natural and Social Philosophy, 11*(1), 342–360.

The Origin of Development, Critical Juncture, and Institutional Inertia

Saleh Ghavidel Doostkouei, Mahmood Mahmoodzadeh, and Mir Hossein Mousavi

1 Introduction

Scientists seek the main cause of nations' backwardness. They seek a response to the questions of what causes nations' rise and fall and why some countries are underdeveloped while others are developed. One of the outstanding works in this field is Why Nations Fail: The Origins of Power, Prosperity, and Poverty 2012, by Acemoglu and Robinson (2012). They proposed four hypotheses as possible causes of nation development: cultural differences, geographical differences, ignorance, and institutional differences. They did not reject the institutional hypothesis. According to them, extractive political institutions represent the primary cause of nations' backwardness, while inclusive political institutions represent the primary reason for nations' development. They considered the institutional change a critical juncture without defining it. Therefore, this chapter aims to define the critical juncture and identify its coordinates. However, the authors rejected the hypotheses of cultural differences, geographical differences, and ignorance.

According to the hypothesis of culture, development is explained by cultural differences between nations. This hypothesis was tested by Acemoglu and Robinson (2012), who used historical samples and quasi-experimental methods. Their results represented that this hypothesis is not sound because one can find countries with the same culture but different degrees of development.

S. G. Doostkouei (✉) · M. Mahmoodzadeh
Department of Economics, Firuzkuh Branch, Islamic Azad University, Firuzkuh, Iran
e-mail: Saleh.ghavidel@iau.ac.ir; Ma.mahmood@iau.ac.ir

M. H. Mousavi
Department of Economics, Faculty of Social Sciences and Economics, Alzahra University, Tehran, Iran
e-mail: hmousavi@alzahra.ac.ir

N. Faghih, A. H. Samadi (eds.), *Institutional Inertia*, Contributions to Economics,
https://doi.org/10.1007/978-3-031-51175-2_4

Culture can be divided into two parts. The first part is highly correlated with geography, such as language, religion, cuisine, social habits, music, and arts, of a particular group of people. The second part stays the same with geography. Some moral behaviors, such as lying, lawlessness, bribery, negligence, and theft, are included in the second part of culture because they are not caused by geography. These behaviors are mainly due to extractive political institutions. For example, the distance between Rapid City in South Dakota and McAllen in Texas, USA, is 1441 miles. The first part of culture differs considerably between the two regions, but the second type is similar. This becomes more obvious when we compare McAllen and Reynosa (a border city in the northern part of Tamaulipas, Mexico). The distance between these two cities is only 16 miles. The first type of culture (food, music, and religion) is very similar in McAllen and Reynosa. Still, the two regions differ in the second type of culture, such as lying, lawlessness, bribery, negligence, and theft. The question arises as to why the two cities' second type of culture differs. The answer is the difference between formal political institutions in the USA and Mexico because McAllen city is in the US and Reynosa in Mexico. Thus, the second type of culture is correlated with the formal institution. The first type of culture is sometimes called an informal institution and is unrelated to the formal institution; it is correlated with geographical areas. Therefore, the culture hypothesis can first be separated into two parts and then merged into the institutions and geography hypotheses. The first type of culture merges the geography hypothesis and the second in the institution's hypothesis. According to the geography hypothesis, the natural environment or geography can drive development. The quasi-historical experimental method rejects this hypothesis. In other words, some countries with the same geography have different development levels.

According to the ignorance hypothesis, ignorance of the authorities is the cause of backwardness. However, this hypothesis, also proposed by Acemoglu and Robinson (2012), has been rejected.

This chapter considers two key questions: 1. What is the root of the change in the institutions? 2. Since other economic elements also change with the institutions change in a country at the same time, no one can claim the change of the institution is the only cause of development. Other economic elements may cause development. Which one: economic elements or institutions?

Factors staying the same with going from backward to development are not the cause of development. The first type of culture and geography provides a vivid example of factors not changing with development. It is easy to find two countries with different developed or underdeveloped geographies.[1]

The factors changing with the development process (e.g., institutional quality, poverty, corruption, and degree of openness) cause development. Still, we cannot identify which one is more important than the others. For example, the institution's

[1]Paired developed countries with different geography: Norway and Australia, Finland and Japan, South Korea, and France. Paired developing countries with different geography: Kyrgyzstan and Nigeria, Lebanon and Nepal, Romania and Jamaica, Georgia and Cuba.

quality cannot be considered the only cause of development because, in the development process, all other factors mentioned above will also change, not the institution's quality only. Before 1945, both North and South Korea had the same development level. There was no difference between these two countries; the difference between North and South Korea was zero. There was not only zero difference between institution quality but also no difference between economic factors like corruption, poverty, and openness of countries. South Korea developed after 1945, but North Korea did not develop. After 1945, we saw differences in institution quality and other economic elements. If the difference between the institution's quality and other elements stayed the same, it could be argued that the increase in institutions led to South Korea's development. In contrast, the reduction in quality institutions led to backwardness in North Korea. A crucial point is the difficulty in detecting development factors' primacy and recency.

We cannot argue that institutions' quality is the main reason for differences. In this case, we have two options: to examine any of the factors involved in the development process or to look for one thing (a reason) that changes everything. Due to the correlation between factors, we cannot argue that the cause of the rise and fall of nations is a dozen or maybe hundreds of factors, each contributing to the development process. We should look for a cause that has changed all factors, including institutions' quality.

In response to the first and second questions, we explain that the cause of the rise and fall is unclear. In the first case, institutional change is the primary cause of nations' rise and fall; it is unknown. In the second case, we should look for a cause that has changed all factors, including institutions' quality; and this is also uncertain. It can be at a historical-critical juncture, such as the institution's divergence between the United States and Mexico. A person, a historical event, a war, a geographical event, a climate change event, or a pandemic like covid-19 can be at a critical juncture. Mahoney (2000) believes that a critical juncture is a situation in which the adoption of various decisions leads to the creation of institutions with specific arrangements that make it difficult to return to the starting point. These decisions may not create institutions with these arrangements in other geographical locations. The critical juncture differs in various countries because they have different historical backgrounds. Critical junctures create paths that lead society in certain directions (Mahoney, 2000). The critical juncture in a society results from previous conditions, cleavage, shocks, and crises.

World War II is a historical-critical juncture for South and North Korea. Captain Arthur Phillip's carrying of British convicts became critical to Australia's development in 1787. The black death in 1346 became a critical juncture in making a parliament in Britain and UK development (Acemoglu & Robinson, 2012). Nelson Mandela and Mahatma Gandhi are two-person that are at critical junctures in changing political institutions in South Africa and India. At first glance, this interpretation is determinism, and the natural description of this event is luck. For this purpose, this issue should be related to infinite regression and distal causes. It emphasizes a kind of cause (involving a big, discontinuous change) and a kind of effect (a persistent effect) (Munck, 2021). The other synonyms for critical juncture are "turning point" and "unsettled times" (Capoccia, 2016).

This chapter will explain that the Historical-critical juncture often is not determinism. However, some scholars believe the critical juncture is an exogenous shock (Mahoney, 2000; Abbott, 1988). This chapter introduces the historical-critical juncture as the root of underdevelopment, and the core identifies the characteristics and coordinates of the historical-critical juncture.

Nevertheless, some researchers have shown that the cause of countries' rise and fall is unknown. Goldstone (2000) found that the West and the East have been roughly the same for 1600 years. Great empires ruled both areas. In these empires, most people were poor in both areas. Goldstone (2000) says progress in the West has no clear cause. Pomeranz (2000) argues, "If the UK had not discovered coal reserves, the industrial exploitation possibility of steam power would not have been possible." Pomeranz (2000) claims that the industrial revolution was initiated in England more by accident than by design.

This concept became very clear when we used the critical juncture for changing institutions. Critical juncture is a part of the path dependence argument that an institution changes at a particular time. However, critical juncture is also used in other disciplines, from medicine to sociology, to account for outcomes as diverse as individual life histories (Capoccia, 2016). Most institutions are path-dependent, resistant to change, and tend to do nothing or remain unchanged; this concept is institutional inertia. The critical juncture can change these institutions.

The most significant findings about the historical-critical juncture will be analyzed in the next section.

This chapter is organized into seven sections. The second session focuses on nations' initial rise and fall characteristics. The first two sessions complete the chapter's theoretical foundations. The third section identifies the main characteristics of the "rise and fall of nations" and defines three key features. This section specifies the methodology. Sections 4, 5, and 6 discuss the research results. The last section is the conclusion.

2 Initial Recognition of the Cause of nation's Rise and Fall

One way of showing the characteristics of the causes of nations' rise and fall is to compare Eastern and Western nations. Before the twelfth century, the East was advanced, and the West was backward (Sarton, 1927). The cause of the turning point is unclear, and it is a common question for researchers. This chapter seeks to identify some features of this turning point (X) in Fig. 1.

The first characteristic: The turning point does not necessarily occur simultaneously in the East and West. The cause of the rise of the West and the collapse of the East may be two different phenomena independent of each other. In Fig. 2, the cause of the East's collapse is X1 at T1, and the cause of the West's rise is X2 at T2.

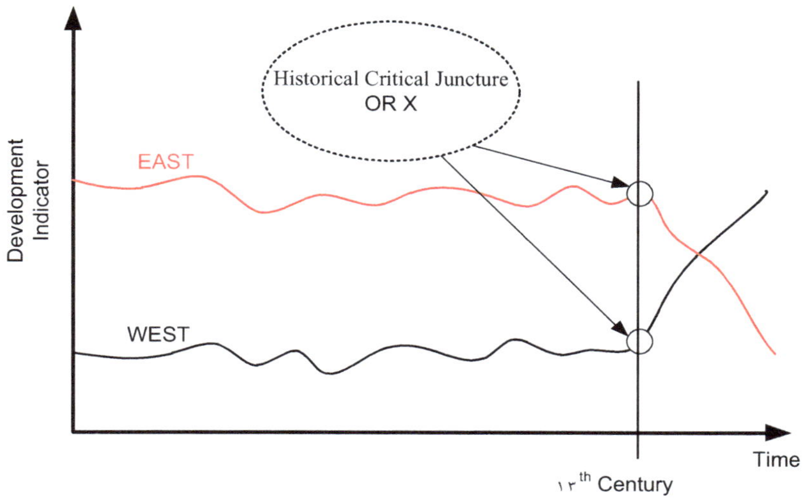

Fig. 1 The rise and fall of Eastern and Western nations
Source: Morris (2010)

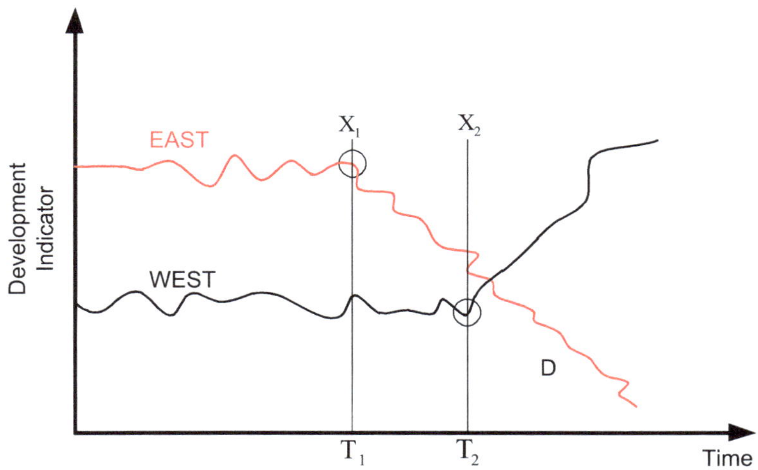

Fig. 2 Turning points of the development path
Source: Morris (2010)

The East's fall and the West's rise are due to separate reasons unless there is a strong reason. It is very difficult to determine whether X1 and X2 are dependent or independent, while X1 and X2 are not understood.[2]

[2]In the next section, we will see that the critical juncture time is unknown. However, whether the conditions for its occurrence exist can be determined.

The second characteristic is that East and West's rise and fall are not unique in history. Most countries with different cultures, geography, and governments have experienced several turning points in history. Figure 3 represents the rise and fall of the West and the East based on historical documents. We see that both the East and the West fell and rose several times. The first period when the West fell was in the fifth century. Most indicators show that the West was higher than the East before the fifth century (Morris, 2010). The factor that caused the West's fall has been named the X5-century. As it is unclear what X5-century is, all turning points in this chapter are represented by 'X.' Various theories have been provided for X5-century. In his famous book, "Introduction to the History of Science," Sarton (1927) considers scholastic ritual to have caused the West's fall in the fifth century. The scholastic ritual was the religion in Europe during Middle Ages. Some researchers believe that the X5-century is not a short-term event, and the conditions of this event have accumulated over centuries. In his book, "Why the West Rules for Now: The Patterns of History, and What They Reveal about the Future," Morris (2010) used energy consumption indicators to show the superiority of the West to the East. Morris's energy consumption indicators show that the West was superior to the East for 14 centuries. Morris believes that the higher energy consumption index in the West than in the East is due to geographic differences. This trend was reversed around 550 AD after the first fall of the West. This indicated that the development in the East was about 30 percent higher than in the West, and this superiority continued until the twelfth century. If we accept the geography hypothesis, we are left with the question of why the energy index improved in the East around 550 AD. However, geography did not change at the same time. It is also unclear why this index was higher in the West in the thirteenth century.

X8-century is the next historical-critical juncture in Fig. 3, representing the turning point for Eastern nations in the eighth century. In the eighth century, Eastern nations significantly grew in the scientific index. The Islamic Golden Age—from the eighth to the mid-thirteenth century—was one of the greatest periods of human knowledge and progress flourishing (Falagas et al., 2006; Farmer, 1970). Many scientists point to the Islamic Golden Age but do not mention the root of this growth (Farmer, 1970; Frieder, 2015; Grierson & Travaini, 1986).

X13-century is the third Historical-critical juncture in Fig. 3; this is a turning point for Eastern countries and the Muslim world in the thirteenth century. Eastern nations declined in the twelfth and thirteenth centuries. Scientific discoveries, which had grown since the eighth century, shut down in the 13th. Saunders (2001) believes that the decline of the East, including the Islamic empire, in the twelfth and thirteenth centuries is associated with the Mongol invasion (Saunders, 2001). Zibakalam (1999) believes this decline occurred because science came from other countries and did not originate in Baghdad. Sarton (1927) believes that the cause of the East's fall in the thirteenth century was scholastic ritual and lack of empiricism.

X15-century is the fourth historical-critical juncture, coinciding with the West Renaissance. Through the Renaissance and science, the West awakened from a thousand-year slumber. Bertrand Russell (2013), in his famous book "A History of Western Philosophy," says that the Renaissance was introduced for two reasons: the

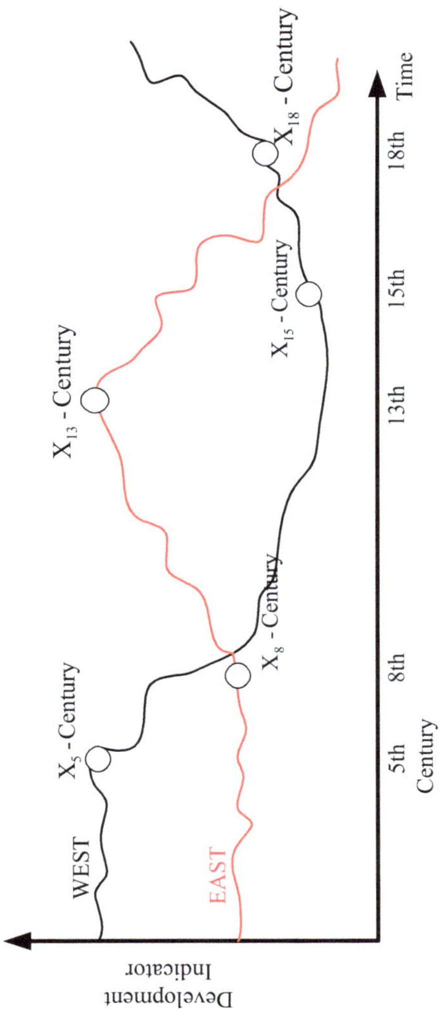

Fig. 3 Turning points of East and West nations
Source: Morris, 2010

reduced role of the church and the increasing power of science. Hollingdale (1979) argues that, by lowering the church's power, science was reinstated again. The question arises as to why such an event did not occur in the East.

Barbour (1966) considers the causes of the Renaissance to include the following: failure of church rule, the changed perspective of humans to God, trade expansion, the invention of the compass, the invention of firearms, the development of the printing industry and news chapter publishing, magazines, and the discovery of American. These factors accelerated the Renaissance. However, with Barbour's theory, the question arises whether these factors cause and affect each other. For example, the compass led to America's discovery. If a factor is the root cause of all the other factors, it is better to identify the key factor than to introduce and list some factors.

Some researchers believe that famous people caused the Renaissance. In "The Story of Philosophy," Will Durant (1961) wrote: The awakening began with Roger Bacon (1214–1294) and was developed by Leonardo da Vinci (1452–1519). Astronomy began with Copernicus (1473–1543) and reached its fullest extent with Galileo (1564–1643). Will Durant's point of view is close to historical criticality?

The fifth Historical-critical juncture X18-century is another turning point for the West's progress. An important phenomenon for the cause of X18-century was Industrial Revolution in England. Scientists have cited a range of reasons for the Industrial Revolution. Allen (2011) argues that apart from economic factors, which were mainly responsible for the Industrial Revolution in England, other factors, such as cultural and political factors, also affected the development of this revolution. Ashton (1997) suggested that the most important factor of the industrial revolution in England was foreign trade, which further expanded to the people worldwide. Some scientists believe that the cause of the Industrial Revolution was laissez-faire or trade. Laissez-faire developed during the eighteenth century, after Adam Smith's "The Wealth of Nations." Some believe that the cause of the West overtaking the East in the past three centuries lies in the racial superiority of Western people over Eastern people. Morris (2010) rejected this hypothesis in a highly detailed archaeological study of the East and West's history. However, he believes in the geography hypothesis.

So, the cause of a country's fall is not the same as another country's rise. For example, it is not necessarily true that the reasons for African nations' backwardness lie in the progress of European countries. Moreover, throughout history, nations have experienced several periods of fall and rise. Therefore, the geography hypothesis that some scientists see as the cause of countries' fall and rise is rejected with high confidence. The next section explains the main coordinates of countries' turning points.

3 Main Coordinates of Nations' Rise and Fall

3.1 The First Coordinate: X Is Unique

If many factors cause development or backwardness, they should be independent. Otherwise, all factors would converge for a unique reason. We now propose two hypotheses:

H1: Each of the above factors contributes to countries' backwardness.
H2: One factor is the main cause of backwardness or development, and the other factors are the effects of that factor.

Consider country A as a developed country and country B as an underdeveloped one. Then, check the development indicators in the two countries. It is clear that, in country B, all the development indicators (extractive institutions and economic factors such as big government, corruption, low degree of openness, poor interaction with the world, lack of meritocracy, weakness of the rule of law, etc.) are in bad condition. In contrast, all development indicators in country A are in good condition. These factors are not independent of each other. When corruption is present in a country, other factors such as a big government size, a low degree of openness, poor interaction with the world, and extractive institutions are also present. Table 1 shows an example of the relationship between development factors in two hypothetical countries.

When X1, X2... Xn is not independent of each other. We cannot estimate their share of Y in the following function:

$$Y = f(X_1, X_2, \ldots, X_n) \tag{1}$$

When X1 and Xn are independent, we can estimate their share. When countries A and B are as seen in Table 2, it could be argued that corruption is the cause of backwardness because all indicators, except corruption, in countries A and B are the same. The corruption index in country A is higher than in country B. In this case, it

Table 1 Relationship between development factors in two assumed countries (Option 1)

Index	A (Developed country)	B (Underdeveloped country)	Difference between AB
Government size	1	8	7
Openness degree	2	9	7
Interaction with the world	1.1	8	6.9
Rule of law	1.5	9.1	7.6
Corruption	2.2	8.5	6.3
Other factors of development	1	8	7

All numbers are assumed and unreal; a higher number indicates a worse index condition

Table 2 Relationship between development factors in two hypothetical countries (Option 2)

Index	A (Developed Country)	B (Underdeveloped Country)	Difference between AB
Government size	8	8	0
Openness degree	9	9	0
Interaction with the world	7.5	8	0.5
Institutions' quality	8.5	8	0.5
Rule of law	9	9.1	0.1
Corruption	***2***	***9***	***7***
Other factors of development	8	8	0

All numbers are assumed and unreal; a higher number indicates a worse index condition

can be argued that the cause of country A's backwardness is corruption because other factors are the same in both countries. In this case, regression analysis was used to estimate corruption's impact on development. In this regression, the dependent variable is the development index, and the corruption index is the independent variable. We can estimate corruption's effect on development by using the following regression:

$$Development\_index = \beta_0 + \beta_1(Corruption\_index) + U \tag{2}$$

In Eq. (2), U includes other factors, such as institutions' quality, government size, openness degree, interaction with the world, etc. As long as these factors do not change from one country to another, they do not need to be controlled. However, Eq. (2) is consistent with Table 2, with no empirical evidence. Stylized fact matches Table 1 conditions.

Table 1 shows the real situation of developed and underdeveloped countries. When the conditions of the two countries are as in Table 1, we cannot estimate the effect of corruption on development by using the regression Eq. (2) because other factors affecting development change along with the corruption index from one country to another. In this case, the regression model should be estimated as follows:

$$Development\_index = \begin{array}{l} \beta_0 + \beta_1(Institution\ quality) \\ + \beta_2(Corruption\_index) + \beta_3(Ignorant) \\ + \beta_4(Globalization) + \beta_5(Other) + U \end{array} \tag{3}$$

However, this model has a major problem: all factors affecting the development index are correlated, and we cannot estimate their partial effect. Thus, the multicollinearity between the explanatory variables in Eq. (3) is the main problem in estimating corruption's effect on development (Wooldridge, 2015; Greene, 2008). If the explanatory variables are independent, the pure effect of each variable can be estimated. For example, if it is clearly stated that corruption is 20 percent, we must control it directly. Unfortunately, it is almost impossible to recognize corruption's pure effect. However, using econometric models, determining the joint effect of all factors on the development index is possible. For this purpose, a joint hypothesis test (F test) is used.

Another way to estimate the effect of one variable on another variable is the quasi-experimental method (Shadish et al., 2002). Some scientists have used this method to estimate corruption's effect on development indicators (Van der Ploeg, 2011). They find two very similar countries, and at a time, the corruption index has increased in one of them, but the other has not changed. Then, the difference in the development index before and after corruption is measured. If corruption has significantly affected the difference between the development index of the two countries, corruption affects development conditions. The simple formula is Eq. (4)[3]:

$$E = \left(Y_{2after} - Y_{1after}\right) - \left(Y_{2befor} - Y_{1befor}\right) \tag{4}$$

$Y_{1before}$ is the development index in country *1* before corruption, $Y_{2before}$ is the development index in country *2* before corruption, $Y_{1before}$ is the development index in country *1* after corruption, and $Y_{2before}$ is the development index in country *1* after corruption. If E is nonzero, the event has been effective.

The most important condition of this test is that all other factors, apart from the corruption, in both countries at the time of the event have not changed.[4] Finding this quasi-experimental condition in the real world is very difficult. When corruption occurs in a country, political and economic institutions such as government size the degree of openness, and, etc. will change simultaneously.

The difficulty of measuring the partial effect of corruption on development indicators in regression and quasi-experiments reflects the fact that corruption is associated with other factors and not independent. We cannot find a pair of countries, one developed and the other underdeveloped, that differ on one factor only. Table 1 shows many pairs of countries.

Figure 4 indicates the correlation between "control of corruption" and "political stability and absence of violence" in various countries. Corruption and political instability (an indicator of political institutions' quality) have a positive relationship. Figure 5 shows the correlation between corruption control and government effectiveness in various countries. Corruption is higher in societies where governments are inefficient.

In most cases, when there is a correlation between the factors, these factors derive from one main cause (main cause). The main cause may be one of the available factors or an unknown factor. In most cases, when the cause of a phenomenon is expressed by several factors that are correlated with each other, the main cause is unknown. Unless the primacy and recentness of these factors are known, a factor that

[3]This method is also called "difference in difference." See Wooldridge, 2015, p. 457.

[4]Unless corruption is a priority in terms of time compared to other factors. In other words, the main cause is corruption, and other factors are caused by corruption.

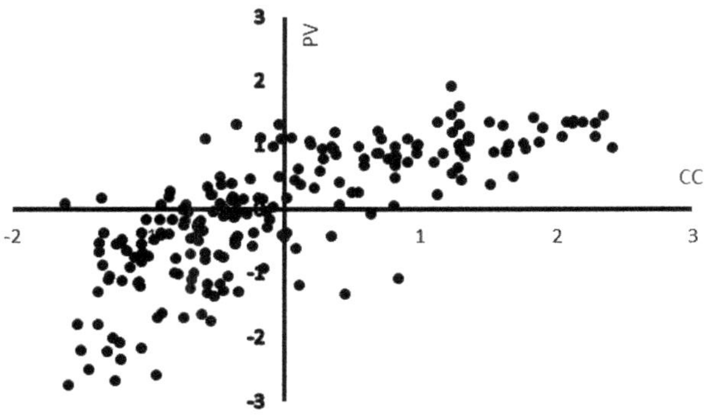

Fig. 4 The relationship between political stability, absence of violence (PV), and control of corruption (CC) for all countries in 2018
Source: The World Bank.

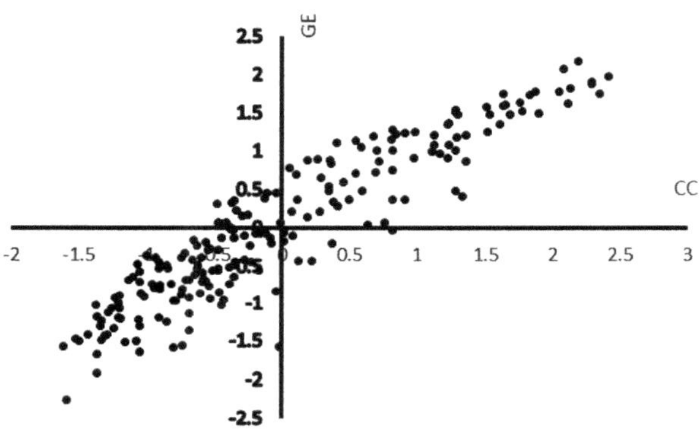

Fig. 5 Relationship between Government Effectiveness (GE) and Control of Corruption (CC) for all countries in 2018
Source: The World Bank

takes precedence over other factors will be the main factor. We can use Paul Edwards (1972) for this: "Suppose five people are standing along the street. The first person is asked: 'Why do you stand here?' They say, 'I am waiting for the bus.' The second person asked, 'I am waiting for my friend.' The third person says, 'I want sunshine.' The fourth person says, 'I stand here to see the sights,' and the fifth person says, 'I am waiting for my mother.' In this case, each person has their specific reasons *because they are independent of each other.*

Now, suppose that five people are not independent of each other. The first and second persons are brothers and sisters. The third and fourth persons are cousins. The fifth person has a family relationship with them. When we ask the first person: 'Why do you stand here?' They say, 'I am waiting for a car.' The second person asked, 'I am waiting for my mother.' The third and fourth persons say, 'We are waiting for our aunt,' and the fifth person says, 'I am waiting for a person from my family.' Note that different people have different answers, but the cause that they are standing along the street is the same because these *people are not independent of each other.* Five people await a woman.

Factors listed for a nation's backwardness are correlated theoretically and empirically. For example, a group of economists argues that corruption is the cause of big government size. Another group argues that the cause of corruption is big government size. Both groups have experimental evidence and theories. Likewise, poor interaction with other countries can be argued as being due to low-quality institutions. On the other hand, low-quality institutions can be argued as the cause of poor interaction with other countries. This argument results in a vicious circle because cause and effect are unclear.

Assume that the primary cause of all these factors is an extra factor called X. One way to find X is to delve into a nation's history. For example, consider two countries, North and South Korea. South Korea is country A, and North Korea is country B in Table 1. Seventy years ago, development was similar in both countries as a single country. In 1945, when World War II ended, Korea was divided into North and South. North Korea established an extractive institution, and South Korea established an inclusive institution. The two countries rank very differently now in terms of development. What caused North Korea's fall and the rise of South Korea? The answer is clear: World War II. If World War II had not happened, Korea would not have been divided into two parts. World War II was the main reason (or X) for North Korea's fall and the rise of South Korea. If further explored, we must introduce X as the cause of World War II. We will later discuss how far this question should continue.

There are many examples, the most famous of which are the causes of development in Western nations and backwardness in Eastern nations. This is mentioned at the beginning of the chapter. Another example of a historical-critical juncture is the Black Death (spread of the plague) in England. This historical-critical juncture is known as the Black Death (Acemoglu & Robinson, 2012).

In general, when Z_1 and Z_2 are factors of Y at time T:

$$Y = f(Z_1, Z_2)T = 1 \tag{5}$$

You cannot say that Z_1 and Z_2 were a factor of Y at T-200 (200 years ago). However, both Z_1 and Z_2 were created from X 200 years ago. We see the X as Z_1 and Z_2, while X is not observed. We can write:

$$\begin{aligned} Z_1 &= G(X) \\ Z_2 &= S(X) \qquad \mathrm{T} = 0 \end{aligned} \tag{6}$$

$$Y = f(Z_1, Z_2) \tag{7}$$

If:

$$Corr\ (Z_1, Z_2) = a \tag{8}$$

Then:

$$Y = f(X) \tag{9}$$

If Z_1 and Z_2 are not correlated: $a = 0$. Each factor causes Y. When Z_1 and Z_2 are correlated (based on theoretical arguments and empirical evidence), the primary cause is X, not Z_1 and Z_2. We know that a is between zero and one. If a is close to unity, the logic of this theory is stronger. For example, consider Z_1 = Corruption and Z_2 = Institutional Quality. We know these two variables are strongly correlated, and both are causes of underdevelopment today. However, T years ago, they did not exist.

Therefore, the primary cause is unique, but it is hard to understand whether it is endogenous or exogenous factors. If the primary cause is endogenous factors, the primacy and recentness of the available factors should be recognized to distinguish a primary cause. This chapter calls it a "Historical-critical juncture.[5]"

3.2 The Second Coordinates: X Emerged in History

To test the hypothesis that endowments are not the cause of backwardness, the difference method is used as a type of quasi-experimental technique:

Suppose that n factors are the causes of development at time t_0 in countries A and B, and the degrees of all factors are the same at time t_0 in the two countries. $m_i^a(t)$ is the factor of i at time t in country A, and $m_i^b(t)$ is the factor of i at time t in country B. As all factors are the same in both countries at t_0:

$$m_i^a(t_0) = m_i^b(t_0) \Rightarrow m_i^a(t_0) - m_i^b(t_0) = 0 \qquad \mathrm{i} = 1, 2, 3, \ldots, \mathrm{n} \tag{10}$$

Suppose that, at t_1, an event known as E occurs. Along with this event, k factors (where $k < n$) will make a difference in the two countries:

$$m_i^a(t_1) - m_i^b(t_1) = \beta_i, \beta_i \neq 0 \ \ for \quad i = 1, 2, \ldots, k \tag{11}$$

While the n-k factor will not make a difference in the two countries:

$$m_i^a(t_1) - m_i^b(t_1) = 0 \ \ for \quad i = k + 1, \ldots, n \tag{12}$$

So, we can say that the event E is associated with k factors, but not connected with n-k number of factors:

$$E = f(m_1, \ldots m_k) \tag{13}$$

$$E \neq f(m_{k+1}, \ldots m_n) \tag{14}$$

May the occurrence of event E and the change in k factors be simultaneous:

[5] This name is from the authors.

$$m_i = f(E) \qquad \mathrm{i} = 1, \ldots, \mathrm{k} \tag{15}$$

$$m_i \neq f(E) \qquad \mathrm{i} = \mathrm{k} + 1, \ldots, \mathrm{n} \tag{16}$$

Equations 13, 14, 15 and 16 suggest that event E is the same as m_1, $m_2 \ldots m_k$ changes, and event E is not changed withm_{k+1}, $m_{k+2} \ldots m_n$.

Geographic, race, and culture are not the main causes of backwardness because we can find many historical quasi-experimental such as those above. One of the quasi-experiments is West and East Germany. Before World War II, the geographical, racial, and cultural differences between Germany's Eastern and Western regions were zero. In addition, the difference in their development indexes was zero. After World War II, Germany was divided into West and East Germany. West Germany was developed, and East Germany was far behind. Differences in geography, race, and culture between the West and the East were zero. However, institutional quality, international interaction, and corruption changed significantly between the East and West. Natural factors did not affect progress between the two countries.

On the other hand, we cannot say that the reason for West Germany's progress and East Germany's lack of progress is the multifactor being changed. This is because, as explained in the previous section, all factors are changed simultaneously. Another quasi-experiment compares Papua New Guinea with Australia. Before 1787, Australia's development level was similar to Papua New Guinea's. The two countries had the same culture and geography. With the arrival of Captain Arthur Phillip's ships carrying British convicts to Australia, many things like inclusive political institutions were formed in Australia but not in New Guinea. Thus, the British convicts' 1787 entry into Australia separated development in Australia and Papua New Guinea. After Australia's development, Australia and Papua New Guinea still have the same culture.[6]

3.3 The Third Coordinates: Doing Philosophy for Backwardness

As long as a single cause cannot be found for a phenomenon like development, every cause is an effect. Suppose you are looking for the main cause of inflation. Economists believe that inflation is caused by liquidity growth. Immediately, the question arises, "What is the cause of liquidity growth?" Therefore, studies on the cause of liquidity growth are conducted. The reason is the central bank's non-independence. The next question is, "Why the central bank is not independent?" So, studies on the cause of central bank independence are conducted. The cause is extractive institutions. This begs the question, "Why have extractive institutions been created?"

[6]Culture is the first type, explained in the introduction.

Acemoglu and Robinson (2012) believe that a historic turning point will change the country's development process, and this critical juncture can be anything.

X is not the last cause when X's cause is found. When Australian prosperity is caused by inclusive institutions by British immigrants, what is the cause of the inclusive institution? When North Korea's backwardness is due to extractive institutions, why have extractive political institutions ruled there? An answer is World War II. If World War II had not happened, North Korea might be an advanced country today.

In this analysis, two problems may occur. First, it seems that the causes of nations' rise and fall are governed by determinism (such as the geography hypothesis). However, this is not true because determinism factors do not correlate with progress according to the second coordinates. In the second coordinates, we proved that geography or any hypothesis related to nature and determinism cannot explain nations' fall and rise. The second problem is the infinite chain of causes/effects (continuum problem); this means how far the chain of questions and answers should continue. Some methodologists believe the infinite causal chain is invalid because there is no chain of events (Gerring, 2011). In other words, if the creation of A from B, B from C, and so on does not end, we will have a continuum problem. This means there is no A. The infinite chain of causes/effects is invalid as long as A exists. Some researchers believe this chain should continue if the reason is convincing (Munck, 2021).

In our topic, A is the progress process. As long as there is a "progression process," there is a cause for that. Identifying the cause requires profound scientific insight. If we know X as the cause, we do not need an infinite chain of causes/effects, but the problem is that we do not know what X is. In other words, "development" has a cause, but its cause is unknown. In this chapter, we identify some X coordinates. This chapter cautions researchers who consider either a list of factors or a non-core reason as the cause of development.

4 Institutional Inertia and the Critical Juncture

The critical juncture changes quiet institutions, especially political institutions. Most institutions tend to be quiet (Rosenbaum, 2021); that is, they have inertia, while institutions have to change themselves in terms of technological, social, economic, political, etc., as societies change.

Five factors generate institutional inertia, especially in political institutions: costs, uncertainty, path dependence, power, and legitimacy (Munck af Rosenschöld et al., 2014). First, to change the institution, nations must pay the cost, which is mostly huge. Second, institutional change brings uncertainty in the future, so people and politicians try to stay in the same old institutions. Third, most institutions, especially political and economic institutions playing an important role in developing societies, depend on their path. Path dependence refers to self-reinforcing or positive feedback processes (Pierson, 2011). Fourth, government power is another factor causing political inertia. If the existing institutions benefit governments and groups of power, especially in non-democratic governments, they will try to maintain them with their power. Institutional changes may affect the distribution of wealth and income (Rosenbaum, 2021; Palley, 2017), which is not pleasant for power groups. Fifth, legitimacy can constrain and encourage institutional change (Munck af Rosenschöld et al., 2014). Many inefficient institutions that hinder development remain stable due to their legitimacy.

When these five factors reinforce each other, the situation worsens.[7] Also, most institutions are self-reinforcing and often complemented by complex culturally transmitted mental models. (Rosenbaum, 2021).

For the reasons mentioned above, it is a critical juncture that can change the path of these institutions. It can also be a turning point for institutional inertia. The evidence shows that most institutional inertia is changed through critical junctures. For example, Gorbachev's shift from Marxism-Leninism to Social Democracy was a historical-critical juncture in transforming institutions as the inertia for the years in Eastern European countries. As a counterfactual, if Gorbachev had not become president of the Soviet Union in 1990, institutional inertia would probably remain in Eastern European countries.

We divide institutions into formal and informal categories. Governments create formal institutions, such as business and regulations, traffic laws, freedom of expression laws, political freedom, etc. The informal institution is rooted in nations' culture, such as religion, customs, tradition, etc. As mentioned earlier, we called the informal institution the first type of culture. Critical juncture cannot change informal institutions because critical juncture happens quickly, while most informal institutions/cultures have not changed immediately. Nevertheless, the critical juncture can change formal/official institutions.

Interestingly, formal institutions (hear extractive institutions) are a major obstacle to development. Most formal institutions tend to be inertia, and seemingly, the main factor to shock them is the historical-critical juncture. So, the critical juncture is the root of the development process through changing the formal institutions.

It should be noted that the change of some informal institutions (not all) takes place gradually after the change of formal institutions. For example, South and North Korean informal institutions/cultures were the same as before World War II. However, some South Korean people's culture now differs from North Koreans' (the second type of culture). This divergence has gradually occurred since World War II.

[7] For example, Mahoney (2000) believes that the path of dependence includes power and legitimacy.

5 Which Priority Is a Political or Economic Institution?

There is much literature on political institutions' impact on development. This chapter argues that political institutions are preferable to economic institutions. Acemoglu et al. (2005) argue that political institutions create economic institutions and implement economic policies. Therefore, the political institutions of a country directly affect the economic institutions and procedures the nature of the country. By changing the nature and function of economic institutions, economic agents are motivated, and better opportunities are provided for production and economic growth. Many researchers have found that although political institutions do not directly affect economic growth, they are a key factor in choosing and applying different economic policies (Flachaire et al. (2014), Owen et al. (2009), Vaio and Enflo (2011) and Bos et al. (2010)).[8] Therefore, countries follow different economic growth and development paths according to their political institutions. Political institutions influence fiscal and trade policies (Persson & Tabellini, 2007). The findings of Eicher and Leukert (2009) support the priority of political institutions. Therefore, political institutions cause changes in economic institutions, and economic policy causes motivations and effects on economic growth and development.

A country with good political institutions will improve economic institutions and stabilize them. If the country only has appropriate economic institutions (for any reason) and no comprehensive political institutions, such a balance will be unstable. This imbalance will gradually change economic institutions and turn them into bad institutions. Therefore, suitable political institutions are necessary for economic institutions and policy stability.

Countries can be classified into four groups within the institutional structure. Good political institutions lead to good economic institutions. Countries with an inclusive political structure have appropriate and rational economic institutions sensitive to people's welfare (Group A in Table 3). Western Europe, the USA, Canada, Australia, and Japan can be placed in this group by ignoring a few differences. Some countries lack a suitable political structure but have relatively suitable economic institutions (B group). This country's long-term survival depends on strategic thinking rather than political institutions. These countries may move to groups "A" or "D" in Table 3. In this group, we can mention China and some Arab countries that have achieved economic growth through economic reforms. Still, this growth is not a guarantee of future stability. Some countries do not have a proper economic and political structure, but through the formation of some political institutions, fundamental changes are observed in their economic institutions. Eastern European countries, Turkey and Brazil, are in this group. Georgia is a new example and experience in this field. According to the latest global business environment ranking, Georgia is among the ten successful countries (Group C). These countries will likely join Group "A" in the long run. It is hard to imagine a prospect for the

[8]Flachaire et al. (2014), Owen et al. (2009), Vaio and Enflo (2011), and Bos et al. (2010).

Table 3 Political and economic institutions' relations

		Political Institutions	
Economic Institutions		Good	Bad
	Good	A (Western Europe, USA, Canada, Australia, and Japan)	B (China)
	Bad	C (Eastern European countries, Brazil, India)	D (North Korea, Venezuela)

countries of group "D." North Korea, Venezuela, and several African countries are included in this group, and it is far from the expectation that they will achieve a stable situation.

Critical juncture is popular in comparative-historical analysis and providesThe tools for studying political origins and reforming important institutional arrangements thatExercise a long-lasting influence on their social and political environment (Capoccia, 2015). This concept covers organizations, formal rules, public policies, political regimes, and political economies. Therefore, in the framework of this concept, the change of political institutions is a trigger and pioneer of other changes, especially the formation of economic institutions.

6 Is the Historical-Critical Juncture a Chance?

We present a philosophical issue about causality. Should any event have a cause, or can it be accepted without one? Is the turning point of nations a cause or a coincidence? To answer these questions, we must answer whether causality can be refused.

Doubts about causality were originated by David Hume (1711–1776) and highlighted by the Heisenberg uncertainty principle in atomic theory (Kenyon & Craig, 1985). Hume challenged accepted wisdom and asked why everything must have a cause. He said that wisdom could not understand such a relationship without experiencing it. In other words, without experience, causation cannot be accepted. Hume considered causality as the habit of the mind resulting from experience. What you see is the time sequence of the events, one after the other, and there is no necessity for the events.

Hume's argument about the principle of causation helps us deepen our search for the cause of nations rotating in the direction of progress or backwardness. When an advanced country is observed, you should not comment quickly on the cause of progress. This includes institutions' quality, interaction with the global economy, corruption reduction, etc. As these experiences have been observed repeatedly, the human mind creates a cause-and-effect relationship between them.

Another reason for doubting causality is quantum physics. If the causality principle is to use current system information for future prediction via universally valid laws, quantum physics can violate this principle. Quantum physics determines the state of any particle system by its wave function. This wave function only determines the particle's probability of occurring at specific locations and speeds. In contrast, classical physics explicitly determines each particle's place and speed.

In economics, we can consider X a historical-critical juncture and believe it happens at any moment and place. We have two types of historical-critical juncture. First, in cases where the historical-critical juncture has already occurred in a nation's history, it is possible to find the probability of the time and place of the historical-critical juncture, but it is not a certainty. Estimating the probability of event X depends on several past events. Second, when the previous Historical-critical juncture has not happened and has not been repeated, the estimation probability is not impossible but very difficult. In this case, we have to go to change the theory.

Luck is defined as nobody trying to be lucky. However, this does not mean that luck's role (regardless of its positive or negative aspects) is equal for everybody. A person who chooses a more adventurous and risky life increases chance's role in life. Conservatives, accountants, and cautious people reduce the role of luck in life. In the past, with fewer tools for prediction and calculation and a more limited discipline, luck played a greater role in human life. In today's world, there is no motive for discovering islands. Nobody has the motive to discover an unknown land because all places in the world have been mapped, and their properties are known. Thus, nowadays, the number of historical-critical junctures has fallen, and the number of rises and falls is smaller than in the past. The materials exposing a nation to a critical juncture are the low quality of political institutions nowadays, including freedom and its derivatives.

7 Conclusion

In this chapter, some coordinates of the rise and fall of nations are explained. Scientists have yet to agree on all the causes of the nation's rise and fall. Consequently, there is no practical solution. Although the cause of the development and backwardness of the countries has been proven uncertain, its coordinates can be identified. When many factors are introduced for development, or when a single factor is introduced, we arrive at a historical-critical juncture by philosophizing. Historical-critical juncture is used in various sciences. Economics uses it for changing political institutions. We have introduced two simple coordinates for a historical-critical juncture. The first coordinate is that a Historical-critical juncture does not happen just once for a single nation and that a country can experience it several times in a different form every time. The second coordinate is that the cause for the rise of a nation is not necessarily the cause of the fall of another nation and vice versa.

In this chapter, we find three main coordinates for historical-critical junctures. First, the cause of each nation's progress (backwardness) is a unique factor and is not a list of factors. This factor may be hidden and appear in other factors. Therefore, researchers point to non-essential factors as the cause of progress or backwardness. Quasi -experimental methods have proved this issue. In this chapter, the quasi-experimental method compares two countries or one country under two different conditions, which the reader may mistakenly consider as examples. Second, "the cause of the rise and fall of a nation" arises in the history of nations and is not historical determinism because many nations have experienced several rises and fall throughout history. Therefore, any hypothesis, such as geography and endowment, considering progress's cause as historical determinism is unacceptable. Many pairs of countries have the same factors of geography, race, and culture both before and after progress; however, progress has only occurred in one of them. Third, the cause of a nation's rise and fall must be persuasive. In other words, the cause-and-effect process should continue. Philosophy is this process. For example, political institutions' hypothesis cannot explain the "cause of a nation's rise and fall because it is the effect of another unknown factor. In this regard, the deeper, the better.

In the third coordinate, the causality principle is discussed. The questions address whether every event must have a cause or can be accepted without a cause. In addition, they address whether a nation's turning point is a cause or a chance. Based on Hume's hypothesis and quantum physics, the Historical-critical juncture can be a chance. We have two types of historical-critical juncture. First, in cases where the historical-critical juncture has already occurred in nations' histories, it is possible to find the probability of the time and place of the historical-critical juncture, but it is not a certainty. Estimating the probability of event X depends on several past events. Second, when a previous historical-critical juncture has not happened and has not been repeated, the estimation of probability is not impossible but very difficult. In today's world, historical-critical junctures have fallen. There are fewer rises and falls of countries now than in the past because there is no motive for discovering islands or unknown land, all places have been mapped, and their properties are known. In other words, nowadays, nations are less exposed to taking their chance.

This chapter has not identified the cause of backwardness and development but omitted unrelated factors. On the other hand, this chapter serves as Occam's razor (a philosophical tool for 'shaving off' unlikely explanations).

Ultimately, nations cannot find their Historical-critical junctures, but they can expose themselves to increase the likelihood of their Historical-critical junctures. For example, an open economy is better than a closed one because the possibility of changing institutional inertia that hinders development is increased. Also, the existence of multiple political parties in society is an expose to create a historic moment.

References

Abbott, A. (1988). Transcending general linear reality. *Sociological Theory, 6*(2), 169–186.

Acemoglu, D., & Robinson, J. A. (2012). *Why Nations Fail: The Origins Of Power, Prosperity, And Poverty* (1st ed., p. 529). Crown.

Acemoglu, D., Johnson, S., & Robinson, J. A. (2005). Institutions as a fundamental cause of long-run growth. In P. Agion & S. Darlauf (Eds.), *Handbook of economic growth* (pp. 384–472). North Holand.

Allen, R. C. (2011). *Global economic history: A very short introduction*. Oxford University Press.

Ashton, T. S. (1997). *The industrial revolution, 1760–1830*. Oxford University Press.

Barbour, I. G. (1966). *Issues in science and religion*. Prentice-Hall.

Bos, J. W. B., Koetter, M., & Kolari, J. W. (2010). Do all countries grow alike? *Journal of Development Economics., 91*(1), 113–127.

Capoccia, G. (2015). In J. Mahoney & K. Thelen (Eds.), *Critical junctures and institutional change, chapter prepared for inclusion in the volume advances in comparative historical analysis in the social sciences*. Cambridge University Press.

Capoccia, G. (2016). *Critical junctures*. Oxford University Press.

Durant, W.. 1885–1981 (1961). *The story of philosophy: The lives and opinions of the great philosophers of the Western world*. Simon and Schuster.

Edwards, P. (1972). *The encyclopedia of philosophy*. Publishing.

Eicher, T., & Leukert, A. (2009). Institutions and economic performance: Endogeneity and parameter heterogeneity. *Journal of Money, Credit, and Banking, 41*(1), 197–219.

Falagas, M., Zarkadoulia, E. A., & Samonis, G. (2006). Arab science in the golden age (750–1258C.E.) and today. *Federation of American Societies for Experimental Biology, 20*, 1581–1586.

Flachaire, E., García-Peñalosa, C., & Konte, M. (2014). Political versus economic institutions in the growth process. *Journal of Comparative Economics, 42*(1), 212–229.

Farmer, H. G. (1970). *Historical facts for the Arabian musical influence*. G. Olms.

Frieder, B. (2015). *Chivalry and the perfect prince: Tournaments, art, and armor at the Spanish Habsburg Court* (Vol. 81). Truman State Univ Press.

George, S. (1927). *Introduction to the history of science*. Carnegie Institution of Washington, by the Williams and Wilkins Company.

Goldstone, J. A. (2000). The rise of the west—Or not? A revision to socio-economic history. *Sociological Theory, 18*(2), 175–194.

Greene, W. H. (2008). *Econometric analysis*. Pearson/Prentice Hall.

Gerring, J. (2011). Social Science Methodology: A Unified Framework. (n.p.): Cambridge University Press.

Grierson, P., & Travaini, L. (1986). *Medieval European coinage: Volume 14, South Italy, Sicily, Sardinia: With a catalogue of the coins in the Fitzwilliam museum* (Vol. 14). Cambridge University Press.

Hollingdale, R. J. (1979). *Western philosophy: An introduction*. Kahn & Averill.

Kenyon, J. D., & Craig, E. (1985). Doubts about the concept of reason. In *Proceedings of the Aristotelian Society, Supplementary Volumes* (Vol. 59, pp. 249–267. 269–283). Wiley. https://doi.org/10.1093/aristoteliansupp/59.1.249

Mahoney, J. (2000). Path dependence in historical sociology. *Theory and Society, 29*(4), 507–548.

Morris, I. (2010). *Why the west rules- for now: The patterns of history, and what they reveal about the future*. Straus and Giroux.
Munck, G. L. (2021). The theoretical foundations of critical juncture research: Critique and reconstruction. Critical Junctures and Historical Legacies: Insights and Methods for Comparative Social Science,. *Forthcoming*.
Munck af Rosenschöld, J., Rozema, J. G., & Frye-Levine, L. A. (2014). Institutional inertia and climate change: A review of the new institutionalist literature. *Wiley Interdisciplinary Reviews: Climate Change, 5*(5), 639–648.
Owen, A. L., Videras, J., & Davis, L. (2009). Do all countries follow the same growth process? *Journal of Economic Growth., 14*(4), 265–286.
Palley, T. (2017). A theory of economic policy lock-in and lock-out via hysteresis: Rethinking economists. *Approach to Economic Policy, Economics: The Open-Access, Open-Assessment E-Journal, 11*(2017–18), 1–18.
Persson, T., & Tabellini, G. (2007). The growth effect of democracy: Is it heterogeneous and how can it be estimated? *NBER Working Chapter, 13150*. https://doi.org/10.3386/w13150
Pierson, P. (2011). *Politics in time: History, institutions, and social analysis*. Princeton University Press. https://doi.org/10.1515/9781400841080
Pomeranz, K. (2000). *The great divergence: China, Europe, and the making of the modern world economy*. Princeton University Press.
Rosenbaum, E. (2021). Mental models and institutional inertia. *Journal of Institutional Economics, 18*(3), 1–18.
Russell, B. (2013). *History of Western philosophy: Collector's edition*. Routledge.
Sarton, G. (1927). *Introduction to the History of Science (Vol. 376)*. Carnegie institution of Washington.
Saunders, J. J. (2001). *The history of the Mongol conquests*. University of Pennsylvania Press.
Shadish, W. R., Cook, T. D., & Campbell, D. T. (2002). *Experimental and quasi-experimental designs for generalized causal inference*. Houghton, Mifflin, and Company.
Vaio, G. D., & Enflo, K. (2011). Did globalization drive convergence? Identifying cross-country growth regimes in the long run. *European Economic Review, Elsevier., 55*(6), 832–844.
Van der Ploeg, F. (2011). Natural resources: Curse or blessing? *Journal of Economic Literature, 49*(2), 366–420.
Wooldridge, J. M. (2015). *Introductory econometrics: A modern approach*. Cengage learning.
Zibakalam, S. (1999). *How did we become what we are: Probing the causes of Iran's backwardness*. Rozeneh Publications.

Inertia in Informal Institutions: Concepts and Effects

Zahra Kheiridoust

1 Introduction

Institutions are the rules of the game and are created to reduce uncertainties and establish order in human societies. The rationale behind the formation of institutions is the limited cognitive capacity of humans and, in the meantime, the necessity to make decisions under uncertain conditions. Therefore, humans impose structures such as institutions on their lifestyles to reduce uncertainty. These structures are the accumulation of prescriptions and proscriptions, together with artifacts that evolved as a part of this accumulation. The outcome is a complex mix of formal and informal institutions that can reduce general uncertainty.[1] The constraints that have been imposed evolve uncertain outcomes, revealing an imperfect understanding of the environment and the equally imperfect nature of the formal rules and informal mechanisms used to enforce those constraints. To improve economic performance, institutional changes must take place toward the formation of more efficient institutions (North, 2005, 1–2); however, it is not possible to change inefficient institutions to efficient ones easily, and institutions are engaged in inertia. "Path dependence" is one of the distinctive features of institutions and is closely related to the concept of institutional inertia. While "institutional inertia" means institutions do not change quickly and show immobility against changing, "path dependence" means that current decisions influenced by institutions get their form from the past and recent institutional arrangements limit future choices.

Concerning path dependence, institutions are born at critical moments, whether due to chance factors or more or less conscious choices of collective actors

[1] For instance, informal social norms adopted in a society can be considered the coordinators of the expectations (or cultural beliefs) of many (rational) players concerning what they carry out within or outside the course of their games (Greif, 2006).

Z. Kheiridoust (✉)
Alzahra University, Tehran, Iran

N. Faghih, A. H. Samadi (eds.), *Institutional Inertia*, Contributions to Economics,
https://doi.org/10.1007/978-3-031-51175-2_5

(Ebbinghaus, 2005). When an institutional pattern is adopted, the benefits of its continued adoption increase. It gradually becomes more difficult to change the adopted patterns or choose the previous ones, even if the alternative options have been more efficient. In other words, after the establishment of an institution, a period of reproduction takes place that stabilizes institutions through path-dependent self-reinforcing processes that increase returns and positive feedback mechanisms (Arrow, 2000; Arthur, 1990; Pierson, 2000 in Greener, 2005).

"Reactive sequences" are a chain of events that follow each other in terms of time and cause. Each event in the chain is a reaction to the previous events and consequently "depends" on the previous steps (Mahoney, 2000).

Different causes explain the persistence of an economic path, some of which include transaction costs (North & Thomas, 1973 in Ebbinghaus, 2005), non-institutionalization of property rights via political factors (North, 1981 in Ebbinghaus, 2005), investment of actors in the dominant path or "sunk costs" (Ebbinghaus, 2005), and the high opportunity cost of cultural interests for challenging the system (Greener, 2005), etc.

Institutional inertia is related to "path dependence". The nature of inertia will vary depending on the sequence type. With self-reinforcing sequences, inertia includes mechanisms that reproduce a particular institutional pattern over time. On the contrary, in "reactive sequences," inertia contains reaction and counter-reaction mechanisms whose "inherent logic" is that one event "naturally" leads to another one (Mahoney, 2000).

So far, the concept of institutional inertia has not been focused separately in informal insinuations. This chapter is dedicated to this topic and reviews inertia in informal institutions. Informal institutions include customs, traditions, conventions, codes of conduct, and norms of behavior (North, 1990: 5, 6–9) that come from socially-transmitted information and are a part of the heritage called "culture" (Ibid:37).

On the one hand, we examine the existence of inertia in informal institutions and, on the other hand, the importance of inertia, i.e., whether it is beneficial for economic growth. In the first case, i.e., the existence of inertia in informal institutions, some elements of informal institutions change, including political factors of innovation (Acemoglu & Robinson, 2021), technology, population (North, 2005), entrepreneurship (Elert & Henrekson, 2021; Kuchař, 2016; Tao, 2016), etc. However, some elements show more inertia than others because stability is a crucial factor in institutions and is necessary for successful functioning. As constraints on human behavior help maintain order and coordinate expectations, institutions are only meaningful if they are durable to some extent (Acemoglu et al., 2021). It is the durability that gives meaning to the existence of institutions. However, it also prevents the attempt for institutional change, avoids the connection of inter-societal institutions, and makes institutional change "incremental" and path dependent.

Meanwhile, informal institutions are more slow-moving. Since informal institutions change in evolutionary form, they generally have a slow pace of change (North, 1990). Remaining stable for a long time, culture creates a powerful incentive for human behavior and economic performance (Williamson, 2000).

As evidence of the stability of informal institutions, some great shocks can be mentioned that have little impact on culture. One of the most important examples is the rise and fall of communism in Central and Eastern Europe. Roland (2004) shows that the fall of communism had a minor impact on the cultures of these countries. The formal institutional changes cannot affect the culture created over a long history. Alesina and Giuliano's (2015) studies about Germans showed that East German people are more advocates of government intervention after the fall of communism, but their other conclusion is that in both West and East Germany, the convergence between the two Germanys is happening rapidly and will probably be established in the next two generations. This result shows that gradual changes in culture are made by rules and answers to daily life.

Whitt and Wilson's (2007) study is another example that can be referred to. Whitt and Wilson (2007) in Dictator Game, showed how people in postwar Bosnia-Herzegovina helped outsiders not known ethnically or as members of their ethnic group. Their result showed that despite the preference of the group, a stable human custom continues among all the Muslim, Croat, and Serb ethnic groups. The result of this study shows that external shocks cannot affect human culture and innate values.

The informal institutional inertia is evident in all the mentioned examples. However, this is just one aspect of the features of informal institutions, and sometimes informal institutions show rapid changes.

The first section of the present chapter deals with the factors on which the inertia of informal institutions depends. From another point of view, the second section of this chapter will examine the usefulness of institutional inertia. In this context, it should be argued that culture as a source of response to individual and social needs is always exposed to new requests in the context of history and time; consequently, it is subject to constant change.

Being affected by inertia does not mean stagnation or lack of transformation. For example, the passage of time may cause some cultural elements to evolve (the paradigm of evolutionism) and some to lose their old functions (the paradigm of functionalism) or enter into a process of self-weakening and decay. In any other way, new needs to be formed, new cultural elements are needed, and the communication and recognition of cultures from and their effects on each other may increase.[2] Moreover, changes in relative prices or changes in taste sometimes lead to their gradual erosion or replacement with other norms. If cultural changes do not occur simultaneously with technological and economic development, society will either stagnate in extreme situations, which results in the death and destruction of a culture and society, or suffer from cultural disintegration. Therefore, stagnation or severe cultural changes are both detrimental to society; instead, simultaneous changes in a way that preserves the continuity of culture are beneficial.

[2]For more information about these two theories, see, for example, Parsons (2017), Mesoudi (2016), Keltner et al. (2022), and Jagiello et al. (2022).

In addition, every country has cultural endowments and values that need to be preserved. Ruttan (2006) mentions that "cultural endowments" can facilitate some types of institutional changes. He gives the example of Japan, where "traditional patterns of cooperation" emerged in the distant past and facilitated modern rural development programs (Ruttan, 2006). Such an endowment of culture exists in all societies that should be preserved, and societies should solve their cultural problems and improve their culture. These issues are discussed in the second section of this chapter.

The purpose of the present chapter is to examine institutional inertia in informal institutions, i.e., culture and values. To this end, examining the relationship between formal and informal institutions is sometimes necessary. The content of this chapter is organized into four general sections, as follows: Second Section is dedicated to investigating the reasons for the formation of inertia of informal institutions. In this regard, the roles of beliefs, habits, bounded rationality, free-rider problem, and institutional complements, organizations, and parameters have been studied. The third Section discusses the usefulness of the changes or inertia of informal institutions and examines the theories of institutional economics, considering rapid changes in culture. The fourth section offers a summary and a conclusion.

2 The Causes of Inertia in Informal Institutions

This section explains why and how the inertia of informal institutions occurs. This section will answer the question of why informal institutions show inertia. The main reason for institutional inertia is the limited cognitive capacity of the human mind for understanding and the complicated relationship between institutions.

Humans have limited cognitive capacity, which, on the one hand, forms beliefs and, on the other hand, human habits. Beliefs and habits concerning institutions and organizations cause institutional inertia because they cannot be changed easily.

On the other hand, limited human cognitive capacity, accompanied by the issues such as human interest and the "free rider problem", forms the inertia of informal institutions in another way. At the same time, there are multifaceted relationships and connections between various formal and informal institutions, which add to the complexity of the existing situation and show resistance to institutional changes. These four cases will be studied further:

First, the role of beliefs is considered. In this context, the relationship between beliefs, institutions, organizations, and socialization in the formation of the inertia of informal institutions is explained. Section 2.2 examines the role of bounded rationality, Veblen, and Simon's points of view on the reason for the formation of habits and their relationship with the inertia of informal institutions. In Sect. 2.3, we address the size of society and the "free-rider problem" from Mancur Olson's point of view. Section 2.4 examines the relationship between formal and informal institutions, the complementary relationship between institutions, and institutional self-reinforcement.

2.1 The Role of Beliefs in the Inertia of Informal Institutions

Beliefs have a significant role in shaping the inertia of informal institutions. Beliefs have an important role in forming institutions. The relationship between beliefs, institutions, and organizations makes the effect of beliefs double. North is one of the scholars who paid special attention to this complexity. He states that humans *"always have an imperfect grasp of "reality"* (Ibid: 23) and make decisions in uncertain conditions (North, 2005: p. 13–17).

Humans' grasp of reality or the environment forms their "beliefs" (North, 2005: p. 4). In other words, individuals shape their mental models to interpret their environment and expectations. Environmental responses confirming the same mental model several times will partially establish the model.

This relatively crystallized mental model is known as beliefs (Mantzavinos et al., 2004). Moreover, there is a possibility that beliefs do not come from experience, like believing in an unseen divine universe. Nonetheless, beliefs are not necessarily compatible with reality and serve as a filter to interpret and comprehend external realities.

Beliefs determine human goals, options, and ways to achieve those goals. The system of beliefs collectively approved (shared mental models) shapes the institutions (formal and mainly informal). "*Belief systems, therefore, are the internal representation and institutions, the external manifestation of that representation*" (North, 2005:49).

Therefore, an institution is recognized as one where beliefs are accepted. Searle believes both linguistic and symbolic acceptances are essential elements of institutions. Furthermore, institutions should be approved by playing many games (Searle, 2005) and being shared as "mutual expectations" between the individuals within a society (Lewis, 1969: 39, 41–2 cited by David, 1994). That is, the players must have similar and consistent expectations about the dominant informal institutions and be mutually aware of them (David, 1994). Furthermore, its regulations and opinions must be constantly executed and reproduced based on the game's strategies and agents. In other words, norms and values are not created through a singular execution, but through a continuous process that requires reconstruction via human interactions. Aoki says:

> *An institution is self-sustaining, salient patterns of social interactions, as represented by meaningful rules that every agent knows and incorporated as agents' shared beliefs about the ways how the game is to be played* (Aoki, 2007).

The cultural transition has three general forms via socialization and social learning: horizontal (among peers), vertical (parents to children), and diagonal (non-parent older to younger ones) (Bowles & Gintis, 2011), which occurs in various

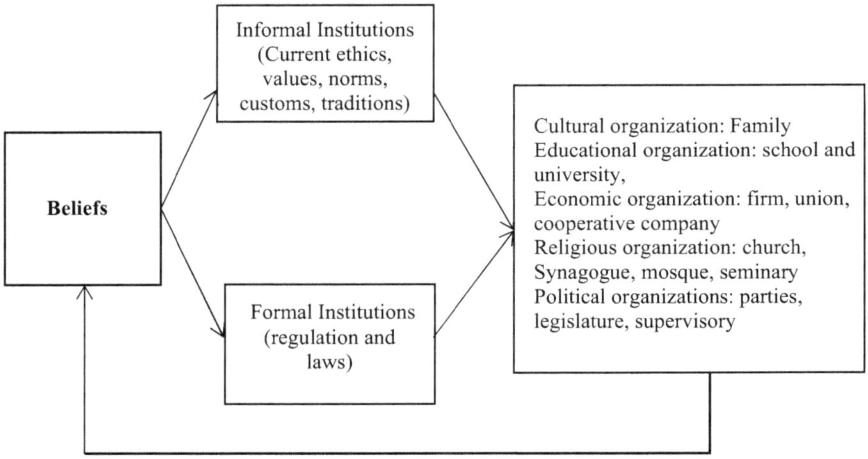

Fig. 1 Stabilization process of culture. (Source: Kheiridoust et al., 2022)

organizations and helps to coordinate and monitor society's endeavors to maintain the prevalence of cultural features over generations (Bisin et al., 2020).

As Mantzavinos et al. (2004) mentioned, this process is related to the connection between the method of human brain functioning, institutions, and various organizations such as cultural organizations (family), educational organizations (school and university), economic organizations (firm, union, cooperative company), religious organizations (boards and religious places such as church, synagogue, mosque, seminary), and political organizations (parties, legislature, supervisory). Institutions create organizations, and beliefs are formed within organizations. Beliefs shape institutions (Fig. 1).

According to Fig. 1, the created cycle results in the establishment of beliefs and institutions and, in other words, creates institutional inertia. Many sublime beliefs are genetically bestowed upon humans. For example, all people consider stealing and lying inappropriate behaviors. Thus, "How are theft and deceit common in some societies?" is in question.

In the model that was mentioned, if the institutional framework rewards theft, lies, and illegal activities, this belief will gradually emerge that nothing can be done without such crimes. In this case, organizations are organized in the direction of crime and theft, and the aforementioned belief is confirmed. If the institutional framework rewards productive activities, the belief in productivity and work replaces the belief in deceit and crime, and organizations promote productive activities.

However, this relationship between beliefs, institutions, and organizations is one of the reasons for the existence of the inertia of informal institutions, which makes it difficult to change towards more efficient cultures in a situation where anti-development culture is institutionalized in a country. Because the organizations benefit from the existing situation, according to the knowledge they have gained from unproductive activities, they resist changes.

2.2 *The Role of Habits and Bounded Rationality in Shaping the Inertia of Informal Institutions*

Another angle from which the inertia of informal institutions can be investigated is the limited cognitive capacity of humans and the formation of their habits. Veblen and Simon are two economists who have paid exclusive attention to this issue. According to the theory of limited cognitive capacity, the limited capacity of the human mind causes the mind to take action to reserve its concentration on various subjects. The formation of "habits" is a way to overcome that limited cognitive capacity in such a way that humans, acquiring "habits" and routines, decrease the time and costs of decision-making and attention (Simon, 1997: p. 89). Habit allows us to exclude aspects of a routine situation from the field of conscious thinking and attend to the novel aspects of a situation needing decision-making (Simon, 1997: p. 100).

Nevertheless, shared habits exist among individuals in society that emerge in informal institutions, saving the resources of society's attention. On the one hand, informal institutions are connected to human beliefs, and there should be belief in their validation to be called institutions. On the other hand, they become habits and are constantly repeated. Veblen says:

> *Settled habits of thought common to the generality of men* (Veblen, 1909).

Institutions are born from habits. The growth of culture is a cumulative sequence of habit-making (Veblen, 1909). An institution has an essence of use that has become evident and essential by habit and general acceptance (Veblen, 1923: 101 cited by Hutchison, 1984).

Veblen and Simon agree on the two following viewpoints: firstly, shared habits are the vital foundation of the social nature of humans. Secondly, shared habits, the foundation of norms and institutions, conduct the essential coordination among individuals. But habits, as their name suggests, have inertia and are also effective on institutional inertia. In other words, it is difficult to quit them. Simon proposes three main features of habits. First, habit is associated with behavioral inflexibility, meaning stable associations between stimuli and behavioral responses. Second, habit is related to the rapid time between the appearance of stimuli and behavioral responses. Third, inflexible cognitive habits are recognized with automated, non-reflective, and even unconscious mental mechanisms (Brette et al., 2017).

The more prolonged the habit, the more unbreakable it is. There are also relationships between habits. Veblen considers habit as the basis of an individual's continuity from a synchronic and diachronic point of view. From a synchronic point of view, the continuity principle means that the fields in which the individual is engaged in the same period are interdependent. The diachronic point of view states that the current behavioral features of an individual are "path dependent." Specifically, it means that the range and intensity of habits that an individual performs at any given time depend on their previous habits (Ibid.).

Another issue, according to Veblen, is the transferability of habits between people and the guarantee of their reproduction over time. As Veblen asserts:

> *In man, [...] habitual acquirements of the race are handed on from one generation to the next, by tradition, training, education, or whatever general term may best designate that discipline of habituation by which the young acquire what the old have learned* (Veblen, 1914: 35).

Moreover, bounded rationality can avoid the recognition of higher efficiencies. Alternatively, the agents may have false beliefs about the possible effects of a proposed institutional change (Ostrom, 2005: chapter 5) or see it as irrational to deviate from the current rules. Therefore, social habits, conventions, and rules would be continued. The persistency of social habits means the persistency of informal institutions, and the difficulty of changing the habits is what shapes the inertia of informal institutions.

2.3 Free-Rider Problem

The free rider problem is one of the concepts related to "institutional inertia." This concept was used and introduced by Mancur Olson in his 1965 book "The Logic of Collective Action".

Olson questioned what he saw as a common idea among political scientists, sociologists, and social psychologists. To explain Olson's approach, in smaller societies, collective reputation, and multilateral reputation mechanisms (Greif, 2006) are adequate to observe moral principles, but with the expansion of societies, these mechanisms alone are not enough. Olson (1971) put forward this idea: "*'The group theory' that dominates the discussions of pressure groups is inadequate for large economic groups, at least, and there is a need for a new theory*" (Olson 1971, p. 131). As the size of the group or community increases, the moral rules are observed less, and as a result, free-riding situations multiply (Fontaine, 2007, p. 15). Buchanan (1965) believes that the crime rate constantly increases with the size of the city. Garbage is usually found more on significant traffic routes than on residential streets. Even the adage "Never trust a stranger" reflects the recognition of this elemental truth, along with, of course, other ethical predictions (Buchanan, 1965, p. 8).

This change in informal institutions, moving toward less obedience to the rules, creates a form of institutional inertia. It is not possible to change the established moral rules easily because the new moral rules are usually connected with the interests of some groups that react to the change.

In this sense, sometimes the need to change informal institutions is felt among a group of society members, which bears the cost, and other groups do not consider it to their benefit. Therefore, the "free-rider problem" is one of the reasons making it difficult to fight against the rent-seeking culture. In these cases, the "free-rider problem" may prevent changes. The greater the perceived legitimacy of the existing institution, the higher the cost required to overcome the "free-rider problem There-fore, the free-rider problem plays a role in shaping the inertia of anti-development informal institutions.

2.4 The Role of Institutional Complementarities, Organizations, and Parameters

Another reason for institutional inertia is the relationship between the institutions. According to Ebbinghaus, the functionalist system theory presented by Parsons and Smelser (1956) and, more implicitly, the new political economy presented by Hall and Soskice (2001) explain the endurance of institutions through their "embedding" into the overall institutional landscape (Ebbinghaus, 2005). Moreover, the application of game theory in the new institutional theory, as an example in Aoki (2007) and Greif and Laitin (2004), has discussed the role of institutional complementarities.

Institutional complementarity means that institutions rarely act alone, but they complement each other to shape an institutional framework in society (Rodrik, 2000; Roland, 2004). Furthermore, in their real dynamics, institutions include interactions between economic, organizational, political, and social factors (Aoki, 2007). Complementary institutions (formal and informal) are interconnected, mutually supporting each other (Milgrom & Roberts, 1994; Schmidt & Spindler, 2002, cited in Ebbinghaus, 2005), and they can sometimes substitute for each other (Park, 2022).

For example, Licht (2005) illustrates that legal families are not separated from the culture of countries, and the correlation between national culture and legal laws remains regardless of other features of the countries (Licht, 2005 cited by Alesina & Giuliano, 2015). By studying the evolution of institutions in America, Fischer shows how cultural beliefs created many differences in the culture that emerged with the four waves of immigration (Fischer, 1989 in Alesina & Giuliano, 2015). Todd also provides a cultural interpretation of the global economic system. He believes the development of political systems in the world is a function of basic values creating an attitude towards liberal or authoritarian ideologies among the youth within the family system (Todd, 1983, 1990 in Alesina & Giuliano, 2015). Alesina & Glaser believe that the individualistic culture and outlook on poverty, along with other reasons, have caused the poor development of a communist party in the United States (Alesina & Glaeser, 2004). Such connections cause institutionalized rules to become salient features of a society (Greif & Laitin, 2004). Therefore, complementary relations between various institutions and organizations cause the institutionalization of institutions and institutional inertia.

However, this is mutual. That is, on the one hand, the relationship between different institutions causes institutional inertia, and on the other hand, institutional inertia prevents institutional changes from reaching their goals without considering other institutions; for example, laws should be compiled and implemented regardless of the cultural environment. Since informal institutions create the motivation for formal institutions, agents prefer to follow the rules and culture of informal institutions (Williamson, 2000; Helmke & Levitsky, 2004; Sankaran, 2022). In other words, mere legislation will not lead to successful enforcement if there is no demand for the law. Change in institutions is not simply achieved by writing rules but only when the fundamental belief system changes accordingly. Berkowitz et al. (2003) call that the "transplant effect," and Levy and Spiller (1994) call it "good fitting" (in Shirley, 2005). Based on this, the fact is that written laws and their changes are not important for their successful enforcement.

For example, Latin American countries that replicated the American constitution, transitioning countries that imitated European and American trade policies and bankruptcy laws, and French colonies in Africa that accepted the French bureaucratic system have had very different and disappointing results (Shirley, 2005). Moreover, the experience of many countries, such as the former communist countries, shows that merely changing laws has a low success rate. Putnam (1993) studied institutional reform in Italy, which is related to the reforms thought to work in the same way all over Italy. However, it worked differently in the north and south of the country. This difference originated from the various cultural features of the two regions formed since the Middle Ages. Experiencing free city arrangements in the Middle Ages resulted in these different cultural features that shaped the levels of cooperation, participation, social interaction, and trust in these two regions differently. Institutional complementarity causes changes to become both slow and difficult, slowing down the changing process. North (2005) says when political and economic entrepreneurs (the current institutional structure decides who will be the policymaker) find new opportunities (although our grasp of reality is not absolute and depends on the mental structures derived from individual experiences and cultural heritage), they try to change the existing institutional structure. However, the existing institutional structure is path-dependent, making changes and predicting the results of the changes to some extent impossible (North, 2005: chapters 1–5). The more an informal institution is completed with other formal and informal institutions, the lesser the probability of change. To maintain informal institutions (for instance, trust), they should be merged with other formal and informal institutions.

Previous institutions provided focal points able to influence the choice of equilibrium in new situations. (Sugden, 1989). Many institutional balances can be imagined in a society. However, one or more equilibria emerge. Equilibrium points are not necessarily Pareto efficient, and there is no guarantee for the formation of efficient institutions. Even if all agents collectively understand the potential of better institutions, engineering the coordinated change of expectations necessary to move toward a better equilibrium may be problematic. Greif and Laitin (2004) generalize these arguments. They explain institutional inertia by defining semi-parameters and recognizing self-enforcing as one of the features of institutions. They also talk about self-reinforcement because of the complementary relationship between institutions. Furthermore, they define semi-parameters along with parameters and variables that are exogenous and constant in the short-term study of institutions but are considered endogenous and variable in the long term. The last change in semi-parameters does not result in a behavior change or expected behaviors related to institutions. Past institutions can influence knowledge, resource ownership, distribution of wealth, and other semi-parameters. They can affect the set of future institutional options (possible equilibrium) and the selection of organizations in that set. Semi-parameters cause institutions to self-reinforce, which is the same as institutional inertia, by increasing the range of institutions' self-enforcing (Greif & Laitin, 2004).

Aoki (2007) highlights the existence of strategic links and complementary relationships between institutions in various "fields" of the economy, for example, between certain types of "the economic exchange domain," "the organizational exchange domain and organizational field," "the political exchange domain," and "the social exchange domain." In the analysis of inter-institutional links, he proposes two equilibrium links from the game theory perspective: first," linked games" in which agents use their strategic choices in one or more other fields, and second, "institutional complementariness". He states:

> *In linked games, each agent coordinates his/her strategic choices across domains and generates a single institution (equilibrium) therein. Alternatively, even if agents may not consciously coordinate their own choices across domains, they regard an institution in another domain as a parameter and accordingly choose strategies in their domains, and vice-versa* (Aoki, 2007).

These connections also cause successful institutional change to require changes in other institutions. It also causes many changes not affecting brokers who consider the game's primary indicators static. (Ibid.).

The combination of this theory with Douglas North's view presented in sections 2.1 shows the relationship between beliefs, organizations, and institutions, indicating several important issues. It shows how a cultural value spreads in an organization and becomes a self-enforcing institution by creating legal and cultural supplements. It shows this self-enforcing institution is penetrated by people in other areas of life, i.e., other social, economic, organizational, and political organizations. Gradually, complementarities are created for it, and its range of self-enforcing expands to become self-reinforcing. In this process, the norms institutionalized in society will become common knowledge among agents. In such situations, the norms that have appeared in each field will depend on each other.

People who have just entered this environment gradually adapt themselves to the conditions. Newcomers are likely to have preferences similar to those who earned higher rewards not so long ago (Boyd & Richerson, 1985). All of these together shape institutional inertia. If semi-parameters (official policies, technologies, game environment, etc.) change in the conditions where the culture is established, agents only change a part of their activities and recognize the indicators of the game to be fixed. Their experiences also do not reject the values. The changed agents exist in the equilibrium state, but the equilibrium properties remain intact as long as they are close to the equilibrium state.

3 Considerations Regarding the Speed of Institutional Changes

Informal institutions are necessary for economic development. Some of the components of informal institutions are universal and some are specific to a society, but the function of both is to preserve and maintain social identity and reduce the uncertainties that we face in life. Therefore, stability is a requirement for the successful performance of institutions. On the other hand, in many cases, the institutions remain inefficient. Thus, institutional change toward more efficient ones is considerable. All societies expect to promote universal values such as truth, trust, and punctuality among their members. Moreover, it is expected that informal institutions change along with technological development, population increase, and knowledge growth because the stagnation of informal institutions hinders the progress of society; however, such a change is not always observed. Therefore, the direction of institutional changes is important for economic development. The speed of institutional changes is also important.

This section investigates if we are constantly facing institutional inertia when there are informal institutions.

First, informal institutions have various components. According to North (2005), culture is divided into two components: moral codes, which have common characteristics across cultures and norms particular to individual societies (North, 2005: 50), and universal and shared societal values (such as honesty, justice, integrity, work, effort, partnership, etc.). Henrich et al. (2005) and Dahlsgaard et al. (2005) have shared their views on this topic. Immanuel Kant calls them "categorical imperatives" or "fundamental principles of morality" that provide and obey universal moral laws (Wood, 2007: 54).

However, another part is the unique values of a society (individualistic or collectivist society, the definition of justice and freedom, etc.) or customs and traditions (clothing, food, language, architecture, etc.). The previous section showed that all societies are interested in rapid changes in this part of the culture and in global values that take root in human societies. However, universal anti-values such as lying and rent-seeking behaviors became institutionalized in society and resulted in institutional inertia. This section discusses how society's unique values, customs, and traditions should be judged. Is inertia also harmful in this part of the culture? Considering that every society is tied to its culture and traditions, are drastic changes in this part of the culture detrimental or beneficial to development? How can this culture be preserved?

The answers to these questions will be provided in this section. First, in Sect. 3.1, we examine the types and speeds of cultural changes as well as those beneficial and those harmful to development. Then, we will discuss how culture accompanies the economy, and then, in Sect. 3.2, we will examine the viewpoints that consider culture to have a fast movement.

3.1 Ethnology of Cultural Changes

Culture does not always contain inertia. Sometimes culture changes very rapidly. For example, culture sometimes changes due to changes in the law. For instance, there was a law in the United States—the "blue law"—prohibiting retailers from Sunday activities. Gruber and Hungerman Grader and Hungerman show that with the removal of this law in many states, attendance and donations to the church have decreased (Gruber & Hungerman, 2008 in Alesina & Giuliano, 2015). Moreover, Di Tella shows that acquiring the title of the land in Buenos Aires has changed a wide range of beliefs such as individualism, the role of competence, and trust (Di Tella, 2007 cited by Alesina & Giuliano, 2015). Here, we discuss whether the pace of cultural changes is harmful or beneficial to development. The emphasis of this section is more on societies with unique cultures.

According to Azadarmaki (2014), there are four different fields proposed for the emergence of diverse types of cultural changes, outlined in Table 1.

There is cultural flexibility and reform in the first field because of the limited range and low intensity of the changes. There is a high intensity of changes with a limited range between the forces that affect incompatible cultures, resulting in anarchy or cultural delay. A cultural delay will occur if some cultural elements, such as infrastructures, material tools, and techniques, are transformed earlier than ideas or social organizations; the elements within that culture are separated and sometimes alienated from each other. A cultural crisis happens when various individual, group, or national identities derange (Azadarmaki, 2014: 231–245).

The changes mentioned in the third field (i.e., cultural reform and changes) occur in a society with structural stability, and the forces of culture coexist alongside each other with the least amount of interference due to the strength within the society. Changes, if they happen, will spread over time and be recognized on an extensive scale. In the last three fields, cultural activists mainly utilized the methods such as diffusion, adaptation, exchange, or cultural policymaking, but in the fourth field,

Table 1 Ethnology of cultural changes

Intensity/ Amplitude	Limited	Spread
Low	**First field:** Cultural adaptability and reforms	**Third field:** Cultural reform, cultural change
High	**Second field:** Cultural anarchy, cultural delay, and cultural crisis	**Fourth field:** Cultural revolution and cultural decay, cultural transformation, and cultural pluralism

Source: Azadarmaki (2014, p. 230)

there are internal conflicts between activists regarding their ideals and how to achieve them. As the primary method, society faces two extremes of change in this field: revolution with institutional changes or complete collapse and degeneration. The Cultural Revolution has roots in structural changes (economically and industrially). Cultural change accompanied by a substantial deviation from traditional values does not necessarily promise a better society with a higher culture.

Cultural decay also occurs as an outcome of material development versus the underdevelopment of culture, and it intensifies shifts in urbanization, changes in population, immigration, class differences, education, etc. The dichotomy between the elites and the people, the impact of foreign culture and the insistence on domestic culture, or the breakdown of the horizontal section of social groups into different ethnicities, religions, and races are among the causes of cultural decay. Cultural disintegration appears when two or more social strata are far away from each other so that, in practice, they become distinct cultures (Ibid: 246–254).

> *A common cultural heritage, therefore, provides a means of reducing the divergent mental models that people in a society possess and constitutes the means for the intergenerational transfer of unifying perceptions* (North, 2005: 27).

Another point that should be considered is cultural diversity. Society accepts either no kind of diversity or sometimes diversity and cultural fluidity.

> *The "melting pot" homogenization result still prevails under conformity bias. On the contrary, an anti-conformist bias preserves cultural diversity in the population* (Bisin et al., 2020: 6).

In other words, hardwired culture accepts only one cultural configuration; however, sometimes culture is so fluid that makes it possible to have more cultural configurations (Acemoglu & Robinson, 2021). It is also possible to witness the formation of minority groups in each of these four fields. However, in the first and second fields, these minorities form the cultural diversity of society alongside each other. Nevertheless, society may be involved in cultural issues due to tension in the third and fourth fields.

Considering this point of view, as mentioned before, the culture involved in stagnant is harmful to economic development. However, it is beneficial for economic growth if the cultural movements are in sync with economic developments and intact with their original authenticity and cultural identity. What Ayres (1994) emphasizes is cultural inflexibility and stasis. He regarded institutions as:

> *impediments to progress, "ceremonial" outgrowths of prior technology, and a negative, "past-preserving" influence* (Ayres, 1944:175 cited by Kingston & Caballero, 2009).

Because if a culture does not grow in sync with material and technological changes or economic changes that do not occur in sync with the culture of a society, the result will be cultural chaos and tension, cultural backwardness, and cultural identity crisis. Also, extreme deviation from traditional values and customs on a large scale will result in revolution, cultural disintegration, transformation, and pluralism, all of which are harmful to economic development. Destroying the foundation of society causes cultural damage and makes economic plans fail. Therefore, for economic development, it is necessary to preserve the specific culture of society via official institutions and laws to prevent society from being involved in cultural problems.

As an example, in this field, Botticini and Eckstein show that Jews got divided into two groups in the first century, before the destruction of the Second Temple: the Sadducees who accepted the written Torah but acted according to the Hellenistic culture, and the Pharisees, who accepted the written and verbal Torah and opposed the spread of the Greek language and culture. The destruction of the Second Temple was an exogenous shock that made the Pharisees prevail. This shock made the uneducated Jews and farmers convert to other religions, leading to the spread of an expensive religious norm that required fathers to teach their children. This norm in an agricultural society could not last in the long term, but in a place where money can be made from literacy. Therefore, having a long-term effect, the initial shock damaged the religion (Botticini & Eckstein, 2005, 2007, cited by Alesina & Giuliano, 2015).

3.2 *Studying the Viewpoints that Ignore The Inertia in Informal Institutions*

A group of economists such as Landes (2015), Acemoglu and Robinson (2012), and Chang (2007) believes that universal cultural values, which are necessary for development, change rapidly with economic development and are the result of development. In other words, economic changes automatically lead to cultural ones. However, specific values of society and customs do not influence development.

In this context, Acemoglu and Robinson mention culture as "*Theories that Don't Work*". Their answer to the question "*Is culture hypothesis useful to understand world inequality?*" is: "*Yes and no. Yes, in the sense that social norms, which are related to culture, matter and can be hard to change, and they also sometimes support institutional differences, this book explanation for world inequality. But mostly no, because those aspects of culture often emphasized—religion, national ethics, African or Latin values—are just not important for understanding how we got here and why the inequalities in the world persist. Other aspects, such as the extent to which people trust each other or can cooperate, are important but they are mostly an outcome of institutions, not an independent cause.*" (Acemoglu & Robinson, 2012: 71).

Chang says:

> *Culture is both the result and cause of economic development. It would be far more accurate to say that economic development makes countries become 'hardworking' and 'disciplined' (and acquire other 'good' cultural traits) rather than the other way around. Since culture changes far more quickly, there is no need for cultural change before economic development. With economic progress, people's behavior and even their underlying beliefs (culture) are changing in a way that contributes to economic development. It is possible to create a 'virtuous circle of economic development and cultural values...* (Chang, 2007: 92).

He cites Japan and Germany as two examples whose cultures have changed with economic development (Ibid: Chapter 9). Landes has the same viewpoint regarding Portugal, the Netherlands, and Thailand (Landes, 2015: 479).

It seems that these new institutional economists have neglected the inertia of informal institutions, universal cultural values, and their complexities, as shown in the first section of this chapter. Moreover, some aspects of culture that are specific to societies have been easily set aside from economic analysis, while these aspects are closely related to economic development. Economic development is impossible without considering the specific culture of society and its cultural endowments. If this part of culture is involved in rapid change, it will cause cultural decay and anarchy and act as an obstacle to economic development. On the other hand, anti-development cultural values cannot be easily modified into suitable values for development because of their close connections with other institutions and organizations and the functioning of the human brain, which is the formation of habits and beliefs. It seems that the societies that these scholars employed as examples have achieved the mentioned results in a back-and-forth movement between overcoming this institutional inertia and economic development.

4 Conclusion

This chapter studied inertia in informal institutions. In Sect. 1, the meaning of inertia in informal institutions and the reason for its formation have been presented, and in Sect. 2, the benefit of institutional inertia and the answer to the perspective of some institutional economists who neglect inertia have been presented.

It was mentioned that informal institutions should be aligned with the evolution of society, technological changes, and population changes. Otherwise, society will be involved in cultural stagnation, or the changes will happen so rapidly that culture will result in disruption and disarray. These changes will prevent the growth and progress of society. Moreover, some cultural endowments and values are so favorable to societies that we should preserve them. Furthermore, societies' unique cultures, like costumes, clothing, and the way they eat, are the items that are protected for identity and cultural cohesion.

In Sect. 1, we talked about institutional inertia and the factors that influence it. According to this section, protecting the culture requires attention to the connections between urges, beliefs, institutions, and culture and the complementary relationship between different institutions. To save culture, we should strengthen it with cultural values, rules, and regulations. We mentioned examples where a culture not supported in this way changed due to changes in laws or external shocks.

However, another crucial point is mentioned in this chapter. But another important point noticed in this chapter is how to transform an anti-development culture into one appropriate to development, considering universal values such as trust, honesty, and meritocracy. We noted that society's values must be changed to form such values for economic development. However, such modifications are not easily attained. As we witness, aligned with the growth of societies and technological developments in the world, developing countries have not yet created the essential institutions to overcome the "free-rider problem", recognize the offenders, and create an appropriate culture for development. In these circumstances, organizations of society formed with an inappropriate culture see their interest in maintaining existing conditions. The deficiency of the laws and the weak process of identifying offenders cause the spread of rent-seeking culture, corruption, and deceit. Organizations have also learned to seek profit instead of production, and the process of bribery and corruption has led to employing corrupt people. This belief has been established showing that nothing can be done without rent, bribery, and deceit. These behaviors have been established as habits in society.

Breaking this vicious cycle that constantly reproduces itself through various individuals in different organizations requires a firm determination among the political elites to make changes and strict laws to identify lawbreakers and offenders. As a result, gradual reverse processes should be formed with assistance from formal and informal institutions. On the other hand, changing the rules is not an important process; instead, the proper adaptation of formal institutions to society's culture is needed for the laws to be accepted. Otherwise, the changes will challenge the existing culture and lead to the aggravation of the chaotic situation. Moreover, reforms should be comprehensive and durable, and the changes should be such that they change beliefs accordingly. According to North, it is possible to overcome the "free-rider problem" of institutional changes through "ideology formation." If the rival ideology of the current institutions is more substantial for the people who consider change appropriate, the price they are willing to pay will be higher, and as a result, the probability of success will increase. (North, 1990: chapter 5). In general, we conclude that change happens when new beliefs within society lead to the formation of new institutions.

References

Acemoglu, D., & Robinson, J. A. (2012). *Why nations fail: The origins of power, prosperity, and poverty*. Crown Publishing Group.

Acemoglu, D., & Robinson, J. A. (2021). *Culture, institutions, and social equilibria: A framework* (Vol. No. w28832). National Bureau of Economic Research.

Acemoglu, D., Egorov, G., & Sonin, K. (2021). Institutional change and institutional persistence. In *The handbook of historical economics* (pp. 365–389). Academic.

Alesina, A., & Giuliano, P. (2015). Culture and institutions. *Journal of Economic Literature, 53*(4), 898–944.

Alesina, A., & Glaeser, E. (2004). *Fighting poverty in the US and Europe: A world of difference*. Oxford University Press.

Aoki, M. (2007). Endogenizing institutions and institutional changes. *Journal of Institutional Economics, 3*(1), 1–31.

Azadarmaki, T. (2014). *Sociology of culture*. Elm Iran.

Berkowitz, D., Pistor, K., & Richard, J. F. (2003). The transplant effect. *American Journal of Comparative Law, 51*, 163.

Bisin, A., Carvalho, J. P., & Verdier, T. (2020). Cultural transmission and religion. In *Handbook of economics and religion* (pp. 1–55). Edward Elgar.
Bowles, S., & Gintis, H. (2011). *A cooperative species: Human reciprocity and its evolution*. Princeton University Press.
Boyd, R., & Richerson, P. J. (1985). *Culture and the evolutionary process*. University of Chicago Press.
Brette, O., Lazaric, N., & Vieira da Silva, V. (2017). Habit, decision-making, and rationality: Comparing Thorstein Veblen and early Herbert Simon. *Journal of Economic Issues, 51*(3), 567–587.
Buchanan, J. M. (1965). Ethical rules, expected values, and large numbers. *Ethics, 76*(1), 1–13.
Chang, H. (2007). *Bad Samaritans: The myth of free trade and the secret history of capitalism*. Bloomsbury.
Dahlsgaard, K., Peterson, C., & Seligman, M. E. P. (2005). Shared virtue: The convergence of valued human strengths across culture and history. *Review of General Psychology, 9*(3), 203–213.
David, P. A. (1994). Why are institutions the 'carriers of history'?: Path dependence and the evolution of conventions, organizations, and institutions. *Structural Change and Economic Dynamics, 5*(2), 205–220.
Ebbinghaus, B. (2005). Can path dependence explain institutional change? Two approaches applied to welfare state reform (No. 05/2). MPIfG Discussion Paper.
Elert, N., & Henrekson, M. (2021). Entrepreneurship prompts institutional change in developing economies. *The Review of Austrian Economics, 34*(1), 33–53.
Fontaine, P. (2007). From Philanthropy to Altruism: Incorporating Unselfish Behavior into Economics, 1961–1975. *History of Political Economy, 39*(1), 1–46.
Greener, I. (2005). The potential of path dependence in political studies. *Politics, 25*(1), 62–72.
Greif, A. (2006). History lessons: The birth of impersonal exchange: The community responsibility system and impartial justice. *Journal of Economic Perspectives, 20*(2), 221–236.
Greif, A., & Laitin, D. D. (2004). A theory of endogenous institutional change. *American Political Science Review, 98*(4), 633–652.
Hall, P. A., & Soskice, D. (2001). *Varieties of capitalism: The institutional foundations of comparative advantage*. OUP Oxford.
Helmke, G., & Levitsky, S. (2004). Informal institutions and comparative politics: A research agenda. *Perspectives on Politics, 2*(4), 725–740.
Henrich, J., Boyd, R., Bowles, S., Camerer, C., Fehr, E., Gintis, H., & Tracer, D. (2005). 'Economic man' in cross-cultural perspective: Behavioral experiments in 15 small-scale societies. *Behavioral and Brain Sciences, 28*(6), 795–855.
Hutchison, T. W. (1984). Institutionalist economics old and new. *Zeitschrift für die gesamte Staatswissenschaft/Journal of Institutional and Theoretical Economics, 140*(H. 1), 20–29.
Jagiello, R., Heyes, C., & Whitehouse, H. (2022). Tradition and invention: The bifocal stance theory of cultural evolution. *Behavioral and Brain Sciences*, 1–50.
Keltner, D., Sauter, D., Tracy, J. L., Wetchler, E., & Cowen, A. S. (2022). How emotions, relationships, and culture constitute each other: Advances in social functionalist theory. *Cognition and Emotion, 36*(3), 388–401.
Kheiridoust, Z., Momeni, F., Khadem Alizadeh, A., & Nasiri, B. (2022). The relationship between cultural changes and economic development. *Iranian Journal of Economic Studies, 10*(1), 193–215.
Kingston, C., & Caballero, G. (2009). Comparing theories of institutional change. *Journal of Institutional Economics, 5*(2), 151–180.
Kuchař, P. (2016). Entrepreneurship and institutional change. *Journal of Evolutionary Economics, 26*(2), 349–379.
Landes, D. S. (2015). *Wealth and poverty of nations*. Hachette UK.

Levy, B., & Spiller, P. T. (1994). The institutional foundations of regulatory commitment: a comparative analysis of telecommunications regulation. *The Journal of Law, Economics, and Organization, 10*(2), 201–246.
Mahoney, J. (2000). Path dependence in historical sociology. *Theory and Society, 29*(4), 507–554.
Mantzavinos, C., North, D. C., & Shariq, S. (2004). Learning, institutions, and economic performance. *Perspectives on Politics, 2*(1), 75–84.
Mesoudi, A. (2016). Cultural evolution: A review of theory, findings, and controversies. *Evolutionary Biology, 43*(4), 481–497.
North, D. C. (1990). *Institutions, institutional change, and economic performance*. Cambridge University Press.
North, D. C. (2005). *Understanding the process of economic change*. Princeton University Press.
Olson, M., Jr. (1971). *The logic of collective action: Public goods and the theory of groups, with a new preface and appendix* (Vol. 124). Harvard University Press.
Ostrom, E. (2005). Doing institutional analysis digging deeper than markets and hierarchies. In *Handbook of new institutional economics* (pp. 819–848). Springer.
Park, S. M. (2022). Domestic formal and informal institutions: Their substitutability and comparative advantage. *Review of World Economics, 159*, 1–34.
Parsons, T., & Smelser, N. J. (1956). A sociological model for economic development. *Explorations in Economic History, 8*(4), 181.
Parsons, T. (2017). The present status of "structural-functional" theory in sociology. In *The idea of social structure* (pp. 67–84). Routledge.
Putnam, R. (1993). *Making democracy work: Civil trading in modern Italy*. Princeton University Press.
Rodrik, D. (2000). Institutions for high-quality growth: What they are and how to acquire them. *Studies in Comparative International Development, 35*(3), 3–31.
Roland, G. (2004). Understanding institutional change: Fast-moving and slow-moving institutions. *Comparative International Development, 38*(4), 109–113.
Ruttan, V. W. (2006). Social science knowledge and induced institutional innovation: An institutional design perspective. *Journal of Institutional Economics, 2*(3), 249–272.
Sankaran, K. (2022). The transition from the informal to the formal economy: The need for a multifaceted approach. *The Indian Journal of Labour Economics, 65*(3), 625–642.
Searle, J. R. (2005). What is an institution? *Journal of Institutional Economics, 1*(1), 1–22.
Shirley, M. M. (2005). Institutions and development. In C. Menard & M. Shirley (Eds.), *Handbook of new institutional economics* (pp. 611–638). Springer.
Simon, H. A. (1997). *Administrative behavior* (4th ed.). Free Press.
Sugden, R. (1989). Spontaneous order. *Journal of Economic Perspectives, 3*(4), 85–97.
Tao, J. (2016). A literature review on institutional change and entrepreneurship. *Open Journal of Business and Management, 4*(04), 629.
Veblen, T. (1914). *The Instinct of Workmanship and the State of the Industrial Arts*, London, Routledge/Thoemmes Press.
Veblen, T. (1909). The limitations of marginal utility. *Journal of Political Economy, 17*(9), 620–636.
Whitt, S., & Wilson, R. K. (2007). The dictator game, fairness, and ethnicity in postwar Bosnia. *American Journal of Political Science, 51*(3), 655–668.
Williamson, O. E. (2000). The new institutional economics: Taking stock, looking ahead. *Journal of Economic Literature, 38*(3), 595–613.
Wood, A. W. (2007). *Kantian ethics*. Cambridge University Press.

Part II
Cognitive Inertia

The Roots of Cognitive Inertia: An Introduction to Institutional Changes

Ali Hussein Samadi, Mojtaba Panahi, and Alireza Raanaei

1 Introduction

In Newtonian physics, inertia[1] is an object's property showing resistance against change in the speed or direction of the object's motion. This concept is frequently used in different contexts as a metaphor to elaborate on human behavior characteristics. For instance, in management and organization science, there are several types of inertia, including insight, action, and psychological inertia. ***Insight inertia*** occurs when there is a considerable interval between fundamental changes in an organization's environment and the organization being informed about the occurrence of these changes. ***Action inertia*** takes place when a managerial insight has been created about the environment as a result of organizational environment analysis. However, the organization's reaction to these alternations might be slow. Moreover, the attempts for change might not occur at the right time (Dierkes, 2003). ***Psychological inertia*** can be considered a barrier to organizational change and transformation. Psychological analyses manifest that stress, anxiety, and psychological mechanisms are behavioral consequences which influence organizational performance (Allcorn & Diamond, 1997).

Therapeutic inertia or ***clinical inertia*** in medical studies means an inappropriate utilization of effective therapies to hinder acute clinical consequences despite abundant evidence regarding the usefulness of these therapies (Phillips et al., 2001; Okonofua et al., 2006). In sociology, ***social inertia*** refers to the resistance to change or the excess stability of social relationships or social groups (Bourdieu, 1985). In psychology, the ***inertia effect*** describes individuals' reluctance to reduce their

[1] To read more about the concept of inertia, refer to Chapter "Inertia: Resistance and Endurance" of this book.

A. H. Samadi (✉) · M. Panahi · A. Raanaei
Department of Economics, Shiraz University, Shiraz, Iran
e-mail: asamadi@rose.shirazu.ac.ir

N. Faghih, A. H. Samadi (eds.), *Institutional Inertia*, Contributions to Economics,
https://doi.org/10.1007/978-3-031-51175-2_6

confidence in a decision following disconfirming information (Pitz & Reinhold, 1968). ***Psychological inertia*** describes the tendency to maintain the status-quo (Gal, 2006).

Summing up, the term inertia describes various phenomena related to resistance against change; these phenomena have been linked to status-quo bias (Samuelson & Zeckhauser, 1988; Ritov & Baron, 1992) and are generally described as a tendency to maintain the defaults either by repeating a decision or avoiding action. So far, however, our understanding of the processes underlying inertia and their connection with economics is rather limited. For instance, the link between ***cognitive inertia*** and ***institutional inertia***[2] and its evaluation and origination in behavioral economics has not been a public concern. The present chapter seeks to extract the roots and causes of inertia in behavioral economics by concentrating on cognitive inertia and presenting it as a factor of institutional inertia.

The rest of this chapter is organized as follows. Section 1 evaluates and defines cognitive inertia and its roots based on the behavioral economics approach (especially issues related to cognitive biases). To elaborate on this issue, first, cognitive inertia is defined, then the issue of the decision-making process in behavioral economics and the role of cognitive biases in the decision-making process are stated. Section 2 identifies and analyzes cognitive biases related to cognitive inertia. Section 3 demonstrates the relationship between cognitive inertia and institutional changes.[3] Section 4 provides the summary and conclusion.

2 Cognitive Inertia

In the 1960s, William J. McGuire, a social psychologist, conducted some research works and experiments and found that people tend to maintain a logical consistency between their behavior and cognition. As a result of his efforts, the concept of cognitive inertia was formed under the influence of two main theories of psychology, i.e., the theory of balance and cognitive dissonance theories, which are fully explored in the following.

1. *Balance theory*: This theory was introduced by Fritz Heider, stating that interpersonal communications should be balanced so that the communicating parties are balanced in their thoughts, emotions, and social relationships. According to Heider, mental balance is a requirement of every human. Human beings seek compatible beliefs, attitudes, and values with those of others, and attempt to be in balance with others in terms of behavior. When there is an imbalance, they set to

[2]To read more about the concept of institutional inertia, and its causes refer to Chapter "An Introduction to Institutional Inertia: Concepts, Types and Causes" of this book.

[3]The effect of cognitive inertia on institutional inertia is explained in Part III of Chapter "Overview of Institutional–Organizational Inertia Nexus" of this book.

create balance (Heider, 1958), so becoming persuaded to keep away from unbalanced structures.

2. *Cognitive dissonance*: It refers to a situation in which a person encounters contradictory attitudes, beliefs, and behaviors, resulting in discomfort and ultimately altering an attitude, belief, or behavior to lower the discomfort and return balance or similar things (Festinger, 1957). According to the cognitive dissonance theory, individuals are motivated to reduce this tension by altering their attitudes, beliefs, or deeds. For instance, smoking people may try to rationalize their behavior by having some beliefs, such as "the medical evidence showing that smoking induces cancer is not convincing" or "most smokers live long, concluding that smoking is harmless for them" (Chapman et al., 1993). Cognitive dissonance theory is founded on the principle that humans pursue compatibility between their expectations and reality. According to Leon Festinger (1957), people are motivated to have lower dissonance, doing it through altering their attitudes, beliefs, and actions.

Accordingly, cognitive dissonance is a crucial factor that justifies cognitive inertia. Indeed, the feeling of sadness and discomfort resulting from the conflict between two different cognitions (beliefs and attitudes) motivates people to reduce dissonance, which can take place via rejecting, avoiding, or changing the perception of contradictory information, which ultimately leads to cognitive inertia.

In his subsequent research works, McGuire (1960) showed that individuals have always an indicated amount of cognitive inertia, so resisting change when processing new and contradictory information. McGuire (1960) conducted an experiment on 120 high school and college students to expand his work regarding cognitive instability and inertia. The participants were given different topics and were asked how they thought about the probability of each topic. A week later, the participants had to read information about the topics that they had predicted previously. Immediately, they were asked again about the probability of these topics. Again, a week later, they were asked about the new information. McGuire (1960) predicted that they would like to alter their probable estimate to be more consistent with the facts due to dissonance of the participants' initial probable estimate; however, he was astonished when he realized that this did not instantly occur. To put it in other words, change in the direction of consistency between the initial estimate and the real information was more difficult as time passed by, and McGuire called it continued seepage of change; later, he termed it cognitive inertia. Indeed, the lack of immediate change was the result of the participants' present thought processes and mental models. This consistency and stability disrupted the correct evaluation of new information and the initial responses' modification (McGuire, 1960).

Overall, cognitive inertia refers to the beliefs' stability after formation. Cognitive inertia is basically the man's tendency to cling to his prior beliefs, even when new evidence does not support those beliefs anymore. This concept is typically a negative concept. Considerable research studies have analyzed its effects (Tripsas & Gavetti, 2000) or its symptoms' reduction (Messner & Vosgerau, 2010; Mclaughlan & Bossarte, 2012); of course, all aspects related to cognitive inertia do not necessarily lead to negative consequences. For instance, cognitive inertia is a main component of love, trust, and friendship. So, cognitive inertia defines human beings' inclination to rely on known presumptions and show disinclination or inability to modify those presumptions, even when there is no supporting evidence or when other evidence questions their validity.

The cognitive inertia concept is linked to similar ideas in social psychology and behavioral decision-making theory, such as status quo bias, belief perseverance bias, confirmation bias, and escalation of commitment bias.

There exist various theories with respect to the formation of cognitive inertia, the most important of which is the theory of behavioral economics. In behavioral economics, considering the cognitive biases in decision-making, the origins of cognitive inertia are investigated. In the following, the origins of the formation of cognitive inertia are examined according to the theories proposed in behavioral economics.

3 Inertia in Behavioral Economics

Behavioral economics is a relatively new field that provides a psychological lens to explain people's decisions and behaviors in various socioeconomic contexts. By combining the insights of psychology with the knowledge of economics, law, political science, and business, behavioral economics offers a deeper understanding of why people in many different situations make choices that are not the best and most beneficial, but also harmful. The fact that people often deviate from choosing the best available option and engage in seemingly irrational behavior contradicts the assumptions that are at the core of contemporary economic arrangements, legal systems, principles of policy design, and even business models (Nikolova, 2020). Behavioral economics tries to deal more with these facts.

In fact, it can be said that behavioral economics is a science that studies the effects of psychological, cognitive, emotional, cultural and social factors on the decisions of individuals or institutions. It also shows how decisions in the real world are different from those described by classical economic theory (Teitelbaum & Zeiler, 2018).

In the following, according to the assumptions of behavioral economics, and by examining the decision processes, the problem of cognitive inertia and its roots will be examined.

3.1 Decision-Making Process in Behavioral Economics

To evaluate cognitive inertia from the behavioral economics perspective, it is crucial to become familiar with the decision-making process. Cialdini (2008) discussed that people are automatically inclined toward their previous decisions due to their inclination to compatibility. When decision-makers decide about an issue,

Table 1 Characteristics of system 1 and system 2

System 1	System 2
Fast	Slow, Gradual
Instinctive	Analytical
Emotional	Structured
Automatic	Logical
Unconscious	Conscious

Source: Kahneman (2011)

compatibility makes them not think about the issue again. So, they do not update their beliefs when encountering new but similar decision-making situations when they encounter new information, resulting in decision-making inertia. The evaluation of a variety of decision-making processes specifies the origins of this inertia.

Decision-making is a process in which an individual selects one among two or more alternatives. This may take place in any part of daily life, personal and professional. There are two key factors involved in the decision-making process:

- *Analytical capacity*: Analytical capacity, i.e., the power to evaluate and understand the context in which a decision is made and its possible repercussions.
- *Emotions*: it refers to the mental status of an individual who makes decisions.

In contrast to the conventional economic theory, (in which the decision-making process is based on precise analysis and calculation of all available alternatives- the rational choice theory in economics), in behavioral economics, decision making as "heuristic" decision-making in which people use cognitive shortcuts and emotional shortcuts. In mainstream economics, individuals' rationality is prevalent over their emotional aspect. However, in behavioral economics, the aforementioned cognitive and emotional shortcuts frequently turn into cognitive and emotional errors. In this regard, Daniel Kahneman (2011) distinguishes two thought systems in his book, *Thinking, Fast and Slow*:

- *System 1* (fast thinking): it operates automatically and quickly, with little or no effort and no sense of voluntary control.
- *System 2* (slow thinking): it allocates attention to the effortful mental activities that demand it, including complex computations.

These systems interact and are always active. System 1 constantly suggests System 2 perceptions, insights, intentions, and emotions. If System 2 confirms them, effects and insights become beliefs, and motivations become voluntary actions. Overall, both systems work smoothly together. Thus, System 2 accepts System 1 suggestions. When System 1 faces a problem, it turns to System 2 to solve the problem with a more accurate method. This task distribution between two systems optimizes task implementation. System 1 works adequately; usually, its short-term predictions are suitable, and its initial responses are fast and suitable. Nevertheless, this system has some biases (systematic biases possibly occurring in certain situations). System 2 is slow and consumes ample energy. The distinctions and features of System 1 and System 2 are provided in Table 1.

In essence, the decision-making process is shaped by one way of thinking based on emotions and intuition that produces fast and automatic responses. Thus, intuition and reasoning are two ways of contemplation. Intuition accounts for fast implications and judgments, and reasoning is much slower, needs more effort, and should be controlled consciously. Most daily decision-making happens by System 1 with a relatively decent result. System 2 merely tries to solve difficult questions that need analysis and critical thinking. Consequently, Kahneman's research shows that the rational agent model does not accurately depict humans, whose decisions are affected by "the quirks of System 1 and the laziness of System 2". Although intuition (System 1) is very efficient in making complicated decisions, the outcomes are not always correct. This difficulty is due to the existence of biases, i.e., certain tricks or mental shortcuts (also called heuristics) that help simplify the multitude of mental processes that are constantly taking place, and make daily life easier. (Kahneman, 2011). Thus, perceiving cognitive biases is crucial for an improved understanding of decision-making theories. The current study evaluates those decision-making biases that affect the formation and enhancement of cognitive inertia.

3.2 Cognitive Bias

Cognitive bias is a systematic, non-random thinking error, i.e., a judgment deviates from what would be considered desirable from the perspective of accepted norms or correct in terms of formal logic (Ariely, 2008). Cognitive psychologists argue that the human brain can be assumed to be an information processor that assesses and solves problems based on input information. In the decision-making process, the main stage is knowing and receiving accurate information about an issue. If this awareness is created better and more completely, decision-making will be followed in a better way; otherwise, the decision-making will not render good consequences. Psychologists have demonstrated that, for various reasons, the cognition process is not correctly performed. Hence, some cognitive biases (i.e., deviation from norm or rationality) have been examined. Humans encounter these biases according to psychological fundamentals, and these biases affect their reactions when encountering phenomena and decisions-makings.

3.3 Cognitive Biases Related to Cognitive Inertia and Its Causes

In behavioral economics, inertia is the endurance of a stable state associated with inaction (Madrian & Shea, 2001). Cognitive inertia is the inclination to resist change and ignore new information that contradicts prevailing beliefs. Cognitive inertia occurs since humans do not want to change, applying it to personal behavior, beliefs, relationships, and commitments. At the societal level, preserving stable behavior and maintaining social roles ensures social integration. In behavioral economics, behavioral nudges can overcome individuals' decision inertia (Jung, 2019). Effective factors affecting cognitive inertia in behavioral economics may include maintaining the status quo bias, confirmation bias, commitment escalation bias, belief persistence bias, *conservatism bias,* and *self-attribution bias*. In the following, the role of these biases in the formation and amplification of cognitive inertia is discussed.

3.3.1 Status Quo Bias

William Samuelson and Richard Zeckhauser (1988) introduced status quo bias for the first time. Samuelson and Zeckhauser, in a series of controlled experiments, concluded that individuals are more inclined to choices maintaining the status quo. Samuelson and Zeckhauser (1988) demonstrated status quo bias using a questionnaire in which subjects faced a series of decision problems, which were alternately framed to be with and without a pre-existing status quo position. Subjects tended to remain with the status quo when such a position was offered to them.

Therefore, the bias of maintaining the status quo is a mental bias that creates a tendency to maintain the status quo in an individual. In this bias, the current situation is considered as a reference situation and any change from this baseline is assumed a loss. Indeed, individuals with status quo bias prefer the current status of affairs to stay the same.

The status quo bias becomes apparent when people would rather have things stable without doing something or adhering to a previous decision (Samuelson & Zeckhauser, 1988). It may even take place when decision-making is so critical; this is often assumed irrational. Adhering to decisions which were effective in the past is regarded as safer and less arduous due to informational and cognitive constraints. For instance, status quo bias is more likely when there are too many alternatives (Dean et al., 2017) or when there is high uncertainty and consultation is costly (Nebel, 2015).

In politics, the status quo bias often refers to conservative thinking. Conservative people focus on maintaining traditions and anything as it is to keep off risks associated with change. This kind of bias is linked to political inertia and results in its formation. The status quo bias may affect the health-related choices of people. Elstad et al. (2012) showed that when people have to choose between their current medicine and a better one, they insist on choosing the current medicine. They prefer to adhere to what they are familiar with rather than use an unknown medicine with unknown influences even if it is not potentially as effective as the alternative medicine.

Social psychology provides several explanations about the reasons why the status quo bias occurs. There are two important concepts related to the status quo bias: loss aversion and regret aversion. The following briefly explains these two concepts.

Loss Aversion Bias

In economics and decision theory, loss aversion refers to the tendency of people to prevent and avoid losses and gains equally. Some studies have shown that psychological losses are almost twice as powerful as gains. Loss aversion was first demonstrated by Amos Tversky and Daniel Kahneman. The psychological studies of these two scholars showed that the disutility or the feeling of dissatisfaction that comes to people from a financial loss with a certain amount is almost equal to the amount of pleasure and utility (satisfaction) from the same amount of profit. This, in turn, leads to risk aversion. Because when people are considering the results of their gains and losses, they prefer not to lose versus to gain.

Kahneman (2011) in the book "*Thinking, Fast and Slow*" points out that: the concept of loss aversion is certainly the most important psychological issue in behavioral economics.

To explain the endowment effect and sunk cost fallacy, the loss aversion theory is used. It also plays an important role in *status quo bias*. In fact, one of the consequences of loss aversion is that people tend to stay in the status quo because the disadvantages of leaving outweigh the advantages.

People behave with the status quo as a reference point or base when they decide to select the default choice or other alternatives. The status quo is known, and people know what they expect from it. Moreover, the selection of an alternative may have risks. This is precisely where the loss aversion bias becomes apparent. Through considering an alternative, individuals give more weight to potential losses as compared to potential gains (Samuelson & Zeckhauser, 1988). Thus, people prefer the status quo.

Regret Aversion Bias

The regret aversion bias theory was proposed by Bell (1982) and Loomes and Sugden (1982) as an alternative to the expected utility model following a set of empirical studies. Regret theory offers an alternative to the traditional expected utility model of decision-making. This theory is an alternative means of describing rational behavior. Regret theory rests on two simple assertions. First, once a decision is made people evaluate the outcome and feel regret if an alternative outcome would have led to a better result. Alternatively, a person rejoices if a different outcome would have made him worse off. Second, regret theory states that people will anticipate these ex-post feelings and shift their preferences ex-ante (Zeelenberg & Beattie, 1997). Additional studies have indicated that regret aversion exists because, like losses versus gains, regret looms larger than rejoicing (Larrick & Boles, 1995).

Therefore, regret theory differs from an expected utility in an important way. Expected utility assumes that the value of individual outcomes is calculated independently. Regret theory states that the value of a given option is a function of its outcomes, and how its outcomes compare with the outcomes of possible alternatives. The choices examined under regret theory are not independent at all but determined concerning each other. Given the uncertainty, this leads to the calculation of "modified utility" by the decision maker.

Modified utility represents expected utility, plus or minus the anticipation of regret or rejoicing. Regret represents a premium that must be overcome to reach a decision consistent with the expected utility theory loss (Bell, 1982).

Bell (1982) and Loomes and Sugden (1982) considered regret as the most relevant sensation in decision-making. Other emotions also affect decision-making including worry, fear, happiness, and joy. Since these feelings are associated with the resulting aspects or uncertainty, they may also appear when there is no decision-making. Regret is directly correlated with a choice or decision. In brief, regret aversion describes the feeling of regret that is caused by a bad choice or at least an undesirable one. Furthermore, the regret aversion bias takes place when a new decision is not made for the fear that it might be wrong (Seiler et al., 2008).

Based on the initial findings of regret theory, researchers sought to investigate regret's relationship to action and inaction. Interestingly, the majority of studies have found that action is regretted more often than inaction. Kahneman and Tversky (1979) demonstrated this hypothesis with their famous investor problem. "In the problem, experimental subjects were told about two investors, Mr. Paul and Mr. George. Mr. Paul owned stock in Company A. The subjects were informed that he considered switching to Company B but elected not to do so. He later learned that he would have gained $1200 had he made the switch. Mr. George owned stock in Company B and he did switch to Company A. As a result, he lost $1200 because he sold B and bought A. Over 90% of the subjects responded that Mr. George would feel more regret" (Gelberg, 2002).

The distinction between action and inaction highlights the importance of the status quo to the regret theory. 4' People may be reluctant to depart from the status quo due to regret aversion associated with actions. Generally, people assume deviation from the status quo to be risky and are not inclined to make risky decisions as they are worried about potential losses or negative consequences. As described above, Kahneman and Tversky (1982) asserted that people regret the adverse consequences of new measures more as compared to the adverse consequences resulting from being passive and inactive (maintaining the status quo). Hence, they set to preserve the status quo and this leads to inertia.

Why Do Individuals Prefer the Status Quo?

Behavioral economics has evaluated reasons why people are inclined to select the status quo; some primary causes are described below.

Prospect Theory Kahneman and Tversky (1979) criticized the expected utility theory as a descriptive model which elaborates on decision-making under risk and developed a new model called prospect theory. This theory is a behavioral model that shows how people decide between alternatives that involve risk and uncertainty (e.g., % likelihood of gains or losses). It demonstrates that people think in terms of

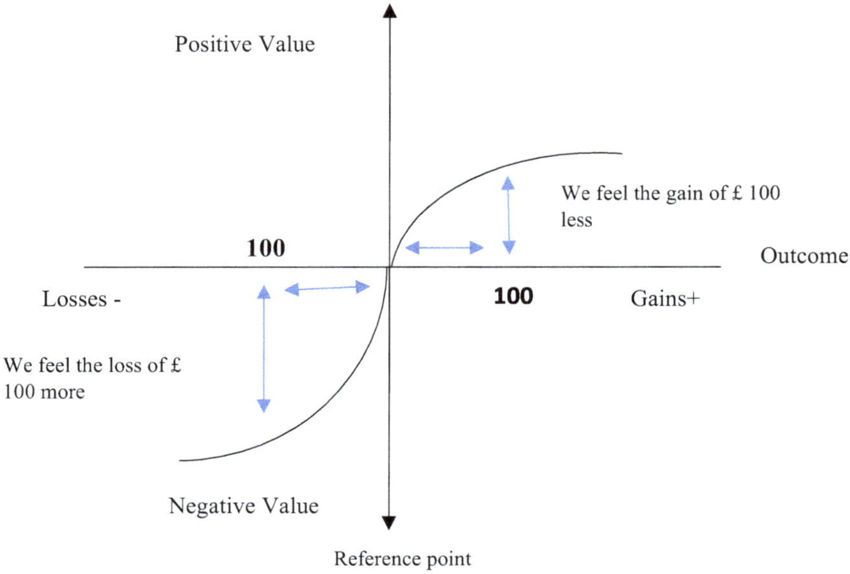

Fig. 1 Value function in the perspective theory. (Source: Kahneman & Tversky, 1977)

expected utility relative to a reference point (e.g., current wealth) rather than absolute outcomes. Prospect theory was developed by framing risky choices and indicates that people are loss-averse; since individuals dislike losses more than equivalent gains, they are more willing to take risks to avoid a loss. Finally, the value function is steeper for losses than for gains. Studies indicate that the mean loss aversion coefficient is 1.955 with a 95% probability that the true value falls in the interval [1.820, 2.105] (Brown et al., 2021). This implies that losing $100 is more unpleasant than gaining $100 is pleasant (see Fig. 1). For example, considering the following two scenarios, we will have:

1. 100% chance to gain $450 or 50% chance to gain $1000
2. 100% chance to lose $500 or 50% chance to lose $1100

Prospect theory suggests that (Kahneman & Tversky, 1979; Kahneman, 2011):

- When faced with a risky choice leading to gains agents are risk averse, preferring a certain outcome with a lower expected utility (concave value function).

Agents will choose the certain $450 even though the expected utility of the risky gain is higher

- When faced with a risky choice leading to losses agents are risk-seeking, preferring the outcome that has a lower expected utility but the potential to avoid losses (convex value function).

Agents will choose the 50% chance to lose $1100 even though the expected utility is lower, due to the chance that they lose nothing at all.

Thus, according to this theory, dissatisfaction with loss is higher than satisfaction with gain; in other words, loss aversion persuades people to maintain their status quo and not alter their conditions.

Endowment Effect It is a cognitive bias that individuals are inclined to overvalue their possessions. It results from the contemplation that people relate their possessions to their identity and assume it is a part of themselves, so they put more value on it. It can be considered as an application of the perspective theory (Weaver & Frederick, 2012). Concerning the endowment effect, people consider their possessions more valuable and do not attempt to alter something.

Choice Costs Samuelson and Zeckhauser (1988) found that the inclination to maintain the status quo rises with an increase in the number of alternatives, suggesting that the higher the number of choices, the higher the decision-making cost and the more attractive the status quo.

Other reasons also make people choose the status quo; Kahneman et al. (1991) and Samuelson and Zeckhauser (1988) pointed to factors such as the fear of the unknown, inertia, familiarity, attachment, and loyalty.

3.3.2 Confirmation Bias

When individuals face information that enhances their prior beliefs and attitudes, confirmation bias takes place (Bessi, 2016: Geschke et al., 2019; Zhao et al., 2020). Confirmation bias is defined as the inclination to interpret, search, remind, and support information to confirm an individual's previous beliefs or assumptions (Westerwick et al., 2017: Gupta et al., 2021), regularly occurring in the face of highly emotional and deeply rooted activities and issues (Zhao et al., 2020).

Generally, people like to search, believe, and share information in line with their beliefs and attitudes but neglect information challenging their beliefs and attitudes (Itzchakov & Van Harreveld, 2018; Knobloch-Westerwick & Kleinman, 2012; van Strien et al., 2016). A user that likes a specific brand and searches for a new purchase may get motivated to surf the net for customer views that favor that brand. Confirmation bias also manifests in the primacy effect and anchoring effect processes, relying on information encountered in the initial stages of a process (Nickerson, 1998). Hence, confirmation bias intensifies the inclination toward beliefs' stability after their formation, resulting in cognitive inertia.

3.3.3 Escalation of Commitment Bias or Sunk Cost Fallacy

An important bias which also creates cognitive inertia and is discussed a lot in behavioral economics is the escalation of commitment bias or sunk cost fallacy. In economics and business decision-making, a sunk cost (also known as retrospective cost) is a cost that has already been incurred and cannot be recovered (Mankiw, 2018).

Almost most human beings encounter circumstances where they perceive it is too late to withdraw since they have invested too much; this perception happens in a broad range of events. For instance, people sometimes order a lot of food and then eat a lot to have their value money returned. Also, a person may have a ticket to a concert worth $20 and may drive for hours in a blizzard because he/she feels he/she has to take part in the concert just because of the initial investment (Thaler, 1999). Accordingly, people have to continue investing time, effort, cost, etc. to promote their situation (Brockner, 1992). Briefly, resource allocation (financial, time, energy) to a plan, strategy, or decision which is not cost-effective anymore is called escalation of commitment bias (Staw & Ross, 1987). Studies show that both rats and humans suffer from sunk cost fallacy (Sweis et al., 2018). A popular example of the sunk cost fallacy influencing large-scale decisions is the Concorde Fallacy. In 1969, France and the United Kingdom invested in a joint undertaking called the Concorde supersonic airplane. It could travel faster than the speed of sound due to its high fuel consumption and powerful engines. Its first flight was on March 2nd, 1969, and officially started traveling on January 21st, 1976. After a while, the joint British-France aircraft crashed on July 25th, 2000, in Paris and its passengers were killed. The experts examined its engine and realized the design defects, the fixing of which was not affordable. However, they could not abandon this project due to political and legal issues. Ultimately, it caused millions of dollars lost, and it worked for less than 30 years (Blasingame, 2011).

One theory about sunk cost fallacy is that humans use the principle of not being wasteful (Arkes, 1996). The escalation of commitment bias is a self-justification, i.e., the inclination to justify the decision made in a person's mind (Brockner, 1992).

Research has been conducted on the escalation of commitment bias, and scholars have listed four primary reasons for the escalation of commitment bias:

- People feel responsible for their decisions.
- Decision-making needs cognitive effort, and when humans decide, they are not inclined to make the cognitive effort again.
- After making the final decision, humans consider their credit as it is dependent on its correctness, and confessing that their decision is not correct is equal to their loss of self-imagery.
- Humans usually justify their initial choice (Bobocel & Meyer, 1994; Staw & Ross, 1987).

3.3.4 Belief Stability Bias and the Backfire Effect

Belief stability or belief persistence is humans' innate desire. To maintain beliefs, humans may confront new evidence that is in contradiction with those beliefs. Its ill form is called the backfire effect, i.e. when people encounter evidence that is in contradiction with their beliefs, they become more determined about their beliefs. This bias causes the fallacy of maintaining the status quo, i.e., neglecting the contradictory evidence and persistence on the claim. Belief stability and confirmation bias are usually applied interchangeably, but it is incorrect. Confirmation bias is the inclination to search, interpret, and retain information based on beliefs. In contrast, belief stability is referred to a state in which an individual refuses to alter his/her beliefs, even if they are wrong.

The backfire effect is a possible psychological effect proposed first by Brendan Nyhan and Jason Reifler in 2010 based on their research work on a survey about conservatism (Nyhan & Reifler, 2010; Wood & Porter, 2018).

Humans' minds reject some information which is not in line with the previous information based on previous values, principles, experiences, preferences, and instructions. In fact, humans encounter problems with respect to new topics that are contrary to their previous mindsets. This is called self-confirmation bias. Nevertheless, there is another bias which is consistent with the self-confirmation bias and in the direction of further enhancing it, and that is called the backfire effect. The backfire effect defines a situation in which an individual persists in his previous position and shows more stability when he/she encounters evidence regarding the rejection or refusal of accepted issues or situations. In an ideal and logical world, when human beings encounter evidence in contradiction with their beliefs, they first evaluate it and then adjust their beliefs. However, this rarely occurs in the real world. Instead of doubting their beliefs, people refuse to accept new information and persist more than ever on their own beliefs. The backfire effect means that if you speak with a person who deeply believes something and you talk about facts completely contradictory to his/her beliefs, you cannot change his/her opinion. This just happens in cognitive inertia and makes a person unwilling to alternate, hence contributing to the escalation of cognitive inertia as well.

3.3.5 Conservatism Bias

Conservatism bias is a mental process in which the mind gives more weight to available data, but ignores new evidence. In cognitive psychology and decision science, conservatism or conservatism bias is a type of bias that refers to a person's tendency to insufficiently revise a belief when new evidence is presented. This bias describes a revision of human beliefs in which people give too much weight to the prior distribution (the base rate). But compared to Bayesian belief revision theory, less weight is given to new sample evidence.

According to the theory, "opinion change is very orderly, and usually proportional to the numbers of Bayes' theorem – but it is insufficient in amount" (Kahneman et al., 1982). In other words, people update their prior beliefs as new evidence becomes available, but they do so more slowly than when they were using Bayes' theorem.

Conservatism can harm the process of processing information in the mind. When the mind receives a lot of complex information, a person experiences anxiety. The easiest option in front of the mind to relieve anxiety is to cling to previous beliefs, and as a result, conservatism occurs.

As stated, this type of bias occurs when people believe previous evidence more than new evidence or information. Therefore, this bias is also related to sticking to the belief system and prevents the formation of new beliefs, and causes cognitive inertia to intensify.

3.3.6 Self-Attribution Bias

Self-attribution bias, sometimes known as *self-serving bias*, occurs when a person attributes the positive outcomes of an event to their good performance, as well as attributing negative results to external factors (Mezulis et al., 2004).

> When individuals reject the validity of negative feedback, focus on their strengths and achievements but overlook their faults and failures, or take more credit for their group's work than they give to other members, they are protecting their self-esteem from threat and injury. These cognitive and perceptual tendencies perpetuate illusions and error, but they also serve the self's need for esteem. (Singh et al., 2020)

For example, students think that the reason for getting a good grade on the exam is their intelligence and preparation, and the reason for getting a poor grade is the teacher's poor teaching ability or unfair test questions. Some studies have shown that this bias may occur in various situations such as the workplace (Pal, 2007), interpersonal relationships (Campbell et al., 2000), sports (De Michele et al., 1998), and consumer decisions (Moon, 2003).

Both motivational processes (i.e., self-enhancement, self-presentation) and cognitive processes (i.e., locus of control, self-esteem) affect self-serving bias (Shepperd et al., 2008). There are both cross-cultural considerations (i.e. individualistic and collectivist culture differences) and special clinical population considerations (such as depression) in this bias (see e.g., Hooghiemstra, 2008; Greenberg et al., 1992).

Therefore, according to the above definition of self-attribution bias, when faced with failure, people attribute the causes of failure to others and are not willing to change their beliefs. Also, if they succeed, they will confirm their current beliefs and strengthen those beliefs. In other words, people who suffer from this bias tend to maintain their previous beliefs in any situation. This issue will intensify cognitive inertia.

4 Cognitive Inertia and Institutional Changes

Cognitive science has the most relationship with economics from two perspectives: (1) It tries to explain the learning process. (2) It tries to explain that: why and how theories are designed and developed considering absolute uncertainty, what expands these theories in society, and what leads to the failure of theories in societies. Why do people believe in them and why do they act based on them (Hodgson, 2004)? In recent decades, economics has benefited from cognitive science in many fields.

By using common theories in cognitive science, a more realistic analysis of institutional changes and their causes can be provided. As said, Cognitive inertia originates from human beings' cognitive biases and results in the stability of many beliefs, and these beliefs are unwilling to be changed. On the other hand, institutional change requires alternation of the mental models previously formed. Indeed, human beings establish mental models and principle-based institutions to assist them in coping with their surroundings and efficiently organizing their society. Individuals invest in these models psychologically and endow them with innate value (Fukuyama, 2011). Since institutions and existing procedures are valued independently of applied or social utility, even when they are irrelevant or even inefficient, they outlive. In the discussions regarding cognitive inertia, it was argued that people still persist in their mental models and beliefs even when encountering contradictory evidence. Fukuyama believes that the genetic inclination to follow rules brings about cognitive and intellectual inertia and also irrational persistence of people in supporting outdated beliefs and institutions (ibid., 2011). Fukuyama (2011) asserts that the lack of Institutional Changes is caused by irrational behavior via individuals' psychological and emotional investment in inefficient or unsuitable institutions and mental models.

In the following, the mechanism of the effect of cognitive inertia on institutional changes is examined according to North's theory about institutional changes.

4.1 The Role of Beliefs Alternation in Institutional Changes in North's Intellect

It was argued in the explanation of cognitive inertia that inclination to beliefs' stability after their establishment results in cognitive inertia. Then, the origins of the tendency to perpetuate beliefs in cognitive bias and mental errors were investigated. In this part, the relationship between the formation of beliefs and institutional changes is inspected according to the viewpoints of a well-known institutionalist economist, i.e., North.

North is one of the institutional economists who has paid special attention to cognitive economics. Using the contributions of this field, he has analyzed the history of economic performance and the causes of their successes and failures.

North considered the individual as the unit of analysis and attempted to elaborate on individuals' beliefs formation and its impact on their actions. He sought to illuminate the role of beliefs in institutions' formation, thus describing their influence on economic performance or institutional changes.

North (2005) believes that people encounter uncertainty all the time and attempt to lower their uncertainty. In fact, humans establish institutions to lower their uncertainty. He believes that initial uncertainty is lowered by teaching two types of experiences that come from the physical and socio-cultural linguistic environment. He pointed out that initial learning develops a structure to interpret different messages perceived by the senses, the primary framework of which is genetic, but its secondary structure is formed by the aforementioned two types of training. North refers to a framework developed and evolved from childhood to organize perception and maintain analytical results. He uses mental models to better perceive this framework. He believes that mental models enhance or modify the approaches to elaborate on and interpret the environment and feedback received from the surroundings.

Ultimately, when environmental responses (almost always) confirm the same mental models, they somehow stabilize them. This mental model is termed belief, which creates a "belief system" from the interconnectedness of beliefs, and enables an individual to survive in his/her past surrounding environment. The belief system is connected to the motivational system. It takes on a common filter' feature for all novel motivational processes. It is accurately assumed that the belief system is more or less resistant to abrupt changes. However, the primary issue is when problems are not resolved based on mental models. According to North, the mind proposes novel models for problem-solving. He emphasizes that although environmental responses can influentially correct the models, their misinterpretation is possible. Furthermore, historical prejudices, myths, superstitions, and ideologies significantly affect this misinterpretation (Nan tzavinos et al., 2004).

North (2005) also brings up the discussion of institutions. In his opinion, mental models, belief systems, and institutions are closely related, i.e., institutions are derived from the belief system. He argues that the belief system preserves the inner representation of the human perspective. Institutions are structures that humans impose on this perspective to attain their desired product. Thus, the belief system is the inner representation, and institutions are the outer representation.

North (1994) defines institutions as humanly devised constraints that shape human interaction. They include both informal constraints (behavioral values, traditions, and codes of conduct), formal constraints (rules, laws, and constitutions), and executive specifications.

North (2005) presented the following model about the relationship between beliefs, institutions, and economic performance:

mental modeling ➡ beliefs ➡ institutions ➡ policies ➡ results

North (2005) considers the biggest challenge of social sciences to explain changes, especially social, political, economic, and organizational changes. In his opinion, institutional changes are related to changes in beliefs, and he states that the starting point of the discussion of changes should be focused on how human learning is. From North's point of view, the ability to learn is the main reason for observing the flexibility of human behavior, and people's learning interactions bring about social, political, economic, and organizational changes.

Mantzavinos (2004) provides a new definition of the phenomenon of change by using cognitive science. In this definition, he considers learning and change in mental models as the main factor in creating institutional changes. In defining the process of learning and human learning, he writes:

> *Learning is the complex modification of the mental models according to the feedback received from the environment. The unique feature of human learning is that the modification of mental models goes hand in hand with "representational re-description," a process in which knowledge stored as the solution to a special problem of the environment is subsequently reordered to serve as the solution to a wide variety of problems.* (Mantzavinos et al., 2004)

He also believes: "*Learning is an evolutionary process of trial and error, and failure to solve a problem leads to the trial of a new solution*" (Ibid). Therefore, changes in mental models can lead to changes in beliefs (through learning) and ultimately social and institutional changes.

As mentioned above, mental models are before beliefs. Hence, belief formation significantly affects institution formation; if the belief change does not occur due to cognitive bias, institutional change will not occur as well. Beliefs change and mental models would be the preface to institutional change. Cognitive inertia refers to the inclination to the lack of change in beliefs and resistance to change. Hence, if cognitive inertia exists, it will lead to institutional inertia. Therefore, it is very important to evaluate and include cognitive inertia in the framework of institutional literature.

5 Conclusion

In recent years, the general belief has emerged that institutions are the main cause of differences in different levels of per capita income, economic growth, and development of countries. A lot of research has been done in this regard. But the problem that has not yet been properly answered is (especially in less developed and emerging market economies): what factors cause institutional changes? In this context, some scholars and institutional economists believe that these changes occur over time and are actually a time-consuming process (Toboso, 1995), and are rooted in changes in belief systems and mental models. But the important issue is that the belief system is relatively resistant to changes (Mantzavinos et al., 2004).

How to change or not change in the system of beliefs and mental models should be searched in cognitive sciences. In fact, the task of cognitive science scholars is to understand the way the mind works and how to make changes in it. Cognitive science has expanded a lot in recent years and economists have paid attention to it in the form of cognitive economics. In the meantime, Douglas North, focusing on mental models, beliefs, and institutions, has tried to use the contributions of cognitive science to explain economic performance and establish a relationship between mind, cognition, and institutions and their effect on institutional changes.

In cognitive science, the lack of change in beliefs is referred to as cognitive inertia. Although a lot of studies have been done in this field of cognitive science, in the field of economics, this issue has not been addressed properly. Therefore, in this chapter, first, the origins of the formation of cognitive inertia were assessed based on psychology and behavioral economics literature. The results confirmed that the notion of cognitive inertia has been generated under the influence of two primary theories in psychology, i.e., the balance and cognitive dissonance theories. In economic literature and behavioral economics, in particular, cognitive inertia originates from cognitive bias. The status quo bias, confirmation bias, commitment escalation bias, belief stability bias, conservatism bias, and Self-attribution bias are the most important cognitive biases related to cognitive inertia.

Regarding the relationship between cognitive inertia and institutional changes, the findings of this study revealed that a point of connection between cognitive inertia and institutional changes is beliefs. On the one hand, cognitive inertia is defined as the beliefs' inclination to be stable after formation; on the other hand, in institutional economics and the literature of Douglas North (a prominent institutional economist), the individuals' beliefs formation and its impact on their actions are considered crucial for institutional changes. North attempted to clarify the role of beliefs in the formation of institutions, hence describing their effect on economic performance and institutional changes. According to North, institutions are derived from the belief system. Thus, the formation of the belief notably affects the institutions' formation. Provided that beliefs do not change due to cognitive inertia, institutional change will not take place. The beliefs and mental models alternation would be the preface to institutional change, while cognitive inertia refers to the inclination to the lack of beliefs' change and resistance to change. If there is cognitive inertia, it will cause institutional inertia, so the institutional change will not take place. Thus, finding out what cognitive inertia is and the factors creating it and trying to lower its influences can accelerate the process of institutional changes.

For future research, it is suggested to investigate the mechanisms of neutralizing the effects of cognitive inertia and also investigate how these mechanisms can cause institutional changes. One of these mechanisms, which is also examined in behavioral economics, is the nudging policy. Research in this field would be a way forward.

References

Allcorn, S., & Diamond, M. (1997). *Managing people during stressful time: The psychologically defensive workplace*. Quorum Books.

Ariely, D. (2008). *Predictably irrational*. Harper Collins.

Arkes, H. R. (1996). The psychology of waste. *Journal of Behavioral Decision Making, 9*, 213–224.

Bell, D. E. (1982). Regret in decision making under uncertainty. *Operations Research, 30*(5), 961–981.

Bessi, A. (2016). Personality traits and echo chambers on Facebook. *Computers in Human Behavior, 65*, 319–324.

Blasingame, J. (2011, October 3). *Beware of the Concorde fallacy*. Forbes. https://www.forbes.com/sites/jimblasingame/2011/09/15/beware-of-theconcorde-fallacy/#5655b8334e22

Bobocel, D. R., & Meyer, J. P. (1994). Escalating commitment to a failing course of action: Separating the roles of choice and justification. *Journal of Applied Psychology, 79*(3), 360–363.

Bourdieu, P. (1985). The social space and the genesis of groups. *Theory and Society, 14*, 723–744. https://doi.org/10.1007/BF00174048

Brockner, J. (1992). The escalation of commitment to a failing course of action: Toward theoretical progress. *Academy of Management Review, 17*, 39–61.

Brown, A. L., Imai, T., Vieider, F., & Camerer, C. (2021). *Meta-analysis of empirical estimates of loss-aversion*. Available at SSRN 3772089.

Campbell, W. K., Sedikides, C., Reeder, G. D., & Elliot, A. J. (2000). Among friends? An examination of friendship and the self-serving bias. *British Journal of Social Psychology, 39*(2), 229–239.

Chapman, S., Wong, W. L., & Smith, W. (1993). Self-exempting beliefs about smoking and health: Differences between smokers and ex-smokers. *American Journal of Public Health, 83*(2), 215–219.

Cialdini, R. B. (2008). *Influence: Science and practice* (5th ed.). Pearson Educations, Inc.

De Michele, P. E., Gansneder, B., & Solomon, G. B. (1998). Success and failure attributions of wrestlers: Further evidence of the self-serving bias. *Journal of Sport Behavior, 21*(3), 242.

Dean, M., Kibris, O., & Masatlioglu, Y. (2017). Limited attention and status quo bias. *Journal of Economic Theory, 169*, 93–127.

Dierkes, M. (Ed.). (2003). *Handbook of organizational learning and knowledge*. Oxford University Press, USA.

Elstad, E., Carpenter, D. M., Devellis, R. F., & Blalock, S. J. (2012). Patient decision making in the face of conflicting medication information. *International Journal of Qualitative Studies on Health and Well-Being, 7*(1), 18523–18511.

Festinger, L. (1957). *A theory of cognitive dissonance*. Stanford University Press.

Fukuyama, F. (2011). *The origins of political order: From pre human times to the French Revolution*. Farrar, Straus, Giroux.

Gal, D. (2006). A psychological law of inertia and the illusion of loss aversion. *Judgment and Decision Making, 1*, 23–32.

Gelberg, G. B. (2002). Regret theory-explanation, evaluation and implications for the law. *University of Michigan Journal of Law Reform, 36*, 183.

Geschke, D., Lorenz, J., & Holtz, P. (2019). The triple-filter bubble: Using agent-based modelling to test a meta-theoretical framework for the emergence of filter bubbles and echo chambers. *British Journal of Social Psychology, 58*(1), 129–149.

Greenberg, J., Pyszczynski, T., Burling, J., & Tibbs, K. (1992). Depression, self-focused attention, and the self-serving attributional bias. *Personality and Individual Differences, 13*(9), 959–965.

Gupta, M., Parra, C. M., & Dennehy, D. (2021). Questioning racial and gender bias in AI-based recommendations: Do espoused national cultural values matter? *Information Systems Frontiers, 1-17*, 1465–1481. https://doi.org/10.1007/s10796-021-10156-2

Hedberg, B., & Wolff, R. (2003). Organizing, learning, and strategizing: From construction to discovery. In M. Dierkes, A. B. Antal, J. Child, & I. Nonaka (Eds.), *Handbook of organizational Learning & Knowledge* (pp. 535–556). Oxford University Press.

Heider, F. (1958). *The psychology of interpersonal relations*. Taylor and Francis.

Hodgson, G. M. (2004). *The evolution of institutional economics*. Routledge.

Hooghiemstra, R. (2008). East—West differences in attributions for company performance: A content analysis of Japanese and US corporate annual reports. *Journal of Cross-Cultural Psychology, 39*(5), 618–629.

Itzchakov, G., & Van Harreveld, F. (2018). Feeling torn and fearing rue: Attitude ambivalence and anticipated regret as antecedents of biased information seeking. *Journal of Experimental Social Psychology, 75*, 19–26.

Jung, D. (2019, March 19). *Nudge action: Overcoming decision inertia in financial planning tools*. Behavioraleconomics.com. Retrieved from https://www.behavioraleconomics.com/nudge-action-overcoming-decision-inertia-in-financial-planning-tools/

Kahneman, D. (2011). *Thinking, fast and slow*. Farrar, Straus and Giroux.
Kahneman, D., & Tversky, A. (1977). *Prospect theory. An analysis of decision making under risk*. https://doi.org/10.21236/ada045771
Kahneman, D., & Tversky, A. (1979). Prospect theory: An analysis of decision under risk. *Econometrica, 47*(2), 263–291.
Kahneman, D., & Tversky, A. (1982). The psychology of preference. *Scientific American, 246*, 160–173.
Kahneman, D., Slovic, S. P., Slovic, P., & Tversky, A. (Eds.). (1982). *Judgment under uncertainty: Heuristics and biases*. Cambridge University Press.
Kahneman, D., Knetsch, J. L., & Thaler, R. H. (1991). Anomalies: The endowment effect, loss aversion, and status quo bias. *Journal of Economic Perspectives., 5*(1), 193–206. https://doi.org/10.1257/jep.5.1.193
Knobloch-Westerwick, S., & Kleinman, S. B. (2012). Pre-election selective exposure: Confirmation bias versus informational utility. *Communication Research, 39*(2), 170–193.
Larrick, R. P., & Boles, T. L. (1995). Avoiding regret in decisions with feedback: A negotiation example. *Organizational Behavior and Human Decision Processes, 63*(1), 87–97.
Loomes, G., & Sugden, R. (1982). Regret theory: An alternative theory of rational choice under uncertainty. *The Economic Journal, 92*(368), 805.
Madrian, B., & Shea, D. (2001). The power of suggestion: Inertia in 401(k) participation and savings behavior. *Quarterly Journal of Economics, 116*, 1149–1187.
Mankiw, N. G. (2018). *Principles of economics* (8th ed.). McGraw-Hill Education.
Mantzavinos, C., North, D. C., & Shariq, S. (2004). Learning, institutions, and economic performance. *Perspectives on Politics, 2*(1), 75–84.
Mcguire, W. J. (1960). Cognitive consistency and attitude change. *Journal of Abnormal and Social Psychology, 60*(3), 345–353.
Mclaughlan, B., & Bossarte, S. (2012, July). *Computationally adjustable cognitive inertia*. Department of Computer and Information Science University of Arkansas, USA.
Messner, C., & Vosgerau, J. (2010). Cognitive inertia and the implicit association test. *Journal of Marketing Research, 47*, 2–386.
Mezulis, A. H., Abramson, L. Y., Hyde, J. S., & Hankin, B. L. (2004). Is there a universal positivity bias in attributions? A meta-analytic review of individual, developmental, and cultural differences in the self-serving attributional bias. *Psychological Bulletin, 130*(5), 711–747.
Moon, Y. (2003). Don't blame the computer: When self-disclosure moderates the self-serving bias. *Journal of Consumer Psychology, 13*(1–2), 125–137.
Nan tzavinos, C., North, D., & Sharig, S. (2004). Learning, institutions and economic performance. *Perspectives on Politics, 2*(1), 76–79.
Nebel, J. M. (2015). Status quo bias, rationality, and conservatism about value. *Ethics, 125*(2), 449–476.
Nickerson, R. S. (1998). Confirmation bias: A ubiquitous phenomenon in many guises. *Review of General Psychology, 2*, 175–220.
Nikolova, M. S. (2020). *Behavioral economics for tourism: Perspectives on business and policy in the travel industry*. Academic.
North, D. C. (1994). Economic performance through time. *The American Economic Review, 84*(3), 359–368.
North, D. C. (2005). Understanding the process of economic change. *Preston University Press.*, 15–155.
Nyhan, B., & Reifler, J. (2010). When corrections fail: The persistence of political misperceptions. *Political Behavior, 32*(2), 303–330.
Okonofua, E. C., Simpson, K. N., Jesri, A., Rehman, S. U., Durkalski, V. L., & Egan, B. M. (2006). Therapeutic inertia is an impediment to achieving the healthy people 2010 blood pressure control goals. *Hypertension, 47*, 345–351. https://doi.org/10.1161/01.HYP.0000200702.76436.4b
Pal, G. C. (2007). Is there a universal self-serving attribution bias? *Psychological Studies*.

Phillips, L. S., Branch, W. T., Cook, C. B., Doyle, J. P., El-Kebbi, I. M., Gallina, D. L., et al. (2001). Clinical inertia. *Annals of Internal Medicine, 135*, 825–834. https://doi.org/10.7326/0003-4819-135-9-200111060-00012

Pitz, G. F., & Reinhold, H. (1968). Payoff effects in sequential decision-making. *Journal of Experimental Psychology, 77*, 249–257. https://doi.org/10.1037/h0025802, 183–206.

Ritov, I., & Baron, J. (1992). Status-quo and omission biases. *Journal of Risk and Uncertainty, 5*, 49–61. https://doi.org/10.1007/BF00208786

Samuelson, W., & Zeckhauser, R. J. (1988). Status quo bias in decision making. *Journal of Risk and Uncertainty, 1*, 7–59.

Seiler, M., Seiler, V., Traub, S., & Harrison, D. (2008). Regret aversion and false reference points in residential real estate. *Journal of Real Estate Research, 30*(4), 461–474.

Shepperd, J., Malone, W., & Sweeny, K. (2008). Exploring causes of the self-serving bias. *Social and Personality Psychology Compass, 2*(2), 895–908.

Singh, R., Singh, R. K., & Singh, S. (2020). Developing intellectual efficiency and "the life challenges"; doing good things and happiness. https://doi.org/10.6084/m9.figshare.11841249.v2

Staw, B. M., & Ross, J. (1987). Behavior in escalation situations: Antecedents, prototypes, and solutions. In L. L. Cummings & B. M. Staw (Eds.), *Research in organizational behavior* (Vol. 9). JAI Press.

Sweis, B. M., Abram, S. V., Schmidt, B. J., Seeland, K. D., MacDonald, A. W., Thomas, M. J., & Redish, A. D. (2018). Sensitivity to "sunk costs" in mice, rats, and humans. *Science, 361*(6398), 178–181.

Teitelbaum, J. C., & Zeiler, K. (Eds.). (2018). *Research handbook on behavioral law and economics*. Edward Elgar Publishing.

Thaler, R. H. (1999). Mental accounting matters. *Journal of Behavioral Decision Making, 12*, 183–206.

Toboso, F. (1995). Explaining the process of change taking place in legal rules and social norms: The cases of institutional economics and new institutional economics. *European Journal of Law and Economics, 2*(1), 63–84.

Tripsas, M., & Gavetti, G. (2000). Capabilities, cognition, and inertia: Evidence from digital imaging. *Strategic Management Journal, 21*, 10–11.

van Strien, J. L., Kammerer, Y., Brand-Gruwel, S., & Boshuizen, H. P. (2016). How attitude strength biases information processing and evaluation on the web? *Computers in Human Behavior, 60*, 245–252.

Weaver, R., & Frederick, S. (2012). A reference price theory of the endowment effect. *Journal of Marketing Research, 49*(5), 696–707. https://doi.org/10.1509/jmr.09.0103.S2CID412119

Westerwick, A., Johnson, B. K., & Knobloch-Westerwick, S. (2017). Confirmation biases in selective exposure to political online information: Source bias vs. content bias. *Communication Monographs, 84*(3), 343–364.

Wood, T., & Porter, E. (2018). The elusive backfire effect: Mass attitudes' steadfast factual adherence. *Political Behavior*, 1–29. https://doi.org/10.1007/s11109-018-9443-y

Zeelenberg, M., & Beattie, J. (1997). Consequences of regret aversion 2: Additional evidence for effects of feedback on decision making. *Organizational Behavior and Human Decision Processes, 72*(1), 63–78.

Zhao, H., Fu, S., & Chen, X. (2020). Promoting users' intention to share online health articles on social media: The role of confirmation bias. *Information Processing & Management, 57*(6), 102354. https://doi.org/10.1016/j.ipm.2020.102354

Cognitive Inertia as a Fundamental Cause of Institutional Inertia

Ali Hussein Samadi, Alireza Raanaei, and Mojtaba Panahi

1 Introduction

First time, Giambattista Vico (1668–1744) used the term ‘institution’ in his book ‘Scienza Nuov’ (1725). Since then, the ‘institution’ has been widely used in the literature. This term has been used by different schools of thought (for example: American Institutionalism, Austrian School, German historical School, French regulation school, Structuralism, etc.) and different fields of science including Economics, Sociology, Philosophy, and Political Science, and also based on it, various scientific topics have been explained and analyzed.

‘Rule, order, and regularity’ which organizing factor of human societies can be seen as a common feature in different definitions of the institution, which are used by different schools and fields of analysis. Institutional analysis covers a wide range: from environmental crisis problems to the poverty of nations, from political elections to economic development, from traffic laws to language. According to Elinor Ostrom (2005, 2010, 2011, 2019) these institutional analysis has three levels: framework, model, and theory.

The discourse of “development” is one of the fields that explain “institution” as the main cause of development and economic growth of nations. Against backdrop of this framework, innovation, capital accumulation or education are not the cause of development and growth, rathe as North said: they “are not causes of growth; they are growth” (North & Thomas, 1973, p. 2) or as Acemoglu et al. (2005) these are proximate causes, but not fundamental, as a result ‘Institutions’ are fundamental cause of development and growth. Therefore, developing countries must make institutional reforms to achieve development. Prior to institutional reforms, it is important to consider institutional changes. Because institutional reforms are in

A. H. Samadi (✉) · A. Raanaei · M. Panahi
Department of Economics, Shiraz University, Shiraz, Iran
e-mail: asamadi@rose.shirazu.ac.ir

N. Faghih, A. H. Samadi (eds.), *Institutional Inertia*, Contributions to Economics,
https://doi.org/10.1007/978-3-031-51175-2_7

accordance with human will and desire to achieve a goal, but institutional changes are the natural path of institutional transformation. The former is human will and the latter is historical destiny. In fact, institutional reforms should be able reorient institutional changes towards the desired goal (development and growth). How do institutions change? Are there obstacles to institutional change or reform? What are those obstacles and how can they be solved?

Efficiency, effectiveness, and economic development are often related to a country's institutional quality. If countries do not enjoy a decent institutional quality or framework, the next step would be the implementation of the policy-related prescription of "institutional reforms". The evidence and experience in different countries reveal that institutional reforms have not always resulted in a desirable outcome but have frequently resulted in failure or an adverse institutional status compared with the initial status; this phenomenon is called the "vicious cycle" (Acemoglu & Robinson, 2012; e Cunha & Tsoukas, 2015; Ghimire, 2021).

Focusing on institutional reforms and changes raises the question of the origin of institution. First of all, one must know what the institution is, and then one must examine how it changes, so that it can be modified to achieve social goals. Most of the researches have dealt with the role of culture, traditions, beliefs, customs, etc. on the formation of the institution, but this research only relates the formation of the institution to another elements, which is not clear from what they were formed. The next question is how the factors of institution formation such as rules and beliefs are formed? The role of cognitive factors in the formation of the institution is brought up, which has been less discussed. In fact, the institution has two general dimensions, one at the cognitive level and one at the external level.

The institutional reforms' failure represents that the creation of an institutional structure is impossible, disregarding the nature of institutions. In institutional reforms, one has to bear in mind that institutions evolve by its essence and change and have dynamic behavior. Institutional changes basically refer to the institutions' origins. Institutional changes and their evolving are related to how they have come into being. Douglas North, Daron Acemoglu, and Avner Grief are institutionalist economists who have taken the issue of institutions' origins into account.

Different theories have elaborated on institutional origins, developments, and changes,[1] among which the role of "cognitive factors" in institutions' creation pursued by institutional evolution has been rarely taken into account. Although little attention is given regarding to the beliefs' impact on the formation of institutions in the new institutionalism compared with the old institutionalism, this does not imply that the eminence if the belief system has been obliterated, rather the eminence of the belief system and cultural norms are analyzed differently. North (2010, p. 42) emphasizes that "the growing literature of the new institutional economics makes abundantly clear that institutions must be explained in terms of the intentionality of humans". North (2010) believes that the beliefs' system and institutional framework are closely related, stating that "belief systems embody the internal representation of

[1] To read more about the theories of institutional change, refer to Samadi and Alipourian (2021a).

the human landscape. Institutions are the structure that humans impose on that landscape in order to produce the desired outcome. Belief systems therefore are the internal representation and institutions the external manifestation of that representation" (North, 2010, p. 49).

There exist numerous definitions for institutions. The current chapter seeks not to get involved with these miscellaneous definitions (see Samadi & Alipourian, 2021a). The objective of this chapter is to evaluate the association of institutions and cognitive factors. Following Aoki (2011), two contentious explanations of institutions can be considered. (1) Institutions imply regularity of behaviors or actions. (2) Institutions act as a social-cognitive aspect, including shared beliefs, knowledge, etc., creating order and behavior regularity. This difference is due to the distinction of the structural/agent-oriented approach to institutions. In the former, institutions are restrictions on human behavior that are imposed by an external factor (for example government), order and regularize individual and social behavior (such as formal laws). But in the latter, institutions are the product of an evolutionary process that appear spontaneously, without an external factor imposing them on human communities (such as norms or social habits). The second explanation, the cognitive approach to institutions, is classified into two sub-categories of mental attitudes vs. materialistic attitudes to institutions. Mental attitude focuses on individuals' internal states such as shared beliefs (Aoki, 2011), collective intentionality (Searle, 2005), and group-mind (Douglas, 1986).

Materialistic attitude focuses on external artifacts such as organizations, money, and symbols that carry some social meanings and generate specific expectations in actors' minds. The following questions are raised: what is artifacts' creation based on in the materialistic attitude? What is their validity based on cognitive aspects? Can artifacts be generated prior to behavioral models? Aoki (2011) responded to these inquiries and concluded that institutions are social artifacts that have the role of media regarding the strategic interactions of actors and their beliefs in social games with respect to cognitive aspects.

The relationship between mental attitudes and materialistic attitudes is as follows: mental beliefs are formed based on the cognitive faculty of humans, then based on mental beliefs, artifacts are formed in the external and social environment. Actually, artifacts are representations of mental beliefs. On the other hand, when the artifacts are formed and established, in a reversed state, individual's minds (in a subjective process) perceive the artifacts (as an object). The explanations are shown in Fig. 1.

Institutional analysis takes place based on cognitive factors, such as the ignored fields of institutionalism. Although Searle, Hayek, and North comprehensively took this issue into consideration, this field is still in its initial stages. We cannot provide an accurate conclusion about institutions' formation, performance, and disintegration without paying attention to the cognitive foundations of institutions (George et al., 2006). Cognitive dimensions are the basis of institutionalism. Consideration of the cognitive features of the institutional environment is the main differentiating property of the new institutionalism. Although scholars believe that an individual's cognition has a role in institutional theory, no convincing and reasonable explanation has been provided regarding how this cognition forms the institutional environment.

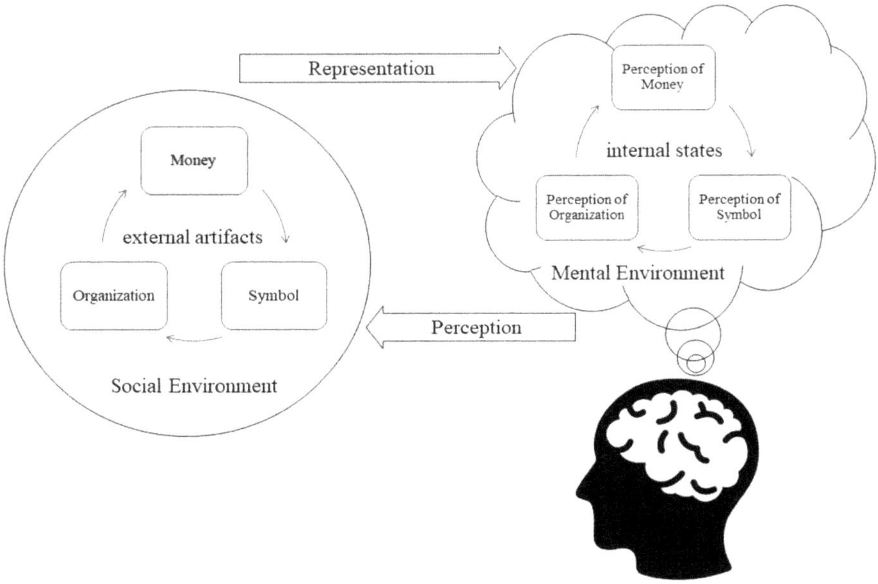

Fig. 1 Mental attitudes vs materialistic attitudes. (Source: Authors' own figure)

Institutional inertia refers to a state that institutions either change slowly or are resistant to change.[2] Zantvoort (2017) argues that it is a privilege that people follow some rules without making questions about them since it results in complicated social behaviors. Human beings create "mental models", and regularity-based institutions overcome the surrounding environment and organize the society towards higher efficiency. Psychologically, human beings give an intrinsic value to mental models. Human beings stick to their beliefs and mental models even when encountering contradictory evidence. So, even if institutions show dysfunction, they are not able to be altered easily since they have been stabilized in individuals' mental models. Zantvoort (2017) asserts that following the regularities by habit proves the existence of cognitive inertia, creating an unreasonable inclination to support beliefs even when changing the beliefs is a necessity. Thus, institutional inertia is caused by behavior based on bounded rationality and individuals' emotional and psychological status in unsuitable and ineffective institutions and mental models.

The inertia of institutionalized rules for change is the outcome of rational trade-off of efficiency and reconciliation. Since the calculation of the optimal consequences in different situations is extortionate and unproductive, blindly pursuing the rules may be economically rational. If we are obliged to continuously negotiate about new rules with our fellow men in all situations, we cannot carry out our

[2]To read more about the concept of institutional inertia, refer to Chapter "An Introduction to Institutional Inertia: Concepts, Types and Causes" of this book.

everyday collective actions. Our innate dependence on specific rules for our goals augments the social life stability. However, institutional inertia is not only created by irrational social behavior, but it can be elaborated on through interpreting more rational political institutions. Institutional inertia is not only a social development feature, but it is an innate feature of institutional performance. Inertia is a structural property of organizations possessing a specific resistance level to alternation, which is significant for political institutions in particular as their effectiveness and legitimacy are broadly dependent on their stabilization in social norms. Thus, political institutions are susceptible to inertia.

Briefly, scholars like Douglas North, John Searle, and Friedrich von Hayek assume cognitive factors significant components in institutional formation and evolution. Thus, cognitive factors should be specifically taken into account for the evaluation of institutional inertia. Moreover, cognition may also face inertia. Thus, this chapter inquires cognitive inertia as the major cause of institutional inertia. To attain prosperous and efficient institutional reforms, this restriction should be omitted. Cognitive inertia is the inclination to a specific orientation in the way individuals contemplate about an issue or belief and their strategy against change. The current chapter seeks to elaborate on the effect of cognitive inertia mechanisms on institutional inertia and does not consider factors causing cognitive inertia.[3] If it is explained that cognitive factors play an essential role in the formation of the institution, then this hypothesis is proved that it is not possible to make efficient institutional reform in the superstructure layer without changing the substructure layer. Institutional resistance to changes and reforms is called institutional inertia. According to the relationship between the institution and cognitive factors, it can be said that cognitive inertia is the cause of the formation of institutional inertia, and the latter cannot be corrected until the former is resolved.

The rest of this chapter is organized as follows: Section 2 defines institution and its synonyms and related concepts to institutional inertia. The objective is to show its significance regarding the ineffectiveness of institutional reforms and the impact of cognitive inertia on institutional inertia. Section 2 assesses how cognitive and institutional inertia can elaborate on institutional changes. The last part of Sect. 2 assesses this gap with regard to bounded rationality and choice theory. Section 3 discusses the association of cognitive inertia with institutional inertia. To perceive cognitive inertia and assess its formation causes, cognitive discussions regarding humans' perception of the surrounding environment should be addressed. The significant issue in humans' perception of their surrounding is the use of mental models. Section 3 mainly focuses on this topic. Emphasizing on humans' perception and cognitive factors regarding their surrounding does not imply that the cognitive analysis of institutional inertia results from a partial or an individualistic view. Section 3 demonstrates that the cognitive analysis of institutional evolutions occurs in a social substrate. Friedrich Hayek, the reputable advocate of the Austrian economics, developed his institutional theory based on cognitive theory, which is

[3]To read more about the factors affecting cognitive inertia, refer to this chapter of this book.

indeed neglected in economics. At the end of Sect. 3, the relevance of sensory and institutional order is discussed. Section 4 presents the conclusion.

2 Institutions, Institutional Changes, and Institutional Inertia: Concepts

Institutions have been defined differently. Their comprehensive definitions are not reviewed in this section[4] (see Samadi & Alipourian, 2021a, b). North (1990) assumes institutions as constraints established by humans that structure interactions, establish order, and reduce uncertainty in exchanges. Institutions form the motivational structure of an economy, i.e., institutions are rules of the game in a society (North, 1990). However, in his book *Understanding the Process of Economic Change*, North (1991) counts on cognitive rules in institutions' functions (North, 1991, p. 97). However, these definitions are related to old institutionalism, mainly founded on humans' perception power and intellectuality. Since it is basically relevant to the mind and contemplation aspect, it can be beneficial to be addressed regarding the association of cognitive and institutional inertia. John R. Commons (1899) confirmed that institutions form people's individuality, stating that people are actually institutionalized minds (Commons, 1934). Veblen also confirmed that institutions are prevalent intellectual habits (Veblen, 1899; Veblen & Samuels, 2017). Hamilton (1932) believed that institution is a conventional thinking procedure which is hidden in the customs of a group or ethnicity, stating that a thinking way is innately an institution. According to the definitions of North and the old institutionalism economists, an institution's advocate resembles a game's rules, habits of thought, and individual thinking ways. The medium between institution, as habits of thought (the shared feature of old institutionalists), and institution, as the rules of the game (North's definition), is the elaboration of the significance of rule. Hodgson (2006) referred to this issue in his definition of institution, defining institution as a system of established and prevalent social rules which structure social interactions.

After emphasizing the cognitive and thought aspect of institutions, the concept of *institutional inertia*[5] will be evaluated. There exist other terms and concepts in institutional economics in addition to institutional inertia which are synonymous with inertia or closely related. Institutional inertia addresses the institutions' stickiness and resistance against changes (Munck af Rosenschöld et al., 2014, p. 640), i.e., resistance against certain reforms and changes. *Institutional rigidity* means situations or states where institutions must change but do not change or do not have conditions for change (Haase et al., 2009). Acemoglu et al. (2021) also talked

[4] To read more about the concept of institutions, refer to Samadi and Alipourian (2021a, b).

[5] To read more about the concept of institutional inertia, institutional rigidity, and institutional stasis refer to Chapter "An Introduction to Institutional Inertia: Concepts, Types and Causes" of this book.

about institutions' strategic stability and *institutional stasis*. Institutions' strategic stability takes place when institutions preserve the status quo as they fear subsequent changes and less productivity following preliminary reforms. Institutional stasis is the plainest form of institutional continuity. Institutional stasis is an unchangeable state of institutional balance, i.e. institutional arrangements that we begin with occur frequently. There are numerous reasons for institutional stasis, the most important of which is that power begets power. In other words, power creates further power, i.e. groups empowered through current institutions benefit from these institutions, hence using their power to preserve them and regenerate their power over upcoming institutions. However, Acemoglu et al. (2021) argue that despite the popularity of ideas based on institutional stasis in economics and politics literature, institutions are mainly in a perpetual status of oscillation and successive alternations; however, their course may still be formed by old institutional choices. Thus, there exists path dependency, showing that it may indicate the initial terms of subsequent institutions' paths and their reaction to impulses. Although there are instances of institutional stasis and many economists' and political scientists' intellectuality is formed through such dynamics, institutional stasis is scarce. In lieu, many institutions are experiencing a perpetual fluctuation. A decent approach is presented with regard to the concept of path dependency change, through which present institutions indicate the future path of institutional changes because of internal dynamics and because minor differences may bring about large divergences when reacting to impulses. Path dependency must not be confused with inertia. North (2010) argues that path dependency is not an inertia but constraint on present choices caused by past historical experiences. Path dependency refers to the fact that a society's past historical choices shape its current possibilities and capacities. For example, if a society, throughout its history, had an autocratic monarchy, in which neither property rights were recognized nor even legislation could limit the authority of the king, such a society would have limited possibilities for legislation and following the law at the political and social level. On the contrary, if a society has experienced a constitutional monarchy throughout its history, it will have more possibilities and capacities to implement various legislations to improve the quality of life and promote social welfare. It may seem that although institutional inertia is different from path dependency, but the latter can play a role in the formation of the former. This assumption is correct, but these two should not be confused with each other. These two societies, regardless of their background and path dependency, may be involved in various institutional inertia for different reasons: legislation, uncertainty, cognitive inertia, etc.

It is concluded that institutional stickiness is a synonym to institutional inertia but an opposite of institutional stasis. Institutional inertia is consistent with institutional oscillations and changes. It is emphasized in the institutional inertia that they do not move towards the desirable reforms and face some barriers. However, institutional inertia does not imply lack of changes or institutional stasis. Thus, Acemoglu's analysis of institutional stasis is not mutually exclusive with regard to institutional inertia.

As previously mentioned, a reason for the significance of cognitive factors in institutional inertia is the requirement for institutional changes and reforms. Among different theories addressing institutional changes[6] and reforms, one group focuses on cognitive factors. Kingston and Caballero (2009) presented five widespread approaches to conceptualization of institutional change: (1) Some theories consider decentralization a principle and take developmental institutional changes into account; (2) Some theories consider centralization and evaluate institutional changes via an intentional political process; (3) Some theories consider the interaction between formal and informal rules a criterion, based on which they evaluate institutional changes; (4) Institutional equilibrium approach; (5) Some theories emphasize cognitive factors' role. In all institutional change theories, institutions are the resultant of purposive and intentional solutions to human-related issues. Human beings attempt to respond to these issues via restricted rationality and deficient information in a changing and complicated environment. Thus, the procedure through which people process information and solve problems may affect the essence of institutional changes (Kingston & Caballero, 2009).

North (2010) proposed five statements responding to the inquiry how institutions change:

1. Competition is the key factor for institutional change.
2. Competition makes organizations invest in skills and knowledge frequently to survive. Individuals' skills and knowledge and their organizations form their perceptions about opportunities and thus choices which incrementally change institutions.
3. The institutional framework motivates the dictation of the types of skills and knowledge perception to attain the maximum pay-off.
4. Perceptions are derived from the mental constructs of the players.
5. The diversity of production and integrated economies and the external effects of the network of an institutional matrix develop institutional changes to a great extent and make them path-dependent.

Statement 4 is mostly associated with cognitive factors. Individuals' perception of their surrounding is the key to their choices. Individuals' choices are dependent on their minds' interpretation of the information received. Economics simply neglects the inquiry of where individuals' perception comes from through the presumption of the rationality of actors and that they know what they do. North (2010) emphasized that the presumption of rationality or having a rational choice might be correct in evaluating the cost of an opportunity in a marketplace, but "this may be true in evaluating opportunity costs at the supermarket, but it is wildly incorrect when it comes to making more complicated choices in a world of incomplete information and of subjective models used to interpret that incomplete information" (North, 2010, p. 64).

[6]To read more about the different theories of institutional change, refer to Samadi and Alipourian (2021).

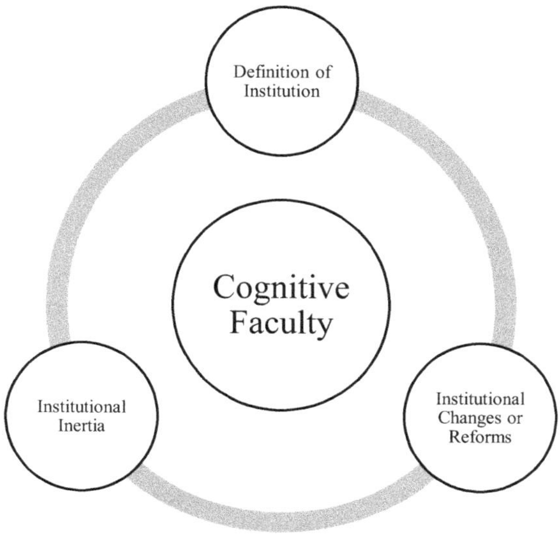

Fig. 2 Cognitive faculty and institutional issues. (Source: Authors' own figure)

The cognitive aspect of the institution is not limited to the definition of the institution, but actually, by identifying the cognitive dimensions of the institution, this characteristic is also extended to all issues related to the institution (institutional dynamics), such as institutional changes and institutional inertia. The cognitive dimensions of institutions can be examined independently both in institutional inertia and in institutional changes. In this way, it is possible to examine the hypothesis that cognitive inertia is the cause of the formation of institutional inertia, and also to test the proposition that prior to the implementation of institutional changes or reforms, changes in mental beliefs must be achieved. However, the key point is that the mental and cognitive aspect is a common feature of the institution, institutional inertia and institutional change. (See Fig. 2).

Economics is assumed a true science based on the theory of choice with outstanding progressions; however, conventional (orthodox) economics neglects the substrate where choices are made. The homo economicus selects from among the alternatives generated by the human mind a priori. People choose based on their perception of the surrounding environment.

The rationality assumption disregards the evaluation of the association of the mind and the surrounding environment. The rational choice is not the outcome of an individual's thought but is achieved through the intricacy of the thought process in a broad institutional and social substrate.

3 Cognitive Inertia and Institutional Inertia

3.1 Institutions and Cognitive Factors

Institutional economics is founded on human choice theories. Institutionalists reject the neoclassical assumption that an economic person's personality is conscious, atomized, and rational, and he always seeks maximization. In contrary, they found their reasoning on the theories of human choice. The modern psychology has offered different approaches for institutional economics to attain an improved understanding of institutions and institutional changes. Cognitive psychology enjoys abundant advances to have a suitable empirical perception of how individuals process information, allowing a better understanding of the basic complication of human choices and social processes.

Stein (1997) believes that despite the novel cognitive psychology findings, these findings have not yet become well prevalent in institutionalism, and the theory of institutionalism is founded on a deficient understanding of the human mind (Stein, 1997). Albeit institutionalism is almost coincident with the initial development of psychology, current developments of cognitive psychology have not affected institutionalism yet. Social analysis of the association of institutions and cognitive factors is essential as well since institutions are somehow individual mental construction as other social phenomena. Institutions influence the organization and selection of information. However, this does not imply that institutions can think or act, but it implies that they can influence humans' performance and then are affected by their actions; hence, an interaction is developed between institutions and activists. Institutions are as structuring principles that exist at the individual cognition level and also in social representations such as rules. Accordingly, the evaluation of cognitive dimensions' role is impossible without assuming the institutions' social aspects.

Economic actors perceive their surrounding world according to the mental models. They use these mental models to evaluate desired conditions for changing a certain rule. Eventually, as actors alter their mental models as they learn about their surroundings, it may even alter their perception of the impact of alternative rules and sets of possible alternative rules. So, mental models derived from human cognition are created. Cognitive rules form humans' mental and behavioral models. Generally, mental models are mental representations of objective, subjective, and social realities. Mental models are assumed a subset of cognitive representations, and any cognitive representation is not a mental model. Mental models visualize our surrounding world's knowledge. They are embedded in our cognitive system but are not programmed in our brains but are transferred by learning processes through imitation and formal and informal instructions. So, mental models may gradually alter, they may also enhance rules.

North (2010) described how humans look for making a mental model to elaborate on facts by an example. An experiment was conducted by Julian Feldman (TV show presenter); he asked guests to predict how many times the numbers 1 and 0 would occur in a sequence of 200 items. Although the presenter randomly indicated which number (0 or 1) would appear, the guests tried to make a pattern for prediction. This example reveals that even when there exists no model, people try to make a mental model to formulate and explain their surrounding world. Thus, the human mental network acts according to a cognitive model and not merely rational arguments. North (2010, p. 26) stated that "thinking occurs in terms of synthesized patterns, not logic, and for this reason it may always exceed in its reach syntactical or mechanical relations".

Mental models are assumed a cognitive structure forming the foundation of reasoning, decision-making, and behaviors (Jones et al., 2011). Mental models are mental representation of objective realities, and mental representation of mental and social realities are the institutions and power structures (Rosenbaum, 2021). Mental models look like architectural models and physical diagrams with similar structures as the structure of the situation they represent. Although the mental models are subjective but not dependent on an individual, they follow intersubjectivity and are transferred through culture-based learning and imitation processes. Hence, they vary over time when we learn about new issues. When mental models change, institutions will certainly and subsequently change because the actors' behavior and the reconstruction ways of these institutions have changed.

North (1981, 2010) pointed to the significance of cognitive rules in elaborating on the human behavior. He believes that institutions present an incentive structure to direct human behavior and structure human interactions. However, this motivational structure cannot be separate from the way of perceiving the world by the mind. On the one hand, institutions structure motivations which direct human behavior; on the other hand, this motivational structure relies on humans' perception of the environment.

The type and content of humans' perception of their surrounding is worth considering in the evaluation of institutional inertia based on cognitive factors. North (2010) argued that humans' perceptions are mental constructs originating from present-time and historical experiences; these perceptions are not isolated from learning. Learning is not merely an accumulation of experiences in the life. He discusses that we must be familiar with the human learning content and how it is shared in the society and changes over time since excess learning structures the culture of a society. It is noteworthy that although institutions are made based on cognitive factors, they rely on the institutional structure that is a combination of formal rules, informal constraints, and functional and executive specifications of institutions. Cognitive factors make possible the humans' perception of their surrounding environment. There exists a joint and dynamic connection between institutions and cognitive factors.

Institutions are established based on shared cognitive rules among human beings. They are social constructs that transfer information (social beliefs and expectations). They must be self-enforcing and self-confirming but not necessarily correct. Cognitive rules are not only based on empirical observations such as the winter-summer temperature difference but also involve beliefs about the nature like that the gravity of the moon is the cause of the tides or smoking induces cancer, i.e. people's beliefs since they are socially accepted cognitive rules.

Incentives that induce reactions are based on cognitive rules socially, i.e. people know that some actions bring about certain outcomes. For instance, if we work arduously, we will be successful, or if we pay tax, good consequences will be attained, and it is basically correct. Cognitive rules are the foundation of behavioral regularities established by institutions. Human beings cannot be acquainted with their surrounding world, their society, marketplaces, and the physical and biological world they live in without these social mechanisms (Greif & Mokyr, 2017).

Established and prevalent social rules in Hodgson's (2006) description of institution are shaped when individuals' beliefs become prevalent as shared and intersubjectively. Indeed, a person's belief obtained through cognitive power becomes a stable rule. Eventually, a system of these social rules forms an institution. Most institutions are stable through the way represented in mental models and reproduced through social interactions created by these models. Institutions are systems of social rules structuring social interactions (Hodgson, 2006). Meyer (2008) confirmed that concentration on the actors' knowledge and their knowledge accumulation do not imply ignorance of and not putting emphasis on the social structure. The social accumulation of knowledge that a society's members share at varying levels originates from old generations' experiences. Man is born in a socio-historical environment. Luckmann (1983) claims that institutionalized classifications make available interpretive frameworks, actors' positions, patterns of action, etc. Therefore, it plots the borders and horizon that people can meaningfully act; beyond these borders and horizon, seeing or understanding is impossible. Interests, preferences, rationalities, choices, and imaginable decisions are within these borders. Innovations, crises, shocks, or change stimulators ought to be interpreted within this horizon to be assumed and have an influence (Luckmann, 1983).

Regarding the impact of social structure, North (2010, p. 61) argues that "the mental constructs individuals form to explain and interpret the world around them are partly a result of their cultural heritage, partly a result of the local everyday problems they confront and must solve, and partly a result of non-local learning. The mix between these sources in interpreting one's environment obviously varies as between for example a Papuan tribesman on the one hand and an economist in the United States on the other (although there is no implication that the latter's perceptions are independent of his or her cultural heritage)."

According to Rosenbaum (2021), institutions should be evaluated from a mental perspective to assess their effect on human behavior. Actors may pursue an institutional rule only when they are aware of it. They may decide not to pursue a rule when they are aware of it. However, conscious pursuation of a rule may sometimes turn into a habit. Actors pursue a rule only when they are aware of it. We cannot imagine an actor who pursues a rule without having awareness about it (Lawson, 1994; Searle, 2005). It is necessary to note that a rule that people are aware of sometimes becomes a habit, so actors do it as a repetitious act (Dequech, 2013). Nevertheless, habits do not negate the principle that people are aware of the rule, because one can gain awareness about a habit, and it is subsequently ignored if it creates an unanticipated or negative result.

Besides the connection between institutions and cognitive factors, cognitive institutions should also be taken into account. Petracca and Gallagher (2020) assume cognitive institutions created based on the mind philosophy with certain social, institutional, and normative dimensions. Cognitive institutions enable actors to pursue certain cognitive processes in social aspects. Also, actors basically may not pursue cognitive processes without cognitive institutions. They asserted that the market is even an economic cognitive institution.

Friedrich Hayek (Nobel prize-winning Austrian school economist) also discussed about cognitive factors' impact on institutions' formation in detail. Hayek can be taken into consideration with Douglas North and John Searle in terms of attending to cognitive factors.

There are three perspectives through which we may link Hayek's (2011) cognitive and institutional theories:

1. Sensory order that is an deficient representation of physical order. There are limitations to what the human mind may be aware of in this process similar to limitations in the process of knowledge from experience.
2. Since the mind renovates its understanding from the surrounding environment, sensory order comprises a fixed learning process. The learning process occurs via cognitive abilities' channel, hence, affecting institutions' behavior. The continuation, retrogression, and evolution of institutions are dependent on how much they have been effective in their formation and knowledge sharing.
3. The connection between mental models and knowledge diffusion should be considered. Our perception of the surrounding world is mostly derived from the representations of the world outside. The human mind filters the world through his mental models and also learns from the external world through language and norms. Thus, knowledge owns a social dimension, and most of what we know, we cannot talk about because they are covert in institutions, norms, and customs. Wenzel (2010) asserts that there is a link between Hayek's institutional and cognitive theory, and the institutional order originates from the cognitive order. Hence, Hayek's support of freedom is based on cognition, not utilitarianism nor a deontological perspective. Hayek (2012) confirms that people live in a world having two orders: the physical order of the surrounding world and the sensory order shaping our understanding of the physical order. He affirms that the physical order is objective, but the sensory order is subjective. Hayek elaborates on the association of the two orders, i.e. psychology explains the correspondence of a physical occurence with its mental imagery. He asserts that perception is always the physical world's interpretation, so it is subjective.

According to Hayek (2011), the mind is consistent with the natural and social environment humans live in and evolves in perpetual interaction with institutions determining the society' structure. The mind is a product of the social environment grown in, but it has not created it. It is rather something that has affected these institutions and altered them. There are some rules pursued by all persons because the environment represents itself in a similar way in people's mind.

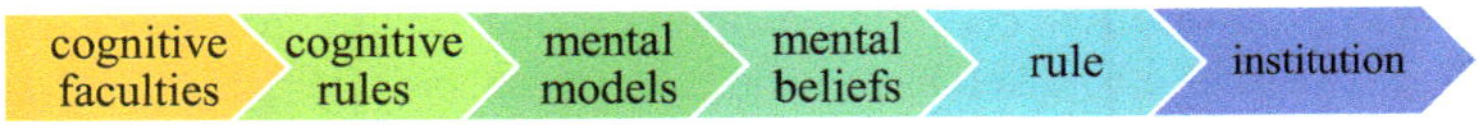

Fig. 3 Formation process of institution; from cognitive faculties to institution. (Source: Authors' own figure)

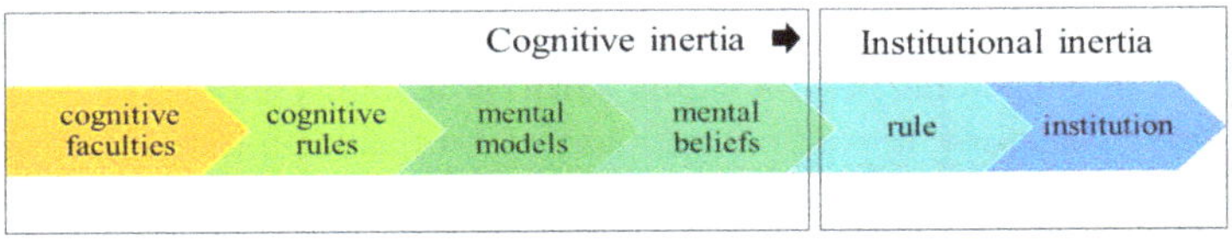

Fig. 4 From cognitive inertia to institutional inertia. (Source: Authors' own figure)

3.2 How Does Cognitive Inertia Result in Institutional Inertia?

Different studies have looked forward finding the sources of institutional inertia.[7] For instance, Munck af Rosenschöld et al. (2014) assumed five factors involved in institutional inertia's formation: costs, uncertainty, path dependency, power, and legitimacy. Genschel (1997) numerated three factors involved: sunk costs, political conflict, and uncertainty. The current chapter argues that cognitive inertia is the foundation for the formation of institutional inertia, and other factors originate from cognitive inertia to some extent, which can be attributed to the formation and roots of institutions. Since the institutions' origin is related to cognitive capacity, cognitive inertia emerging in the institution formation process is the foundation of institutional inertia. The present chapter merely discusses the relationship between cognitive inertia and institutional inertia.

Individuals attain a perception of their surrounding world according to their mental faculties. Of course, it is clear that there is no such thing as an institutional vacuum. Cognitive faculties always analyze the surrounding environment in an institutional framework. Humans generate mental and behavioral models in their minds to present a specific and coherent interpretation of phenomena in repeatous situations. The interpretation of the mental models' outcomes when becoming intersubjective and social can become a rule. When a sustained system is generated from these rules, new institution is emerged. In this mechanism, if there exists cognitive inertia from the mind to institution, an institutional inertia will be created.

Figure 3 displays the formation process of institution based on cognitive faculties.

If cognitive inertia is developed in this process, institutional inertia will be unddoubtedly created (Fig. 4).

The institutions' formation is based on cognitive faculties. Cognitive faculties generate cognitive rules and mental models, and actors perceive their surrounding

---

[7] To read more about the concept of institutional inertia, and sources of institutional inertia refer to Chapter "An Introduction to Institutional Inertia: Concepts, Types and Causes" of this book.

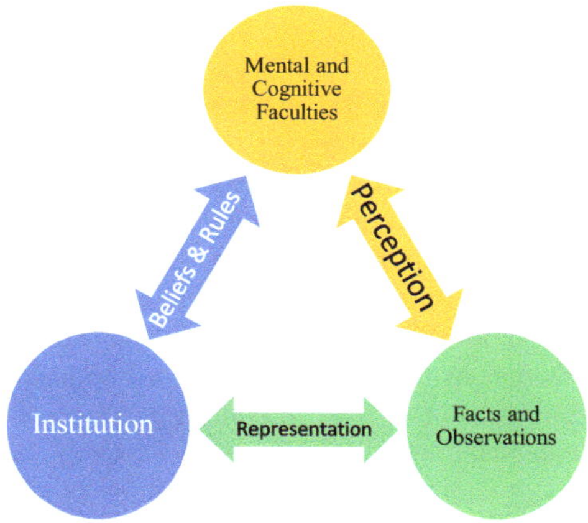

Fig. 5 Mind, observation and institution. (Source: Authors' own figure)

world based on these mental models, and their mental beliefs are formed. Social rules are developed on the basis of these individual mental beliefs based on which individuals organize their interactions. Ultimately, these social rules systematically form institutions. In this trend, regarding cognitive faculties and the human mind, the formation of cognitive inertia is feasible. This cognitive inertia may develop in any of the so-called phases. After the creation of cognitive inertia, the institutions' formation rules face dysfunction and in turn result in institutional inertia.

But what is cognitive inertia? What other factors affect the formation of institutional inertia besides cognitive inertia? Why does this chapter contends that cognitive inertia is the foundation of institutional inertia?

Cognitive inertia is the inclination to the duralabity of beliefs after formation. Cognitive inertia is basically the tendency of humans to maintain old beliefs even when new evidence does not support them, i.e. cognitive inertia explains the human's inclination to count on familiar assumptions and to be reluctant or incapable to alter those assumptions even when there is not supporting evidence or when other evidence questions their validity.

Mental and cognitive faculties of humans generate mental beliefs according to their perception of their observations and realities. These beliefs turn into rules and institutions. In cognitive inertia, mental models do not change and mentally formulate realities and observations based on old models even if new evidence does not advocate previous beliefs. New evidence and realities require novel institutions and rules. Movreover, institutions formed based on previous evidence cannot act properly in new situations. Therfore, institutional reforms are a necessity. So, mental models should alter first based on new evidence and then form the proper institution. Institutional reforms will fail even if they are applied imperatively without considering cognitive inertia because the media is from observations to institutions, minds, and cognitive rules. The mental faculties cannot perceive institutions applied as imperative reforms. Figure 5 depicts the association of the mind, observation, and institution.

4 Conclusion

The main idea of this chapter is based on the synthesis of institutional economics and behavioral economics. Institutions are a matter of the mind and mental beliefs are a matter of the institution. Individuals are institutionally embedded, Human behavior is largely governed by cognitive rules. As mentioned Hayek shows the choice process. He explains that the human mind shapes individual behavior. Individual reasoning differs from person to person, as it is based on subjective perceptions. The human mind is the product of the environment in which it has grown up. The mind emerges from the complexity of the connections between the physical world and the sensory world. The relationship between the structure and the agent is key to understanding the relationship between the institution and the mind. Institutions are structures, and individual actions as rule-following behavior are in agent level. Institutions interacts with and individual behaviors, the former influences the latter, and the latter shapes the former. The process enable the individuals to interact with external reality. Change in mental beliefs, change individual's actions, and finally change institutions. Thus "a key to understanding institutional evolution is an understanding of how individuals modify their mental models. Institutional evolution is an endogenous phenomenon with a cognitive dimension" (Teraji, 2018: p. xi). This chapter elaboarated on the institutional inertia with regard to the significance of institutional reforms. Then, it confirmed the definitions of North, Hodgson, and old institutionalists, showing the differences and similarities of institutional inertia with related concepts. Afterward, the importance of cognitive factors in the institutional changes' theories was emphasized. Ultimately, the institution formation mechanism was explained according to cognitive rules. Since there exists cognitive and mental inertia, this inertia will become institutional inertia as well. Institutions behave dynamically. In different situations, institutions may develop or show resistance against changes and remain stable. Alternations in various factors that influence institutions' dynamic behavior, directly or indirectly, can bring about change in the institutions. However, the changes in these factors do not result in institutional changes since the institutional inertia hinders the influence of these factors and neutralizes deliberate reforms for institutional changes. Furthermore, institutional inertia inhibits institutions' transfer among societies and causes institutional changes to be extremely laborious.

Cognitive inertia is a fundamental cause of institutional inertia because it influences the institution's formation and development. For institutional reforms, we ought to take institutional inertia into account; secondly, its emergence causes should be considered. Thirdly, cognitive inertia must be specifically taken into consideration as the primary cause of institutional inertia, assuming all other causes. To overcoming institutional inertia, cognitive inertia must be overcomed to efficiently attain institutional reforms (Fig. 6).

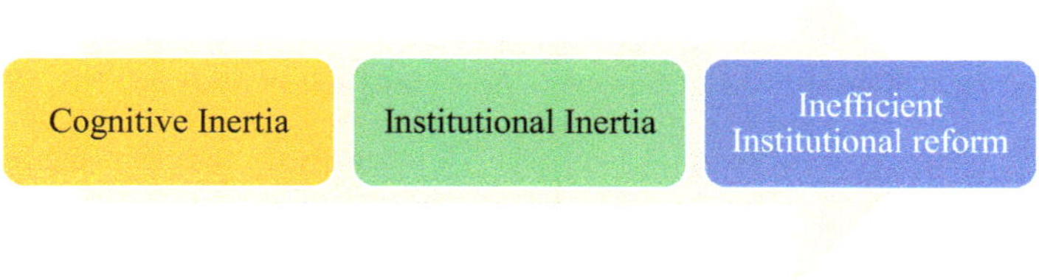

Fig. 6 Cognitive inertia, institutional inertia and institutional reform

References

Acemoglu, D., & Robinson, J. A. (2012). *Why nations fail: The origins of power, prosperity, and poverty*. Currency.

Acemoglu, D., Johnson, S., & Robinson, J. A. (2005). Institutions as a fundamental cause of long-run growth. In *Handbook of economic growth* (Vol. 1, pp. 385–472). Elsevier.

Acemoglu, D., Egorov, G., & Sonin, K. (2021). Institutional change and institutional persistence. In *The handbook of historical economics* (pp. 365–389). Elsevier.

Aoki, M. (2011). Institutions as cognitive media between strategic interactions and individual beliefs. *Journal of Economic Behavior & Organization, 79*(1–2), 20–34.

Commons, J. R. (1899). A sociological view of sovereignty. I. *American Journal of Sociology, 5*(1), 1–15.

Commons, J. R. (1934). *Institutional economics–Its place in political economy*. Macmillan.

Dequech, D. (2013). Economic institutions: Explanations for conformity and room for deviation. *Journal of Institutional Economics, 9*(1), 81–108.

Douglas, M. (1986). *How institutions think*. Syracuse University Press, Syracuse, NY.

e Cunha, M. P., & Tsoukas, H. (2015). Reforming the state: Understanding the vicious circles of reform. *European Management Journal, 33*(4), 225–229.

Genschel, P. (1997). The dynamics of inertia: Institutional persistence and change in telecommunications and health care. *Governance, 10*(1), 43–66.

George, E., Chattopadhyay, P., Sitkin, S. B., & Barden, J. (2006). Cognitive underpinnings of institutional persistence and change: A framing perspective. *Academy of Management Review, 31*(2), 347–365.

Ghimire, K. M. (2021). Natural disasters and weak government institutions: Creating a vicious cycle that ensnares developing countries. *Law and Development Review, 14*(1), 59–104.

Greif, A., & Mokyr, J. (2017). Cognitive rules, institutions, and economic growth: Douglass North and beyond. *Journal of Institutional Economics, 13*(1), 25–52.

Haase, M., Roedenbeck, M., & Söllner, A. (2009). A sketch of a mechanism-based explanation of cognitive path processes, lock-in of individual mental models and institutional rigidity. In *Methoden in der Betriebswirtschaftslehre* (pp. 21–46). Springer.

Hamilton, W. H. (1932). Institution. In *Encyclopedia of the social sciences* (Vol. 8, pp. 84–89). Macmillan.

Hayek, F. A. (2011). *Law, legislation and liberty, volume 1: Rules and order* (Vol. 1). University of Chicago Press.

Hayek, F. A. (2012). *The sensory order: An inquiry into the foundations of theoretical psychology*. University of Chicago Press.

Hodgson, G. M. (2006). What are institutions? *Journal of Economic Issues, 40*(1), 1–25.

Jones, N. A., Ross, H., Lynam, T., Perez, P., & Leitch, A. (2011). Mental models: An interdisciplinary synthesis of theory and methods. *Ecology and Society, 16*(1), 46.

Kingston, C., & Caballero, G. (2009). Comparing theories of institutional change. *Journal of Institutional Economics, 5*(2), 151–180.
Lawson, C. (1994). The transformational model of social activity and economic analysis: A reinterpretation of the work of JR Commons. *Review of Political Economy, 6*(2), 186–204.
Luckmann, T. (1983). *Life-world and social realities*. Heinemann Educational Publishers.
Meyer, R. E. (2008). New sociology of knowledge: Historical legacy and contributions to current debates in institutional research. In *The SAGE Handbook of Organizational Institutionalism* (pp. 519–538). Sage.
Munck af Rosenschöld, J., Rozema, J. G., & Frye-Levine, L. A. (2014). Institutional inertia and climate change: A review of the new institutionalist literature. *Wiley Interdisciplinary Reviews: Climate Change, 5*(5), 639–648.
North, D. C. (1981). *Structure and change in economic history*. Norton.
North, D. C. (1990). *Institutions, institutional change and economic performance*. Cambridge University Press.
North, D. C. (1991). Institutions. *Journal of Economic Perspectives, 5*(1), 97–112.
North, D. C. (2010). *Understanding the process of economic change*. Princeton University Press.
North, D. C., & Thomas, R. P. (1973). *The rise of the western world: A new economic history*. Cambridge University Press.
Ostrom, E. (2005). Doing institutional analysis digging deeper than markets and hierarchies. In *Handbook of new institutional economics* (pp. 819–848). Springer.
Ostrom, E. (2010). Institutional analysis and development: Elements of the framework in historical perspective. In *Historical developments and theoretical approaches in sociology* (Vol. 2, pp. 261–288). EOLSS Publications.
Ostrom, E. (2011). Background on the institutional analysis and development framework. *Policy Studies Journal, 39*(1), 7–27.
Ostrom, E. (2019). Institutional rational choice: An assessment of the institutional analysis and development framework. In *Theories of the policy process* (pp. 21–64). Routledge.
Petracca, E., & Gallagher, S. (2020). Economic cognitive institutions. *Journal of Institutional Economics, 16*(6), 747–765.
Rosenbaum, E. (2021). Mental models and institutional inertia. *Journal of Institutional Economics*, 1–18. https://doi.org/10.1017/S174413742100059X
Samadi, A. H., & Alipourian, M. (2021a). Institutions and institutional change: Concepts and theories. In *Dynamics of institutional change in emerging market economies* (pp. 107–132). Springer.
Samadi, A. H., & Alipourian, M. (2021b). Measuring institutional quality: A review. In *Dynamics of institutional change in emerging market economies* (pp. 143–171). Springer.
Searle, J. R. (2005). What is an institution? *Journal of Institutional Economics, 1*(1), 1–22.
Stein, J. (1997). How institutions learn: A socio-cognitive perspective. *Journal of Economic Issues, 31*(3), 729–740.
Teraji, S. (2018). *The cognitive basis of institutions: A synthesis of behavioral and institutional economics*. Academic.
Veblen, T. (1899). *The theory of the leisure class*. Oxford University Press.
Veblen, T., & Samuels, W. J. (2017). *The place of science in modern civilization and other essays*. Routledge.
Wenzel, N. G. (2010). An institutional solution for a cognitive problem: Hayek's sensory order as foundation for Hayek's institutional order. In *The social science of Hayek's 'The Sensory Order'*. Emerald Group Publishing Limited.
Zantvoort, B. (2017). Political inertia and social acceleration. *Philosophy & Social Criticism, 43*(7), 707–723.

Part III
Organizational Inertia

Overview of Institutional–Organizational Inertia Nexus

Adeleke Oladapo Banwo, Henry Omache, and Josiah Chukwuma Ngonadi

1 Introduction

Organizations and institutions undergo diverse transformations and evolutions due to forces of change in the internal and external environment. Though the organization-institution nomenclature might differ across disciplines, they are still subject to uncertainties and environmental influences (Aksom, 2022; McGinty, 2021). The response and reactions to these forces and influences vary and sometimes result in change, resistance, and different forms of inertia.

In recent times, the forces of change and inertia[1] arise because of the current winds of disruptive change occasioned by a global pandemic, recession, declining profitability, uncertainties in the business environment, rising levels of unemployment, technological innovations, labor supply, the emergence of the new face of work, organizational design and structure. The facets and dimensions of disruptive change continue to permeate all facets of life in social contexts with shades of the positive and negative effects on different stakeholders (Banwo et al., 2021; Faghih & Samadi, 2021). Institutions and organizations are seen as complementary and used interchangeably. This study aims at providing an overview of institutional –

[1]To read more about the concept of inertia, refer to Chapter "" of this book.

A. O. Banwo (✉)
Doctoral Supervision, KMU Akademie & Management AG, Linz, Austria

Faculty of Management Studies, Islamic University In Uganda, Mbale, Uganda

H. Omache
School of Business, Uganda Christian University, Mukono, Uganda

J. C. Ngonadi
School of Finance and Economics, Jiangsu University, Zhenjiang, China

N. Faghih, A. H. Samadi (eds.), *Institutional Inertia*, Contributions to Economics,
https://doi.org/10.1007/978-3-031-51175-2_8

organizational inertia nexus through an expository perspective of how inertia could have positive and negative benefits. The first section provides an overview of Institutional inertia[2]; the second section consists of an organizational-institutional nexus literature review. In the third section, the inertia dimension confluence and the importance of institutional-organizational age and size dynamics are discussed. The fourth section provides insights into the spheres of inertia using Rumelt (1995) work on inertia and transformation. The last section provides insights and conclusions.

2 Overview of Institutional-Organizational Inertia

Scholars have continually used diverse perspectives and theories to decipher and postulate the change–institutional inertia nexus (Armenta et al., 2022; Jerger et al., 2019; Kang et al., 2020). It is glaring that the construct and dimensions attest to the non-uniformity in views on institutional inertia vis-a-vis the constant flurry of change forces. The extant literature attests to the diverse perspectives that scholars have used in construing this multidisciplinary construct. Efforts at conceptualizing inertia have continued to vary across the research spectrum. Attempts at defining inertia reflect non-uniformity across studies. These variations arise from the simple premise that inertia is sometimes used interchangeably with organizational change.

Munck af Rosenschöld et al. (2014) define inertia as a situation that arises when institutions slowly resist the forces of change. Organizational inertia[3] refers to when an organization prefers to maintain the status quo in its operations, organizational structure, strategies, and practices and chooses to change incrementally instead of succumbing to external environmental changes (Jui-Chan et al., 2020). In the telecommunications and healthcare domain, institutional inertia is presumed to act as a barrier to adaptation, limit policy change, and foster an environment that does not favor change (Genschel, 1997). Rumelt (1995) conceptualization of inertia shows that "Inertia is the strong persistence of existing form and function". Woelders (2020) defines inertia as "the organizational change crisis that inhibits significant changes, which cause organizations to misalign with their respective external environment".

Attempting to define inertia would further confirm the complexity and evolving nature of the construct across disciplines and contexts. Despite the various typologies, inertia is inherent in humans and organisms and its semblance depicts a natural process that is essential, automatic, and inevitable depending on the nature of the forces of change (Zantvoort, 2015). The need for self-preservation is at the basic core

---

[2]To read more about the concept of institutional inertia, and sources of institutional inertia refer to Chapter "An Introduction to Institutional Inertia: Concept, Types and Causes" of this book.

[3]To read more about the some definitions of organizational inertia refer to Chapter "Trade and Institutional Inertia" of this book.

of cultures, economic agents, and societies and the state of inertia is transient with time.

On the flip side, formal and informal organizations and institutions pursuing diverse goals and objectives exist in every stratum of society regardless of the context. The multidisciplinary facet and dimensions of problems organizations solve and the cause remains a topical area of interest to different interest groups in the academia and organizational stakeholders. The organizational change ecology depicts a series of exchanges with the environment, selection process, adaptation process, and structural inertia (Abbott et al., 2016; Hannan & Freeman, 1989; Tucker et al., 1992).

Change is a constant factor in organizational studies and a major cause of organizational and institutional inertia. The level and rate of organizational changes and frequency of environmental changes can either cause or inhibit inertia in organizations. Untangling the organizational change construct remains complex despite the preponderance of organizational change literature and the realities in the organizational life- cycle (Bennis, 1965; Hughes, 2018; Khan et al., 2017; Kotter, 2012; Srivastava & Agrawal, 2020). For instance, several organizations still experience failures despite making efforts to implement some of the organizational change stages in practice. Some of the root causes of these failures may be due to the organizational context, organization structure, communication process, cognition, timing, distrust, lack of adequate information, competing interests, level of resistance, and inertia in different units. Inertia can also arise due to the mistake of non-considering the organizational behavior dynamics and poor adaptation to suit local context and needs (Huber et al., 1993).

Regardless of the perspective adopted, the pieces of literature on the continuum of organizational-institutional inertia reflect robust scholarly works aimed at shedding light on a different dimension and broadening understanding in different contexts (Ahlstrom et al., 2020; Islam, 2018).

Therefore, organizational and institutional studies should be construed using a broad and system perspective that investigates multiple push and pull factors that shape organizational behavior and resultant organizational inertia forms. For instance, human behavior dynamics, cognitions, structure, environment, culture, context, interests, and life cycles are soft and fundamental areas that shape and influences outcomes of organizational and institutional studies (Huber et al., 1993). Their connection and interface with institutions are interwoven and dependent on unlimited factors.

3 Organizational-Institutional Nexus

Understanding organizations and institutions are complex, changing, contextual and thus resulting in the formulation of endless theories and perspectives related to specific subsets of the organizations. Some of these include; organizational theory, organizational change (Stouten et al., 2018); organizational ecology (Abbott et al.,

2016); organizational structure (Burton & Obel, 2018); organizational environment (Boyd, 1990; Thompson, 1967); organizational Inertia, organizational culture (Schein, 1990), institutional theory (Peters, 2000; Zilber, 2017), the resource-based view (Hillman et al., 2009), boundary-spanning (Schotter et al., 2017), open and closed systems (Scott & Davis, 2015).

This raises the question of why organizational-institutional studies are complex given the preponderance of theories and scholarly literature across disciplines. We advance that the starting point to resolving this complexity requires understanding that the term organization is a general construct that exists in different forms and purposes within a given period. Common examples include formal organizations, informal organizations, open organizations, closed organizations, virtual organizations, government organizations, private organizations, non-governmental organizations, industry-based organizations, and social organizations. The defining features of these organizations and institutions are dependent on the activities of the principal stakeholders, economy, size, context, human cognitions, behaviors, and motives (Hoppmann et al., 2019). For instance, the forms and structures of informal and government organizations in developing countries are distinctly different from those in developed countries due to human factors, culture, and environment. The imperativeness of having a broad insight into the underlying human-environment nexus in organizational and institutional inertia studies remains topical. Thompson et al. (2017) reaffirmed that environmental turbulence can result in organizational structure inertia; a diverse environment provides threats and opportunities; environmental pressures and changes; disruptive shifts in the organizational environment could necessitate strands of organizational change. The environmental ambit of institutions and organizations is broad and comprises the regulatory, political, and business environment (Faghih & Sazegar, 2021). Likewise, the conceptualization of institutions is broad, multifaceted, and scholarly evidence attests to the non-uniformity in construing this concept. Banwo et al. (2021) emphasized that the evolution of institutions occurs through conscious and unconscious decisions, actions, and behaviors of economic agents that become the shared norms and culture that mold behaviors. However, the discourse on institutions and institutional change is incomplete without reference to the scholarly works and immense contributions of leading scholars in this domain. North (1991) defined Institution as "humanly devised constraints that structure political, economic and social interactions. They consist of both informal constraints (sanctions, taboos, customs, traditions and codes of conduct) and formal rules (constitutions, laws, property rights). This conceptualization has become the most widely cited and guiding framework for studies related to institutions and institutional change.

3.1 Inertia Dimension Confluence

Premised on the insight that the inertia dimension confluence is multidisciplinary, it might be a utopian task to discuss the facets in a single research. Nevertheless, we attempt to provide some insight and factors that can shape the construct. Within the confluence of institutional inertia are diverse premises, perspectives, and positions on how this construct can be viewed. For example, resistance to change, and institutional and organizational inertia is easily construed as negative. These preconceptions are shaped by popular extant literature and studies on organizational and institutional change (Faghih & Samadi, 2021; Micelotta et al., 2017; Woelders, 2020). We advocate using an onion model approach or systems method since it is important to view the varying perspectives and postulations. Using this approach can help broaden the understanding of the multiple facets of inertia and organizational change.

From primordial times, it is evident that disruptive, planned and normal changes have had good and bad consequences on human existence, the ecosystem, and economics (Schumpeter, 1942). Many cultures and institutions have resisted changes in a bid to preserve their heritage, protect their sovereignty, and reduce the negative effect of external disruptions on their way of life. Institutions and systems at the core are often modeled to have some form of inertia. For example, the judiciary system, government establishments such as the army, and other units that preserve the national integrity of an economy are not likely to change frequently.

At the individual level, it is sometimes impossible to adapt to every wind of change. For example, the human body is designed to resist unwanted changes that might negatively affect the body and the human cells produce antibodies to fight this to prevent infections and sicknesses.

In some situations, resistance to change and inertia have positive benefits for the individual or institution since it is impossible to adapt to the constant flurry of change. Suffice to assert that the need for survival, stability, and effective functioning of the institutions might be an underlying factor that makes inertia and resistance to change necessary.

It is possible to draw inferences from the dimension confluence of inertia domain in Fig. 1 below and posit that the inherent act of maintaining some levels of status quo is predicated on the organization structure, culture, operations, goals, human dynamics, and institutional and regulatory environment. The process of maintaining the status quo helps the organizations and stakeholders filter or resist the forces of change to decipher how to adapt or respond to the perceived risk from the external influences.

The inertia dimension confluence denotes some essential dimensions that should be considered in institutional-organizational inertia studies. Adopting a holistic approach broadens the knowledge of how the factors are interrelated and the soft factors that influence outcomes. Each dimension in the inertia dimension confluence represents a possible area of research and several scholarly studies have investigated and highlighted how they influence inertia and change. This micro-level and systematic approach offer perspectives on how the board of directors, biased managerial cognition, levels of incentive to change, institution size, context, organizational objectives, human behavior motivations, uncertainty and anxiety, sunk costs, social and political conflicts, stability and security, nature of institutional strategy,

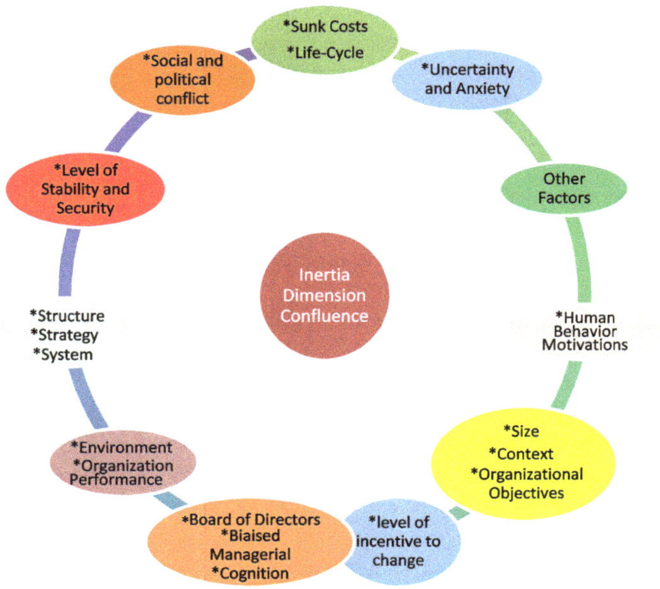

Fig. 1 Inertia dimension confluence
Source: Author's design

structure, systems, internal and external environment, organizational performance, life-cycle, and other factors shape inertia.

Gilbert (2005) attempted to unbundle inertia through the proposition that the perceptual dimension of threat is a major premise that shapes the two inertia dimensions of resource rigidity and process (routine) rigidity. The perception of threat is dependent on environmental scanning competencies, availability of resources, and response rate to change. Several scholars have attempted to investigate these dual dimensions using a microscopic lens to understand the combination of soft and hard factors. Several insights and dimensions of organizational inertia exist in the works of literature and scholars have attempted to unbundle these dimensions using different scopes and perspectives. Godkin and Allcorn (2008) posited that the nature of the tripartite forces of action, insights, and the nature of psychological influences are major hindrances to change in organizations. Using a system model perspective, this dimension considers the impact of time lag, environmental scanning competencies, timeliness of actions, and resultant decisions based on contextual and psychological forces.

Recent studies by Moradi et al. (2021) reinforce the scope of the organizational inertia dimensions to include structural and economic inertia based on (Haag, 2014) propositions about business model innovation and organizational performance. When a cue is taken from the big data study conducted in 27 European firms, it is seen that the dimensions of organizational inertia are multifaceted, complex, and contextual based on several factors. Mikalef et al. (2021) study showed that these dimensions include environmental factors such as political inertia, socio-cognition inertia, economic inertia, and technical inertia. It is pertinent to investigate and construe the dimensions of organizational inertia using a systematic model and change dynamics.

3.1.1 Triple Forces Underlying Institutional – Organizational Inertia

3.2 Institutional-Organizational Age Dynamics

Empirical evidence shows that the dimensions, sphere, and strength of forces of inertia would vary in organizations and institutions. The underlying triadic forces comprise age, size, and level of complexity which are construed to be major determinants of the level of institutional inertia (Hannan & Freeman, 1984). We expand on Hannan and Freeman (1984) proposition by advocating the need to adopt a microscopic view of the triadic forces and propose factors that need to be considered in each dimension.

Using a simple analogy, it is plausible to deduce that the age of existence of an entity or institution is likely to determine its level of inherent inertia and resistance to change. Moreover, the age dimension is broad and goes beyond how old or young an institution is and encompasses time, age range, year of establishment, available resources, context, level of experience, and technology (see Eqs. 1 and 2). For instance, an institution established in 1940 and an institution established in 2022 would ordinarily have two reactions and levels of inertia.

Hypothetically, the former is likely to have inertia institutionalized in its process and the latter is likely to have low resistance. Shinkle and Kriauciunas (2008) study on transition economies reveal that age is likely to have an asset value in developed environments compared to transition environments. They found that the age-size dimension has varying effects and inertia is inherent in older institutions and organizations in less developed environments. C.-A. Chen (2014) asserted that is important to always consider organizational age in organizational studies in resolving the various problems confronting organizations. The study also shows that organizational age dynamics are dependent on the stage or nature of the organizational ecology and adaptability. Since the dimension confluence of age is dynamic, we propose that the age variable can be represented in the equation

$$If = F(Ag + Sz + Cm + N) \tag{1}$$

Where
If = Institutional Inertia;
Ag = Age;
Sz = Size;
Cm = Complexity:

N = other variables;
F = Function

$$Ag = Cap + La + Es + Ar + C + Ex + At + Th + Obc + Lcg + N \tag{2}$$

Where:
Cap = Capabilities;
La = level of adaptability;
Es′ = ecology stage;
Ar = Available Resources;
C=Context;
Ex = Experience;
At = Available technology;
Time Horizon = Th;
Obc: Organizational Behavior and Culture;
Lcg = Level of Cognition
N = Other Internal and External Factors

From the above equation, the ambit of organizational, institutional age, and inertia nexus is influenced by diverse variables that vary in contexts. Organizational and institutional studies should not just view age or organizational life cycle using a nominal approach. Age is not just a number rather it has a concomitant relationship with other intervening variables. These variables determine and influence its nexus with inertia and change. Some studies show that older organizations develop inertia from their structures and the other variables as shown in Eq. 2.

Likewise, it is also possible for a young organization also to have a high level of inertia based on the dynamics of the variables. The interdependence of these variables and their outcomes should be critically considered using a system analogy. Interestingly, a microscopic overview of the variables can further shed light on why and how institutional inertia varies in institutions in the same context and different climes. Institutions have different capabilities and these capabilities might be inbuilt by design or acquired in the course of operations and existence (Valderrama-Ferrando, 2006). For instance, Government institutions sometimes have inherent capabilities derived from government funding, legislation, and established codes of conduct. Likewise, the level of capabilities derived by private institutions and organizations is dependent on an endless array of factors. Capabilities and competencies can be developed within different time frames (Pihkala et al., 2007; Živčicová & Gullerová, 2017). Nevertheless, the same institutions established in the same year might not develop the same capabilities. For instance, Universities established in the same year within a country or different countries might develop different capabilities due to other intervening variables within the context. It, therefore, does not suffice to assume that institutions have or do not have inertia without understanding how these soft intervening variables shaped their existence.

Similarly, the level of adaptability is a reflection of the robustness or rigidity of the institution and environmental forces. Institutions in volatile business environments are subject to an array of intervening push and pull variables that impact their ability to handle the forces of change and level of inertia. The sphere of inertia might be strong or weak due to inconsistencies in government policies, overbearing influences, dictates of international organizations, and a lack of required skill sets and resources. For example, the decision to introduce a new technology or automate the judiciary system in fragile or developing countries can be perceived as a good intention and yet still fail or experience strong inertia due to levels of adaptability. Several studies on the adaptability-inertia nexus show different findings and relationships (Moradi et al., 2021; Pihkala et al., 2007). Recent examples during the outbreak of COVID-19 showed that the speed of change varied across institutions in different sectors and contexts irrespective of age.

The concept of the ecology stage embodies the different life cycle stages vis a vis the dictates in the operating environment, hard and soft factors (Abbott et al., 2016; Hannan & Freeman, 1989). The proposition that institutions are like organisms with evolutionary tendencies shows the inherent change process that occurs at different stages during the institutional life cycle. Ecology and life cycle are subsumed within periods that affect its behavior at different ages.

Scholarly discourse and literature depict the role the environment plays in this domain. Using Schumpeter's creative destructive analogy and organizational ecology theory it can be seen that the ability or inability of an institution to survive a particular stage in its life cycle is not only dependent on its internal capabilities but also on the selection and replacement process that occurs in the environment (Baum, 1999; Chen, 2014). Important considerations should also be given to the entry and exit processes and how this interface is causing inertia or preventing inertia. For example, institutions established during colonial rule in most developing countries might have a form of inertia inherent in the period vis a vis new institutions created during reforms. Furthermore, it is necessary to emphasize that stability is good for institutions and the need to protect the sovereign integrity of a country or some sensitive institution might necessitate having inertia as a form of control and preservation.

The age dimension also includes the level of available resources available and unavailable to an organization. It might not suffice to just assert that some organizations have inertia or resist change without considering the resource dimension. For instance, the resource-based view theory enhances our understanding of how this relates to firms and institutions (Barney, 2001; Hart, 1995). The resource factor transcends all disciplines and scholarly evidence attests to its diverse effect on institutions. The level of resources available to an institution has an effect on its age experience over a period. Rezkalla et al. (2018) show that resource availability affects rotational inertia. Resource dependency might decrease or increase in the age of an institution depending on the environment, industry, and goals. Hannan and Freeman (1984) study reiterate that different units of institutions require different resources and there is always a constant interface with the environment to gain access to scarce resources.

It is obvious that institutions and organizations do not exist in a vacuum and therefore can exist in natural, virtual, or artificial environments (contexts).

Understanding the context-institution dimensions is necessary for organizational studies. Valuable insights can be gained into how the various layers of contexts affect the growth and behavior of the institutions over the years (Campos, 2000; Johns, 2006, 2018). For example, there is abundant evidence in developed, developing, and emerging economies that shows that the multiple influences in contexts are a major source of differences in their behavior, performance, and survival.

In addition, the institutional environment reflects the survival and variations in the forms and structures in different settings and often provides the prevailing norms, policies, and regulations for the local business environment (Nye, 2008; Usman et al., 2021). Given the dynamics of exchanges with the environment, it is evident that the spate of pressures and the ability to manage this would have varying effects on institutions. For example institutions in developing countries are usually exposed to a flurry of external influences and multiple policy changes that can affect their growth and survival. This probably gives credence to why some old organizations have survived all environmental pressures compared with younger institutions in the same context.

Regardless of the context, it is plausible for similar institutions and organizations to have different experiences due to the availability and non-availability of several internal and external factors. For instance, two institutions established in different countries would certainly have different experiences, despite the organizational policies and resources due to environmental pressures and opportunities.

Perkins (2014) depicts the experience variable as a learning process that is reliant on environmental contexts. Institutional experiences and learning are dependent on other variables and reliant on how these institutions can use the knowledge gained to navigate the complex business terrain. Furthermore, suffice to state that the level of access to available technology and time horizons have joint impacts on an institution's age and performance.

Several studies attest to how they interface and affect organizations (Buchta et al., 2003; Dong & Saha, 1998; Grudin, 2018). The emergence of COVID-19 and technological innovations is a reference case with resultant levels of changes and inertia across global contexts. More than ever the spate of innovations related to technology and time horizons has caused major disruptions in almost every facet of life globally. Other factors to be considered include the organizational and institutional culture, the level of cognition of the principal stakeholders and decision-makers, and boundary-spanning activities relating to other internal and external factors.

The pervasive nature of culture and how it plays out in organizations has remained a topical area of interest in all disciplines (Persson & Tabellini, 2021). Its multidisciplinary nature necessitates understanding how this affects the survival and decline of institutions when faced with external pressures. Since human beings are most often at the core of organizational design, operations, and decision-making, it is imperative to consider the cognition levels at different strata vis a vis the quality of human capital and group dynamics. The variations in cognition level are a pointer to why institutions vary in different countries and how they are classified as weak or strong institutions.

3.3 Organizational Size Dynamics

Hannan and Freeman (1984) study on structural inertia and organizational change remains the most cited work relating to the size-inertia relationship. Much extant literature and studies show there is a relationship between the institution, size, and the level of inertia (Armenta et al., 2022; Chen et al., 2021). Size matters in organizational and institutional inertia studies and this has been widely acknowledged in all disciplines. Moreover, the size-inertia relationship consists of several elements and factors that shape the interactions and outcomes in different contexts. Kelly and Amburgey (1991) indicated that organizational and institutional history constrains organizational actors within the purview of the culture, policies, and antecedents.

In understanding, what size means it is pertinent to look beyond the nominal connotation that suggests it refers to how big or small an organization is or the number of human resources in the institution. Scholars and institutions have used size in various dimensions and classifications of organizations and institutions; organizational size and structure (Kimberly, 1976), organizational size and job satisfaction (Beer, 1964), organizational innovation, firm growth and size (Corsi et al., 2019), organizational change (Hughes, 2018).

For example, small and medium enterprises are classified based on their size in different countries; also, size plays a great role in organizational design in institutions. It is therefore expedient for considerations to be given to the level or strength of inertia forces vis a vis the size dimensions in every environment (Aldrich & Pfeffer, 1976; AlKayid et al., 2022; Chen, 2014).

We reiterate the need to consider the stage of the institutional and organizational life cycle when investigating its level of inertia. The life-cycle dimension and size are interdependent and justify the evolutionary and selection process that confronts organizations (Adizes, 1979; Gupta & Chin, 1993). Hannan and Freeman (1984) show that there is a relationship between organizational size and structure and this is shaped by the organizational life cycle. They provide evidence that the inertia pressures that institutions encounter are continuous and dependent on their size, complexity, and life cycle stages (Adizes, 1979). They also assert that size affects the level of inertia and the relationship is complex. These complexities arise from the broad and evolving sphere of size and its influence on other organizational forms.. In addition, the institutional size-age linkage depicts that as organizations grow in age, they are likely to develop more resistance to change, have inbuilt inertia, and ability to manage the several internal and external forces due to established and complex web of exchanges. As new forms of organizations emerge with distinct structures it might be expedient to take a cue from past studies related to structural inertia, structure, and organizational size and see how variations occur in different contexts. Kelly and Amburgey (1991) posit that not every area of the organization would change as its sizes change. Their finding shows organizational core units in the airline industry are unlikely to change regardless of the forces of change through other units or features that might change with variations in size. Further evidence suggests that the high level of bureaucracy and formalization in large institutions is inherent and a major cause of innate inertia and low level of flexibility (Kelly & Amburgey, 1991).

3.4 Organizational Complexity Dynamics

The conundrum of organizational complexity dynamics is multidisciplinary, multidimensional, and essential in organizational studies. The import of organizational complexity is evident in the extant literature and studies conducted in different contexts. In principle, a basic understanding of the level and nature of organizational complexity, and human behavior complexity provides invaluable insights into its relationship with organizational change and organizational inertia. This concept has been used extensively in understanding how the dynamics of organizational structure and other factors within the organization and its environment result in different variants of organizational complexity.

Dooley (2002) dual definitions of organizational complexity include "the amount of differentiation that exists within different elements constituting the organization" and "embodies organization's: core processes, technologies, clientele, product offerings, supply chain channels, markets, and geographical networks".

In addition, organizational complexity can be easily understood when consideration is given to the level of environmental and technological complexity. The import of Dooley triadic model of organizational-environmental-technological complexity results in processes that shapes the behaviors and decisions to manage organizational complexity, it is imperative to determine whether it's embedded in its organizational structure, organizational life cycle stage, and effect on organizational actors. Beyer and Ulrich advance the need to use structural and dynamic models within the ambit of the time element and posit that the degree of complexity in an organization can harm the performance where the cognitive levels of the organizational actors are not at par.

Godkin and Allcorn (2008) posited the need to have an in-depth knowledge and perspective of organizational complexity as a precursor to managing inertia and organizational change.

Hannan and Freeman (1984) propositions on the dynamics of organizational change asserted the negative effect of organizational complexity embedded in structural inertia. These insights enhance our understanding of why some big organizations with complex structures and frameworks respond slowly to the forces of change dynamics. For example, the failure of IBM, NOKIA, and other organizations to anticipate and respond swiftly to the forces of change could be traced to organizational complexity and success bias.

Thompson et al. (2017) classical work operationalizes that complex organizations comprise multiple strands of uncertainty, open systems, and complexity of the organization's environment. Furthermore, organizational complexity dynamics and dimensions include structural design, levels of authority, technological competence,

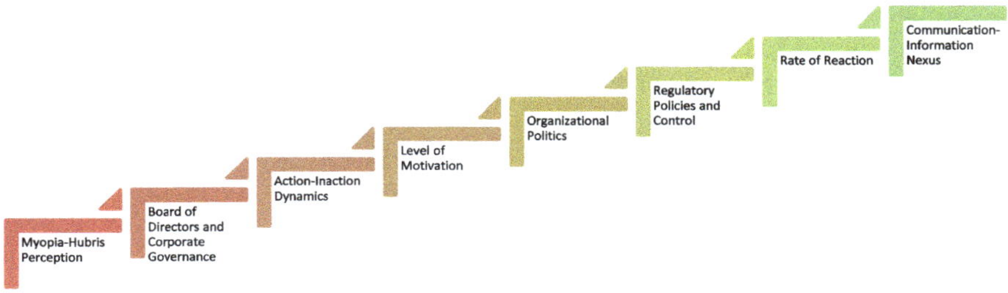

Fig. 2 Sphere of inertia
Source: Author's adaption

product types, locus of control, the composition of the labor force, and skillsets within the organization (Dooley, 2002). Typical examples of complex organizations are common in public sector organizations due to the local institutional environment effect.

3.4.1 Dynamic Behavior Perspective in Inertia Based on Rumelt's Sphere of Inertia

Inertia is inherent and it is evident that the sphere, theories, and direct and indirect causes are complex and multidisciplinary. We argue that unbundling inertia is evolving and the dynamics vary across contexts., Rumelt (1995) adopted the behavioral perspective and dynamics in unbundling the inertia-transformation process of institutional –Organizational nexus and provides practical and empirical insight into the evolving sources, spheres, and confluence of inertia. This behavioral approach complements the inertia confluence garnered from various literature.

Rumelt (1995) emphasized that five main sources of inertia include variations in perception, level of motivation, rate of reaction, organizational politics, and action-inaction dynamics of stakeholders (see Fig. 2). It is evident that the sources of inertia are interwoven and require a holistic approach to understanding the complexity of the multiple sources of inertia.

4 Myopia-hubris Perception

The dynamics in the myopia-hubris perception stem from the inherent variation in contexts and the way organizational decision-makers see and analyze the diverse forces of influence. Since human behavior, cognition levels, and attitudes differ, it is possible to have situations where a short-term approach is adopted. This myopic mindset can arise due to the interplay of internal and external group dynamics at the various cadre of the organization that shapes the individual and group perception (Gilbert, 2005; Rumelt, 1995; Swaminathan & Wade, 2016). Moreover, myopic perceptions may be due to limited resources, a volatile business environment, unstable policies, and uncertainty. Similarly, successful organizations are likely to suffer from the assumption of invincibility, brand immunity, and the tendency to ignore new information and innovations. Rumelt (1995) showed evidence of past success; overconfidence and information filtering problems can cause hubris perception and resultant negative effects. For example, many big brands have lost market share due to myopia-hubris perception and experienced disruptive changes due to subtle innovations and changes in customer preferences.

5 Level of Motivation

The desire or non-desire to embrace forces of change is relative to the motivation dynamics of social actors (Deemer et al., 2021). Several factors can influence the interest to embrace or resist change depending on perceptions of cost-benefit analysis, rational-irrational thinking logic, diverse interests, perceived disruptions, and effects on stakeholders. Rumelt (1995) points out that there is a connection between organizational resistance to change and the level of motivation and need to embrace change.

6 Rate of Reaction

Since organizations vary in size, contexts, complexity, dynamics, and boundary-spanning capabilities there are certainly going to be variations in their response rate due to the level of reactiveness. The structure, import of adequate information, ability to meet information need demands, cognitive levels, and timeliness of strategic analysis and interpretation of environmental cues influence the reaction framework of organizations. Technical, government institutions, and organizations with a high level of bureaucracy are more likely to resist forces of change that threaten their core and design (Ford et al., 2008; Sandlin, 2022). Rather staggered reforms and innovations are likely to be introduced at segments where it is necessary. Organizations using technical equipment and technology would not easily switch over to new or emerging technology and innovation due to the negative effect such a change can have on the continued survival of the business and risk hazards to the environment, and internal and external stakeholders. For example, banks use different banking software and are not likely to switch to another software overnight due to the disastrous effects. Moreover, Airlines are not likely to switch any technical component to another innovative component in the short run due to compatibility issues and the risks of loss of lives.

7 Organizational Politics

The prevalence of organizational politics permeates any social group and institution. Using the group dynamics analogy, inertia can arise due to groupthink, group polarization, in-out-group problems, and competing interests of the different stakeholders (Forsyth, 2018). The sphere of organizational politics is evident within formal and informal relationships and at all levels where decision-making and interests are core issues (Drory & Romm, 1990; Ferris et al., 2019). As Rumelt (1995) suggested, the personal interest of stakeholders, beliefs, and values often conflict during the process of decision-making. When the interests of major stakeholders are threatened, it triggers a sharp inertia bias, since it can result in loss of power, control and desire to preserve status-quo. As long as social systems exist and human behaviors vary, individual personality differences, experience can either favor or hinder change.

8 Action-Inaction Dynamics

The timeliness of organizational action and period of inaction has multiple effects on the organizational change framework. Scholars have reiterated the importance of considering the time effect in inertia and change studies (Ford et al., 2008). Even when the organizational change stages process is reviewed, it is evident that several forces could hinder the action process of implementing changes. The action-inaction continuum is the complex and resultant effect of diverse factors that can be either within or outside the purview of the organization. Using the Ajzen theory of planned behavior as a basis, empirical evidence confirms that the inherent cause of inertia could arise from the fact that intention does not always result in actions or behavior (Ajzen, 1985, 1991). Leaders and major stakeholders may subtly embrace change but might not know how to design and implement a successful change process. This can likely lead to the desire to maintain the status quo and resultant inaction. Inaction dynamics are also multifaceted, extend beyond the human resistance to change, and include structural elements such as the level of complexity in the organizational process, design and networks of relationship (Feldman et al., 1999; Terris & Tykocinski, 2016). Several studies have shown that the size and age of an organization cause various forms of inertia (Ranger-Moore, 1997). Beyond this, empirical findings show that both action and inaction could also lead to positive effects depending on the level of stability and strength of the forces of change. For example, the advent of new technologies or innovations might cause some organizations to take actions towards making some changes and some organizations might refuse to react to the change forces due to superior information, depth of networks, size and ability to use diverse strategies to undercut the anticipated effects.

9 Board of Directors and Corporate Governance Framework

It is rational for frontline workers and junior employees that interface regularly with customers and clients to desire changes either in response to changes in customer preferences, competitors' actions, the decline in market share, or the emergence of new technologies. Yet the rational basis for these desired changes might not materialize due to the decision-making process, quality of information available to make informed decisions, and competing interests of the board of directors (Hoppmann et al., 2019). At the helm of affairs, information is critical to decision making and inertia is automatically triggered if the desired change is outside their capacity, legal provisions, and regulatory policies that guide the purview of their operations and actions. Where this is even available there might still be inaction until the desired changes are communicated and approved by the various stakeholders such as shareholders, government agencies, and other interest groups.

10 Regulatory Policies and Control

This is an external source of inertia that acts as a constraint for regulating and controlling the activities of organizations in different contexts (Faure-Grimaud & Martimort, 2003). Several cultural, social, and environmental factors shape the nature of prevailing policies and controls based on the peculiarities of the industry and the need to maintain economic and social stability. Institutions and organizations are subject to the laws and regulations of their operating environment and may be restrained from embracing some changes without due approval and consultation. Even where the cost of the proposed change is minimal, organizations that attempt to implement changes might risk serious fines and penalties that can lead to business closure, loss of investors' confidence, and a decline in market share.

11 Communication-Information Nexus

Lack of proper, timely communication and detailed information is a major source of inertia and resistance to change (Severin & Tankard, 1997). Human behavior and organizational activities rely on different forms of verbal, and non-verbal communication and cues in and outside the organization to make informed decisions or actions. For example during the outbreak of COVID-19, the lack of information, misinformation, and communication issues resulted in the rapid spread of the pandemic and inertia in most settings. The web of communication is complex and requires multidimensional approaches due to differences in language, culture, context, cognition, and channels adopted. Although some forces of change are good, apparent issues arise in communicating or satisfying the information need nexus (Case, 2012; Cole, 2011; Derr, 1983). Arising from this, it is normal for the recipients or parties involved to develop automatic inertia due to the uncertainties that could arise. However, depending on the context, level of formality, and informality in the organization and organizational climate, the need for organizational change can be disseminated through a multi-level approach (Guzley, 1992; Neill et al., 2019). Hannan et al. (2003) stressed the need to consider the effect of the structural process, learning process, institutional process, and political process (SLIP) in cascading the need for organizational change.

How the communication-information nexus and processes are handled within appropriate periods influences the active or latent power of all inertia sources and reactions to change. Several studies attest to the relevance of timing in organizational communication, change information dissemination, and inertia (Moscarini, 2004). In addition, proponents and studies related to organizational ecology shed light on the timing, and communication dimension in the process of transition and life cycle stages (Abbott et al., 2016; Adizes, 1979; Gupta & Chin, 1993).

12 Conclusion

Discourses and research on organizational–institutional change and inertia nexus would continue evolving due to increasing levels of disruptive change and uncertainties in the local and global economies. The boundaries and facets of inertia and resistance to change are declining due to push and pull factors in the external environment and increasing controls of government and international agencies. Nevertheless, there are wide variations in levels of inertia due to the multiplicity of factors and elements within the inertia sphere and dimension confluence. Differences in human behavior motivations and contextual factors are critical elements that would continue to shape the findings related to this construct.

Recommendations It is also advocated that studies and research related to Organizational-Institutional inertia should adopt a holistic perspective that considers the dynamics of the internal-external environment, soft-hard factors continuum, and push and pull factors that relate to inertia within the context of the study. There is a need for institutions and organizations to evolve as learning and adaptable organizations in their environment to predict and manage the positive and negative effects of diverse forces of change that are envisaged and emergent.

References

Abbott, K. W., Green, J. F., & Keohane, R. O. (2016). Organizational ecology and institutional change in global governance. *International Organization, 70*(2), 247–277.

Adizes, I. (1979). Organizational passages – diagnosing and treating lifecycle problems of organizations. *Organizational Dynamics, 8*(1), 3–25.
Ahlstrom, D., Arregle, J. L., Hitt, M. A., Qian, G., Ma, X., & Faems, D. (2020). Managing technological, sociopolitical, and institutional change in the new normal. *Journal of Management Studies, 57*(3), 411–437.
Ajzen, I. (1985). *From intentions to actions: A theory of planned behavior.* Springer.
Ajzen, I. (1991). The theory of planned behavior. *Organizational Behavior and Human Decision Processes, 50*(2), 179–211.
Aksom, H. (2022). Institutional inertia and practice variation. *Journal of Organizational Change Management., 35*, 463–487.
Aldrich, H. E., & Pfeffer, J. (1976). Environments of organizations. *Annual Review of Sociology, 2*(1), 79–105.
AlKayid, K., Selem, K. M., Shehata, A. E., & Tan, C. C. (2022). Leader vision, organizational inertia and service hotel employee creativity: Role of knowledge-donating. *Current Psychology, 42*(4), 3382–3394.
Armenta, A., Alvarez, M. J., Aguilera, R., Hitlan, R., Federico, C., & Zárate, M. A. (2022). Cultural Inertia: Framework of change and Intergroup Relations. *Personality and Social Psychology Bulletin, 49*(5), 659–672. https://doi.org/10.1177/01461672221076209
Banwo, A. O., Onokala, U., & Ametepe, P. K. (2021). Overview of institutional change contexts and dynamics. In N. Faghih & A. H. Samadi (Eds.), *Dynamics of institutional change in emerging market economies: Theories, concepts and mechanisms* (pp. 87–105). Springer.
Barney, J. B. J. J. (2001). Resource-based theories of competitive advantage: A ten-year retrospective on the resource-based view. *Journal of Management, 27*(6), 643–650.
Baum, J. A. (1999). *Organizational ecology. Studying organization: Theory and method* (pp. 71–108). University of Toronto.
Beer, M. (1964). Organizational size and job satisfaction. *Academy of Management Journal, 7*(1), 34–44.
Bennis, W. G. (1965). Theory and method in applying behavioral science to planned organizational change. *The Journal of Applied Behavioral Science, 1*(4), 337–360.
Boyd, B. (1990). Corporate linkages and organizational environment: A test of the resource dependence model. *Strategic Management Journal, 11*(6), 419–430.
Buchta, C., Meyer, D., Pfister, A., Mild, A., & Taudes, A. (2003). Technological efficiency and organizational inertia: A model of the emergence of disruption. *Computational & Mathematical Organization Theory, 9*(2), 127–146.
Burton, R. M., & Obel, B. (2018). The science of organizational design: Fit between structure and coordination. *Journal of Organization Design, 7*(1), 1–13.
Campos, N. F. (2000). *Context is everything: measuring institutional change in transition economies.* The World Bank.
Case, D. O. (2012). *Looking for information: A survey of research on information seeking, needs and behavior.* Emerald Group Publishing.
Chen, C.-A. (2014). Revisiting organizational age, inertia, and adaptability: Developing and testing a multi-stage model in the nonprofit sector. *Journal of Organizational Change Management., 27*, 251–272.
Chen, J., Hui, L. S., Yu, T., Feldman, G., Zeng, S., Ching, T. L., et al. (2021). Foregone opportunities and choosing not to act: Replications of inaction inertia effect. *Social Psychological and Personality Science, 12*(3), 333–345.
Cole, C. (2011). A theory of information need for information retrieval that connects information to knowledge. *Journal of the American Society for Information Science and Technology, 62*(7), 1216–1231.
Corsi, C., Prencipe, A., & Capriotti, A. (2019). Linking organizational innovation, firm growth and firm size. *Management Research: Journal of the Iberoamerican Academy of Management, 17*(1), 24–49.

Deemer, E. D., Derosa, P. A., Duhon, S. A., & Dotterer, A. M. (2021). Psychological momentum and inertia: toward a model of academic motivation. *Journal of Career Development, 48*(3), 275–289.

Derr, R. L. (1983). A conceptual analysis of information need. *Information Processing & Management, 19*(5), 273–278.

Dong, D., & Saha, A. (1998). He came, he saw, (and) he waited: an empirical analysis of inertia in technology adoption. *Applied Economics, 30*(7), 893–905.

Dooley, K. (2002). Organizational complexity. *International Encyclopedia of Business and Management, 6*, 5013–5022.

Drory, A., & Romm, T. (1990). The definition of organizational politics: A review. *Human Relations, 43*(11), 1133–1154.

Faghih, N., & Samadi, A. H. (2021). *An introduction to dynamics of institutional change in emerging markets: Theories, concepts, and mechanisms dynamics of institutional change in emerging market economies* (pp. 1–8). Springer.

Faghih, N., & Sazegar, M. (2021). Dynamics of institutional change within the group of twenty (G20) and the European Union, and an assessment of brexit impact: A taxonomic study. In *Dynamics of institutional change in emerging market economies* (pp. 11–86). Springer.

Faure-Grimaud, A., & Martimort, D. (2003). Regulatory inertia. *RAND Journal of Economics, 34*, 413–437.

Feldman, J., Miyamoto, J., & Loftus, E. F. (1999). Are actions regretted more than inactions? *Organizational Behavior and Human Decision Processes, 78*(3), 232–255.

Ferris, G. R., Ellen, B. P., III, McAllister, C. P., & Maher, L. P. (2019). Reorganizing organizational politics research: A review of the literature and identification of future research directions. *Annual Review of Organizational Psychology and Organizational Behavior, 6*, 299–323.

Ford, J. D., Ford, L. W., & D'Amelio, A. (2008). Resistance to change: The rest of the story. *Academy of Management Review, 33*(2), 362–377.

Forsyth, D. R. (2018). *Group dynamics*. Cengage Learning.

Genschel, P. (1997). The dynamics of inertia: institutional persistence and change in telecommunications and health care. *Governance, 10*(1), 43–66.

Gilbert, C. G. (2005). Unbundling the structure of inertia: Resource versus routine rigidity. *Academy of Management Journal, 48*(5), 741–763.

Godkin, L., & Allcorn, S. (2008). Overcoming organizational inertia: A tripartite model for achieving strategic organizational change. *The Journal of Applied Business and Economics, 8*(1), 82.

Grudin, J. (2018). Innovation and inertia: Information technology and education in the United States. *Computer, 51*(10), 40–47.

Gupta, Y. P., & Chin, D. C. (1993). Strategy making and environment: An organizational life cycle perspective. *Technovation, 13*(1), 27–44.

Guzley, R. M. (1992). Organizational climate and communication climate: Predictors of commitment to the organization. *Management Communication Quarterly, 5*(4), 379–402.

Haag, S. (2014). *Organizational inertia as barrier to firms' IT adoption–multidimensional scale development and validation*. Goethe University Frankfurt.

Hannan, M. T., & Freeman, J. (1984). Structural inertia and organizational change. *American Sociological Review, 49*, 149–164.

Hannan, M. T., & Freeman, J. (1989). *Organizational ecology*. Harvard University Press.

Hannan, M. T., Pólos, L., & Carroll, G. R. (2003). Cascading organizational change. *Organization Science, 14*(5), 463–482.

Hart, S. L. (1995). A natural-resource-based view of the firm. *Academy of Management Review, 20*(4), 986–1014.

Hillman, A. J., Withers, M. C., & Collins, B. J. (2009). Resource dependence theory: A review. *Journal of Management, 35*(6), 1404–1427.

Hoppmann, J., Naegele, F., & Girod, B. (2019). Boards as a source of inertia: Examining the internal challenges and dynamics of boards of directors in times of environmental discontinuities. *Academy of Management Journal, 62*(2), 437–468.
Huber, G. P., Sutcliffe, K. M., Miller, C. C., & Glick, W. H. (1993). Understanding and predicting organizational change. *Organizational Change and Redesign: Ideas and Insights for Improving Performance, 215*, 265.
Hughes, M. (2018). *Managing and leading organizational change*. Routledge.
Islam, R. J. (2018). *One more time: what are institutions and how do they change?* (World bank policy research working paper no. 8422).
Jerger, J., Mullineux, A., & Welfens, P. J. (2019). Institutional changes and economic dynamics of international capital markets in the context of BREXIT. *International Economics and Economic Policy, Springer, 16*, 1–4.
Johns, G. (2006). The essential impact of context on organizational behavior. *Academy of Management Review, 31*(2), 386–408.
Johns, G. (2018). Advances in the treatment of context in organizational research. *Annual Review of Organizational Psychology and Organizational Behavior, 5*, 21–46.
Jui-Chan, H., Lu, C., Hao-Ming, W., Ching-Tang, H., & Hui-Wen, W. (2020). The study of organizational inertia, business model innovation and organizational performance in Taiwan financial institutions: Organizational learning perspective. *Revista Argentina de Clínica Psicológica, 29*(5), 104.
Kang, S. P., Chen, Y., Svihla, V., Gallup, A., Ferris, K., & Datye, A. K. (2020). Guiding change in higher education: An emergent, iterative application of Kotter's change model. *Studies in Higher Education, 47*(2), 270–289.
Kelly, D., & Amburgey, T. L. (1991). Organizational inertia and momentum: A dynamic model of strategic change. *Academy of Management Journal, 34*(3), 591–612.
Khan, S. T., Raza, S. S., & George, S. (2017). Resistance to change in organizations: A case of general motors and nokia. *International Journal of Research in Management, Economics and Commerce, 7*(1), 16–25.
Kimberly, J. R. (1976). Organizational size and the structuralist perspective: A review, critique, and proposal. *Administrative Science Quarterly, 21*, 571–597.
Kotter, J. P. (2012). *Leading change*. Harvard Business Press.
McGinty, P. J. (2021). *Organizations and institutions The Routledge International Handbook of Interactionism* (pp. 181–193). Routledge.
Micelotta, E., Lounsbury, M., & Greenwood, R. J. J. (2017). Pathways of institutional change: An integrative review and research agenda. *Journal of Management, 43*(6), 1885–1910.
Mikalef, P., van de Wetering, R., & Krogstie, J. (2021). Building dynamic capabilities by leveraging big data analytics: The role of organizational inertia. *Information & Management, 58*(6), 103412.
Moradi, E., Jafari, S. M., Doorbash, Z. M., & Mirzaei, A. (2021). Impact of organizational inertia on business model innovation, open innovation and corporate performance. *Asia Pacific Management Review, 26*, 171–179.
Moscarini, G. (2004). Limited information capacity as a source of inertia. *Journal of Economic Dynamics and Control, 28*(10), 2003–2035.
Munck af Rosenschöld, J., Rozema, J. G., & Frye-Levine, L. A. (2014). Institutional inertia and climate change: a review of the new institutionalist literature. *Wiley Interdisciplinary Reviews: Climate Change, 5*(5), 639–648.
Neill, M. S., Men, L. R., & Yue, C. A. (2019). How communication climate and organizational identification impact change. *Corporate Communications: An International Journal, 25*, 281–298.
North, D. (1991). Institutions. *Journal of Economic Perspectives, 5*(1), 97–112.
Nye, J. (2008). *Institutions and the institutional environment. New Institutional Economics, a guidebook'* (pp. 67–81). Cambridge University Press.

Perkins, S. E. (2014). When does prior experience pay? Institutional experience and the multinational corporation. *Administrative Science Quarterly, 59*(1), 145–181.

Persson, T., & Tabellini, G. (2021). *Culture, institutions, and policy The Handbook of historical economics* (pp. 463–489). Elsevier.

Peters, B. G. (2000). *Institutional theory: Problems and prospects*. University of Pittsburgh.

Pihkala, T., Harmaakorpi, V., & Pekkarinen, S. (2007). The role of dynamic capabilities and social capital in breaking socio-institutional inertia in regional development. *International Journal of Urban and Regional Research, 31*(4), 836–852.

Ranger-Moore, J. (1997). Bigger may be better, but is older wiser? Organizational age and size in the New York life insurance industry. *American Sociological Review, 62*, 903–920.

Rezkalla, M., Pertl, M., & Marinelli, M. (2018). Electric power system inertia: Requirements, challenges and solutions. *Electrical Engineering, 100*(4), 2677–2693.

Rumelt, R. P. (1995). *Inertia and transformation Resource-based and evolutionary theories of the firm: Towards a synthesis* (pp. 101–132). Springer.

Sandlin, E. W. (2022). The trump administration versus human rights: Executive agency or policy inertia? *Human Rights Review, 23*, 1–27.

Schein, E. H. (1990). *Organizational culture* (Vol. Vol. 45). American Psychological Association.

Schotter, A. P., Mudambi, R., Doz, Y. L., & Gaur, A. (2017). Boundary spanning in global organizations. *Journal of Management Studies, 54*(4), 403–421.

Schumpeter, J. J. C. (1942). Creative destruction. *Capitalism, Socialism and Democracy, 825*, 82–85.

Scott, W. R., & Davis, G. F. (2015). *Organizations and organizing: Rational, natural and open systems perspectives*. Routledge.

Severin, W. J., & Tankard, J. W. (1997). *Communication theories: Origins, methods, and uses in the mass media*. Longman.

Shinkle, G., & Kriauciunas, A. (2008). *Determinants of export growth in transition economy firms: Instituions, aspirations, incentives, and inertia*. Purdue University.

Srivastava, S., & Agrawal, S. (2020). Resistance to change and turnover intention: a moderated mediation model of burnout and perceived organizational support. *Journal of Organizational Change Management., 33*, 1431–1447.

Stouten, J., Rousseau, D. M., & De Cremer, D. (2018). Successful organizational change: Integrating the management practice and scholarly literatures. *Academy of Management Annals, 12*(2), 752–788.

Swaminathan, A., & Wade, J. (2016). *Institutional environment. The Palgrave encyclopedia of strategic management* (pp. 1–7). Palgrave Macmillan.

Terris, L. G., & Tykocinski, O. E. (2016). Inaction inertia in international negotiations: The consequences of missed opportunities. *British Journal of Political Science, 46*(3), 701–717.

Thompson, J. D. (1967). *Organizations in action: Social science bases of administrative theory*. Transaction Publishers.

Thompson, J. D., Zald, M. N., & Scott, W. R. (2017). *Organizations in action: Social science bases of administrative theory*. Routledge.

Tucker, D. J., Baum, J. A., & Singh, J. V. J. H. (1992). The institutional ecology of human service organizations. *Human Services as Complex Organizations, 47*.

Usman, M., Shabbir, R., Ahmad, I., & Zubair, A. (2021). Host countries' institutional environment and multinational enterprises: Does home-host developmental status matter? *Journal of the Knowledge Economy, 13*, 1–25.

Valderrama-Ferrando, L. (2006). In Citeseer (Ed.), *Institutional inertia*.

Woelders, S. (2020). Unravelling the relationship between organisational inertia, change resistance and (un) learning.

Zantvoort, B. (2015). On inertia: resistance to change in individuals, institutions and the development of knowledge. *Cosmos and History: The Journal of Natural and Social Philosophy, 11*(1), 342–361.

Zilber, T. B. (2017). *A call for "strong" multimodal research in institutional theory multimodality, meaning, and institutions*. Emerald Publishing Limited.

Živčicová, E., & Gullerová, M. (2017). *Evaluation of managerial competences through self-reflection.* Paper presented at the CBU International Conference Proceedings.

Internal Empowerment Dynamics of Organizational Inertia Management

Fatemeh Rezazadeh, Sima Rezazadeh, and Mina Rezazadeh

1 Introduction

The administrative system is undoubtedly considered any country's essential political system, so any progress and development of the society depend on healthy and consistent functioning. This lack of compatibility is rooted in organizational stagnation and immobility, or inertia. Adaptive and necessary organizational changes are usually stopped due to organizational inertia. In organizations, impatience towards changes and laxity in practical action for changes are observed. According to Schon (1971), some organizations try hard to remain what they are. Today, organizations must either be able to adapt to the rapid and sometimes sudden changes in the surrounding environment or dissolve.

Organizational survival requires functioning as open systems and connecting with their external environment. Inertia does not allow the organization and the employees to adapt to environmental changes and exchange information with the environment. Consequently, it causes personal stagnation and inertia in the entire organization (Hasannezhad et al., 2022).

Therefore, a correct understanding of organizational inertia can help managers properly deal with resistance to change in the organization and prevent the failure of the change process. Because of the rapid progress of science and technology and the complexity of the organizational environment, the need to create organizational

F. Rezazadeh (✉)
Faculty of Management and Accounting, Allameh Tabataba'i University, Tehran, Iran
e-mail: f.rezazadeh@atu.ac.ir

S. Rezazadeh
Faculty of Management and Accounting, Islamic Azad University Shiraz Branch, Shiraz, Iran

M. Rezazadeh
Industrial Engineering, Faculty of Engineering, Islamic Azad University Shiraz Branch, Shiraz, Iran

N. Faghih, A. H. Samadi (eds.), *Institutional Inertia*, Contributions to Economics,
https://doi.org/10.1007/978-3-031-51175-2_9

change has become highly noteworthy. Organizational survival and dynamism require continuous innovations and changes. The world is constantly changing and evolving with unprecedented speed, and change is the only constant thing in today's world (Senge, 2007). If a change, evolution, and innovation are not necessary, the organization will remain in the early stages of its formation, and no change or evolution will be achieved. On the other hand, rapid environmental changes threaten many organizations' life. Organizations' ability to adapt to environmental changes and, as a result, their survival is effective. Accordingly, organizational resource empowerment should be considered the organization's most important issue, and seemingly, this vital issue provides the organization flexibility for internal changes. Organizational resource empowerment and flexibility cause dynamic and improved employee organization relationship (EOR). These dynamic and improved relationships enable and facilitate organizational inertia management. However, this chapter's primary goal is how and in what direction the empowerment of organizational resources can be realized. Undoubtedly, answering this question is the main achievement of this chapter. The current review intends to describe organizational inertia based on reliable and valid research results and explain and clarify the path of organizational inertia management through empowering organizational resources. Thus, different parts of the chapter have been designed and linked to achieve this goal. By reviewing the literature and conceptualizing organizational inertia, the determinants of organizational inertia are explained from two organizational and individual perspectives. Furthermore, according to human resources' importance and inevitable role, groups prone to organizational inertia and its dimensions and components are also explained. In the following, to clarify and facilitate the path of organizational inertia management, this research aims to explain and interpret organizational resource empowerment through the description of organizational inertia management and from the four perspectives of employees, organization context, manager, and employment relationship (ER). In addition, the contents of the chapter are discussed and analyzed. Finally, after summarizing the contents, future research proposals are also presented. Writing this chapter will hopefully be a practical step for improving and dynamism EOR and the optimal management of organizational inertia through powerful organizational resources.

2 Literature Review

According to Godkin and Allcorn (2008)|, a significant negative relationship exists between organizational inertia and organizational planning for change. Because organizations with higher organizational inertia have fewer strategic changes, in this regard, Carvalho et al. (2018) concluded that strategic inertia, as a complicated relationship between interpreted performance and negotiated strategic measures in formal planning, is subject to the mechanisms of path reinforcement that interfere with the strategic change conditions. Wang and Yang (2013) found that knowledge inertia in organizations and among employees negatively affects employees' innovation and creativity. Reportedly, individuals with high organizational inertia have less innovation and creativity in their organizational relationships and job. Based on the research conducted by Ebrahimi (2015), knowledge inertia is the essential factor affecting the three dimensions of organizational inertia. Similarly, Javadi et al. (2017) designed the organizational inertia model through four factors of knowledge management, predisposing measures to change, change management, and psychological considerations, in which knowledge management and psychological considerations lead to improvement of the predisposing measures to change and change management. Haag (2014) identified five cognitive, behavioral, social, economic, and political dimensions of organizational stress. Hanaysha & Tahir (2016) believe that employee empowerment, teamwork, and employee training can positively and meaningfully affect individuals' job satisfaction. Farzin Nia (2020) also believes that a significant and negative relationship exists between managers' basic skills and components of managers' perceptive, humanistic, technical skills, and organizational inertia.

As seen in the previous section of this literature, most research has focused more on the factors affecting organizational inertia, and less attention has been paid to the exclusive role of individuals as the organization's essential and valuable resources. In contrast, successful organizational changes go through the channels of individuals' organizational performances. It is employees who see, evaluate, and interpret management decisions, then, based on their interpretation; they form their interactive behavior about organizational decisions.

3 Organizational Inertia (OI)

The principle of inertia in physics states that if no force is applied to an object or the resultant of the applied forces to it is zero, the static one will always remain static, and the moving one will continue its straight and uniform movement. Changes in the path occur only when the movement of an object is interrupted by external forces. This means that external forces cause any change in inertia. Inertia or immobility is the object's tendency to maintain its current state. Expressly, a static object tends to maintain its immobility, and a moving object tends to continue moving in a straight line with a constant speed. Force is necessary to overcome inertia. In addition to the physical concept of inertia in the world of inanimate objects, inertia can also be found in the world of humans and around them. Wherever there is change, inertia exists (Ebrahimi, 2015). Inertia is a characteristic of an object that resists changing the speed or direction of the object's movement. Newton's first law states that a static object or an object moving in a straight line remains in the same situation unless an external force is applied. This expression is an example of inertia (Franklin, 1976).

In addition to natural sciences, inertia is also used in the field of humans, organizations, and communities. Organizational inertia is the phenomenon of an organization's resistance against not changing the current direction of movement or

Table 1 Some definitions of organizational inertia (Authors' own)

Source	Definitions
Huff and Huff (2000)	The desire to remain in the current situation and resistance to renewing the organization's strategy outside its current form.
Liao (2002)	The organization's desire to maintain the organization's current situation.
Smith et al. (2005)	A set of factors that prevent the identification of environmental threats for the organization and slow down the speed of the organization's compatibility with the environment.
Liao et al. (2008)	The strength and resistance that the organization shows against environmental changes.
Majid et al. (2011)	A set of factors and obstacles in creating organizational change, evolution, and effectiveness.
Boyer and Robert (2006)	A set of factors causing organizational resistance to change.
Haag (2014)	Inertia means idle and lazy, and it is a phenomenon of stagnant organizations; it reflects excessively stable conditions in the organization's product, production method, and policies.
Henriksen and Dayton (2006)	A collective phenomenon in which people show very little participation in responding to issues and problems that the organization faces.

resistance to change from immobility to movement. In other words, the tendency to maintain the current situation in an organization is called organizational inertia. Organizations often show disinterest in change and evolution, and a kind of lethargy is seen in organizations. Lack of necessary changes and weakness in an organization's ability to adapt to environmental uncertainties cause organizations to be trapped in the swamp of organizational inertia and create undesired organizational relationships (Sepahvand et al., 2017). Organizational inertia manifests in various forms, such as suppression of valuable information from the organization, rigid laws, and inflexibility (Hasannezhad et al., 2022). Furthermore, organizational inertia is considered an obstacle to adopting technology by employees in organizations (Zhen et al., 2021).

Although extensive research on organizational inertia has been integrated to some extent with related organizational theories, the general concept of organizational inertia needs to be clarified. The concept of organizational inertia was first defined by Hannan and Freeman (1977) and further strengthened by Hannan et al. (2003) (Heimonen, 2011). The following definitions selection of organizational inertia is shown in Table (1).

Although the origin of inertia goes back to the science of physics, and it means immobility and maintaining the current situation, scientists and researchers have used this concept to analyze many behaviors in their field of study, one of which is human resource management and organizational behavior (Dostar et al., 2011). In organizational behavior, inertia is defined as the organization's tendency to continue using the existing system. Inertia causes inflexibility or rigidity, making it difficult for the organization to adapt or change efficiently along with environmental changes (Trudel et al., 2017). The concept of inertia can also be used for human behavior because it shows that people often use old methods when facing problems. Common problem-solving approaches and similar reasoning are used to save time, as well as avoid risk. In the context of strategic change, inertia is defined as the tendency to remain in the current status and resistance to redesigning the organization's strategy outside its current form (Shahabi & Jalilian, 2011). Also organizational inertia is defined as an organizational behavior: Conscious avoidance of expressing the ideas, information, and opinions related to work (Najari, 2020).

4 Determinants of OI

Organizational inertia is an individual experience and, at the same time, specific to the employment field and relationships. Javid Milani et al.'s (2008) research has focused on three factors related to organizational inertia such as organizational and interpersonal factors. Other researchers have also identified these factors. Therefore, based on the studies conducted in this field, as a general summary, predisposing factors of organizational inertia can be separated from two perspectives, each of which has a close relationship with organizational inertia:

4.1 From the Perspective of Organizational Factors

1. **Role Ambiguity** occurs when an organization's expectations of an individual in the work environment need to be clarified and may be due to a lack of understanding of the expectation, lack of familiarity with how work is done, or lack of knowledge of its results.
2. **Role Conflict** occurs when contradictory and non-contradictory demands or requests are applied to individuals.
3. **Employment Expectations** are a factor that is caused by two types of organizational expectations. The first is the expectation of progress, and the second is the organizational expectation. The expectation of progress is related to what the individual will be able to do, and the organizational expectation is related to the nature of the job and the systems in which the individual acts as an employee.
4. **The Workload** includes qualitative and quantitative components. Quantitative workload components include excessive requests and a limited time to deal with them, and qualitative workload components are related to employment complexity.
5. **Other Internal-External Organizational Factors Having Close Relationships with Each Other** include depreciation expenses, information limitation, internal political pressures, internal institutional pressures, entry and exit barriers, external legal restrictions, limitations of collective rationality, learning limitations, organizational structures and policies, creating common perceptions through collective conceptualization, and lack of demographic similarity (Heimonen, 2011).

4.2 From the Perspective of Interpersonal, Intrapersonal, and Managerial Factors

1. **Interpersonal Factors**: Lack of awareness to get a job, demographic variables, individuals' personality traits, and lack of planning (humans themselves) are known as intrapersonal factors in organizational inertia. Individuals who have not received the necessary training to get a job are more prepared to suffer from organizational inertia. Demographic variables (gender, age, level of education, marital status, and work experience) have an influential role in organizational inertia (Sharafi, 2019). Lack of planning is a factor of organizational inertia. The meaning of planning is to specify priorities; for example, what the priority in our lives is. People often strive for their rare and essential priorities and goals, so they know their critical priorities and goals and strive for them. An individual's personality traits can act as a context for organizational inertia. In other words, humans cause organizational inertia because they cannot make good decisions and do not know where to start and that a person who cannot make good decisions suffers from a lack of identity (Izadpanah, 2019).
2. **Intrapersonal Factors**: Various studies that have been conducted on the role of support in psychological pressure and organizational inertia have identified social support as a source of support for individuals to deal with psychological pressure and organizational inertia. Social support facilitates individual adaptive strategies, which of course, goes back to the individual social nature. In other words, it is formed when deep ERs show interest and concern for each other (Sharafi, 2019).
3. **Managerial Factors**: Due to the manager's influential and determinative role in the formation and stability of employee-organization relationship (EOR) followed by organizational inertia identification and management, these factors are crucial and can be expressed in four general categories such as managerial actions and behaviors, manager's leadership style, manager's fear of receiving negative feedback and manager's implicit beliefs about organizational inertia (Najari, 2020).

5 Groups Prone to Organizational Inertia

The following groups are more exposed to organizational inertia:

5.1 Dedicated and Committed Employees

This group is more prone to organizational inertia because they seek to help others, like those who serve people in counseling, crisis prevention centers, and other institutions. In this type of job, committed employees face additional pressures. First of all, they feel the internal force and pressure to perform better; on the other hand, they are under psychological pressure from their employers. If we add these mental pressures to the organizational pressures that are constantly imposed on them, they will face exhausting pressure.

5.2 *Employees with Negative Work-Life Balance*

These individuals are too committed to work, and life outside the office is unsatisfactory. Excessive commitment is considered a real risk and indicates that the employee has abandoned life outside the office.

5.3 *Individuals/Employees with Domineering Personality*

These individuals feel a great need to control others. They believe they need help to do their job as well as they do. They may even prevent others from receiving the necessary training for their job. The dominance of these individuals has many adverse effects on organizational relationships and leads to negative attitudes, pessimism, and even hatred of the organization's individuals towards them. Since these individuals try to control everything, they gradually experience organizational inertia.

5.4 *New and Active Managers Are Also Exposed to This Risk*

When these individuals start their activities in the organization, they do their work quickly. Initially, they have such power to keep the organization active and monitor everything. In the long run, these managers suffer from burnout and gradually feel alone and separate themselves from others. Along with this isolation, they hinder their progress and even the progress of others (Sharafi, 2019).

6 Dimensions and Components of Organizational Inertia

Hedberg and Ericson (1997) believe that inertia in various dimensions is a critical obstacle in how an organization develops and implements organizational macro-strategic orientations. Organizational inertia will lead to a lack of innovation and expected behavior that may endanger an organization's life and survival and destroy its competitive advantage in a competitive environment. Therefore, the organization or company needs to avoid the negative effect of inertia on the ability to learn, and also it should use innovation, creativity, and knowledge effectively and efficiently. Generally, the dimensions and components of organizational inertia are as follows:

6.1 Knowledge Inertia

Based on theoretical foundations, knowledge orientation is the key component. In many contexts, the concept of knowledge orientation has been considered synonymous with knowledge management. Knowledge orientation means the intelligent design of organizational processes, instruments, and structures intending to increase innovation, knowledge, sharing knowledge, or improving the use of it, which is reflected in each of the three elements of intellectual capital (structural, humanistic, and social elements). Knowledge is both a power factor and a strategically important resource for innovation (Donate & Sanchez de, 2015). Knowledge is like water, which is necessary to circulate among individuals and organizations. If knowledge does not flow and is not updated, its stagnation, like water stagnation, will lead to its decay. If only past knowledge and experience are used in solving problems and the methods are not updated, the problem-solving approach will suffer from inertia. Knowledge inertia is an obstacle to innovation, change, and flexibility and endangers the organization's survival in the competitive environment. Although the knowledge inertia and the use of standard approaches to problem-solving save time and energy, they prevent risk and risk-taking (Ebrahimi, 2015).

Learning inertia and experience inertia are two components of knowledge inertia:

1. Learning Inertia

   Stagnation in the organization and organizational boundaries is created through existing system knowledge perception and fear of how to use data. Organizations usually create procedures for using certain information in specific ways, which can hinder learning (Ahmadian et al., 2011). Anticipating an organization's thinking and actions by competitors in a competitive environment will cause the organization failure and loss. The organization's members affected by learning inertia usually do not use new knowledge to solve new and upcoming problems, and their problem-solving methods lack innovation and mostly rely on past and outdated knowledge and experience. This phenomenon is called learning inertia (Liao et al., 2008).
2. Experience Inertia

   Experience inertia occurs when the organization members use their previous experience and knowledge to face a new and different problem. Organizations can reduce learning inertia by encouraging individuals to acquire and learn new ideas and methods, supporting their employees in dealing with the experience inertia and encouraging them to acquire new knowledge and explore new approaches and ideas. Sharing the organization's members' knowledge and experience can lead to developing and improving experience inertia and creating a win-win situation for both individuals and the organization. Managers can also motivate individuals to change old behaviors and thoughts, use initiatives to find new sources of knowledge, and accept suggestions about new ways to solve problems. They can create conditions in the organization where members feel safe to share constructive ideas and criticism, receive mental help from others, and change the usual way of doing things (Liao et al., 2008).

6.2 Vision Inertia

Hedberg and Wolff (2003) believe that vision inertia is the need to properly understand the organization's environmental changes. In other words, the management may need a better interpretation and view of the signs and symptoms of the internal and external environment to determine and adapt the organization's behavior to face the external environment or internal demands for change. In vision inertia, organizational members do not adequately understand the environment and cannot understand why changes occur (Ebrahimi, 2015). Vision inertia appears when there is a significant time gap between fundamental changes in the organization's environment and awareness of these changes.

6.3 Action Inertia

Action inertia occurs when the management response to environmental activities needs to be faster or when the information gathered needs to be more sufficient to implement a beneficial conscious action for the organization. Notably, inertia in action, in contrast to vision inertia, is formed after analyzing the environment and environmental exploration (Farzin Nia, 2020). In other words, inertia in action occurs when the organizational environment analysis creates a managerial vision of the environment. However, the response and the organization's reaction to these changes could be faster, and the efforts made to change only occur at the appropriate and valuable time. Practices underlying change play a fundamental role in overcoming inertia in action. Increasing the organization's flexibility, revising the vision, preparing a coherent and step-by-step plan for change, management skills in matching environmental changes, the organization's structural dimensions, reconstruction, renovation, strategic goal setting, and continuous improvement in human relationship dimensions using influential employees and informing employees about the results of previous successful experiences are examples of actions that lead to change.

6.4 Psychological Inertia

Psychological inertia is created by fear and anxiety caused by the change in the organization's employees. In addition to improving actions that underlie and promote the change, psychological considerations play an essential role in overcoming psychological inertia. Organizational resistance to change is often known as psychological inertia. Organization members often strongly resist change regardless of whether change is needed or not. Resistance to change is a psychological phenomenon that indicates an individual's internal tendency to accept change. Resistance to change is one of the unique characteristics of change, such a way that if an individual's interest in change is threatened, they will resist change. The phenomenon of individual resistance is not necessarily resistance to change itself but rather a resistance to the loss of valuable things during the change process. Psychological readiness for change through reducing ambiguity, stress, distress, and anxiety, creating psychological security by creating an atmosphere of trust and mutual respect, preventing rumors and misunderstanding about change, and having an open relationship with employees to explain the steps in the path of change and giving importance to the feelings and emotions of subordinates in making changes by the manager are among the things that should be considered to overcome the psychological dimension of inertia (Godkin & Allcorn, 2008).

6.5 Structural Inertia

Haag (2014) believes structural inertia refers to the organization's structure and processes. This type of inertia occurs when the organization cannot change its processes (Farzin Nia, 2020). The best solutions for reducing or managing the structural inertia and reorganizing the organizational hierarchy are possible through using new technologies and improving human resource management practices because these factors increase the probability of successful organizational changes and evolution (Bel et al., 2017).

6.6 Strategic Inertia

Tripsas and Gavetti (2000) analyzed strategic inertia as a cognitive phenomenon. They believed that the organization's tendency to maintain the strategy in the existing situation and resist the renewal of the strategy is related to the mindsets and perceptions of the middle and senior management (Carvalho et al., 2018).

Generally, we can use Godkin and Allcorn's (2008) organizational inertia questionnaire with 15 items to measure the organizational inertia variable, which has three dimensions: (1) Inertia in vision, (2) Inertia in action, and (3) Psychological inertia.

Scholars have identified five types of inertia:

1. **Cognitive Inertia:** This type of inertia states that key managers consciously insist on using the existing system and procedures, even though they know there may be better, more effective, and more efficient alternatives.
2. **Behavioral Inertia:** This type of inertia states that the organization managers continue to use the existing methods because they are used to these methods and have become accustomed to them in the past.
3. **Social Cognitive Inertia:** The organization managers continue to use the existing processes and methods because changing the existing procedures and methods is faced with the employees' resistance, and changing the organization's values and norms are simply impossible.
4. **Economic Inertia:** Economic inertia refers to cost savings and how much the organization spends on changing processes for new approaches because organizations usually resist creating a new system or providing a new solution economically. According to Haag (2014), changing existing organizational processes is complicated due to high costs. Therefore, it is easier for managers to act according to existing processes.
5. **Political Inertia:** organization managers insist on using traditional processes because changing the existing procedures is faced with opposition or hindrance from strategic partners and stakeholders (Polites & Karahanna, 2012., Zhen et al., 2021).

7 Organizational Inertia Management

The central goal of the organizational inertia management process is to improve the ability of organizational change. Organizational changes happen when the company changes from its current situation to its desired situation in the future. Promoting organizational changes is planning and implementing changes in the organization. The changes should be implemented with the lowest cost for the organization and the lowest level of employee resistance and, at the same time, has maximum efficiency. Training and proper relationships with employees are critical factors in minimizing negative reactions to change. Another way to overcome employee resistance is to ask them to actively participate in the change processes and interfere in the design and implementation of change stages. Bel et al. (2017) have modeled the interaction between relationships, manager characteristics, and the probability of the organization's success in implementing a significant change. Although change requires support and strong relationships to help overcome inertia within the organization, they believe frequent relationships can be costly for managers and larger organizations. These theoretical predictions are consistent with the empirical analysis. However, frequent relationships have been moderated in organizations that have implemented significant changes, and their managers have a severe focus on results. Therefore, organizations interested in change promotion should consider the interaction between manager characteristics and the quality of interpersonal and organizational relationship protocols.

8 Empowerment

The history of first definition of the term empowerment goes back to the year (1788) in which empowerment was considered a delegation of authority in its organizational role, and this authority should be granted to the individual or understood in her/his organizational role. Empowerment in the sense of an individual desire to accept responsibility was a word that was officially interpreted as accountability for the first time. Groo (1971) refers to standard dictionary definitions of empowerment, which include delegation of legal authority, a delegation of authority, mission assignment, as well as empowerment. Gandz (1990) conceptualized empowerment as the delegation of decision-making to employees, but Zimmerman (1990) points to the inimitable simplicity of its definition and believes that it is easy to define empowerment when we want to pay attention to it without considering words such as helplessness, powerlessness, and alienation, and it is challenging when we want to define it according to different people. In general, since interpersonal and organizational relationships are of particular importance, the formation, improvement, stability, and dynamics of these relationships are not solely dependent on the empowerment of employees or other organizational resources. Instead, the quadruple empowerment of employees, managers, organizational context, and ER is one of the successful solutions in the direction of organizational inertia management. These strategies will be discussed in detail (Zamani, 2019).

8.1 Employee Empowerment

Traditional organizations only need employees who do specific and defined tasks and do not have excessive curiosity and challenges. Nevertheless, today's work environments need individuals who can make decisions, find new solutions to problems, be creative, and be responsible for work results. Therefore about the necessity of (employee empowerment) and change in power (autonomous employees) is that the changes that are transforming the work now, including employee empowerment, are not the result of the altruism of confused, aimless, and distracted people but rather, is the result of development and changes that are necessary for the success of the organization in producing wealth (Zamani, 2019).

Employee empowerment is an entirely different solution for individuals to work together and in the organization. In the framework of this new solution:

- Employees feel that they are responsible not only for doing their tasks but also for the whole organization's better functioning.
- Work teams, including self-regulating work teams, continuously work together to improve performance and achieve higher productivity levels.
- The organization structures are designed so that the employees can work to achieve their desired results, not that they only work to fulfill their duties and receive rewards (Dust et al., 2018).

These are the individuals employed in the organizational field to reach the comprehensive and ultimate goals of the organization. Accordingly, individuals in organizational relationships are not passive receivers; they see the organizational context and interpret it with their behavioral backgrounds and form, present and promote their interaction and participation in organizational relationships according to their perception and interpretation results. The successful implementation of employee empowerment is directly related to the implementation of specific strategies such as informing of goals and consequences of morality, paying attention to the individual value system, internalizing organizational goals in individuals, clarifying and improving job security, seeking the committed and analyst expert participation in decision-making, youth-oriented internal and local elite selection, individual role clarification in the service chain and employee creative research-training empowerment in the path of entrepreneurship (Rezazadeh, 2022).

8.2 *Organizational Context Empowerment*

At the most basic level, the context and what surrounds it is the place of obligations and includes the terms and conditions of the relationship. Context includes constraints and opportunities that affect the links through which individuals and organizations can communicate with each other and other agents; therefore, the context is multilateral and multidimensional (Rezazadeh, 2022). Individuals' behavior is not only a simple intrapersonal phenomenon but also is related to organizational factors (Yoon, 2017). In a powerful work environment, the employees and the organization are considered partners of each other; each individual is not only responsible for her/his work and duty but also has a sense of ownership towards the entire organization. Groups and work teams respond to official duties and orders and are innovators and designers of operations and actions. The employee is not a subordinate but a decision-maker; everyone is continuously learning and developing their skills to respond to new demands and participate effectively in new opportunities and challenges (Dust et al., 2018). Organizational context empowerment is directly related to the implementation of solutions such as creating a structure that facilitates positive interactions between individuals and organizations, institutionalizing the culture of persuasion and sanctity of work in managers and employees, reengineering and clarifying the framework and processes, preventing a fungal and parasitic system formation, strategic and targeted planning and integrated management of human resources and the research and development system (Rezazadeh, 2022).

8.3 Manager Empowerment

According to Hanaysha & Tahir (2016), as companies grow and technology becomes more complex, only some individuals can shoulder the entire burden of knowledge, decision-making, and management. This is why business owners gradually need managers and rely on them. Workplace democracy, like political democracy, will not succeed when people are misinformed. With the spread of advanced technology, unskilled and poorly educated workers will be dismissed and left behind a more educated group that cannot be managed in a traditional autocratic way and in the style of (you have no right to ask me anything). Gradually questioning and challenging the assumptions will become a part of everyone's work (Zamani, 2019). Paying attention to the crucial role of the manager in the EOR, in such a way that the managers are considered as the mediators between the organization and the employees, plays a highly influential role in this relationship and how it is formed, promoted or sustained in organizations and relationships where managers are critical, and their competence and ability are highly efficient in directing the organization and its success. Therefore, it is logical to say that the competencies required for a manager include a wider field of a manager, including manager empowerment to fulfill the multiple roles of managers. Manager empowerment is directly related to the implementation of strategies such as creating and training the belief in the unity of individual and organizational goals, training managers (traveling managers),[1] creating executive guarantees of bilateral contracts and laws, strengthening self-awareness, social identification, and manager entrepreneurial futurology, clarifying the manager perspective and self-image in decision-making with a focus on organizational capital, eliminating parallel management, and managing the employee behavior diversity due to employee multiplicity (Rezazadeh, 2022).

8.4 Relationship Empowerment (Employee Organization Relationship)

With the change in the economic and social environment during the last two decades and its continuation in the new century, a general agreement exists that the nature of ER between the employee and the employer has also undergone significant changes. Furthermore, the research field of EOR has increasingly become the focus of

[1]– The managers who seek to identify and solve the employee problems and do not sit behind closed doors to be referred to them, but they themselves appear among the employees and take action to find and solve the employee problems.

research on organizational behavior, human resource management, and industrial relationships. The need to integrate this literature as an instrument to improve the understanding of EOR has attracted special research attention (Rezazadeh, 2022). Because the first method by which the employees can actively shape their EOR is the formation of their ER by guaranteeing entry into a specific employment situation (Meijerink, 2014). Empowerment literature has undergone many transformations until finally, empowerment as a context for increasing critical thinking dialogues and activities in small groups and that allowing the activities to move beyond sharing, dividing, and refining experiences, thinking, seeing, conversations and ER are the main components of empowerment (Dust et al., 2018). ERs are the degrees to which an organization and its employees trust each other and include mutual control, satisfaction, and commitment concerning who has the necessary power to influence (mutual control), the degree of satisfaction with each other (satisfaction) and commitment of one person to another (commitment) (Men & Robinson, 2018). Moreover, show the evaluation of the scope of employees' interaction and interpersonal dynamics with each other on the one hand and the organization on the other (Shore et al., 2012). Employment relationship empowerment is directly related to the implementation of solutions such as ethical role modeling with a perspective of public interest, surfing to monitor informal relationships, practical pathology along with mutual feedback, succession, and stabilization of expertise structure and management short life, improvement of service quality and optimal behavior analysis with a dynamic system perspective (Rezazadeh, 2022).

9 Discussion

An employment relationship is considered a crucial factor of human development in individual and collective life to the current performance of organizational life (Men & Robinson, 2018). The challenges of this relationship can be related to the incompatibility of the organization's expectations of employee participation and interactions with the employee expectations and demands against the provided incentives. According to Tsui et al. (1997) and Shore et al. (2015), such incompatibility damages the relationship and negatively impacts performance outcomes for both the employee and the organization. This results in a negative EOR, far from an improvement path, and will be accompanied by increased costs in different dimensions for both the organization and the employees (Livne-Ofer, 2015). The concept of organizational performance is the final result of each employee's activities in the organization and has an effective role in the organization's productivity, so it is vital in the organization. In other words, organizational performance shows the level of job achievement, implementation of organizational regulations, and persuasion of employee expectations and organizational requirements for each employee. Studies have shown that organizational performance is a multidimensional phenomenon and a social structure whose improvement in the organization appears in objective and tangible parts, such as economic and financial results (Faridi et al., 2020).

Therefore, human forces, as an organization's crucial, valuable, and costly resources of an organization can use all the other facilities and resources to provide optimal services. In other words, the employee's unwillingness and diligence to participate in organizational activities and procrastination in it, if it becomes widespread, will have unfortunate consequences for the organization and endanger its effectiveness of the organization (Rezazadeh, 2022). Therefore, indicatively, the EOR is like an umbrella that researchers use to evaluate the scope of interaction and interpersonal dynamics between employees on the one hand and the organization on the other. An umbrella under which all comprehensive programs are implemented through individual work and the interaction of individuals with the organization, and ignorance of the process of adjusting its mechanism will cause serious challenges and problems in the progress of growth and development processes (Meijerink, 2014). EOR forms an emerging process concerning human resource management and organizational behavior through creating and maintaining interpersonal and valuable relationships within the organization. Therefore, research in this field needs to focus on the comprehensive principles of management based on knowledge of human resources and organizational behavior to solve the fundamental problems of effective management of the individual and organization (Shore et al., 2012). Because EOR has helped organizations improve and develop affairs as a comprehensive term to describe the EOR to achieve sustainable competitive advantage, a prerequisite for effective and creative organizational performance and cohesion. Moreover, it is considered a vital driver for connecting human resource management procedures, strategies, and organizational behavior to tangible business results such as customer service quality, employee loyalty, and effective job performance.

Today, empowerment is considered one of the valuable instruments for improving the quality of organizational resources and increasing organizational effectiveness. Organizational success in a changing environment requires knowledge, opinion, energy, and creativity of all organizational resources, including frontline employees, organizational context, ERs, and high-level managers. On the other hand, the desire to maintain the current situation makes the organization unable to react appropriately to environmental changes. This phenomenon of organizational resistance to change is called organizational inertia. According to Boyer and Robert (2006), inertia manifests itself in different forms, such as suppression of valuable information in the organization, rigid and inflexible rules, and the like. Organizational survival requires functioning as an open system and relationship with its environment. Inflexibility does not allow the organization and its employees (organizational resources) to adapt to environmental changes and to exchange information with the environment and, as a result, causes personal stagnation and, after that, the state of inertia in the organization's relationships and resources (Ghaffari & Rostamnia, 2017). In response to environmental and internal changes, organizations need to create capabilities in organizational resources. Therefore, if the organization does not have the property of changeability and modification, it will remain in its original framework, and the way of this progress will be blocked.

The phenomenon of organizational inertia and, generally, resistance to change and the application of new procedures have always been a problem and concern for managers and organizational researchers. Thus, with the rapid progress of science and technology and the complexity of the organizational environment, the need to create organizational change has become particularly important. Today, all aspects of life are changing at an unprecedented speed, and organization survival and dynamism require continuous and permanent innovation and changes. As a result, according to the mentioned topic, individuals and human capital, and overall organizational resources are undoubtedly the sources of creating creative solutions in the organization. For example, as processors of the organizational process, employees should show creativity and innovation and provide innovative and creative solutions in response to issues and changes. Therefore, empowerment can create a spirit of employee participation by involving and delegating responsibility to them. This method encourages employees to make decisions about their affairs and has more power and skill at work. The organization's human resources should be empowered in such a way that they can react appropriately to issues and changes and take the organization out of inertia. Empowerment is a vital element of organizations in the modern world. Achieving goals such as service improvement and continuous innovation happens by empowering employees. Empowerment is a permanent move, and its importance is constantly increasing. Organizational inertia appears when a lack of change and stagnation are institutionalized in the organization, and empowering organizational resources is one of the solutions to eliminate inertia in the organization.

10 Conclusion

Human force changes other resources of the organization in the direction of service. This is realized when the organization's employees have enough motivation and enthusiasm to work and are satisfied with their jobs, and see the level of motivation provided by the organization as aligned and proportional with the level of organizational expectations in the context of the organization's background factors. Nevertheless, if, for any reason, human factors do not have enough motivation and desire to work and participate in efforts to achieve goals, the organization will lose its original dynamism and will suffer from organizational stagnation and inertia. In conclusion, the four organizational resource empowerment strategies can be considered effective by focusing on managing organizational inertia and using the advantages of stopping and limiting organizational inertia. These strategies are (self-conscious and traveling) manager, (committed, analytical, and specialized) employee, organizational context (with the approach of reengineering and clarifying frameworks and processes), and ERs (with the perspective of public interest and surfing to monitor informal relationships). Notably, a desired realization of these strategies can determine the path of relationship formation in the atmosphere of a positive, enthusiastic, compassionate, collaborative, and humanistic organizational unit. Unquestionably, it can be along with an integrated organizational plan according to social identity.

In other words, the employee's interactive behavior toward the organization determines the level of his/her resistance to change. If individuals are adequately justified about the decisions made for organizational change, they will have better collaborative participation in the successful implementation.

Here, the managers' basic skills play an essential role. Therefore, the EOR and the desirability of its formation, maintenance, and stability depend on exceptional attention to employee empowerment from various aspects. In addition, managers play an essential and determinative role in this stage because managers connect individuals with the organization. Suppose organizational managers have an optimal level of basic skills. In that case, the process of human resources empowerment and EOR will be realized. This way, all organizational factors, including managers, employees, ERs, and organizational context, can predict and experience successful organizational inertia management and take advantage of its multiple benefits. Subsequently, researchers are recommended to evaluate the impact of empowerment of organizational resources on organizational inertia and the effect level of each one to be used by the organization managers as an effective strategy for managing organizational inertia. Correspondingly, they are recommended to fulfill the extent of organizational resource utilization of quadruple empowerment and measure the effect of each on reducing inertia separately. Based on the results of Al Hasnawi & Abbas's study (2020) that a manager's contradictory behavior in the organization causes inertia and ultimately leads to a decrease in organizational performance among employees, we understand the managers' influential and determinative role in employees' effective performance from various aspects. On the other hand, managers play the role of the connector of individuals with the organization and determine the quality and stability of the EOR. Therefore, some research directions can consider the Effect of Managers' Basic Skills (Perceptive, Humanistic, and Technical Skills) on the Reduction of Employee Resistance to Change. Other areas include investigating the factors affecting organizational inertia in industrial and competitive environments or measuring the effect of organization inertia on the variables that have a proper semantic affinity with the concept of inertia. Besides, considering the lack of a model for organizational inertia, it is suggested that the researchers present a native model for this phenomenon using the interpretive structural modeling technique.

References

Ahmadian, S. A. A., Shekari, H., & Afshari, M. A. (2011). Investigating the relationship between knowledge stagnation, organizational learning and innovation. *Organizational Culture Management, 9*(2), 131–154.

Al Hasnawi, H., & Abbas, A. A. (2020). Workplace ostracism as a mediating variable in the relationship between paradoxical leader behaviors and organizational inertia. *The Organ, 53*(2), 342–362.

Bel, R., Smirnov, V., & Wait, A. (2017). Managing change: Communication, managerial style and change in organizations. *Economic Modelling, 69*(4), 1–27.

Boyer, M., & Robert, J. (2006). Organizational inertia and dynamic incentives. *Journal of Economic Behavior & Organization, 59*(3), 324–348.

Carvalho, D. M., Filho, E. G., & De Almeida, V. E. (2018). Organizational performance and strategic inertia: The case of a Brazilian heavy construction company. *Revista de Gestão, 25*(1), 25–46.

Donate, M. J., & Sanchez de, P. J. D. (2015). The role of knowledge-oriented leadership in knowledge management practices and innovation. *Journal of Business Research, 68*(2), 360–370.

Dostar, M., Babazadeh, T., & Moradi, M. (2011). Examining the effect of learning on innovation with the moderating role of organizational inertia. *Scientific Journal of Innovation and Creativity in Human Sciences, 9*(2), 165–198.

Dust, S. B., Resick, C. J., Margolis, J. A., Mawritz, M. B., & Greenbaum, R. L. (2018). Ethical leadership and employee success: Examining the roles of psychological empowerment and emotional exhaustion. *The Leadership Quarterly, 29*(5), 570–583. https://doi.org/10.1016/j.leaqua.2018.02.002

Ebrahimi, S. A. (2015). An introduction to organizational inertia and its influencing factors in Iran's public sector organizations. *Quarterly Journal of Government Organizations Management, 4*(13), 101–120.

Faridi, Z. A., Moharamzadeh, M., & Imanzadeh, M. (2020). Designing a model organizational inertia based on employees' empowerment of sport and youth general offices in north west of the country. *Scientific Journal of Organizational Behavior Management in Sport Studies, 7*(1), 53–64.

Farzin Nia, J. (2020). *Investigating the relationship between Managers' basic skills with organizational inertia in Semnan gas company.*, Thesis for receiving a Master's degree, tendency: Evolution. Islamic Azad University, Shahrood Branch.

Franklin, A. (1976). Principle of inertia in the middle ages. *American Journal of Physics, 44*(6), 529–545.

Gandz, J. (1990). The employee empowerment era. *Business Quarterly, 55*(2), 74–79.

Ghaffari, R., & Rostamnia, Y. (2017). Organizational inertia and social laziness; Misfunctions of bureaucratic organizational culture. *Public Management Journal, 2*(9), 332–307.

Godkin, L., & Allcorn, S. (2008). Overcoming organizational inertia: A tripartite model for achieving strategic organizational change. *Journal of Applied Business and Economics, 8*(1), 82–95.

Groo, E. S. (1971). Choosing foreign locations: One company's experience. *Columbia Journal of World Business, 6*(1971), 71–78.

Haag, S. (2014). Organizational inertia as barrier to firms. In *IT adoption– Multidimensional scale development and validation* (pp. 1–11). Twentieth Americas Conference on Information Systems.

Hanaysha, J., & Tahir, P. R. (2016). Examining the effects of employee empowerment, teamwork, and employee training on job satisfaction. *Procedia- Social and Behavioral Sciences, 219*, 272–282.

Hannan, M. T., & Freeman, J. (1977). The population ecology of organizations. *American Journal of Sociology, 82*(5), 929–964.

Hannan, M. T., Pólos, L., & Carroll, G. R. (2003). Cascading organizational change. *Organization Science, 14*(5), 463–482.

Hasannezhad, R., Safania, A. M., & Afarinesh Khaki, A. (2022). Correlation of organizational laziness with organizational performance mediated by organizational inertia in the staff of the Ministry of Sports and Youth. *Journal of Health Promotion Management (JHPM), 11*(1), 73–84.

Hedberg, B. L. T., & Ericson, A. (1997). Insight inertia and action inertia in organizational reorientation. In B. L. T. Hedberg & S. E. Sjöstrand (Eds.), *From organizational crisis to industrial politics* (pp. 54–66). Liber.

Hedberg, B., & Wolff, R. (2003). Organizing, learning, and strategizing: From construction to discovery. In M. Dierkes, A. B. Antal, J. Child, & I. Nonaka (Eds.), *Handbook of organizational learning & knowledge* (pp. 535–556). Oxford University Press.

Heimonen, M. (2011). *Organizational inertia in a strategic public sector merger: Case Aalto University* (p. 5). Aalto University publication series, CROSSOVER.

Henriksen, K., & Dayton, E. (2006). Organizational silence and hidden threats to patient safety. *Health Service Research, 41*(4), 1539–1554.

Huff, A. S., & Huff, J. O. (2000). *When firms change direction*. Oxford University Press.

Izadpanah, M. (2019). *The relationship between talent management and organizational trust with organizational inertia in the educational Office of Lamerd*, Thesis for Receiving the Master's Degree in Educational Sciences, Training and Improving Human Resources, Tabnak Institute of Higher Education.

Javadi, S. M., Alodari, H., Amirkhani, A., & Jamshidi, A. (2017). Presentation of organizational inertia management model in North Khorasan University of Medical Sciences. *Management of Governmental Organizations, 5*(4), 39–47.

Javid Milani, M., Bamdadi, J., & Niknam, M. (2008). Investigating the effect of organizational structure of Tehran Girls' high schools on the job burnout of their managers. In *The degree of doctor of philosophy (Ph.D.) in the field of educational management*. Shahid Rajaee Teacher Training University.

Liao, S. H. (2002). Problem solving and knowledge inertia. *Expert Systems with Applications, 22*(1), 21–31.

Liao, S. H., Fei, W. C., & Liu, C. T. (2008). Relationships between knowledge inertia, organizational learning and organization innovation. *Technovation, 28*(4), 183–195.

Livne-Ofer, E. (2015). *Perceived exploitative employee – Organization relationship: A multi- study investigation of a new construct*, A Thesis submitted to the employment relations and organizational behavior Group in the Department of management, at the London School of Economics and Political Science, for the degree of doctor of philosophy.

Majid, A., Abdullah, M. T., Yasir, M., & Tabassum, N. (2011). Organizational inertia and change portfolio: An analysis of the organizational environment in developing countries. *African Journal of Business Management, 5*(2), 383–388.

Meijerink, J. (2014). Practicing social innovation: Enactment of the employee–Organization relationship by employees. *In Human Resource Management, Social Innovation and Technology Advanced Series in Management, 14*, 135–153.

Men, R. L., & Robinson, K. L. (2018). It's about how employees feel! Examining the impact of emotional culture on employee–Organization relationships. *Corporate Communications: An International Journal, 4*(23), 470–491.

Najari, M. (2020). *Investigating the effect of organizational climate on organizational inertia in the management of North Khorasan Maskan Bank*, Thesis for Receiving a Master's Degree, Human Resource Development. Islamic Azad University, Shahrood Branch.

Polites, G. L., & Karahanna, E. (2012). Shackled to the status quo: The inhibiting effects of incumbent system habit, switching costs, and inertia on new system acceptance. *MIS Quarterly, 36*(1), 21–42.

Rezazadeh, F. (2022). *The pattern of employee – organization relationship based on positive organizational behavior*. The degree of doctor of philosophy (Ph.D.). In *Public administration – Organizational behavior. Faculty of Management and Accounting*. Allameh Tabataba'i University.

Schon, D. A. (1971). *Beyond the stable state: Public and private learning in a changing society*. Temple Smith.

Senge, P. (2007). *Dance of change*. In A. N. Mashayekhi, H. Akbari, & M. Soltani (Eds.), (3rd ed.). Publication of Ariana Industrial Research Group.

Sepahvand, R., Arefnejad, M., & Shariatnejad, A. (2017). Identifying and prioritizing factors that create organizational inertia using the fuzzy Delphi method. *New Researches in Decision Making, 2*(1), 95–118.

Shahabi, M., & Jalilian, H. (2011). Examining the relationship between knowledge inertia, organizational learning and organizational innovation (Case study of west oil and gas exploitation company). *Management and Human Resources Research Quarterly in the Oil Industry, 4*(15), 137–158.

Sharafi, A. (2019). *Impact of talent management on reduce organizational inertia with the innovative role of intermediary organizational climate of employees of the Administration for Civil Registration of Ardabil Province.*, A Thesis Submitted in partial fulfillment of the requirements for the degree of M.A in governmental management. Islamic Azad University, Branch Gerami.

Shore, L., Coyle-shapiro, J. A. M., & Tetric, L. (2012). *The employee – Organization relationship applications for the 21st century*. Routledge. Taylor & Francis Group.

Shore, L. M., Tetrick, L. E., Taylor, M. S., Coyle-Shapiro, J. A. M., Liden, R. C., McLean Parks, J., Morrison, E. W., Porter, L. W., Robinson, S. L., Roehling, M. V., Rousseau, D. M., Schalk, R., Tsui, A. S., & Van Dyne, L. (2015). The employee-organization relationship: A timely concept in a period of transition. In J. Martocchio (Ed.), *Research in personnel and human resource management, 23* (pp. 291–370). Elsevier Ltd. https://doi.org/10.1016/S0742-7301(04)23007-9

Smith, M. F., Lancioni, R. A., & Oliva, T. A. (2005). The effects of management inertia on the supply chain performance of produce-to-stock firms. *Industria Marketing Management, 34*(6), 614–628.

Tripsas, M., & Gavetti, G. (2000). Capabilities, cognition, and inertia: Evidence from digital imaging. *Strategic Management Journal, 21*(10–12), 1147–1161.

Trudel, M. C., Marsan, J., Paré, G., Raymond, L., De Guinea, A. O., Maillet, E., & Micheneau, T. (2017). Ceiling effect in EMR system assimilation: A multiple case study in primary care family practices. *BMC Medical Informatics and Decision Making, 17*(1), 1–14.

Tsui, A. S., Pearce, J. L., Porter, L. W., & Tripoli, A. M. (1997). Alternative approaches to the employee-organization relationship: Does investment in employees pay off? *Academy of Management Journal, 40*, 1089–1121.

Wang, P., & Yang, X. (2013). A review of knowledge inertia: How can we explain the hindrance on individual innovation, *Atlantis press, advances in intelligent systems research: International academic workshop on social science, (IAW-SC 2013)*, 312–316.

Yoon, D. J. (2017). Compassion momentum model in supervisory relationships. *Human Resource Management Review, 1-18*, 473–490. https://doi.org/10.1016/j.hrmr.2017.02.002

Zamani, B. (2019). *Presenting a model for identification the effective factors on organizational inertia with the approach of empowering human resource*, Thesis for Master Degree in Strategic Management. Institution Tolo Mehr.

Zhen, J., Cao, C., Qiu, H., & Xie, Z. (2021). Impact of organizational inertia on organizational agility: The role of IT ambidexterity. *Information Technology and Management, 22*(1), 53–65.

Zimmerman, M. A. (1990). Taking aim on empowerment research: On the distinction between individual and psychological conceptions. *American Journal of Community Psychology, 18*(1), 169–177.

Part IV
Trade, Energy and Environments

Trade and Institutional Inertia

Saeed Rasekhi

1 Introduction

Institution is defined as the rules of the game in a society or, more formally, constrictions that are designed by humans and shape their interactions (North, 1990). Formal constraints such as laws and informal constraints such as norms are considered lasting. Formal constraints are those explicitly written and enforced by the government or those enforced by actors with specialized roles (Milgrom et al., 1990), while informal constraints are endogenously and enforced by members of a group. In an effort to model institutional changes, it should be noted that informal institutions are difficult to change and takes centuries, and in this framework, they may not even allow any changes. Those that allow this change may have different short run and long run effects on the change pattern. For example, according to Libecap (1989), different property rights frameworks that govern daily interactions have different distributional consequences, so groups and individuals engage in lobbying and bargaining and try to change these rules to their advantage. Libecap (1989) refers to such activities as contracts, which together with other activities and perceptions of the players shape the direction of institutional change of low-level rules, i.e. property rights. In Libecap model, whether an institutional change ultimately occurs depends on higher level rules and how decision makers perceive the potential effects of the change (Kingston & Caballero, 2009). Also, the likelihood of institutional change depends on the distributional effects of change and the behavior of beneficiary players. Institution is a broad concept from the behaviour of individuals and organizations to government policies. Table 1 shows some institutional features.

S. Rasekhi (✉)
University of Mazandaran, Babolsar, Iran
e-mail: srasekhi@umz.ac.ir

N. Faghih, A. H. Samadi (eds.), *Institutional Inertia*, Contributions to Economics,
https://doi.org/10.1007/978-3-031-51175-2_10

Table 1 Some institutional features and their relationship with foreign trade

Some features	Expected impact	Examples
Global organizations	WTO promotes the trade of new members.	Dos Reis et al. (2021)
Globalization	Increased trade is a result of globalization.	Surugiu and Surugiu (2015)
Globalization	There is some evidence of the relationship between globalization and institutional change.	Samadi (2019)
Exchange rate regimes	Intermediate exchange rate regimes promote trade.	Santana-Gallego and Pérez-Rodríguez (2019)
Trade Policies	Trade restrictions have a negative impact on trade.	Noureen and Mahmood (2022) Estefania-Flores et al. (2022)
Arrangements of economic, social and political interactions	Institutional factors influence trade positively.	Rasekhi et al. (2016)
Trade Agreements	Trade agreements lead to potential bilateral trade.	Walter (2022)
Good Governance	Good governance has a positive effect on overseas sales.	Abreo et al. (2021)
Trade Diplomacy	Trade diplomacy is a tool to promote exports.	Rose (2005)
Sanctions	Sanctions have a negative impact on trade.	Splinter and Klomp (2022) Larch et al. (2022)
Transaction costs	Transaction costs are frictional for trading.	Chen and Qi (2022)
Property Rights	Property rights have an overall positive effect on exports.	Brunel and Zylkin (2022)
Law enforcement	Law enforcement facilitates trade.	Araujo et al. (2016)
Cultural distance	Cultural distance has a negative effect on trade.	Ghaffari (2021)
Tastes and Preferences	Tastes explain the variation in export.	Aw et al. (2019)
Corruption	Corruption is as an obstacle to trade.	de Jong and Bogmans (2011)
Trust	Trust boosts trade.	Chen and Qi (2022)

Reference: Source: Author's own table

Interaction of institution and economy has a long history in such a way that the rise of Western Europe after 1500 is tied to institutional changes. The rise of Western Europe is largely attributed to the growth of Atlantic trade. The growth of trade, along with the initial political institutions that controlled the monarchy, strengthened a group of merchants that limited the power of the monarchy and helped create new institutions to protect property rights. These institutions played a key role in the subsequent economic growth of Europe (Acemoglu et al., 2005). The case of medieval Venice (ca. 800–1600) was a little different. Specifically, the growth of long-distance trade made a large group of merchants rich. They innovated in terms of institutional changes to facilitate trade. This group used their newfound economic power to limit executive and created modern institutions such as Colleganza to facilitate long-distance trade. But there was also a small group of particularly wealthy merchants who blocked economic and political power. They inherited parliamentary participation, and created barriers to participation in the most profitable aspects of long-distance trade. Over the next two centuries, this caused a fundamental social change from political openness, economic competition and social mobility to political closure, extreme inequality and social stratification (Puga & Trefler, 2014).

Regardless of the results, Table 1 indicates a significant relationship between the institutional aspects and international trade. One of the important reasons for the suboptimal economic performance of countries, especially developing countries, can be the lack of formation of productive institutions, resistance to institutional transformation, and the existence of high institutional inertia. It is worth noting that Inertia is related to Newton's first law of motion in physics, which states that any matter resists changes in speed and/or direction unless acted upon an external force. According to Newton's second law, mass is one of the most important factors affecting inertia. Although Inertia is not new to social science, especially Economics, and has a long history, as Afonasova et al. (2020) mentioned, this issue is in its early theoretical stages. Researchers such as Vetlo (2000), Jung (2019) and Kursakova (2010) studied inertia for different areas such as inflation, financial issues and marketing (Navickas & Bačiulienė, 2021). Various versions of inertia have been presented in studies. For example, in this regard, loyalty in marketing (Turner & Wilson, 2006), status quo and locking to current positions in social sciences (Samuelson & Zeckhauser, 1988) and path dependence in the systems approach can be mentioned. Perhaps it is because Zhuravsky (2019) has emphasized the possible changes in the methodology of inertia in Economics. Inertia may cause people to make irrational decisions. According to Samuelson and Zeckhauser (1988), this inertia increases with the cost of change. This is the reason that Firend (2015) argues that countries may voluntarily put themselves in a situation that lacks economic growth due to institutional and social factors. In his study for Malaysia, he concluded that the country is stuck in the middle of its global competitive position.

This chapter seeks to answer the question of whether there is any relationship between foreign trade and institutional inertia. To answer this question, while reviewing the literature, a simple theoretical model based on Gartner (1993) has been used.

The chapter is organized in such a way that after the introduction in the first section, the theory of institutional comparative advantage is presented in second 2. Then, in the third section, the impact of institutional inertia on foreign trade has been examined. Summary and results are presented in Sect. 4.

2 Theory of Institutional Comparative Advantage

Most researchers believe that institutions have played an important role in economic development and transition economies (e.g. Knack & Keefer, 1995, 1997; Havrylyshyn & Van Rooden, 2003; Stone et al., 1996).[1] The influence of institutions and policy mechanisms, known as social infrastructure, has been widely considered in the literature of economic growth, productivity and trade in various ways. Institutions affect economic growth and trade by influencing transaction costs, which are mainly driven by opportunistic behaviour and uncertainty in the economic environment. Also, according to North (1990), the security of property rights and private sector contracts as formal institutions affect background variables. Economic policy itself is a double-edged sword because good policy may bring stability to society and bad policy may destabilize the macroeconomic environment. Good government plays an important role in the design and implementation of these policies and in this framework, the independence and autonomy of the government structure is vital. In addition, according to Wei (2000), the effect of good governance on transaction costs may be greater for foreign trade than for domestic trade. De Groot et al. (2004) state that trade, on the one hand, often requires long run investment in business relationships, and on the other hand, partners have more options in international markets. But since competition and uncertainty are significant in international markets, the influence of institutions on foreign trade is more obvious. Good governance increases foreign trade through other factors, particularly investment in export infrastructure and research and development. As De Groot et al. (2004) point out, citing Wei (2000), the incentive to invest in good governance is greater in countries that seek greater participation in international markets. According to Deardorff (2001), international competitiveness is mainly attributed to unobservable trading costs resulting from inefficient institutions rather than factor endowments and technology. On the other hand, unobserved barriers to trade are often related to asymmetric information and uncertainty in trade, and in this regard, institutions can directly and indirectly help to reduce these barriers and increase trade.

Economic institutions help allocate resources for their best use (Iwanow, 2012). Without these institutions, the gains from trade are not exploited and resources are misallocated. In addition to theoretical explanations for foreign trade drivers such as productivity and relative endowment, institutional environments are also effective in international trade. As an example, we can refer to Leontief's paradox, one of the reasons for which is the neglect of non-physical capital. Also, missing trade refers to a part of trade that is not explained by trade theory and this part can be caused by other factors such as institutional factors. In addition, the border effect refers to asymmetry in trade patterns and this asymmetry can be related to institutional factors. This is in accordance with North (1991), who points out that institutions determine transaction and production costs, and therefore profitability and the

[1] For more information, see Raiser et al. (2000)

possibility of entering into economic activities. Anderson and Marcouiller (2002) show that weak institutions increase hidden international transaction costs, which cause insecurity in exchanges and hamper foreign trade. On the other hand, with strong institutions, trade expands dramatically. This is related to the transaction cost effect, according to which institutions positively affect trade by reducing transaction costs. Institutions may affect trade through production cost effects, thereby altering comparative advantage, especially if they are immobile across countries. These two effects determine the volume and pattern of international trade. Also due to weak institutions (such as weak contract enforcement), companies often prefer to vertically integrate their production process (Antras & Helpman, 2008). In particular, as Williamson (1979) pointed out, this vertical integration is the firm's response to the hold-up problem because this type of integration, as a better organizational structure, moves the flow of production within the firm's boundaries, and the effect of contract enforcement settings on performance reduces. In this framework, different industries will have an inherent capacity for vertical integration and thus a different comparative advantage in the product space. If vertical integration is not technically possible, outsourcing is a solution but this depends heavily on institutional arrangements regarding trade and production.

As a strong institutional feature, property rights significantly influence investment decisions and facilitate trade benefits. Specifically, in a productive economy, assets are allocated to people who can invest in the most productive way, and improving property rights facilitates this issue (Besley & Ghatak, 2010). Based on the proposition that firms in developing countries have fewer intangible assets, it can be claimed that these countries protect property rights less (Iwanow, 2012). This leads to different trade patterns and different comparative advantages, so that intangible assets-intensive industries are concentrated in developed countries with high level of property right protection. In addition, weak institutions may lead to changes in the pattern of trade in such a way that countries with weak institutional frameworks enter into barter trade or countertrade, which imposes higher transaction costs on foreign trade. However, institutional characteristics seem to have a greater impact on intra-industry trade (IIT), which is more sensitive to intangible assets.[2] Also, it seems that at least part of the missing trade, which is the gap between actual and theoretical trade, can be attributed to intangible factors, especially institutional aspects.

The importance of institutions for new trade is such that the current global trade is not only related to relations with other countries but also non-border regulations reaching deep into the domestic economy and its institutions. Meanwhile, based on the border effect, national borders are important issues even for developed countries, and in this regard, each country is expected to trade more with its neighbors than with other countries. However, the role of institutions has not yet been formalized as

[2]For instance, see Rasekhi and Shojaee (2012) who examined the determinants of IIT types in selected developing countries. In this research, the level of development and the Linder factor as well as other factors have been used to explain the types of IIT.

a part of comprehensible trade theory. But institutions with governance and transparency have a greater impact on international trade.

Despite some researchers claim that international trade theories are unable to provide a systematic explanation for various types of institutions (Yarbrough & Yarbrough, 1987), Saad (2021) argues Institution can theoretically be a source of comparative advantage. He has developed a theoretical model of trade with heterogeneous firms and imperfect contracting institutions to investigate the effect of trade liberalization on the quality of economic institutions. His model has three important implications: (1) institutions are a source of comparative advantage, (2) in an open economy, weak institutions benefit some firms, and (3) those firms lobby for sub-optimal institutions in a political game. Greater trade openness increases the distributive influence of institutions and firms' incentive to engage in political lobbying. Under these circumstances, trade reforms are most likely to be detrimental to institutions in countries specializing in goods requiring bad institutions. Institutions play two roles in this model: they are a source of comparative advantage and have different effects on firms' performance. Institutional quality itself is determined in a political economic equilibrium with lobbying firms. Some firms benefit from the deterioration of institutions and thus naturally engage in political activities to lobby for sub-optimal institutions. The relative power of firms lobbying for bad institutions is greater in a country with a comparative advantage in goods requiring inferior institutions than in a country specializing in goods requiring good institutions. In sum, if a country has a comparative advantage in goods that require inferior institutions, greater trade openness is most likely to worsen economic institutions. In this study, the institution is entered into the model in the form of a relationship-specificity. In such a way that firms use intermediate inputs to produce final goods and independent suppliers produce intermediate goods and undertake some relationship-specific investments for their production. Consistent with the literature, stronger institutions are shown to lead to higher aggregate productivity and economic welfare. However, the gains of institutional reforms are not evenly distributed. In the model presented by Saad (2021), there are two symmetrical countries with different institutional quality and two sectors in the world economy. Sectors 1 and 2 produce homogeneous and differentiated goods, respectively. Furthermore, differentiated goods are the institutions-intensive. According to this model, a country with better institutions in sector 2 will be a net exporter. Free trade leads to the expansion of the sector with comparative advantage and the contraction of the sector with no comparative advantage. Only the most productive firms choose to export in sector 2. Better institutional quality increases the productivity of all firms in sector 2, subsequently, more firms are encouraged to enter the market, the aggregate price index decreases, and domestic market competition increases. In a closed economy, the positive effect of higher productivity on the company's profit counterbalances the negative effect of increased competition and leaves the company's profit unchanged. In an open economy, better institutions significantly increase firms' expected profits from entering sector 2. This forces many firms to enter sector 2 and leads to very intense competition in the domestic market. Therefore, the profits of firms in the domestic market will decrease. However, the few firms that have exports, due to the improvement of productivity and the expansion of exports in the comparative advantage sector, will enjoy higher exports and profits. By solving the model, Saad (2021) shows that greater trade openness changes the extent to which institutions redistribute resources among firms, thereby changing the optimal level of institutional quality for each political group. Thus, trade may lead to institutional change in the absence of profound changes in political power. Trade is most likely to empower anti-reform groups and weaken pro-reform groups in a country with initially weak institutions and a comparative advantage in sector 1. Furthermore, the model predicts that the proportion of firms opposed to institutional reforms is higher in a country with initially weak primary institutions than in a country with initially strong primary institutions. According to Saad (2021), the benefits from trade may be larger (smaller) than most trade models predict. Also, According to Nunn (2007), countries with better contract enforcement export relatively more in industries for which relationship-specific investments are most important. Interestingly, according to the author's estimates, contract enforcement explains more of the pattern of trade than physical capital and skilled labor combined.[3]

As institutional formation and development promote international trade through transaction costs, protection of property rights and contracts, and good governance, institutional quality and similarity can also be effective on mutual trade. Researchers show economic institutions have a more positive effect on trade compared to political institutions, and on the contrary, military conflict has a negative effect on the trade, but the effect of military cooperation on bilateral trade is ambiguous (Kim et al., 2008). Some researchers have shown that institutional similarities increase the on bilateral trade by 12–18% (De Groot et al., 2004).

International organizations such as WTO and PTAs can also have a positive effect on foreign trade by stabilizing prices and reducing trade volatility (Mansfield & Reinhardt, 2008). According to this research, higher quality of international institutions is associated with higher trade through lower transaction costs, and these costs increase due to market opportunism and uncertainties in the economic environment and in this case, trade institutions can provide a reassuring atmosphere regarding private sector ownership and contract implementation. These institutions themselves need good governance with effective and impartial policies, which in turn requires an independent government structure.

Bad policy destabilizes the economy, and in this framework, bad governance has negative externalities on private transactions, which subsequently increase transaction costs. In this case, in addition to the negative impact on the value of the domestic currency, investment and the economic environment, the government has more considerations about the international political economy. The latter effect is more for international trade than domestic trade. In particular, foreign trade requires long term investment and trade patterns are more external options. Due to more

[3]Nunn (2007) has examined the hypothesis by constructing a variable to measure the proportion of intermediate inputs of each good that requires relationship-specific investments, and with the United States input-output tables.

competitive conditions and greater uncertainty in global markets, the influence of institutions on foreign trade is stronger, and in this framework, countries that pursue cooperation with the world are more motivated to invest in good governance.

Institutions may be influenced by other structural factors in influencing comparative advantages and their impact on foreign trade may be distorted and ambiguous. In this regard, Levchenko (2008) has examined the relationship between institutional changes and trade. This study emphasizes on the importance of institutions in economic performance, as well as the persistence of institutions, so that their change is rare and accompanied by large and one-time changes in the economic environment. Moreover, institutions are a source of comparative advantage in trade, although with ambiguous welfare implications.

In Levchenko's (2008) study, institutions have two key roles, including rent generating units and a source of comparative advantage for some parties. Then, based on Grossman and Helpman (1994), the study uses a lobbying game to determine and endogenize institutional quality. Based on this research, with the assumption of internationally same technology, the countries involved in trade race to the top in quality thanks to rent-seeking. In contrast, if one country has a strong technological advantage in rent bearing goods, the institutional quality will not improve with trade opening. Consequently, with strong comparative advantages not due to institutions, there may be no relationship between changes in institutions and trade. This research shows that countries with potential comparative advantage in institution intensive sectors have very high institutional quality.

Levchenko (2008) justifies the persistence of institutions by the redistribution of rents created by political parties in economic sectors. Therefore, the redistributive effect can change institutions through foreign trade. Imperfect contracts and property rights as sources of holdup problem worsen institutional quality because they generate rents for political parties that in turn make parties prefer the status quo and even its deterioration for their own interests.

With the opening of trade, the country with better institution exports institution-intensive rent-bearing goods. All countries try to upgrade their institutions to the top in order to benefit from the institutional advantage. The rents that bad institutions lobby for are lost thanks to trade, and each country tries to improve its institutional quality compared to its partners. The result will be the best institutional quality in equilibrium. If rent does not disappear after free trade, trade will not improve institutional quality. Also, with significant technological differences, the race to the top does not occur. In fact, trade creates rents in this case, and for this reason, institutional quality may deteriorate in countries producing institution-intensive goods.

In his model, Levchenko (2008) assumes that the economy produces three goods including K-good, H-good, and a composite good which is M-good. The latter good is produced by Leontief technology using one unit of entrepreneurship and x units of capital. Institutions in this model facilitate communication between economic sectors, so this facilitation is important for the composite goods. It is natural to assume that when two sectors make a joint investment they must have a joint product, M-good. Irreversibility discourages sectors from investing, which creates inefficiency, the well-known holdup problem. A way to control the holdup problem is to make a binding long term contract. Another way is to consider property rights in order to distribute the remaining rights of property.

In the above model, H and K are inside capital and outside or unorganized capital, respectively. Regarding the composite product, the specific factor of this product is a combination of two other inputs. Weights are different depending on the country, and in this regard, a lower weight of K indicates better institutions, which means good performance of property rights and contracts in the country. When the weight assigned to K is zero, the model is frictionless and the institutions are perfect and at their optimal level. If country A has better institutions, a lower proportion of outside capital becomes a specific input for the composite good, that is, contracts in this country are less imperfect.

For the rest of the model, Levchenko (2008) assumes that technology is the same in the two countries and then concludes that in this case, as in Ricardo's model for labor; institutions appear to be a source of comparative advantages and create the M-trade. As trade begins, the country with inferior institutions loses M and its associated rents, but the rival country produces M more productively and at a lower price. If the second country B is well endowed in labor or technology, it may end the trade pattern with M, in which case institutional differences may not be the sources of advantage. Therefore with the introduction of another productive factor, the pattern of trade will become ambiguous.

The Institutional environment may be changed by foreign trade, for example, the lower the trade barriers to trade and the greater the competition in the global market, the less incentive there is to corrupt. In this framework, governance and institutional quality increases as trade begins. International trade can also lead to more cronyism. On the other hand, if public investment in trade-related infrastructure generates high rents for firms linked to the political body, Institutional conditions can worsen (Hochman et al., 2013).

3 Impact of Institutional Inertia on Foreign Trade

Inertia[4] is the ability of an entity not to change or to change its parameters in a downward direction towards disappearance, provided that there is no external force (Navickas & Bačiulienė, 2021). During transformation, inertia in an economy means that its important competitive components, such as innovation and productivity, have no incentive to change, and that is why innovation is generally considered the opposite of inertia, as Schumpeter (1987) talked about creative destruction. In an extreme case, the economy is isolated from internal and external conditions in a state of inertia. As a theoretical example, an autarkic equilibrium in international trade

[4]To read more about the concept inertia refer to Chapter "Inertia: Resistance and Endurance" of this book.

theories can be considered as inertia. According to international trade theories, free trade has benefits for the economy beyond autarky. These benefits are due to the optimal allocation of economic resources based on comparative and competitive advantages. In this situation, the welfare of consumers increase due to the consumption of differentiated goods at a lower price than autarky. Also, producers reach better conditions due to their greater competitiveness and market share. Therefore, if inertia is taken to maintaining the status quo, it can deprive society of significant benefits from economic dynamism. High inertia in the sense of low sensitivity of the economy to external disturbances in economic crisis conditions can also be considered as a positive aspect of the socio-economic system with high inertia. Therefore, as Afonasova and Ryzhkova (2017) suggest, inertia as an ambiguous and contradictory phenomenon acts as a double-edged sword in economic theories.

Many researchers have tried the answer the question why inertia exists? Some attribute it to bounded rationality and the cost of accessing information and the cost of their backup, transmission and related processes in decision making under uncertainty (Colombo & Delmastro, 2002). Since there is no guarantee that the decision will be optimal, organizations prefer not to change the status quo unless they are performing very poorly. Also, based on evolutionary theories, organizations need repetition for reliability and accountability. In this framework, these organizations need some standard routines which itself leads to high resistance to changes. Another way to explain inertia is related to sunk costs. In fact, adjustment cost can be considered as sunk costs without specific returns. In this case, it may be optimal to delay decisions resulting in changes, leading to inertia. Inertia may be caused by this attitude and the fact that any change may cause the effects of rent redistribution among economic factors and the deviation of resources from efficiency. By ignoring this change, the organization will not adopt efficient policy and will be locked in inertia. There are two driving factors for the changes; the first factor is related to the condition in which the organization functions so poorly that its existence is endangered and the other is related to the emergence of new technologies that act as the driving force of the organization.

According to technological gap theory, the formation and continuation of international trade requires continuous creation and change of technology, and this structural change requires overcoming the inertia of the closed economy. Also, according to traditional trade theories, comparative advantage is the result of structural differences such as differences in productivity and relative endowments, and as the magnified theorem of Heckscher-Ohlin-Samuelson model shows, when trade begins; it redistributes the benefits of trade among economic factors. Therefore, inertia is likely in this situation and the result can be locking of the economy in no-trade situation or at least losing competitive advantages.

Considering that a significant change causes uncertainties, inertia can be justified from this aspect because in this situation the performance of the system improves due to the reduction of uncertainty (Stryja et al., 2017). For example, with a case study for Chile, Cerda et al. (2018) showed that the economic uncertainty weakens macroeconomic performance. Although inertia may improve the performance of the system by reducing uncertainty, due to the system's resistance to changes, it is likely that the adopted policies will face the resistance will only lead to the deviation of the economy from the optimal allocation of resources and the deterioration of the system's performance. For example, one of the important reasons for applying trade restrictions such as import tariffs is to protect domestic industries. This policy has been challenged in some international trade theories because it causes inefficient allocation and distribution of resources and sometimes leads to trade wars. If we accept that the tariff is applied with a positive intention to protect industries that are likely to have competitive advantages, it may not only have no protective effect, but due to the high inertia of the system and increase in corruption in these conditions, competitive companies may lose their ability to produce, export and innovate. Even if the policymaker has employed subsidies (as an exogenous institution[5]), the incentive of economic actors to innovate to ensure trade growth is reduced. In response to constraints, institutions tend to be stable and inertial. This may lead to their insensitivity to various threats and opportunities from the external environment (Jui-Chan et al., 2020). In this case, trade liberalization can stop politicians' reform programs (Busse et al., 2007).

At the firm level, as Schwarz et al. (2020) point out that inertia harms firms facing environment risks because such inertia prevents them from moving forward as much as external changes. Old firms may not be able to adapt to such conditions. Of course companies try to accept a degree of inertia for accountability and predictability, but subsequently they may lose through this stasis. In fact, inertia may prevent firms from achieving competitive advantage. To deal with this incompatibility (structural inertia[6] and competitive advantage), companies must have sufficient resources to be flexible to environmental changes and commit to new initiatives. If not, they may move more slowly and lag behind environmental changes. Uncertainty about resources creates a similar situation. A producer concerned about providing reliable production factors may not strive for competitive advantage, as doing so may cause the firm to fail miserably and even drive it out of the market. So simply, the company prefers to accept the status quo and inertia. The institution is locked in inertia due to routine activities, and as a result there is no incentive to restructure. Sometimes, organizations recognize inertia, but accept it purposefully to manage available resources, and this inertia may be reinforced over time.

Also the reasons of the existence of the inertia phenomenon can be examined with institutional theories. But as North (1990) states, we need to know more about informal rules and how they interact with formal rules. In this regard, Kingston and Caballero (2009) emphasize the institutional equilibrium approach, based on which the focus is shifted from the rules governing the behavior to the behavior

[5] For the definitions of exogenous and endogenous institutions see Robertson and Langlois (1994) and Samadi and Alipourian (2021).

[6] As Colombo and Delmastro states that business firms quite rarely change their organizational structure, a phenomenon usually referred to in the literature as structural inertia. It refers to the tendency of institutions to maintain the status quo or to resist deviating from existing structure.

itself. In this view, institutional change[7] does not fundamentally lead to changing rules, but to changing expectations. They continue to discuss institutional inertia[8] in the framework of different theories. In collective choice theory, the free rider problem may be a source of inertia. Another source of inertia is informal rules change slowly according to evolutionary theory. Also, the interconnectedness of different institutions makes them incapable of fundamental change, and this creates a kind of inertia. Moreover, as Kingston and Caballero (2009) also stated, path dependence is another source of institutional inertia. Another potential source of inertia is the endogeneity of preferences. In this view, individuals shape institutions and as long as the preferences of individuals do not change, inertia will continue. The way people process information and solve problems may determine institutional changes, and in this framework, bounded rationality as well as the formation of mental models can create institutional inertia to some extent.

Inertia, whether caused by real factors such as demand and resources, or influenced by the competence, can have profound effects on society, especially the economy. For example, the latter form of inertia was responsible for the economic recession of Britain in the years after 1870 (Robertson & Langlois, 1994). Also, cognitive problems related to new methods or changes may lock institutions into the inertia. Cultural incompatibilities may undermine the system of innovation and entrepreneurship that Britain experienced in the late nineteenth century. Institutional adaption to new technology is also important because it helps society to be flexible to adapt new technologies and overcome inertia. Depending on their type, these entities may be endogenous or exogenous. For instance, training in the company and at the macro level are endogenous and exogenous, respectively. No matter which kind of institutions we have, they are interacting and the result may be balancing or reinforcing. For example, employment policy may create a specific labor relationship as well as specific labor unions, which in turn affect the company.

Overall, inertia has two effects on firm innovation. On the one hand, inertia is the product of the company's successful adaptation to the previous technology, and in this framework, the company prefers not to accept changes new and technologies due to the high cost of adaptation. In this case, the transmission to the new state will be slow. On the other hand, with the existing inertia for previous firms, new entrants who have not been affected by the changes, may quickly learn adaptations and cope with innovations. The most important lock in this case is the response of the leader firms that may see the existing innovations as a significant trend and cannot successfully make this transition. This issue is important because innovation, as well as understanding how much and why innovation is critical for companies and their competitive advantage, as well as the economy in which they operate is one of the most important driving factors for competitive advantage. According to

[7] To read more about the institutional change, see Samadi and Alipourian (2021).

[8] To read more about the concepts of inertia, institutional inertia, and sources of institutional inertia refer to Chapters. "Inertia: Resistance and Endurance" and "An Introduction to Institutional Inertia: Concepts, Types and Causes" of this book.

Schumpeter (1987), innovation is a kind of creative destruction and inertia prevents this process. Therefore, we expect that inertia will lead to stasis and non-acceptance of new developments and prevent the achievement of competitive advantages. Remember that comparative advantages are formed based on endowments and can result from any structural differences such as productivity and resources while competitive advantage is based on learning, innovative and creative processes over time.

Path-dependent utility as another reason for inertia can lead to higher product prices (MacKay & Remer, 2022). Path dependence is also effective on system's performance in such a way that if there is no external force in path-dependent systems, we will witness an unstable equilibrium and this can keep the system in the initial stage. Especially if the initial state is characterized by bad governance, the state of the economy can lead to retrogradation. As North (1981) emphasizes, a predatory ruler may design the rule based on goals other than economic growth and output, and in this case, institutional change may deviate from the optimal path, implying the importance of political structure along the path.

The process of being dependent on the path for institutional change can lead to inertia because the change to achieve consensus is merely incremental (Libecap, 1989). In other words, beneficial institutional changes may be blocked by powerful groups, if losers are not compensated (Ostrom, 1990). These changes, if they occur, will be inefficient due to factors such as bounded rationality, whereby players may have false beliefs about the likely impact of the changes. If players recognize their own bounded rationality, they will taste other successful institutions and then change will be intentional. Of course, some researchers reject the definition of inertia as static and immutable and state that inert structure can be patched up with new structures or transposed to new functions (Genschel, 1995). In this framework, inertia prevents the replacement of old institutions with new ones, but it is still compatible with other forms of institutions. Thus, inertia in itself is not opposed to institutional change, but it may be a perquisite for it. Genschel (1995) claims that institutions with coordination improve static efficiency but worsen dynamic efficiency due to adaptation-specific problems. In this framework, over time, all institutional virtues may turn into vices. This research emphasizes that institutions are used as durable capital goods for a long time and this specific institutional capital cannot be transferred easily and if it can, it will be have a high cost, which creates inertia due to sunk costs. Furthermore, the uncertainty caused by bounded rationality makes it difficult to replace old institutions as well as to predict new ones due to their unknown nature. In conditions of high uncertainty and risk aversion, inertia will be normal. Finally, political conflicts act as a source of inertia. As mentioned, institutional change has distributional effects and this casts doubt on the possibility of change. All related measures to adapt to the new situation may impose significant costs with unknown results. In the framework of the above discussion, the role of institutions in comparative advantage can be investigated through the special factor model. As assumed in the latter model, some factors are considered sector-specific in the short run. In this situation, the distributional effects will be different from HOS model, although the pattern of trade is still determined by the relative endowment. If we consider institutions as sector-specific factors that are not easily moveable, the state of inertia can be attributed to the specific factor model, while in the long run, institutions are expected to overcome inertia.

By clarifying these reasons of the existence of institutions, we can find ways to overcome inertia. In this regard, Yarbrough and Yarbrough (1987) developed transaction cost approach to explain types of institutions in the framework of trade opportunism. Given the benefits of multilateral trade, countries will have incentives to develop institutions as well as limit opportunism. The approach has two important implications related to international trade. First, the observed institutions should embody the enforcement mechanism in the face of public and private opportunism. Second, the greater the uncertainty in a given transaction, the more complex the governance structure. These researchers claim that trade theories are unable to provide systematic explanations for a variety of institutions. For example, according to their study, trade theories do not explain why the emphasis on bilateral trade is persistent, why technical barriers to trade are difficult to overcome, why customs unions exist, and why successful unions are rare. They believe that the emphasis on specific historical episodes has prevented the development of a single framework for explaining institutional diversity and institutional change. Considering the transaction costs, institutional diversity would actually be alternative governance structures to international agreements. It is noteworthy that international organizations play a role as a proxy for international governance. In this framework, institutional inertia may result from international transaction costs, locking of international trade into various types of trade restrictions, highlighting the role of geography in international trade, e.g. bilateral trade between neighbors, and the emergence of protecting organizations such as customs unions, which may be the result of moving away from free trade.

Institutional inertia also affects foreign trade in another way. In this regard, as Broner et al. (2011) showed that by reducing environmental regulations, countries have more incentives to export pollution-intensive goods, which is consistent with the pollution haven hypothesis. In this regard, institutions influence regulations as an important source of comparative advantage. First, electoral incentives influence the tendency to emphasize environmental quality. Second, democratic institutions are associated with better government performance. Of course as the authors point out, institutions may create comparative advantages in skill intensive industries by investing in education.

As mentioned earlier, high-quality formal and informal institutions facilitate development processes. They can improve (destroy) the performance of a society through structural, behavioral, and policy-induced changes. We expect good institutions to at least increase the economic growth rate and reduce the inflation rate. In this framework, we model an economy with institutions that are an inevitable part of a society. This model is based on the neoclassical view presented by Gartner (1993).

To start, the supply side of a neoclassical open economy is assumed to be based on Eq. 1:

$$y_t = \alpha(\dot{p}_t - \dot{p}_{t-1}) \tag{1}$$

Where y_t, $\dot{p}_t$ and $\dot{p}_{t-1}$ are aggregate output in time t, inflation rate at times t and t–1, respectively. On the aggregate demand side, the following IS schedule describes the goods market equilibrium. The implicit Eq. 2 postulates behavioral functions explaining consumption, investment, government expenditure, exports and imports, thus it depends on aggregate output (y_t), interest rate (i_t), price level (p_t) and exchange rate (e_t):

$$y_t^d = \beta(e_t - p_t) + \rho y_t - \sigma i_t \tag{2}$$

Also, the equilibrium of money market is described based on the LM curve, which consists of money demand (m_t^d), money supply (m_t^s), and the equilibrium condition ($m_t^d = m_t^s = m_t$). Money demand depends on income and interest rate; the former part is related to transaction demand of money and the latter part is related to speculative demand of money. Money supply (m_t^s) is assumed to be exogenous. Then we can write the implicit LM Eq. 3:

$$m_t = p_t + \mu y_t - \delta i_t \tag{3}$$

The asset market reach the equilibrium based on the interest parity condition, which equalizes the rate of return of domestic and foreign assets, and as a result, the exchange rate can be determined in equilibrium. The equilibrium in the asset market can be written as Eq. 4:

$$i_t = E(\dot{e}_t) \tag{4}$$

In this relation, the formation of exchange rate expectations is considered as relation 5:

$$E(\dot{e}_t) = \phi(\overline{e}_t - e_t) \tag{5}$$

Where, $\overline{e}_t$ and E are the equilibrium exchange rate and the mathematical expectation operator, respectively.

Before solving the dynamic model, we introduce the institutions in Cartesian coordinate ($\dot{p}_t, y_t$) as Eq. 6:

$$I_t = -\dot{p}_t^2 + \eta y_t \tag{6}$$

Where, I_t indicates the institutional quality index in such a way that a higher index is associated with a lower inflation rate and positive economic growth. Thus, institutions are assumed to be beneficial to society.

This relation for an inert institution ($I_t = \overline{I}_t$), which can be called Iso-institutional quality curve, is a hyperbola in Cartesian coordinates, the curve showing all

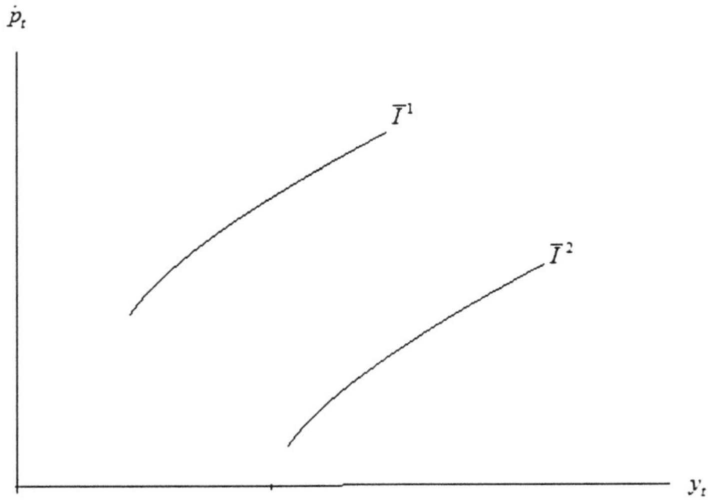

Fig. 1 Iso-institutional quality curves. (Reference: Present research)

combinations of output and inflation rate that can create the same level of institutional quality (Fig. 1). By moving this curve from northwest to southeast, institutional quality improves. So for a higher quality institution, the objective is to shift the cure downward (from $\overline{I}^1$ to $\overline{I}^2$).

Equation 7 is obtained by solving Eq. 6:

$$[-I_t + \eta y_t]^{\frac{1}{2}} = \dot{p}_t \tag{7}$$

Next, we solve the model described by relations 1, 2, 3, 4, and 5. For this purpose, we first obtain the following equilibrium relations (8) from Eqs. 2, 4, and 5:

$$\overline{e}_t = \overline{p}_t = \overline{m}_t, \quad \overline{y}_t = 0 \tag{8}$$

Also, we drive the exchange rate Eq. 9 from Eqs. 3, 4, and 5:

$$e_t = \overline{e}_t - \frac{1}{\delta\phi}(p_t + \mu y_t - m_t) \tag{9}$$

In the following, we obtain the dynamic aggregate demand curve 10 from Eqs. 2, 8, and 9:

$$\dot{p}_t = \dot{m}_t - \frac{\delta\phi(1-\rho) + (\beta + \sigma\phi)\mu}{\beta(\delta\phi + 1) + \sigma\phi}\dot{y}_t \tag{10}$$

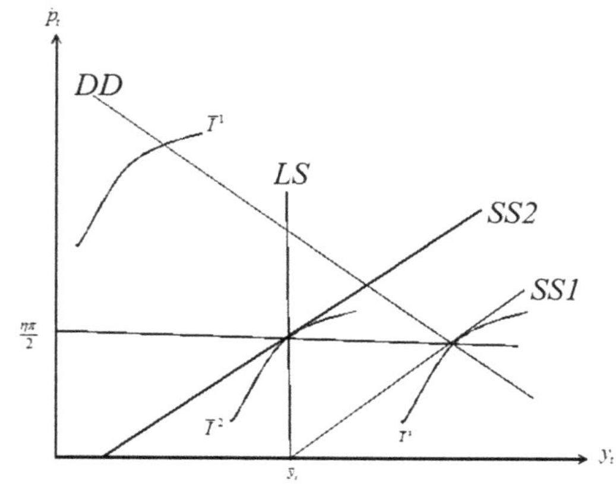

Fig. 2 Dynamic trajectories of institutional quality and macroeconomic variables. (Reference: Present research based on Gartner (1993))

Considering that all parameters of the model are assumed to be positive and also that the marginal propensity to consume is less than one, the signs of coefficients in Eq. 10 are in accordance with the theoretical expectation.

We also drive the short-run supply curve 11 from Eq. 1:

$$\dot{p}_t = \dot{p}_{t-1} + \frac{1}{\alpha} y_t \tag{11}$$

To check the optimal institutional quality in this model, first we solve the above differential equation. Then, using the graphical method, we will examine the institutional quality and inertia. The analytical solution of the differential equation is Eqs. 12 and 13:

$$\dot{p}_t = \frac{\eta\pi}{2} \tag{12}$$

$$y_t = \frac{\eta\pi^2}{2} \tag{13}$$

If institutional quality is in an unfavorable state, as we see for undeveloped countries, the indifference curve of institutional quality is expected to lie to the left side and higher in Fig. 2. This situation is associated with a very high inflation rate and a very low level of aggregate output. While for developed countries that experience higher institutional quality, this curve is close to full employment, and institutional arrangements contribute to economic and social satisfaction through various mechanisms.

Suppose the indifference curve of institutional quality is in an unfavorable position (in the northwest of Fig. 2). In this situation, the inflation rate is high and the level of aggregate output is low, and accordingly, foreign trade is also at a low level, because the export is a surplus of supply that is at a low level, and of course it is also a function of competitiveness that is at a low level in these conditions. National income and import are also at a low level. If institutional quality characteristics improve, for example, because transaction costs are reduced or doing business conditions improve, or property rights are respected in such a way that the macroeconomic environment improves, this will lower inflation expectations. In this situation, the short-run supply curve shifts to the right.

Given macroeconomic dynamics, the dynamic demand is expected to move toward long-run equilibrium. Also, the indifference curve of the institutional quality will expectedly shift to the right and institutional quality will increase. In this way, one-to-one changes in institutional quality and macroeconomic mobility lead to achieving equilibrium, and full employment and long run macroeconomics equilibrium are achieved with maximum institutional quality. In this situation, increasing demand and short-run supply can increase foreign trade and encourage the country towards a more open economy.

If the structures of the country's macroeconomics do not change, it is expected that the further increase of institutions (For example, the increase in inputs requiring relationship-specific investment in the study of Nunn, 2007) beyond the level of full employment will lead to a crowding effect and the reverse reaction will lead to the formation of inflationary expectations and the SAS and DAD curves (in Fig. 2) will shift to the left. Again long run equilibrium will be achieved. Thus in this situation, although in the short run, institutional improvement may lead to a better situation in terms of inflation rates and production levels, but this situation will not last.

It should be noted that the primary goals of macroeconomics is to reach a long-run equilibrium, also considering that stable economic growth and inflation control to maximize standard of living are among the most important goals of macroeconomics, and considering the relationship between these variables and institutional quality, another goal can be to reach the highest institutional quality. If these goals are not achieved, according to the model, it will not be possible to achieve macroeconomics equilibrium.

The noteworthy point in this simplified model is that the change in institutional quality with the implementation of economic policies. In a situation where the government focuses on institutional quality, the simultaneous change of institutional quality and trade policies is also taken into consideration by the policy maker. In other words, the government can adopt favorable economic policies by targeting institutional quality. On the other hand, if the government relies only on the interests of a particular group and, for example, overvalues the currency, although the interests of certain groups are met by increasing imports, exports will decrease. In this situation, institutional quality is at a low level, which means system inertia for both institutional quality and foreign trade. It should be noted that inertia does not only mean steady state, but can also be interpreted as a decrease in the quality of socio-economic variables.

Another issue is related to the impact of institutional quality on economic and trade policies. As we move from left to right in Fig. 2 and institutional quality increases, economic policies also change due to improved institutional quality. For example, by improving work culture and labor productivity or improving property rights, it is expected that economic policies and their effectiveness will also change. In this way, institutional quality and trade policies will change together. For example, if in a relatively labor-abundant country, tariffs on imported capital-intensive goods are reduced or eliminated, powerful capital owners and import competing firms may resist the policy. On the other hand, this policy may increase the pressure of interest groups, and as a result, by moving away from economic freedom, due to the increase of corruption and lack of optimal allocation of resources, the possibility of rent-seeking and reduction of institutional quality will be provided. In this situation, the increase in the general level of prices through the import cost channel will cause inflationary expectations and reduce economic growth. On the other hand, by improving the business environment, regulating and reforming policies to improve investment and economic activities, not only economic prosperity, but also the effectiveness of economic policies will increase.

4 Summary and Conclusion

The main purpose of this chapter is to explain the relationship between foreign trade and institutional inertia. Theoretical and empirical literature shows the mutual relationship between institutional quality and economic performance as well as foreign trade. In general, institutions act as intangible factors of production and any country with stronger institutions is expected to perform stronger in the goods associated with these institutions. Also, if the institution is considered as a specific agent, although in this situation the redistribution of benefits from trade differs from the neoclassical HOS trade model, the pattern of trade based on relative endowment continues.

Inertia is interpreted as steady state or unfavorable change. In this framework and by using a simplified model based on Gartner (1993), we showed that if there is no favorable change in institutional quality, it will be difficult to favorably change the environment and economic conditions. Also, according to the literature of this chapter, although institutions change based on necessity and according to economic and social conditions, governments should pay more attention to changing institutional quality for the effectiveness of economic and commercial policies. Changing laws and regulations, recognizing property rights, reducing exchange costs, establishing democracy and other important institutions can help the effectiveness of economic policies, and on the other hand, favorable economic policies can lead to the growth of high-quality institutions and overcoming inertia.

Considering that the phenomenon of inertia is ambiguous and like a double-edged sword, future studies can theoretically develop this issue, and of course extensive empirical studies in various economic subjects, especially international trade, can help to clarify the effect of this phenomenon.

Acknowledgments I would like to thank the editors of this book as well as the respected reviewers of this chapter for their valuable comments.

References

Abreo, C., Bustillo, R., & Rodriguez, C. (2021). The role of institutional quality in the international trade of a Latin American country: Evidence from Colombian export performance. *Journal of Economic Structures, 10*(24), 1–21.

Acemoglu, D., Johnson, S., & Robinson, J. (2005). The rise of Europe: Atlantic trade, institutional change, and economic growth. *American Economic Review, 95*(3), 546–579.

Afonasova, M. A., & Ryzhkova, M. V. (2017). Economic inertia and economic growth: Is there any contradiction? In K. Anna Yurevna, A. Igor Borisovich, W. Martin de Jong, & M. Nikita Vladimirovich (Eds.), *Responsible research and innovation, European proceedings of social and behavioural sciences*. Future Academy.

Afonasova, M. A., Bogomolova, A. V., & Dobrynin, A. S. (2020). *Inertia of the regional economic system: Distinctive features and manifestations, proceedings of the international conference on economics, management and technologies*. Atlantis Press.

Anderson, J., & Marcouiller, D. (2002). Insecurity and the pattern of trade: An empirical investigation. *Review of Economics and Statistics, 84*(2), 342–352.

Antras, P., & Helpman, E. (2008). *Contractual frictions and global sourcing, the organization of firms in a global economy*. Harvard University Press.

Araujo, L., Mion, G., & Ornelas, E. (2016). Institutions and export dynamics. *Journal of International Economics, 98*, 2–20.

Aw, B. Y., Lee, Y., & Vandenbussche, H. (2019). The importance of consumer taste in trade, CESifo Working Paper. CESifo.

Besley, T., & Ghatak, M. (2010). Property rights and economic development. In D. Rodrik & M. Rosenzweig (Eds.), *Handbook of development economics*. North-Holland.

Broner, F., Bustos, P., & Carvalho, V. M. (2011). *Sources of comparative advantage in polluting industries*. CREI and ERWIT.

Brunel, C., & Zylkin, T. (2022). Do cross-border patents promote trade? *Canadian Journal of Economics/Revue canadienne d'économique, 55*, 379–418.

Busse, M., Borrmann, A., Fischer, S., & Groening, S. (2007). *Institutions, governance and trade: An empirical investigation of the linkages*, in view of the proposed ACP / EU economic partnership agreements, Hamburg Institute of International Economics (HWWI), Program World Economy.

Cerda, R., Silva, Á., & Valente, J. T. (2018). Impact of economic uncertainty in a small open economy: The case of Chile. *Applied Economics, 50*(26), 2894–2908.

Chen, H., & Qi, C. (2022). The trade effect of trust: Evidence from agricultural trade between China and its partners. *Sustainability, 14*(729), 1–22.

Colombo, M. G., & Delmastro, M. (2002). The determinants of organizational change and structural inertia: Technological and organizational factors. *Journal of Economics and Management Strategy, 11*(4), 595–635.

De Groot, H. L. F., Linders, G.-J., Rietveld, P., & Subramanian, U. (2004). The institutional determinants of bilateral trade patterns. *Kyklos, 57*(1), 103–123.

De Jong, E., & Bogmans, C. (2011). Does corruption discourage international trade? *European Journal of Political Economy, 27*(2), 385–398.

Deardorff, A. V. (2001). International provision of trade services, trade, and fragmentation. *Review of International Economics, 9*(2), 233–248.

Dos Reis, M., da Silva Pôrto, S., & de Azevedo, A. F. Z. (2021). The impacts of the World Trade Organization on new members. *The World Economy, 44*, 1944–1972.

Estefania-Flores, J., Furceri, D., Hannan, M. S. A., Ostry, M. J. D., & Rose, M. A. K. (2022). *A measurement of aggregate trade restrictions and their economic effects* (Vol. 16919). International Monetary Fund.

Firend, A. R. (2015). The phenomenon of economic inertia. *The International Journal of Business and Management Research, 8*(1), 14–20.

Gartner, M. (1993). *Macroeconomics under flexible exchange rates*. Harvester Wheatsheaf.

Genschel P. (1995). The dynamics of inertia: Institutional persistence and institutional change in telecommunications and health care, MPIFG Discussion Paper. Max-Planck-Institut für Gesellschaftsforschung.

Ghaffari, M. (2021). Evaluating the effect of cultural and institutional distance on the proportion of B and R countries' imports from China. *Open Journal of Social Sciences, 9*, 425–457.

Grossman, G., & Helpman, E. (1994). Protection for sale. *American Economic Review, 84*, 833–850.

Havrylyshyn, O., & Van Rooden, R. (2003). Institutions matter in transition, but so do policies. *Comparative Economic Studies, 45*(1), 2–24.

Hochman, G., Tabakis, C., & Zilberman, D. (2013). The impact of international trade on institutions and infrastructure. *Journal of Comparative Economics, 41*(1), 126–140.

Iwanow, T. (2012). *Essays on institutions and international trade* (Doctoral dissertation, The University of Manchester).

Jui-Chan, H., Lu, C., Hao-Ming, W., Ching-Tang, H., & Hui-Wen, W. (2020). The study of organizational inertia, business model innovation and organizational performance in Taiwan financial institutions: Organizational learning perspective. *Revista Argentina de Clínica Psicológica, 29*(5), 104.

Kim, M. H., Kim, D., & Han, Y. (2008). The impact of international institutions on bilateral trade: Economic and political. *Global Economy Journal, 8*(4), 1–20.

Kingston, C., & Caballero, G. (2009). Comparing theories of institutional change. *Journal of Institutional Economics, 5*(2), 151–180.

Knack, S., & Keefer, P. (1995). Institutions and economic performance: Cross-country tests using alternative institutional measures. *Economics and Politics, 7*(3), 207–227.

Knack, S., & Keefer, P. (1997). Does social capital have an economic payoff? A cross-country investigation. *The Quarterly Journal of Economics, 112*(4), 1251–1288.

Larch, M., Shikher, S., Syropoulos, C., & Yotov, Y. V. (2022). Quantifying the impact of economic sanctions on international trade in the energy and mining sectors. *Economic Inquiry, 60*(3), 1038–1063.

Levchenko, A. A. (2008). International trade and institutional change, Discussion Paper. University of Michigan.

Libecap, G. D. (1989). Distributional issues in contracting for property rights. *Journal of Institutional and Theoretical Economics (JITE)*, 6–24.

MacKay A., & Remer M. (2022). Consumer inertia and market power, Working Paper. Harvard University.

Mansfield, E. D., & Reinhardt, E. (2008). International institutions and the volatility of international trade. *International Organization, 62*(4), 621–652.

Milgrom, P. R., North, D. C., & Weingast, B. R. (1990). The role of institutions in the revival of trade: The law merchant, private judges, and the champagne fairs. *Economics and Politics, 2*(1), 1–23.

Navickas, V., & Bačiulienė, V. (2021). Impact of economic inertia on economics: A methodological framework. *Nr, 44*, 46–53.

North, D. (1981). *Structure and change in economic history*. W.W. Norton and Company.

North, D. C. (1990). *Institutions, institutional change and economic performance*. Cambridge University Press.

North, D. C. (1991). Institutions. *Journal of Economic Perspectives, 5*(1), 97–112.

Noureen, S., & Mahmood, Z. (2022). The effects of trade cost components and uncertainty of time delay on bilateral export growth. *Heliyon, 8*(1), 1–13.

Nunn, N. (2007). Relationship-specificity, incomplete contracts and the pattern of trade. *Quarterly Journal of Economics, 122*(2), 569–600.

Ostrom, E. (1990). *Governing the commons: The evolution of institutions for collective action*. Cambridge University Press.

Puga, D., & Trefler, D. (2014). International trade and institutional change: Medieval Venice's response to globalization. *Quarterly Journal of Economics, 129*, 753–821.

Raiser, M., Di Tommaso, M. L., & Weeks, M. (2000). *The measurement and determination of institutional change: Evidence from transition economics*. Faculty of Economics, University of Cambridge.
Rasekhi, S., & Shojaee, S. (2012). Determinant factors of vertical intra industry trade in agricultural sector: A study of Iran and her main trading partners. *Agricultural Economics (Zemědělská Ekonomika), 58*(4), 180–190.
Rasekhi, S., Sheidaei, Z., & Asadi, S. P. (2016). A causal relationship between trade efficiency and economic efficiency: Evidence from dynamic simultaneous equations models. *The Journal of International Trade and Economic Development, 26*(4), 473–487.
Robertson, P. L., & Langlois, R. N. (1994). Institutions, inertia and changing industrial leadership. *Industrial and Corporate Change, 3*(2), 359–378.
Rose, A. (2005). The foreign service and foreign trade: Embassies as export promotion. *The World Economy, 30*(1), 22–38.
Saad, A. F. (2021). Institutional change in the global economy: How trade reform can be detrimental to welfare. *Economic Modeling, 95*(C), 97–110.
Samadi, A. H. (2019). Institutional quality and globalization in developing countries. In N. Faghih (Ed.), *Globalization and development economic and socio-cultural perspectives from emerging markets* (pp. 135–161). Springer.
Samadi, A. H., & Alipourian, M. (2021). Institutions and institutional change: Concepts and theories. In N. Faghih & A. H. Samadi (Eds.), *Dynamics of institutional change in emerging market economies* (pp. 107–132). Springer.
Samuelson, W., & Zeckhauser, R. (1988). Status quo bias in decision making. *Journal of Risk and Uncertainty, 1*, 7–59.
Santana-Gallego, M., & Pérez-Rodríguez, J. V. (2019). International trade, exchange rate regimes, and financial crises. *The North American Journal of Economics and Finance, 47*, 85–95.
Schumpeter, J. A. (1987). *Capitalism, socialism and democracy*. Counterpoint.
Schwarz, G. M., Yang, K. P., Chou, C., & Chiu, Y. J. (2020). A classification of structural inertia: Variations in structural response. *Asia Pacific Journal of Management, 37*(1), 33–63.
Splinter, M., & Klomp, J. (2022). Do sanctions cause economic growth collapses? In R. Beeres, R. Bertrand, J. Klomp, J. Timmermans, & J. Voetelink (Eds.), *NL ARMS Netherlands annual review of military studies* (NL ARMS). T.M.C. Asser Press.
Stone, A., Levy, B., & Paredes, R. (1996). Transaction costs and economic development, in empirical studies in institutional change. In L. J. Alston, T. Eggertsson, & D. C. North (Eds.). Cambridge University Press.
Stryja, C., Dorner, V., and Riefle, L. (2017). *Overcoming innovation resistance beyond status quo bias-a decision support system approach* (Research-in-Progress).
Surugiu, M.-R., & Surugiu, C. (2015). International trade, globalization and economic interdependence between European Countries: Implications for businesses and marketing framework. *Procedia Economics and Finance, 32*, 131–138.
Turner, J. J., & Wilson, K. (2006). Grocery loyalty: Tesco Clubcard and its impact on loyalty. *British Food Journal, 108*(11), 958–964.
Walter, T. (2022). Trade and welfare effects of a potential free trade agreement between Japan and the United States. *Review of World Economics, 158*, 1–32.
Wei, S. J. (2000). Natural openness and good government, NBER Working Paper, 7765.
Williamson, O. (1979). Transaction-cost economics: The governance of contractual relations. *Journal of Law and Economics, 22*(2), 233–261.
Yarbrough, B. V., & Yarbrough, R. M. (1987). Institutions for the governance of opportunism in international trade. *Journal of Law, Economics, and Organization, 3*(1), 129–139.
Zhuravsky, Y. A. (2019). Economic inertia and acceleration in the methodology of economic dynamics. *Economics and Innovation Management, 4*, 20–34.

The Transition to Sustainable Energy and Institutional Inertia

Ali Hussein Samadi and Masoumeh Alipourian

1 Introduction

Today, the necessity of transition to sustainable energy has been widely recognized for several reasons. First, Climate change due to global carbon dioxide emissions is increasing and current energy systems are unsustainable by all economic, social, and environmental criteria (Grubler, 2012: 8) Second, the future of energy systems is one of the policy-oriented challenges facing industrialized countries (Miller et al., 2013: 136). Third, the transition to newer and cleaner energy systems, such as renewable electricity sources and electric vehicles, often requires significant changes not only in technology, but also in political contexts, regulations, tariffs and pricing systems (Painuly, 2001, Sovacool, 2009, Sovacool & Hirsh, 2009, Nielsen et al., 2015).

One of the measures taken in response to the question of "how to take a step towards a low-carbon economy and transition to sustainable energy?" is the signing of the Kyoto Protocol, which obliges different countries to cooperate in reducing climate change. But complying with the provisions of this protocol is facing difficult obstacles, including free rides in some countries. The main mechanism thought in this agreement to achieve the goal of slowing climate change is based on market mechanisms (carbon emission pricing and carbon tax) with the aim of reducing the use of carbon-generating goods and services, increasing energy efficiency, using low-carbon technologies and fuels, and developing clean and renewable energies. This approach, using economic incentives, is the least expensive and most flexible mechanism to implement the agreement on carbon reduction. But the market mechanism (even if the carbon pricing mechanism can sufficiently and fundamentally modify the behavior of the actors) alone is not enough to make the necessary adjustments in the climate changes in the remaining time. Because, the carbon

A. H. Samadi (✉) · M. Alipourian
Department of Economics, Shiraz University, Shiraz, Iran
e-mail: asamadi@rose.shirazu.ac.ir

N. Faghih, A. H. Samadi (eds.), *Institutional Inertia*, Contributions to Economics,
https://doi.org/10.1007/978-3-031-51175-2_11

market (due to the existence of asymmetric information problems, incompleteness of the market, weak protection of intellectual property rights, existing infrastructure) cannot create enough incentive for carbon license trading to change the behavior of actors (Gunningham, 2012: 121). Therefore, the change of infrastructure, along with the adoption of policies that increase investment in low-carbon technologies, the expansion of large-scale research and development projects (which only the government can afford), along with following the initial development of renewable technologies and the intellectual property law (that facilitate and develop such technologies), becomes necessary (Aldy & Pizer, 2008: 21).

Another question that is raised in relation to the best solution to achieve a low-carbon economy and transition to sustainable energy is "which sectors of the world economy are responsible for the most carbon emissions, and how much is the share of each of these sectors?" The honest answer that can be given to this question is that: approximately 70% of greenhouse gas emissions are caused by energy production and consumption. Therefore, without changing the shape and transformation of the energy sector, it is almost impossible to calm down and reduce climate changes. This does not mean that in order to slow climate change, we should only focus on the energy sector, rather, on the contrary, this issue should be addressed from several aspects (such as preventing deforestation, or transforming other sectors, especially transportation). However, due to the high impact of the energy sector on greenhouse gas emissions, the transformation of this sector is at the heart of all actions and solutions (International Energy Agency, 2009: 3) and the most important tool to mitigate climate change.

So, we must know: (1) What does the transformation of the energy sector include? (2) What are the biggest obstacles to achieving this goal? and (3) What is the role of governance, regulation and legality in removing these obstacles and facilitating the transition to a low carbon and sustainable energy economy?

In response to the first question, the International Energy Agency (2010) put the changes in the energy sector on four bases: energy efficiency, use of renewable energy, use of nuclear energy, and carbon capture and storage. The answer to the second question is complex and multi-dimensional, and depends on the different governance paradigms (approaches) in the energy sector; the economic, social, and political approaches of different nations; the global and regional dimensions of the issue; and the implementation of long-term projects. The answer to the third question shows how, in different dimensions, governance, regulation and legality are basic and fundamental in the transformation of the energy sector into a low-carbon sector. For this purpose, the way of governance of countries should be determined in relation to energy transition (Gunningham, 2012: 122–123).

Analysts of the transition to sustainable energy believe that countries that have historically had a desire for active governance to achieve a sustainable energy transition have the capabilities and capacities that the liberal free market does not benefit from it (Crouch, 2005: 441). Some other researchers argue that countries that are able to support a variety of welfare policies experience a more equitable distribution of the effects of changing the energy system, thus having a greater chance of long-term success (Crepaz, 1998: 61). Because a fairer distribution of the benefits resulting from system change will lead to greater community support for sustainable innovations. Moreover, in countries where larger groups of green energy advocates have been replaced in formal political organizations (through the voting system), governments are able to use new policy tools to prioritize changing the existing energy system (Kuzemko et al., 2016: 100).

The goal of governance for transition is to achieve the goals of reducing greenhouse gas emissions by moving away from centralized and fossil fuel-based energy systems through sustainable energy innovations. However, despite the tendency to focus on these innovations, energy systems show different degrees and types of change, and different countries, governance to create a deep change in the energy system (while ensuring affordable and secure energy services), have experienced in different ways. One of the main reasons for the difference in energy governance among different countries is the uneven geographical distribution of fossil fuels in the world. Countries with an abundance of fossil resources such as oil and gas (due to major investments, the creation of extensive infrastructure, the use of human resources in fossil industries, dependence on the income from the sale of fossil fuels, and due to the economic, social and political consequences of replacing the existing energy systems with new systems), are not very inclined to transition to renewable energy sources. In various ways, it has tried to support the existing energy regimes and innovations such as carbon capture and storage, which are designed to improve the current energy systems (and not fundamental changes in the energy system). In fact, the interest groups in the fossil fuel industries emphasize the necessity of innovation in ways that guarantee their survival by lobbying. But the countries that do not have the gift of fossil resources, and are forced to create political and economic networks to access fossil fuels and are more vulnerable in energy crises such as the oil shock of the 1970s, have a longer history in creating sustainable energy systems and changing common energy systems. Some of these countries, such as Germany, Denmark and Sweden, by saving, increasing energy efficiency, encouraging the production of renewable energy (which is decentralized and owned by smaller groups in society) and supporting new technological innovations in the energy sector has started transitioning to sustainable energy systems. In contrast, the UK considers nuclear energy to be a sustainable energy source, and has enabled relatively less renewable energy generation, with almost all renewable energy generation owned by large corporations (Kuzemko et al., 2016: 100).

In this chapter, to answer the question why the governance for the transition to sustainable energy has been very different among different countries, and under what conditions and with what consequences is it possible, from the new institutionalist approaches, especially from the socio-technical transition (STT) literature (in which innovation is very important for sustainable change, and in this regard, governance becomes important in enabling sustainable innovations), have been used. In addition, to understand why different countries are transitioning to more sustainable energy systems at different speeds and paths, the viewpoint of institutionalists on institutional changes, institutional inertia, and the role of path dependence in this regard are also analyzed.

This chapter is organized in 5 sections. In the second section, after referring to the idea and concept of transition, three approaches of new institutionalists (technological social transition approach; co-evolutionary approach to transitions; and social conflict approach) have been analyzed in relation to the transition to sustainable energy. In the third section, the analytical framework of governance for the transition to sustainable energy is presented. The fourth section is dedicated to the analysis of the relationship between institutional inertia and the transition to sustainable energy. In the fifth section, we have drawn conclusions.

2 Transition to Sustainable Energy

The modern economy is highly dependent on energy and access to energy is necessary to have a standard life and provide public goods. However, the increase in energy consumption has made the world community face many environmental challenges. This issue has increasingly led to the understanding that addressing climate change (and other environmental problems) requires a transition from fossil fuel-based energy to low-carbon systems based on clean and renewable energy technologies (such as wind and solar).

2.1 *The Idea of Transition to Sustainable Energy*

For the first time in 1976, Lovins proposed the idea of "sustainable energy transition" by suggesting that America is facing two different paths for its energy system. The first path was the continuation of the existing policy and the development of high-level fossil fuel technologies to increase energy supply. The second path was a combination of policies such as increasing energy efficiency, rapid development of renewable energy sources, and increasing energy quality, to respond to final needs, and the transition of fossil fuel technologies to renewable technologies. Lovins (1976: 187) has described these two pathways as *"hard" and "soft" energy pathways*.

According to Lovins (1976), the distinction between *hard and soft energy paths* does not depend on the amount of energy consumption, but rather on the technical and socio-political structure of the energy system. A hard energy path (which is based on energy technology infrastructure and energy supply), requires central control and thus concentrates political and economic power; It constantly distorts political structures and social priorities; increases the bureaucracy; It is inappropriate for equal distribution among the members of society; and provides an incorrect analysis of costs and benefits. Therefore, by following a hard energy path, the existing energy systems have become impenetrable and undemocratic, the people who consume energy are mostly unable to participate in the planning and understanding of the complex details of these systems, and it is very difficult for energy consumers to understand the complex details of these large systems. On the other hand, soft track technologies are technologies that are distributed on a small scale, designed based on local social and ecological conditions and under local ownership and control, and can help to community well-being and flexibility, and democratic participatory policies (Lovins, 1978: 477–478). Therefore, these technologies are a tool to promote and facilitate public support for the future of renewable energy.

According to Lovins (1978: 478), the two approaches to energy development are culturally incompatible because they have completely different environmental and socio-political consequences. In his opinion, the trend of hard path energy systems will continue until a change in social philosophy is achieved; in a way that considers the provision of "sustainable energy" as a human and social right and specifies the value and relationship between energy production networks and their socio-political consequences.

Years after the publication of Lovin's theory, most countries started using cheap fossil fuels (that is, the hard energy path). But after a few decades, after seeing environmental challenges and climate changes, some countries took the approach of soft energy and transition to renewable energies and increasing energy efficiency. Therefore, the energy paths have increasingly diverged, so that the movement in the path of soft energy is much faster and more stable in some countries than in others. In fact, these countries have achieved environmental and energy sustainability at the lowest cost with the growth of renewable energy, demand management and energy efficiency (moving towards soft energy) (Lockwood et al., 2013: 3).

Here we can raise the question: why and how some countries are able to implement policies that lead to rapid and sustainable changes in the energy system, while others are not? In other words, why is there a divergence in the transition to a sustainable energy system among different countries (such as UK and Germany)? The answer to this question goes back to choosing different paths to reach a sustainable energy system. The lack of success of UK in transitioning to a sustainable energy system is due to the nature of the country's institutional system and policy paradigm. The prerequisite for this country's success in achieving sustainable energy is the establishment of a proper governance system or managed energy transition, in which both the relationship between the institutions in charge of energy, actors and policy makers have been paid attention to, and the change in performance and consequences have been emphasized.

2.2 *The Concept of Transition to Sustainable Energy*

From the point of view of Markand, Raven and Truffer (2012: 956) in the literature of socio-technical transition, "transition" is: A set of processes that lead to fundamental changes in socio-technical systems and lead to change in various technical, material, organizational, institutional, political, economic, and socio-cultural aspects. "Transitional sustainability" is also a multi-dimensional and fundamental long-term transformative process through which the established socio-technical systems are moved towards a more sustainable system of production and consumption. "*Energy transition*" or *energy change* means changing the function of a wide range of actors in the energy system (including electricity producers, wholesalers, supply companies, network operators, energy service providers and energy users). Such changes could include selling energy services in retail markets instead of selling electricity and gas, investing in renewable electricity generation technologies instead of conventional gas turbines, or choosing more economical home appliances in energy consumption by consumers, or the decision of small businesses to use automatic lighting controllers (connected to sensors). Whether in business models or investing in new technologies or in new procedures for using energy, moving in the direction of soft energy means innovation.

How far the energy system of a country moves towards a "soft transition" path depends on the laws and regulations, incentives and institutions in the system. This approach to the nature of energy transition (changing functions, laws and regulations, incentives and institutional infrastructures), together with the diverse experience of different countries, raises key questions about the poor performance of some countries in the transition to sustainable energy, including two basic questions, as follows:

(a) Why laws and regulations, incentives and institutional infrastructures have evolved in different ways in different energy systems?
(b) Why have the laws and regulations, incentives and institutional infrastructures in the energy systems of some countries moved faster towards the transition to soft energy?

The answers to these questions are different according to the different approaches of the new institutionalists, which are mentioned below.

2.3 New Institutionalist Approaches to Analyzing Sustainable Energy Transition

The three important approaches of the new institutionalists in relation to the transition to sustainable energy are: (1) the "socio-technical transition" (STT) approach proposed by the sociological institutionalists. (2) the "co-evolutionary approach to transitions" which is the idea of historical institutionalists. And (3) the "social conflict and predominance of political power" approach, which belongs to rational choice institutionalists.

2.3.1 The Socio-Technical Transitions Approach

The main framework of the theory of transition to sustainable energy is the STT approach. Socio-technical systems of transition are one of the concepts used by sociological institutionalists regarding political institutions, decision-making processes, and changes, which is used for how energy systems function and change. Socio-technical systems are defined as systems that relate the function (performance) of technology to social needs (Smith et al., 2010: 436), and includes a wide range of separable subjects (and at the same time dynamically interrelated) such as environment, infrastructure, technology, industry, civil society, institutions, policies, etc. (Rotmans et al., 2001: 16).

To describe how transitions, occur, STT theory uses concepts such as regimes, niches, and landscapes. Energy systems are regimes that show the interaction between niche innovations and the socio-technical landscape. Regimes provide the context for the realization of diverse social functions, the environment and suitable conditions for new technologies and other innovations (Smith et al., 2010: 440). A socio-technical regime is a very broad concept and not only including "technological regimes" consisting of the normal work of engineers and companies, complex engineering laws and practices, skills, characteristics of the output of institutions and infrastructures, but also includes the rules and procedures of other groups such as: users, policy makers, social groups, suppliers, capital banks, etc. (Geels, 2002: 1259–60). This set of rules and procedures stabilizes the existing paths (the existing situation) and more importantly, the new changes and developments are out of the focus of the uninformed actors. The socio-technical landscape includes social and physical factors such as broad political coalitions, socio-cultural norms, paradigms and economic growth. In addition, fundamental innovations are providers of new methods of meeting social demands (Geels & Schot, 2007: 400).

The nature of change and innovation in the regimes is progressive, in contracts; radical innovations related to STT are created in niches. Niche innovations, emphasizing on technical innovations, have been pioneers in meeting social demands and include R&D, learning-by-doing processes, and the creation of supportive social networks such as supply chains, etc. (Geels, 2002: 1261). In the beginning, niches are expensive, have poor performance, and unstable status. For this reason, they should be supported against the common option in the market, so that they can go through the period of incubation and development (Schot, 1998, cited by Lockwood et al., 2013: 9). But niches, by creating a gap and tension, and by challenging the existing energy systems, provide pressure to change and replace these systems. For example, new scientific and technical achievements regarding climate change have put pressures on the existing systems of energy production and consumption to change (Kuzemko et al., 2016: 98).

The trajectory of technological changes, (which is a set of deep structural trends such as cultural and normative values, environmental problems, oil price growth, economic growth, war, immigration, broad political coalitions (Smith et al., 2010: 440) are described, placed in a "socio-technical landscape". From the landscape of the regime and niches, the "landscape level" represents the "external structural context" (Lockwood et al., 2013: 9). In this framework, "transitions defined as regime change are created through mutual processes within and between these levels" (Geels, 2010: 495). Unlike regimes that tend to reproduce normal patterns of innovation, niches are known as exogenous sites of "evolutionary change" (Smith et al., 2010: 440). Nevertheless, if changes in the external landscape create pressures (such as climate change) on the regime in a way that leads to gaps, tensions, and windows of opportunity, niches will disappear (Geels, 2010: 495). Therefore, transitions do not happen easily because the elements in the socio-technical body are aligned and resist change (Geels, 2002: 1258). Resistance patterns (Patterns of lock-in) include behavioral patterns, granted benefits, infrastructure, favorable subsidies, attracted investments, laws and regulations (Geels, 2010: 495). In such a situation, niches can hardly be used because laws and regulations, infrastructure, user practices, maintenance networks are all in accordance with existing technologies. However, the transition is possible and has historically occurred in various cases, including in energy systems (Lockwood et al., 2013: 10).

The transition consists of a series of interconnected changes at different levels, which often occur over a considerable period of time (Kuzemko et al., 2016: 97). The socio-technical transition is a change from a relatively stable state of an energy system to another state. Thus, transitions are profound and large-scale transformations (Verbong & Loorbach, 2012: 6). Transition to low-carbon energy, including changes in energy efficiency, innovation and the use of a wide range of low-carbon technologies, extensive changes in industries, changes in markets, the performance of actors, policies and cultural concepts at the level of the national and global economy (Foxon, 2011: 2258).

According to the STT approach, the transition is most likely to occur where, simultaneously with the pressures of the landscape on a regime, there is an unexpected progress in niches. In a targeted transition (where the actors (governments) are trying to accelerate the transition, and niches can be better nurtured or managed through strategic management, and in cases where the factors of the landscape put more pressure on the regimes), the transition will happen faster.

From the point of view of comparative institutionalism, such an approach to transition has limitations. The first limitation is not stating the cause and roots of policymaking. Since transitions represent profound changes on a large scale, they not only imply procedures and functions, but also represent different social groups (for example, producers, distributors, and new retailers) that are affected by the trend. The transition benefited or suffered (Fouquet, 2010: 6591). Hence, some groups are heavily involved in imposing their economic and political power and resisting change or at least influencing the type of change (ibid, 2010: 6592).

The theory of STT has been criticized for ignoring such issues and not analyzing the causes of policy-making or political decision-making (ibid, 2010: 6591). Instead of analyzing the political and institutional conditions (which lead to the adoption of some policies), this approach focuses on the prohibition of individual policies (Meadowcroft, 2011: 73). As a result, in theoretical discussions, policy-making in managed transition seems completely straightforward and easy; while the realities in different countries show the opposite of this issue. The lack of analysis of policies in the transition to sustainable energy, especially the managed transition, is very problematic (Markand et al., 2012: 957). Although the theory of STT includes interpretive frameworks, structural value of culture, norms and power structures in a historical sense, but how these aspects affect the choice of policies, laws and regulations and procedures should be considered. (Ibid, 2012: 956).

The second criticism of the theory of STT is that its explanatory power how actors and institutions interact in regimes, niches and landscape, is limited. For example, although the landscape of scientific knowledge about climate change (which puts pressure on current regimes of energy production and consumption) is common in all countries, this theory does not explain why the reactions of the regime are very different. The heterogeneity of the factors in the landscape, the complexity and the number of processes in the regime and niches, and the fact that several regimes and niches may interact with each other, means that they are different and that the energy transition is likely to occur historically (Smith et al., 2010: 443).

2.3.2 A Co-evolutionary Approach to Transitions

From Faxon's point of view, any certain socio-technical system, in addition to intra-system communication, is in communication with other socio-technical systems and influences them (Foxon, 2011: 2262). For example, transportation systems and fossil fuels are historically intertwined, and increasing path dependence over time has prevented sustainable change. This definition of energy system is based on path dependency and includes a wide range of actors. These actors are affected by changes in the economic environment (supply chain and markets) and the socio-political environment (relationships between industry activists and policy makers, civil society and people) (Kuzemko et al., 2016: 97).

Foxon (2011: 2262), argues that change is the result of interaction between five key system elements including Ecosystems, technologies, institutions (i.e. regulatory frameworks, property rights and standard forms of business organization), business strategies (tools and processes by which companies organize their activities to achieve their socio-economic goals), and the way users act. These different systems evolve under their own dynamics, they are simultaneously evolving with each other, and they mutually affect each other. For example, user practices, (which plays an important role in the formation of energy demand), can be influenced by technologies, business practices and organization, and enable or disable specific methods. From Foxon's point of view, the co-evolutionary approach (simultaneous evolution) provides a single framework in which it is possible to simultaneously consider changes at the micro, medium and macro levels of the energy system, that is, in addition to considering the dynamics within the systems, it also pays attention to the causal interactions between them. This framework represents an attempt to capture the complexities, dynamic interactions, and bilateral stability that can exist between different elements and actors in the energy system.

The framework provided by Foxon (2011) has some limitations. This framework does not provide details about what is in each system and, most importantly, what is happening and who is involved in the interactions between them. In addition, it does not specify how we expect these different elements to interact with each other, or why they interact in different ways in different countries, or why the interaction changes over time.

2.3.3 The Social Conflict, and Predominance of Political Power Approach

In the rational choice theory, actors seek to maximize a specific set of their preferences or tastes, and their behavior is based on strategic interactions (Hall & Taylor, 1996: 45–944). In practice, these preferences are often defined as financial benefits, political power or electoral advantage. Institutions that emerge from these strategic interactions have arrangements that minimize transaction costs (Coase, 1937; Williamson, 1985; North, 1990) and solve collective action problems (Ostrom, 1990). Since the existence of institutions is usually explained by reference to their functions, they tend to be seen as socially optimal and therefore inherently stable (Hall & Taylor, 1996: 46–945).

In the social conflict approach, the maximum benefits belong to the actors who have the most political power. In fact, the emphasis is on the primacy of political power, whether created through formal political institutions or informally through military or economic means. Nevertheless, even the social conflict approach considers institutional arrangements to be stable in the absence of external drivers of change, because they represent the most powerful actors in the system, who have no motivation to change. (Lockwood et al., 2013: 13, cited in Acemoglu et al., 2005).

Hall and Soskice (2001: 8–9) have chosen the rational choice approach as a solution to minimize the transaction cost, which presents certain hypotheses about the relative advantage of different systems with different types of innovation. However, this approach of institutional economics is completely static compared to dynamic approaches in which ideas play a greater role (especially in explaining the different rates of institutional change in different countries).

Institutionalists' description of rational choice of institutional changes, like the theory of socio-technical systems, is based on exogenous shocks such as changes in relative prices or technological changes (Geels, 2010: 497). However, this approach is difficult to analyze how to change in the managed technological transition. Moreover, the assumption that actors always know what is in their best interest has been criticized in this approach. On the contrary, in the approach of sociological institutionalism, behavior is not based on pursuing fixed financial or political benefits, but is based on social status or relations derived from specific cultural practices (Hall & Taylor, 1996: 949).

In Table 1, the approach of new institutionalists to the energy transition and the criticism of these approaches are briefly presented.

The approaches of new institutionalists, by themselves, do not provide a comparative explanatory analysis to understand "why different countries are transitioning to sustainable energy at different speeds and paths". The answer to this question goes back to the issue of institutional diversity of capitalist systems, which is mentioned below.

Table 1 New institutionalist approaches to analyzing energy transition

Approaches	Theoretical foundations	Criticism
Socio-Technical Transition (STT) Approach (The theory of sociological institutionalists)	Energy systems are regimes that show the interaction between niches and the socio-technical landscape. (Smith et al., 2010: 440). Socio-technical systems relate the function of technology to social needs (Smith et al., 2010: 436) Unlike regimes that tend to reproduce normal patterns of innovation, emerging innovations are known as exogenous places of "evolutionary changes" (Smith et al., 2010: 440). From the perspective of the regime and niches, the "landscape level" represents the "external structural context" (Lockwood et al., 2013: 9). Transitions do not happen easily because the elements in the social technical body are aligned with each other and resist change (Geels, 2002: 1258). The transition is possible and has historically occurred in various cases, including in energy systems (Lockwood et al., 2013: 10). The transition is most likely to occur where, at the same time as the pressures of the landscape on a regime, unexpected niches occur. (Kuzemko et al., 2016: 98). In the approach of sociological institutionalism, behavior is based on the status or social relations derived from specific cultural practices (Hall & Taylor, 1996: 949). Achieving a sustainable energy system depends on the political conditions governing the society, and the power of pressure groups in limiting changes (Kuzemko et al., 2016: 98).	This approach does not analyze the causes of policy-making or political decisions (Meadowcroft, 2011). In the theory of STT, there is no mention of how culture, norms and power structures influence the choice of policies, laws and regulations and procedures historically. (Markand et al., 2012). The power of this approach to explain how actors and institutions interact in regimes, niches and perspectives is limited and weak (Smith et al., 2010).
Co-evolutionary approach to transitions (Historical Institutionalist Theory)	Any given socio-technical system, in addition to intra-system communication, is in communication with other socio-technical systems and influences them (Foxon, 2011: 2262). Different systems evolve under their own dynamics, and they are evolving simultaneously with each other, and they mutually influence each other (Foxon, 2011: 2262). The co-evolutionary approach, in	This approach does not provide details about what happens in each system and who is involved in the interactions between the system components (Kuzemko et al., 2016). In this approach, how the different elements of the system interact with each other, the reason for their difference in different countries, and the reason for their

(continued)

Table 1 (continued)

Approaches	Theoretical foundations	Criticism
	addition to considering the dynamics within the system, it also pays attention to the causal interactions between them (Foxon, 2011: 2262). Change is the result of the interaction between five key elements of the system including: ecosystems, technologies, institutions, the strategies of business, and user practices (Foxon, 2011: 2262). This framework, represents dynamic interactions and two-way stability that can exist between different elements and actors in the energy system (Kuzemko et al., 2016: 98). This approach is based on path dependence and includes a wide range of actors. Actors are influenced by changes in the economic, social and political environment (Kuzemko et al., 2016: 98).	change over time have not been determined. (Kuzemko et al., 2016).
Social conflict approach (Theory of rational choice institutionalists)	Actors seek to maximize a certain set of their preferences or tastes, and their behavior is based on strategic interactions (Hall & Taylor, 1996: 45–944). Actor's preferences are often defined as financial benefits, political power or electoral advantage. Institutions that emerge from these strategic interactions have arrangements that minimize transaction and solve collective action problems (Ostrom, 1990). The maximum benefits belong to the actors who have the most political power Lockwood et al., 2013: 13) In this approach, the emphasis is on the primacy of political power, whether it is through formal political institutions, whether it is informally through military or economic means (Lockwood et al., 2013: 13, quoted by Acemoglu et al., 2005). The school of social conflict, in the absence of exogenous drivers of change, considers institutional arrangements to be stable, because they represent the most powerful actors in the system, who have no motivation to change (Lockwood et al., 2013: 13). Rational choice institutionalists' description of institutional changes, is	Rational choice institutionalists do not pay attention to how change occurs in a managed technological transition (Kuzemko et al., 2016). The assumption that actors always know what is in their best interest has been criticized in this approach (Kuzemko et al., 2016). This approach is completely static compared to dynamic approaches in which ideas play a greater role (Lockwood et al., 2013).

(continued)

Table 1 (continued)

Approaches	Theoretical foundations	Criticism
	based on exogenous shocks such as changes in relative prices or technological changes (Geels, 2010: 497).	

Source: Author's own table

2.3.4 Institutional Diversity of Capitalist Systems in the Transition to Sustainable Energy

One of the most important applications of new institutionalist theories is to discover institutional diversity in capitalist systems and its consequences for economic performance. The approach of institutional diversity in the capitalist system relates the significant differences in the speed of transition to sustainable energy to the conflict between the previous liberal market institutions and the neoliberal policy paradigm and managed markets and social market policies. The institutional diversity of capitalist systems explains the question why it was easier for Germany, as a coordinated (and balanced) economy, to step into the path of transition to sustainable energy, compared to the UK. Achieving this success for Germany is most likely due to having a long-term plan and its proper management, and an institutional structure that is appropriate to it. The public tendency to support the transition to sustainable energy in Germany has led to collective action in support of the "Green Energy Ideal" as a mechanism to prevent climate change (which is considered a social goal). While, the UK energy system is formed in such a way that the regime resists change, the protection of niche innovations is less effective, and the landscape factors, compared to managed market systems (Germany, Denmark) are destabilizing (Lockwood, 2013). The more complete and more realistic the neoliberal policy paradigm is adopted, the desire and will of the government to invest in networks that support technological innovations in the private and public sectors (for example, universities, technology companies, development banks) will be more. For example, Germany accelerated the transition to sustainable energy by restructuring institutions that provided low-cost facilities to niche technologies, and by adopting control policies (Meadowcroft, 2011: 72). Most of the countries with coordinated market economies (such as Denmark and Germany) have electoral systems tailored to environmental policies, while countries such as the UK with liberal market economies maintain electoral systems based on the majority vote which work against smaller parties, including pro-green energy parties. The welfare system of countries with managed capitalism has less inequality and a higher level of welfare services. However, in liberal market economies, real wages have grown less, and a larger share of national income has been invested, and welfare services have grown less. As a result, inequality has increased dramatically, there is more poverty in the lower deciles, and the real income of the middle deciles has decreased (Lockwood et al., 2013).

Institutional diversity of capitalist systems emphasizes different aspects of institutional formation, performance and change, including financial or political benefits, ideas, strategic behavior and limitations of existing institutions. However, according to Hall and Taylor (1996: 955), these different approaches to energy transition "have a lot of common analytical ground" and can complement each other in certain combinations. The **first** of these common themes is that the difference between countries is due to having different institutional systems that have evolved simultaneously, are linked to each other, and support each other. Such systems are not unchangeable and are not always found equally in all sectors of the economy. These differences in the dominant institutional systems have disappeared to some extent with globalization, but it is very unlikely to eradicate them.

The **second** common theme is that the institutional diversity of capitalist systems shows a kind of contrast between what is in the "coordinated" or "managed" institutional systems prevailing in the northwest of the European continent (Germany) (as a type of policy paradigm), with the "liberal" or "market-oriented" systems governing the countries of UK and America (as a different type of policy paradigm). In the approach of Hall and Soskice (2001: 8–9), (rational choice approach) in liberal market-oriented economies, exchange takes place between enterprises that work competitively in the long term. In contrast, the economic enterprises in the coordinated market economy are more focused on non-market relations including: wider relations or incomplete contracts, network management based on the exchange of private information within networks, and cooperation based on mutual trust, in compared to competitive relationships, they are dependent. Governments in the liberal capitalist system and the coordinated and managed capitalist system have roles that they play by using different institutional systems. Schmidt (2002: 113) argues that in a liberal market economy, the state has a liberal arbiter character with distant relations with the private sector, while in coordinated or managed capitalism; the state plays the role of a facilitator.

The **third** common theme in all types of capitalist systems is focusing on basic economic institutions (including labor markets and educational organizations, corporate governance and how companies access resources, and how to manage relationships between companies in the supply chain). Therefore, the relative advantage of different countries in all kinds of innovations (which makes these countries superior compared to other countries) is derived from these institutions. Companies in liberal market-oriented economies due to the flexibility in the labor market and the relationships between companies in such economies, have a tendency to radical innovations, while companies in a coordinated and managed market economy have an increasing tendency for progressive (developmental and profitable) innovations (Hall & Soskice, 2001: 36–44).

In Table 2, the differences and common themes of institutional diversity in capitalist systems are mentioned.

Table 2 Institutional diversity of capitalist systems: differences and common themes

Institutional diversity of capitalist systems	The differences	Common themes
"coordinated" or "managed" institutional systems	Economic enterprises in the coordinated market economy are dependent to non-market relations including: broader relations or incomplete contracts, network management based on the exchange of private information within the networks, and cooperation based on mutual trust, compared to competitive relationships (Hall & Soskice, 2001). In coordinated or managed capitalism, the government plays the role of a facilitator (Schmidt, 2002). Firms in a coordinated and managed market economy have an increasing desire for progressive (developmental and profitable) innovations (Hall & Soskice, 2001). In a coordinated and managed market economy, the desire and willingness of the government to invest in networks that support technological innovations in the private and public sectors (for example, universities, technology companies, development banks) more than. Most of the countries with coordinated market economy (such as Denmark and Germany) have electoral systems in accordance with environmental policies. The welfare system of countries with managed capitalism has less inequality and a higher level of welfare services.	In all types of capitalist systems, the focus is on basic economic institutions (including labor markets and educational organizations, corporate governance and how companies access financial affairs, and how to manage relationships between companies in the supply chain). (Hall & Soskice, 2001). The relative advantage of different countries in all kinds of innovations (which makes these countries superior compared to other countries) is derived from basic economic institutions (Hall & Soskice, 2001). Ideas and especially policy paradigms play a key role in the institutional diversity of capitalist systems under the influence of liberalization caused by globalization and European integration (Schmidt, 2002).
"Liberal" or "market-oriented" institutional systems	In liberal market-oriented economies, exchange takes place between firms that work competitively in the long term. (Hall & Soskice, 2001). In a liberal market economy, the government has a liberal arbiter character with distant relations with the private sector (Schmidt, 2002). Firms of market-oriented liberal economies tend to radical innovations due to the flexibility in the labor market and the relationships	

(continued)

Table 2 (continued)

Institutional diversity of capitalist systems	The differences	Common themes
	between companies that exist in such economies (Hall & Soskice, 2001). In a liberal market economy, the electoral system is based on the majority vote, which works against smaller parties, including those in favor of green energy. In liberal market economies, welfare services are less developed. As a result, inequality has increased significantly, there is more poverty in the lower deciles, and the real income of the middle deciles has decreased.	

Source: Author's own table

2.4 Transition Conditions to Sustainable Energy

Based on the characteristics of energy systems, special conditions can be considered for the transition to sustainable energy. **The first** and basic condition is related to the **nature of investment in energy**. To change the outcome and performance of actors in the energy system (especially private sector actors), new methods (taking into account any support mechanism through public policy) should be less cost or more profitable and at the same time, the risk of these actions, including political risk, should be sufficiently reduced. The overall profit adjusted under risk conditions should be more than the profit that can be achieved in other situations and should be in accordance with the time schedule required by investors, including shareholders.

The second condition is related to the **nature of institutional arrangements** in energy markets, both at the wholesale and retail levels. Institutional arrangements that include a wide range of market entrants are more conducive to innovation in practices and outcomes than exclusive ones.

The third condition is that the successful implementation of sustainable practices and outcomes depends on the **risk-return adjustment** to attract investors, but this adjustment is not such that to imposes unacceptable costs on energy consumers. This issue is applied not only in relation to large companies, but also in the situation where a large number of actors are private households that have invested in sustainable energy.

The fourth condition for the success of the policies designed to move the energy system towards sustainability is that **these policies reinforce each other**. Such policies should have increasing returns or spillovers, both economically (for example, reducing the costs of developing sustainable technologies) and politically (for example, creating interest groups or new institutions adopting reforms).

The fifth condition is to **have knowledge of climate change** as a potential factor and driver for changing energy systems and transitioning to sustainable energy. However, the extent of its effectiveness depends on the extent to which the climate crisis is an acceptable reason for change. The deeper the understanding of the climate change crisis, the greater the possibility of fundamental changes in the energy system. In practice, in most fields, climate change is seen as a long-term problem, whose effects are uncertain and scattered. For this reason, other issues such as energy security and its price are usually more important for most people. In most cases, these households are the ones who have to bear the costs of transition. So it is very important for households to understand the crisis of climate change, because they impose restrictions on policy makers.

The sixth condition is related to the **nature of the dominant policy paradigm**(-s). If the dominant policy-making paradigm is compatible with sustainability and gives it a lot of value, the effectiveness of policies that support new practices and achievements for a sustainable future is greater (Kuzemko et al., 2016).

The degree of alignment of these factors is different in different conditions and places. For this reason, we do not expect the transition to sustainable energy to happen at the same speed and in the same way everywhere. Such differences give rise to the question: "How do interactions between actors create different settings and why?". We will find the answer to this question in the third section.

3 Analytical Framework of Governance for the Transition to Sustainable Energy

Historical studies on the transition to energy show that "technological innovations", "market actors" and "governance in the distribution of benefits from new technologies in society" are the main factors of change. Today, in the transition to sustainable energy, conscious and targeted efforts to create laws, incentives and institutions, in order to guide and initiate the transition, play a very important role (Markand et al., 2012: 956). Emphasizing the importance of governance for the transition to sustainable energy, the researchers of STT considered necessary the government's political interventions in the form of tariff exemptions to protect technological innovations until they are ready to emerge and spread, because the actors of the existing systems resist technological changes (Geels, 2014: 37). From the point of view of these researchers, the success of governance depends on a long-term and targeted stance on the positive relationship between technological innovations and important social political programs (Raven et al., 2015: 5).

In the analytical framework of the new institutionalists, based on the STT approach, policy-making institutions and their relationship with policy-makers, how to choose policies and how to govern to change procedures in the transition to sustainable energy are determined. Policy-making institutions include a wide range of policy packages within a country, including formal and informal laws and norms that affect the type of voting system as well as the extent of providing citizens' welfare. In addition, policy-making institutions for prioritizing economic goals, energy and climate policies, and how energy and climate are related, policy makers and market actors, in achieving energy goals, have also been considered. The question raised here is: should the change of the energy system be left to the market, or should the government play the role of leadership and coordination through targeted governance? The answer to this question will be different depending on the political conditions, local energy sources, political goals, governing laws and regulations, market conditions for the activities of energy companies, etc. The forces influencing sustainable change use different procedures to influence energy policy makers and governance decisions. These effects will be different according to the political contexts and local energy sources, which in turn, will affect the nature of energy governance, including the hierarchy of policy goals, the choice of policy tools, regulations, and market conditions for emerging technology firms, and therefore, performance and outcomes. Finally, the energy system changes when the procedures change. By establishing new procedures over time, new forces and conditions provide governance grounds for sustainable innovations. This issue helps us understand the complexity and diversity of governance for sustainable energy innovations, and the transition to sustainable energy (Kuzemko et al., 2016: 102–103).

Due to the importance of the elements of dominant institutional systems, policy paradigms and the interests of actors (especially important political and economic groups), it is necessary to describe the governance relationship with them and how each of them affects the energy sector, which we will discuss further.

3.1 Energy Governance and Policy-Making Paradigm

The policymaking paradigm is based on ideas. These ideas are used in the form of formal and informal rules over time. The importance of ideas in the policy-making process is that they are the intermediate link between institutions and behaviors. Ideas play a role both in the formation of political action and in the restructuring of political values and interests (Schmidt, 2010: 2).

In the framework of ideas and standards, policy makers specify not only the policy goals and the type of policy tools that can be used to achieve those goals, but also the main nature of the problems. Ideas, or the policy paradigm, in addition to influencing important decisions such as the selection of goals and policy tools, also influence the more precise regulation of policies. Ideas, after being accepted in the policy-making process, are considered obvious and customary (Hall, 1993: 279). In fact, the set of established ideas become knowledge that can be transferred through education in society. The framework of ideas is embedded in the form of institutions, and the institutions, under the influence of governance decision-making processes, become regular behaviors, norms and rules.

In the STT approach, both the governance change process for the energy system and the changes within the energy system have been considered. From the point of view of sociological institutionalists, governance is a dynamic and changeable process over time. With the transfer of power to another political party because of general elections (in critical and uncertain conditions), or gradual changes and the accumulation of new rules and norms over time, governance undergoes changes. If it is recognized that there is a problem and existing technologies and governance cannot solve this problem, change is possible. Therefore, new policy ideas and paradigms should be replaced. These changes do not happen easily and new ideas should be involved with the presuppositions in previous policies and challenge them to prove their legitimacy. Therefore, policy-making is a continuous effort to gain power and transform the existing conditions. In other words, existing institutions often form new forms of governance, because changes are relative and there is a kind of compromise between the status quo and the continuity of change (Kuzemko et al., 2016: 100).

3.2 Energy Governance, Performance and Consequences of Energy Transition

The change in the performance of the energy transition actors and the resulting consequences lead to the formation of a transition through the laws and incentives applied by governance institutions on the energy system. Using the institutionalism approach, we can see these institutions evolving through the interaction between political and economic interests, policy paradigms, general tendency, and the inertia of existing institutions (including economic and political institutions).

The main role is played by policy-making paradigms (through political projects stimulating the public opinion of the majority of the society). Institutionalized policy paradigms are not only through influencing policy objectives, tools and rules, but also in the design of institutions that are established to manage policy areas (Kuzemko, 2013: a51). These, in turn, also have impacts on performance and outcomes at the business, industry and individual levels – for example within energy systems. Therefore, there are interrelationships between different levels of governance system, policy paradigm, goals, tools, rules, structure of energy organizations and general tendency. In this approach, the main focus is on the relationship between economy and transitional politics (up to technical procedures, usage practices and technologies). Because in cases where there are sufficient economic incentives or political will to change the nature of energy demand, the usage procedures are often susceptible to change (Unruh, 2000). Technical factors are less important for comparative analysis, because technologies are mostly available everywhere and therefore cannot play a major role in explaining the difference between the paths of different countries and the speed of transition. In contrast, investments in certain technologies throughout history (and especially in infrastructure) create a major path dependency and therefore play a more prominent role.

3.3 Energy Governance, Actors, and Mutual Relations

Interest groups in the energy sector are formed, limited, established through institutions and are influenced by ideas. It is important to describe the three main groups of actors in the energy sector (i.e., suppliers, policymakers, and energy consumers) for a better understanding of the transition to sustainable energy. The relations between groups of actors lead to the creation of institutions that manage the energy system in each particular country. The change in these relationships causes the change in governance. These entities include energy markets, investment methods, technological changes and their effects on environmental systems (such as greenhouse gas emissions) which have more feedback effects on actors (Scrase & Smith, 2009: 710).

In most countries, at the beginning of energy transition, energy production, supply and investment are under the control of existing energy companies (which are mostly large private sector companies and basically seek to maximize profit and minimize risk). However, energy suppliers' perspective on short-term and long-term profits is different, and it depends on corporate governance, access to financial markets, their relationships with other companies, and the extent of their interaction with social goals. When suppliers invest in certain technologies, these investments lead to subsequent actions in energy markets and investment development and due to the existence of very long-lived infrastructures in the energy sector, it gives the nature of path dependence to regimes and transitions. Suppliers may influence the policy process through a range of tools, such as direct lobbying, obtaining government support, and participating in technical committees related to markets. Since large energy companies are the center of providing energy goods and services, they become the main channel of energy policy. A common strategy of large energy companies is to threaten the government with investment strikes or capital outflow abroad, which can lead to the downfall of the government. This gives them political power and high influence in policy-making (Meadowcroft, 2005: 492).

One of the main tools of large companies to influence regulation and policy making is their financial ability to bear the very high costs of the energy sector, which itself is an obstacle for newcomers to enter the energy markets (mostly innovators of low-carbon and sustainable energy industries). The relative power of newcomers to penetrate energy markets, and accelerate the transition to low-carbon and sustainable energy depends to some extent on their degree of integration. The lack of unity among the innovators of low-carbon and sustainable energy industries will maintain the existing situation.

The regulation of energy sector policies is influenced by various factors, including the relationship between politicians and energy industry activists and energy users (especially households who are also voters). For this reason, since the 1980s, governments have tried to depoliticize the energy sector. Therefore, at the beginning of the transition to sustainable energy, there is little desire to invest in this sector (Kuzemko et al., 2016). In this regard, there are differences between different countries regarding the level of concern of people and business owners (as energy users) about climate change, and their will to move towards low-carbon energy. How much these concerns affect policymakers depends on the influence of environment friendly parties and civil society organizations in governments. To the extent that environmental issues, especially climate change, are important to energy users, policy makers are likely to pay more attention to changes in greenhouse gas emissions. Nevertheless, the importance of these issues for households is often lower than the cost of energy services and concerns about energy security, and there is little willingness to pay for low-carbon energy (Lockwood, 2013). As a result, policy makers will also worry about the costs of policymaking, and in fact, this approach will lead to the formation of dominant institutions.

As an energy user, the commercial sector is important for policy making for two reasons: 1. a number of voters are employed in this sector, 2. they can be a threat to capital outflows abroad. Large energy consumers tend to lobby against policies that increase energy costs. Nevertheless, other businesses may support the transition to sustainable energy because it creates opportunities to earn money through the sale of low-carbon products and services and the acquisition of renewable energy-related assets. Business leaders are also influenced by ideas related to climate change and may try to adopt long-term strategies that sacrifice short-term profits for corporate action ahead of expected regulations. Business leaders are also influenced by ideas related to climate change and may try to adopt long-term strategies that sacrifice short-term profits for corporate action ahead of expected regulations.

Politicians (policy activists), in addition to political or electoral interests, are also influenced by ideas. The question that is raised in this regard is how the ideas related to environmental issues interact with the dominant policy paradigm to carry out reforms in the energy sector (related to climate change). It is expected that such sets of ideas will affect all actors, but they will affect policy makers more than they will affect others. Political power is the success factor of politicians in framing and representing problems in order to provide potentially acceptable interpretation frameworks and solutions. The best situation is that their solution is sufficiently welcomed by the public, political and business opinion in such a way that it makes possible policy changes in times of crisis. For example, changing the energy structure in UK and other countries as a security issue, made these countries follow policies aimed at encouraging green energy production, which in turn has strengthened nuclear energy in some countries (Kuzemko, 2013).

Therefore, actors in the energy system led to the evolution of institutions through their interactions. This work is done using economic, social and technical fields and under the conditions of path dependence and restrictions imposed by technologies, institutions and personal interests. These effects in the energy sector can be long-term because energy infrastructures are expensive and have a very long lifespan.

4 Institutional Inertia and Transition to Sustainable Energy

The term inertia has entered the social sciences from physics to include a range of characteristics related to social systems (such as resistance to change). The first law of motion in physics is based on the assumption that: an object remains at rest or in uniform linear motion until no external force acts to change that state. Three important results regarding inertia as an inherent characteristic of matter can be deduced from this assumption. First, an object does not need external forces to maintain its direction and motion. Second, an object maintains its motion and direction without external forces acting on it, and a force must be applied to change the current state of the object. Third, an object resists any attempt to change its motion and direction. In general, inertia as the default state of the system is the resistance of any physical object to any change in its velocity. This means that whether an object is at rest or constantly moving, a force must be applied to change its speed and/or direction. For a body retains any new state it acquires only by its own inertia, and the preservation of the present state means resistance to any attempt to change this state of rest or motion. In other words, no historical dependence remains after the change in physical phenomena. In this sense, inertia in social phenomena is fundamentally different from physical phenomena. Because, after overcoming institutional inertia and new orientation, inertial characteristics (due to path dependence) may be temporarily overshadowed, but they do not disappear (Aksom, 2021: 17–18). For this reason, it can be said that dependence on the historical path in social phenomena is an important factor in institutional inertia. Other factors also affect institutional inertia. The explanation of these factors and the mechanism of their effect is beyond the goals of this chapter.

4.1 Concept of Institutional Inertia

Transition is a set of change processes in socio-technical systems (in various technical, material, organizational, institutional, political, economic, and socio-cultural aspects). Different types of exogenous or endogenous parameter changes can lead to institutional changes. However, not all parameter changes lead to institutional change due to the resistance of institutions.[1]

[1] Institutions are "the rules of the game in a society or the human-designed constraints that shape human interactions." Institutions "reduce uncertainty by providing structure to everyday life." Institutions include both formal rules such as laws and constitutions and informal constraints such as contracts and norms (North, 1990: 3). Fundamentally, institutions are seen as enduring rules that govern human interactions, and are also designed "by human hands."

"Stickiness" and the tendency of institutions to "resistance to change" and as a result the stabilization of policy leads to institutional inertia.[2] Institutional inertia and resistance to change is a defining characteristic for institutions, because they have considerable stability and predictability. The stability of institutions makes them meaningful, but hinders attempts at institutional change and makes institutional change "extremely gradual" (North, 1990: 89). The response of institutions to new challenges, which aim to support changes, is often very slow, leading to specific types of support for existing institutions that do not match social needs. The institutional inertia resulting from these resistances indicates several obstacles for innovations in favor of sustainable transition, and leads to blocking the path of change and creating an obstacle to replace sustainable innovations in the energy transition (Seyfang & Smith, 2007; Knickel et al., 2009; Pierson, 2011; Hoffman, 2011; Munck af Rosenschöld et al., 2014; Ingram, 2015).

4.2 Institutional Changes, Institutional Inertia and Path Dependence in the Transition to Sustainable Energy

Institutional change[3] is the result of the accumulation of many small changes rather than sudden large changes. The process of institutional change is also path-dependent because individuals learn, organizations develop, and ideologies are formed within a specific set of formal and informal rules. These organizations may then try to change the formal rules to their advantage, and over time this may in turn (indirectly) affect the informal rules. In general, there are multiple trade-offs and there is no guarantee of an efficient outcome. Bounded rationality, which leads to unwanted results or inertia due to pre-existing informal rules, can prevent the implementation of an efficient institutional change (North, 1990). Institutional inertia is closely related to the role of history because "past political agreements on property institutions provide a framework for compensating new common losses, the identity of agents and opponents of change, their effectiveness in political bargaining, and the range of possible alternatives". Existing institutions create groups that have a vested interest in maintaining the status quo, which can impede institutional change and enable dysfunctional institutions to persist. Moreover, institutional change is usually incremental because, often, it is easier to reach

[2] To read more about the concepts of inertia, institutional inertia, and sources of institutional inertia refer to Chapters. "Inertia: Resistance and Endurance" and "An Introduction to Institutional Inertia: Concepts, Types and Causes" of this book.

[3] In the analysis of how institutions change over time based on the "source of change", four theories of institutional change can be mentioned: collective choice theory, evolutionary theory, equilibrium theory, and deinstitutionalization theory. The first three theories discuss the emergence of new beliefs and practices, while the last theory discusses the weakening and disappearance of beliefs and practices (for further reading, see Samadi & Alipourian, 2021).

consensus on small adjustments than to make major changes to existing rules (Libecap, 1989: 16).

Path dependence explains institutional inertia as the inability to change development paths due to past choices and decisions. In the transition to sustainable energy, energy systems depend on the historical path and can be strongly influenced by past events related to geographical and geological location (such as the presence of coal or oil reserves in a country) or historical background (especially the degree of acceptance of a country's military nuclear force) (Libecap, 1989; Mahoney, 2000; Unruh, 2000; Foxon et al., 2013; Munck af Rosenschöld et al., 2014). An example of inertia caused by historical path dependence is "technological lock-in ".”Technological lock-in" (where relatively open development futures are limited or closed due to the dominance of carbon-based technology) results from a lack of political or technical support for change. That is, institutional legacies protect the status quo and political regulations, tax laws, and even banks and educational institutions along with related coalitions support a particular energy path. Overall, these technological and behavioral forces lock us into a carbon-dependent energy system that is highly resistant to institutional change (Unruh, 2000; Goldthau & Sovacool, 2012; Knox-Hayes, 2012; Steinhilber et al., 2013).

4.3 Path Dependence in the Transition to Sustainable Energy: Evidence

Path dependence in energy transition is not decisive by itself, but it is effective through political decisions and the political power of the resulting lobbies. Some countries have access to large sources of native fossil fuels, which are historically considered strategic assets. The production and consumption of these special resources is deeply embedded in the national and transnational political economy of these countries, and as a result has had an impact on energy policy in these countries. This historical and geographical heritage has shaped not only the attitude towards the transition, but also the way different countries reacted to energy shocks or past crises (for example, in the 1970s and early 1980s) in different ways. In these countries, fossil fuels have strong lobbies, and energy transition is slow and faces resistance from interest groups. In the transportation sector, the main lobby is oil. In other energy sectors, the main lobbies are coal and gas (usually oil is part of the lobby of these sectors). Coal is often a strong lobby because it creates more employment than oil (Mitchell, 2011). In Germany and Denmark, the coal lobby (including lignite) is still strong and reinforces the continued presence of coal in the energy mix despite strong pressure to move towards a more sustainable energy system. The British government has been reducing the coal industry for the past half century by banning new coal-fired power plants. A strong lobby in the UK is North Sea gas, which is now a major factor in accelerating the move towards sustainable energy.

Path dependence also affects the transition to sustainable energy through the political power of nuclear lobbies. Countries with a history of military nuclear energy tend to inherit a nuclear lobby with considerable political power. Britain and France, with the commitment to independent nuclear deterrent power, after World War II, gave nuclear technology a high status and made a wave of investments in this regard in the 1960s and 1970 have done. In contrast, Germany was prevented from developing nuclear military capacity after World War II, and Denmark, as a very small geopolitical actor, has not been able to enjoy such ambition. Both Germany and Denmark actually felt threatened by the nuclear weapons of the Cold War and strong anti-nuclear movements were formed in both countries, which in turn influenced their energy policies. In fact, strong anti-nuclear movements prevented Denmark's nuclear development or limited Germany's nuclear energy as a substitute for oil in electricity production. These two countries, which did not have oil and gas reserves, have taken measures to improve energy efficiency by using heating energy and combined energy (at a time when the pricing of these products suffered serious political shocks). In the United States, major efforts have been made to improve energy efficiency. In California, major institutional reforms were made at the energy retail level, but as in UK, the nuclear program continued.

The nuclear lobby has the ability to reinvent itself, and recently, due to the accreditation of low-carbon energies as well as the issue of energy supply security, the political power of nuclear energy in these countries is still standing. A nuclear lobby will not stop or slow the transition to sustainable energy, but will distort it by trying to acquire existing resources (which support the transition to low-carbon energy policies and the substitution of renewable energies). These two groups of technologies are not compatible with each other and after the establishment of one, and the completion of the technologies with the network infrastructure of one of them, the other group will probably disappear (Katz & Shapiro, 1985: 424–25).

4.4 Experience of Some Countries in the Transition to Sustainable Energy

The history of energy transition shows the success of different countries in overcoming institutional inertia and making changes in energy systems, in line with the transition from fossil fuels to renewable energies. Successful experiences show that energy transition is based on the framework of powerful energy policies designed by governments that can accelerate energy transition and determine its direction. Well-designed transition policies consider both the characteristics of energy systems and energy supply and demand (NEA, 2016). Indeed, there is an alternative combination of resources, technologies and policies in future energy pathways that make it possible to achieve improvements in energy access, air quality and energy security simultaneously while avoiding dangerous climate change (Riahi et al., 2012). In the meantime, renewable energy technology has played a key role in the global energy transition, so that the global investment in renewable energy reached 241.6 billion dollars in 2016. In 2017, the world's newly installed renewable electricity capacity reached a new record of 167 GW. This year was another record in which more than 60% of the total new electricity capacity was from renewables. Solar PV capacity has grown more than any other source of electricity generation (IRENA, 2017a, b). 2017 marked the fifth year in a row that new investment in renewable power generation capacity was nearly twice as much as investment in fossil power generation capacity. The root of this acceleration is the significant reduction in renewable technology costs (IRENA, 2016). Renewable energies, too, could potentially provide between 41 and 54% of CO2 emission reductions by 2050. The remaining 46% is achieved through energy efficiency, fossil fuel replacement, continuous use of nuclear energy, and carbon capture and storage (IRENA and International Energy Agency (IEA), 2017).

Among the countries that have had a successful experience in energy transition through the use of renewable energies are the G20 countries. These countries have allocated about 85% of the deployment of renewable energy (including China 26%, the United States 15%, India 12%, the European Union 9%) until 2050. This limited number of countries and some others play an important role in energy transition. For example, the European Union revised its binding 2030 target, set in 2014, to 32% in June 2018. In Germany, the energy transition is the result of a national consensus to abandon nuclear power and reduce greenhouse gas emissions by 80% by 2050 through the rapid uptake of renewable energies (Renn & Marshall, 2016; Morris & Jungjohann, 2017). However, the energy transition remains a policy in the electricity sector (with little impact on coal production in the heating and transport sectors) (Kemfert, 2017). In Denmark, there is also a consensus on climate goals combined with a policy of implicit support for the renewable energy supply industry (IRENA, 2013).

In 2016, Portugal produced 57% of its electricity using renewable energy sources (APREN, 2017), and less than half of the annual electricity supply comes from fossil fuels. Almost doubling in the last decade, Portugal's total installed electricity capacity is over 20 gigawatts (GW) or 20,000 megawatts (MW). This amount is much higher than the national demand, which has reached 9 gigawatts in recent years. Two thermal power plants (using coal) and existing natural gas power plants can regulate supply and enable grid flexibility. The geophysical conditions of Portugal make solar photovoltaic cost competitive with other sources. Combined with impressive renewable resources and emerging energy flexibility, conventional PV could enable Portugal's rapid transition to very low carbon sources (Brown et al., 2018; Jacobson et al., 2015).

The Russian Federation, which owns one of the largest fossil fuel resources in the world, accelerates the deployment of solar and wind energy through auctions to create benefits for employment, science, technology and energy security for marginalized populations (IRENA, 2017a, b). More than 5 GW of wind and solar capacity have been installed since 2013, indicating that the country will likely exceed its 2024 target of 5.9 GW of installed renewable energy capacity (including geothermal) (IRENA, 2017a, b; Power Technology, 2018).

In Asia, China, as the largest energy producer and consumer, plays an important role in the global energy transition. China is turning to renewable energy to meet its growing energy demand and reduce air pollution. China has also set targets to reduce carbon emissions per unit of GDP by 60 to 65% by 2030 from 2005 levels, in which renewable energy will play a central role. The goal of non-fossil fuel share in China's total energy demand is 20% by 2030 (NDRC, 2016), which accounts for more than half of the total global photovoltaic capacity of 94 GW. However, in 2018, the Chinese government adopted a policy of solar PV installation quotas and decided to phase out feed-in tariffs (incentive tariffs), which is expected to reduce installation capacity (IEA, 2018).

The Indian government has set an ambitious renewable energy target of 175 GW by 2022, which includes 60 GW of wind and 100 GW of solar energy (MNRE, 2022). As the country has made good progress in this regard, the Indian government has increased the target to 227 GW by 2027. This (despite the heterogeneity of the energy sector and the distinct differences and priorities of actors in individual energy markets with more than 3000 utilities in each of the 50 states) provides a success story for the energy transition. Domestic production of natural gas and the efforts of determined policymakers, driven by mechanisms such as tax incentives for renewable energy, have transformed the country's energy sector.

As an emerging economy, Turkey is exploring ways to increase its share of solar and wind energy with an urgent need to reduce its energy imports. In this country, to meet short-term renewable energy targets by 2023, the use of feed-in tariffs for solar PV to reach 5 GW of installed capacity in 2018 has been successful. Large-scale capacity auctions, which are primarily aimed at creating a local renewable energy equipment industry, have pushed out of the market small-scale actors who suffer from a lack of financial resources (Saygin et al., 2018).

According to the latest 2017 data from the United States, 11% of total energy demand and 17% of total electricity generation in the United States come from renewable energy sources (U.S. Energy Information Administration, 2018). These results were made possible by strong network planning and innovation. For example, Hawaii in the United States aims to achieve 70% energy independence by 2030, of which 40% will come from renewable energy. Energy policymaking in the United States also shows the importance of continuously updating and improving energy transition policies (especially in the electricity and transportation sectors), so that the scope of their policy impacts is frequently expanded and their timing exceeds goals (Stokes & Breetz, 2018).

In Brazil, in 1975, the Proalcool program (a combination of policy instruments that have evolved over time) was initiated to meet the needs of both the supply and demand sides. Government policies related to this program have increased the demand for biomass-based ethanol (Meyer et al., 2014). But the long-term success of this sector is still affected by economic cycles and changing government priorities (Altenburg & Assmann, 2017).

5 Conclusion

In this chapter, the analysis of the transition to sustainable energy, governance for the transition and the impact of institutional inertia and dependence on the transition path were considered. Therefore, at the beginning, after referring to the idea of transition and its concept, different approaches to transition, especially the STT approach have been analyzed. The STT approach is the main framework of the theory of transition to sustainable energy, and connected the function of technology with social needs and including a wide range of different topics such as: environment, infrastructure, technology, industry, civil society, institutions, policies, etc.). Then, to answer the question why different countries have experienced the transition to sustainable energy in different ways, the institutional diversity of capitalist systems has been pointed out. In addition, using the STT approach on governance for the transition to sustainable energy and the contexts in which such processes occur, the relationship between governance and the elements of dominant institutional systems, policy-making paradigms and interests of actors (especially important political and economic groups), is described.

Transition to sustainable energy includes a set of interconnected changes such as changes in energy efficiency, innovation and the use of a wide range of low-carbon technologies, extensive changes in industries, changes in markets, actor's performance, policies and cultural concepts are described at the level of national and global economy. In this transition, not only the pattern of production and consumption will change, but different social groups such as new energy companies, producers, distributors, and retailers will benefit from the transition process, while others may face significant losses. In the transition process, political, legal and economic rules and regulations (and people who have invested heavily in energy systems based on fossil fuels with high carbon production), against any changes in energy systems are resisted, which is the result of institutional inertia.

Institutional inertia refers to the "stickiness" of institutions or the tendency of institutions to move slowly and resist change. One of the most important sources of institutional inertia is path dependence. Path dependence shows that the transition to sustainable energy is strongly influenced by past events related to geographical and geological location or historical background. In addition, path dependence through political decisions and the political power of lobbies resulting from it has an effect on the transition. Therefore, the transition to sustainable energy depends on the economic, social and political conditions governing the society and the power of pressure groups in limiting changes (and the resulting institutional inertia). Changing these conditions in favor of the transition can facilitate the transition to sustainable energy.

In the fourth section of the chapter, evidence of the influence of dependence on the historical path (an important factor of institutional inertia) has been mentioned, which shows that the transition is difficult to occur, and also, examples of the successful experience of some countries in the transition to sustainable energy through the use of renewable technologies (overcoming institutional inertia) have been given, which show that the transition is possible.

References

Acemoglu, D., Johnson, S., & Robinson, J. (2005). Institutions as the fundamental cause of long-run growth. In P. Aghion & S. Durlauf (Eds.), *Handbook of economic growth*. Elsevier.

Aksom, H. (2021). *A theory of institutional inertia. I. Organizational change and practice variation*. University of Jyväskylä. https://www.researchgate.net/publication/351774271

Aldy, J., & Pizer, W. (2008). *'Issues in developing us climate change policy', resources for the future*, Discussion Paper, RFF DP 08-20, June 2008, at p. 21. Available at: http://www.rff.org/documents/RFF-DP-08-20.pdf

Altenburg, T., & Assmann, C. (Eds.). (2017). *Green industrial policy. Concept, policies, country experiences*. UN Environment; German Development Institute. https://www.die-gdi.de/uploads/media/GREEN_INDUSTRIAL_POLICY.Endf_07.pdf

APREN (Portuguese Renewable Energy Association). (2017). *Yearbook 2017*. APREN.

Brown, T., Bischof-Niemz, T., Mathiesen, B. V., Lund, H., & Blok, K. (2018). Response to 'Burden of proof: A comprehensive review of the feasibility of 100% renewable electricity systems'. *Renewable and Sustainable Energy Reviews, 92*, 834–847.

Coase, R. H. (1937). The nature of the firm. *Economica, 4*(16), 386–405.

Crepaz, M. (1998). Inclusion versus exclusion—political institutions and welfare expenditures. *Comparative Politics, 31*(1), 61–80.

Crouch, C. (2005). Models of capitalisms. *New Political Economy, 10*(4), 439–456.

Fouquet, R. (2010). The slow search for solutions: Lessons from historical energy transitions by sector and service. *Energy Policy, 38*(11), 6586–6596.

Foxon, T. J. (2011). A co-evolutionary framework for analyzing a transition to a sustainable low carbon economy. *Ecological Economics, 70*, 2258–2267.34.

Foxon, T. J., Pearson, P. J., Arapostathis, S., Carlsson-Hyslop, A., & Thornton, J. (2013). Branching points for transition pathways: assessing responses of actors to challenges on pathways to a low carbon future. *Energy Policy, 52*, 146–158.

Geels, F. W. (2002). Technological transitions as evolutionary reconfiguration processes: a multilevel perspective and a case-study. *Research Policy, 31*(8/9), 1257–1274.

Geels, F. (2010). Ontologies, socio-technical transitions (to sustainability), and the multi-level perspective. *Research Policy, 39*, 495–510.

Geels, F. (2014). Regime resistance against low-carbon transitions: introducing politics and power into the multi-level perspective. *Theory, Culture and Society, 31*(5), 21–40.

Geels, F., & Schot, J. (2007). Typology of sociotechnical transition pathways. *Research Policy, 36*, 399–417.

Goldthau, A., & Sovacool, B. K. (2012). The uniqueness of the energy security, justice, and governance problem. *Energy Policy, 41*, 232–240.

Grubler, A. (2012). Energy transitions research insights and cautionary tales. *Energy Policy, 50*, 8–18.

Gunningham, N. (2012). Confronting the challenge of energy governance. *Transnational Environmental Law, 1*(1), 119–135. Cambridge University Press.

Hall, P. A. (1993). Policy paradigms, social learning, and the state: the case of economic policymaking in Britain. *Comparative Politics, 25*(3), 275–296.

Hall, P. A., & Soskice, D. (2001). *Varieties of capitalism: The institutional foundations of comparative advantage*. OUP.

Hall, P. A., & Taylor, R. C. (1996). Political science and the three new institutionalisms. *Political Studies, 44*(5), 936–957.

Hoffman, A. J. (2011). Talking past each other? Cultural framing of skeptical and convinced logics in the climate change debate. *Organization & Environment, 24*(1), 3–33.
IEA, Market Report Series: Renewables. (2018). OECD/IEA, 2018. https://www.iea.org/renewables2018/
Ingram, J. (2015). Framing niche-regime linkage as adaptation: an analysis of learning and innovation networks for sustainable agriculture across Europe. *Journal of Rural Studies, 40*, 59–75.
International Energy Agency, (IEA). (2009). *World energy outlook.* Available at: http://www.iea.org/textbase/npsum/weo2009sum.pdf
International Energy Agency, (IEA). (2010). *Combining policy instruments for least-cost climate mitigation strategies.*
IRENA. (2013). *30 years of policies for wind energy: Lessons from 12 wind energy markets.* IRENA. http://www.irena.org/menu/index.aspx?mnu=Subcat&PriMenuID=36&CatID=141&SubcatID=281
IRENA. (2016). *The power to change: Solar and wind cost reduction potential to 2025.* IRENA. http://www.irena.org/menu/?mnu=Subcat&PriMenuID=36&CatID=141&SubcatID=2733
IRENA. (2017a). *Renewable capacity statistics.* IRENA, Abu Dhabi. http://www.irena.org/menu/index.aspx?mnu=Subcat&PriMenuID=36&CatID=141&SubcatID=3831
IRENA. (2017b). *Renewable energy prospects for the Russian Federation.* IRENA, Abu Dhabi. https://www.irena.org//media/Files/IRENA/Agency/Publication/2017/Apr/IRENA_REmap_Russia_paper_2017.pdf
IRENA and International Energy Agency (IEA). (2017). *Perspectives for the energy transition – Investment needs for a low-carbon energy system.* IRENA & Paris: IEA, Abu Dhabi. http://www.irena.org/DocumentDownloads/Publications/Perspectives_for_the_Energy_Transition_2017.pdf
Jacobson, M., Delucchi, M., Cameron, M., & Frew, B. (2015). Low-cost solution to the grid reliability problem with 100% penetration of intermittent wind, water, and solar for all purposes. *Proceedings of the National Academy of Sciences., 112*(49), 15060–15065.
Katz, M. L., & Shapiro, C. (1985). Network externalities, competition, and compatibility. *The American Economic Review, 75*, 424–440.
Kemfert, C. (2017). Germany must go back to its low-carbon future. *Nature, 549*, 26–27.
Knickel, K., Brunori, G., Rand, S., & Proost, J. (2009). Towards a better conceptual framework for innovation processes in agriculture and rural development: from linear models to systemic approaches. *Journal of Agricultural Education and Extension, 15*(2), 131–146.
Knox-Hayes, J. (2012). Negotiating climate legislation: Policy path dependence and coalition stabilization. *Regulation & Governance, 6*(4), 545–567.
Kuzemko, C. (2013) Problematizing Governance for Low Carbon Transition IGov Working Paper 1, Energy Policy Group, University of Exeter.
Kuzemko, C., Lockwood, M., Mitchell, C., & Hoggett, R. (2016). Governing for sustainable energy system change: Politics, contexts and contingency. *Energy Research & Social Science, 12*, 96–105.
Libecap, G. D. (1989). *Contracting for Property Rights.* Cambridge University Press.
Lockwood, M. (2013). The political dynamics of green transformations: Feedback effects and institutional context. In I. Scoones, M. Leach, & P. Newell (Eds.), *The politics of green transformations.* Routledge.
Lockwood, M., Kuzemko, C., Mitchell, C., & Hoggett, R. (2013). Theorizing governance and innovation in sustainable energy transitions, EPG Working Paper: 1304, 1–37.
Lovins, A. B. (1976). Energy strategy: The road not taken. *Foreign Affairs, 1976*(55), 186–217.
Lovins, A. B. (1978). Soft Energy Technologies. *Annual Review of Energy, 3*, 477–517.
Mahoney, J. (2000). Path dependence in historical sociology. *Theory and Society, 29*(4), 507–548.
Markand, J., Raven, R., & Truffer, B. (2012). Sustainability transitions: An emerging field of research and its prospects. *Research Policy, 41*(2012), 955–967.

Meadowcroft, J. (2005). Environmental political economy, technological transitions and the state. *New Political Economy, 10*(4), 479–498.

Meadowcroft, J. (2011). Engaging with the politics of sustainability transitions. *Environmental Innovations and Societal Transitions, 1*(2011), 70–75.

Meyer, D., Mytelka, L., Press, R., Dall'Oglio, E. L., de Sousa, P. T., Jr., & Grubler, A. (2014). Brazilian ethanol: unpacking a success story of energy technology innovation. In A. Grubler (Ed.), *Energy technology innovation: Learning from historical successes and failures*. Cambridge University Press.

Miller, C. A., Iles, A., & Jones, C. F. (2013). The social dimensions of energy transitions. *Science as Culture, 22*(2), 135–148.

Mitchell, T. (2011). *Carbon democracy: Political power in the age of oil*. Verso.

MNRE. (2022). *Tentative State-wise break-up of Renewable Power target to be achieved by the year 2022 so that cumulative achievement is 175,000 MW*. MNRE. https://mnre.gov.in/file-manager/UserFiles/Tentative-State-wise-break-up-ofRenewable-Power-by-2022.pdf

Morris, C., & Jungjohann, A. (2017). Energize the people to effect policy change. *Nature, 551*, 138–140. https://doi.org/10.1038/d41586-017-07508-x

Munck af Rosenschöld, J., Rozema, J. G., & Frye-Levine, L. A. (2014). Institutional inertia and climate change: a review of the new institutionalist literature. *Wiley Interdisciplinary Reviews: Climate Change, 5*(5), 639–648.

National Energy Administration of China, Government of Jiangsu Province (NEA), International Renewable Energy Agency (IRENA), Suzhou Declaration of the Second International Forum on Energy Transitions. (2016, 31 October). Suzhou, Jiangsu Province (People's Republic of China) http://www.nea.gov.cn/2016-10/31/c_135794708.htm (in Chinese).

NDRC. (2016). *The 13th five-year plan for energy development*, NDRC. http://www.ndrc.gov.cn/zcfb/zcfbghwb/201701/W020170117350627940556.pdf.

Nielsen, J. R., Hovmøller, H., Blyth, P.-L., & Sovacool, B. (2015). Of "white crows" and "cash savers": A qualitative study of travel behavior and perceptions of ridesharing in Denmark. *Transportation Research, Part A, 78*, 113–123.

North, D. C. (1990). *Institutions, institutional change and economic performance*. Cambridge University Press.

Ostrom, E. (1990). *Governing the commons: The evolution of institutions for collective action*. Cambridge University Press.

Painuly, J. P. (2001). Barriers to renewable energy penetration: A framework for analysis. *Renewable Energy, 24*, 73–89.

Pierson, P. (2011). *Politics in time: History, institutions, and social analysis*. Princeton University Press.

Power Technology. (2018). *Is Russia finally ready to embrace renewable energy?* https://www.power-technology.com/features/russia-renewableenergy/.

Raven, R., Kern, F., Verhees, B., & Smith, A. (2015). Niche construction and empowerment through socio-political work. A meta-analysis of six low-carbon technology cases. *Environmental Innovation and Societal Transitions, 18*, 164–180.

Renn, O., & Marshall, J. P. (2016). Coal, nuclear and renewable energy policies in Germany: from the 1950s to the "Energiewende". *Energy Policy, 99*, 224–232.

Riahi, K., Dentener, F., Gielen, D., Grubler, A. Jewell, J. Klimont, Z. Krey, V. McCollum, D. Pachauri, S. Rao, S. van Ruijven, B. van Vuuren, D., Wilson, C. (2012). Global energy assessment chapter 17: Energy pathways for sustainable development, Cambridge University Press. http://pure.iiasa.ac.at/id/eprint/10065/1/GEA%20Chapter%2017%20Energy%20%20Pathways

Rotmans, J., Kemp, R., & van Asselt, M. (2001). More evolution than revolution: transition management in public policy. *Foresight, 3*(1), 15–31.

Samadi, A. H., & Alipourian, M. (2021). Institution and institutional change: Concepts and theories. In N. Faghih & A. H. Samadi (Eds.), *Dynamics of institutional change in emerging market economies: Theories, concepts and mechanisms*. Springer International Publishing.

https://doi.org/10.1007/978-3-030-61342-6_4, https://doi.org/10.1007/978-3-030-61342-6, Series ISSN: 1431-1933, https://www.springer.com/gp/book/9783030613419
Saygin, D., Hoffman, M., & Godron, P. (2018). *How Turkey can ensure a successful energy transition*. Center for American Progress.
Schmidt, V. (2002). *2002*. The futures of European capitalisms.
Schmidt, V. (2010). Taking ideas and discourse seriously: explaining change through discursive institutionalism as the fourth new institutionalism. *European Political Science Review, 2*(1), 1–25.
Scrase, I., & Smith, A. (2009). The (non-) politics of managing low carbon socio-technical transitions. *Environmental Politics, 18*(5), 707–726.
Seyfang, G., & Smith, A. (2007). Grassroots innovations for sustainable development: Towards a new research and policy agenda. *Environmental politics, 16*(4), 584–603.
Smith, A., Voß, J.-P., & Grin, J. (2010). Innovation studies and sustainability transitions: The allure of the multi-level perspective and its challenges. *Research Policy, 39*(4), 435–448.
Sovacool, B. K. (2009). Rejecting renewables: The socio-technical impediments to renewable electricity in the United States. *Energy Policy, 37*(11), 4500–4513.
Sovacool, B. K., & Hirsh, R. F. (2009). Beyond batteries: An examination of the benefits and barriers to plug-in hybrid electric vehicles (PHEVs) and a vehicle-to-grid (V2G) transition. *Energy Policy, 37*, 1095–1103.
Steinhilber, S., Wells, P., & Thankappan, S. (2013). Socio-technical inertia: Understanding the barriers to electric vehicles. *Energy Policy, 60*, 5319.
Stokes, L. C., & Breetz, H. L. (2018). Politics in the U.S. energy transition: case studies of solar, wind, biofuels and electric vehicles policy. *Energy Policy, 113*, 76–86.
U.S. Energy Information Administration, Renewable Energy, (EIA). (2018). Washington, DC, https://www.eia.gov/energyexplained/?page=renewable_home.
Unruh, G. C. (2000). Understanding carbon lock-in. *Energy policy, 28*(12), 817–830.
Verbong, G. P. J., & Loorbach, D. (2012). Introduction. In G. Verbong & D. Loorbach (Eds.), *Governing the energy transition: Reality illusion or necessity?* Routledge.
Williamson, O. E. (1985). *The economic institutions of capitalism: Firms, markets, relational contracting*. Free Press.

Legitimacy, Institutional Inertia, and Climate Change

Ali Hussein Samadi and Sajjad Afroozeh

1 Introduction

With the growing importance of climate change and the need for policies to reduce its negative effects, removing the obstacles facing these issues should be prioritized. Some of these obstacles are related to the institutional environment and rules of the game. Relationships between power holders, parties, interest groups, beneficiaries of the status quo, and owners of industries and technologies are among the most important factors in creating obstacles or making environmental policies less effective. These factors cause systemic resistance to change, which is called institutional inertia. In the field of climate change, five factors of costs, uncertainty, path dependence, power and legitimacy cause institutional inertia (Munck af Rosenschöld et al., 2014). This chapter will investigate the effect of legitimacy on creating institutional inertia in climate change policymaking. The issue of state's legitimacy can be a factor to improve or weaken the environmental performance of a country by influencing political institutions.

The reason for paying attention to legitimacy in this chapter is because of the basic role of this factor. The legitimacy of political power leads to the creation of a suitable institutional platform for the implementation of institutional change policies and the improvement of institutional quality and, as a result, the improvement of environmental performance. If a state is not recognized as legitimate, its decisions and policies will either not be implemented by individuals or will be implemented very poorly. Legitimacy is a necessary condition for the efficiency of a state and implies the implementation of its policies. Also, a state that is not considered legitimate within its borders or has a lower degree of legitimacy will also have less legitimacy in the international arena.

A. H. Samadi (✉) · S. Afroozeh
Department of Economics, Shiraz University, Shiraz, Iran
e-mail: asamadi@rose.shirazu.ac.ir

N. Faghih, A. H. Samadi (eds.), *Institutional Inertia*, Contributions to Economics,
https://doi.org/10.1007/978-3-031-51175-2_12

In the field of climate change, decisions and policies are generally long-term, costly, require structural changes in the existing situation (such as technological changes and changes in consumption habits), and require international cooperation. Naturally, there will be resistance and obstacles against these decisions and policies from the people, groups in power, and economic agents. If a political system is not recognized as legitimate among the people under its rule, it is not possible to make fundamental decisions and policies. Also, low legitimacy, the crisis of legitimacy, or the recognition of the illegitimacy of a political order causes resources to be used for creating legitimacy, suppressing protesters, or state propaganda and patronage. In this case, there will be no necessary resources, power, or even will for long-term environmental policy-making.

Less attention has been paid to the issue of legitimacy of state in the implementation of climate change policies. In previous studies, the relationship between state legitimacy and environmental performance has not been evaluated. Also, the issue of the legitimacy of the state has not been investigated completely and in all dimensions. In this chapter, the following hypothesis has been tested:

H: The higher the degree of legitimacy of a government, the better its environmental performance.

This hypothesis will be examined in the fifth section of this chapter. It seems that many policy failures to solve the problems of climate change are related to the legitimacy of the states. This chapter is an attempt to understand the effect of government legitimacy on environmental performance.

The rest of this chapter is organized as follows. In Sect. 2, the concept of legitimacy and its relationship with power will be explained. In Sect. 3, legitimacy and power are examined as a mechanism creating institutional inertia. Section 4 is dedicated to examining the relationship between institutions and the environment. In Sect. 5, the proposed hypothesis has been tested using regression analysis. Section 6 is devoted to conclusions.

2 Legitimacy and Political Power: Concept and Importance

The legitimacy of the political system and state has always been a concern of many philosophers. In this section, we study the primary and basic theories of the legitimacy of power from the point of view of the great theorists of the second half of the twentieth century. Many scientific works in the field of legitimacy have been proposed by scholars such as Weber, Habermas, Kant and Beetham. In this section, we provide a quick overview of some views in social and political sciences to clarify the concept of legitimacy and its relationship with power.

The *Oxford English dictionary* defines legitimacy and legitimate as follows (Schaar, 1984):

> ***Legitimacy:*** *(a) of a government or the title of a sovereign: the condition of being in accordance with law or principle ... (b) conformity to a rule or principle; lawfulness. In logic, conformity to sound reasoning.*
>
> ***Legitimate:*** *(a) etymologically, the word expresses a status, which has been conferred or ratified by some authority; (b) conformable to law or rule. Sanctioned or authorized by law or right, lawful, proper; (c) normal, regular; conformable to a recognized standard type; (d) sanctioned by the laws of reasoning; logically admissible or inferable.*

The legitimacy of an institution (formal or informal) is a very important issue. Because to build or rebuild an institution, legitimacy is needed. Legitimacy is not given in any system. Power holders can give legitimacy to an institution or deny it legitimacy. In fact, it is the power structures that are responsible for maintaining and reproducing legitimacy for the system in which they exercise power. In addition, legitimacy is necessary for any democratic system. It is the legitimacy that transforms "power" into "authority" and provides the possibility of governance without using force and conflict (Beetham, 2013; Connelly et al., 2006; Schmitter, 2001).

(Rousseau, 1978) believes that:

> *Man is born free, and everywhere he is in chains ... How did this change occur? I do not know, what can make it legitimate? I believe I can answer this question ... But the social order is a sacred right that serves as a basis for all others. However, this right does not come from nature; it is therefore based on convention. The problem is to know what these conventions are* (Connolly, 1984).

Rousseau believes that the legitimacy of power to create social order is established through a social contract. Legitimacy is not naturally or inherently granted to a state and is not given. States should create legitimacy for themselves and their decisions by interacting with society. Legitimacy must be accompanied and supported by society. Rousseau's problem is to find this social contract. This issue has remained unsolved in many societies. In order to achieve social order, dominant powers must reach a common understanding of their values and beliefs with their subordinate society. It is through this social contract that the dominant power can limit the free-born man with his consent. One of the factors that create the legitimacy of power is the satisfaction of subordinates to the rules limiting their behavior.

Habermas has linked laws and legitimacy together. He considers legitimate laws to be the objective manifestation of a political society, and the means of maintaining and sustaining that society. From his point of view, legitimacy means that the social order should be recognized based on being right and fair. Legitimacy is the worthiness of a political order to be recognized (Habermas, 1979). According to Habermas, a law is legitimate when the people who follow it are somehow the author of that law (Wheeler, 2001). In fact, Habermas explains a kind of self-regulation in the democratic framework; A framework in which people participate in policy and legislative affairs, and laws are formulated according to their wishes. This participation of the people legitimizes the actions of the political system and creates the foundation for their sustainability. According to Habermas (1998), legal legitimacy should not be merged with moral validity. Of course, this issue does not mean the complete separation of law from morality. Law complements weak post-traditional morality.

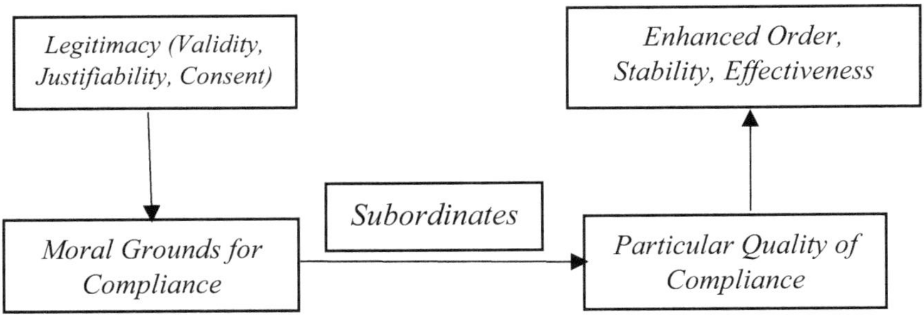

Fig. 1 The effect of legitimacy on the order, stability, and effectiveness of a political system. (Source: (Beetham, 2013))

Power is considered legitimate by having the following conditions (Beetham, 2013):

(i) Compliance with established laws (legal validity)
(ii) The justification of laws according to the common beliefs between dominant and subordinate people (justifiability)
(iii) The existence of evidence that the subordinates consent to the power relationship (consent).

These are the pre-conditions according to which the power dominating the society can be considered legitimate or illegitimate. Obviously, if a state does not have these three conditions at the same time, it will not be able to govern the society effectively and there will be obstacles against its decisions. The **legitimacy crisis** can be seen as a factor for creating institutional inertia.

Some scholars (e.g. (Luhmann, 1969)) consider "legitimacy" and "efficiency of the political system" or its stability to be the same. Legitimacy is important because of its effects on the behavior of subordinates and the characteristics of power relations. Legitimacy, with the three characteristics of validity, justification, and satisfaction, creates grounds for acceptance of dominant power among subordinates. Legitimacy creates moral grounds for accepting power in society. The degree of legitimacy (according to the 3 characteristics), and as a result, the amount and quality of acceptance of the dominant power can be different in different countries. The level of social acceptance and legitimacy of power will establish a degree of order, stability and effectiveness for the political system. These relationships are given in Fig. 1.

In Max Weber's view, the legitimacy of power originates from people's belief in its legitimacy, and power is legitimate where both dominant and subordinate people consider it legitimate (Weber, 1968). Weber expresses the need for power for legitimacy as follows:

> *Legitimacy is much more than a matter of theoretical or philosophical speculation; it rather constitutes the basis of very real differences in the empirical structure of domination. The reason for this fact lies in the generally observable need of any power, or even of any advantage of life, to justify itself.*

Table 1 Different conditions of legitimacy and effectiveness

	High effectiveness	Low effectiveness
High legitimacy	A	B
Low legitimacy	C	D

Source: Lipset (1984)

From Weber's point of view, the legitimacy of authority is generated in three major ways: tradition, charisma, and law. Tradition is the authority of the eternal yesterday. This type of authority is related to traditional and ancient authority, in which people considered an ancient dominion as legitimate; Like royal dynasties. Charisma, through extraordinary personal gifts, attracts the attention of subordinates and creates legitimacy. In this case, the subordinates are willing to sacrifice for their leader with complete trust. This power can be exercised by a hero, a prophet, a ruling party leader, a populist, a war commander, and so on. The third way to generate the legitimacy of the state and authority is the law. This path of legitimization is based on rational rules. In this case in modern governments, legitimacy is given to those in power through the law (Weber, 1984).

(Beetham, 2013) using the theories of sociologists completes Weber's definition of legitimacy with several points. From his point of view, people's beliefs originate from the cumulative effects they are exposed to. The existence of propaganda and the media can strengthen the opinion that it is the states that instill their legitimacy in the people by dominating the media and propaganda. Legitimacy is in the hands of those in power and it depends on their ability to convince the people under their rule.

In terms of (Lipset, 1958), the legitimacy of a political system is the ability of that system to create and maintain the belief in the people of the society that the political institutions of the established system are the best .(Lipset, 1984) considers the legitimacy of the democratic systems dependent on the methods of solving the key issues of society. These issues are the main issues that societies have faced throughout history and have caused the creation of different groups in society. These groups compete with other groups according to their interests and values. Different groups consider that state as legitimate or illegitimate according to their subjective value system and its comparison with the state's values. Understanding the different degrees of legitimacy of a country's political institutions can help to better analyze the stability of that country's political system when an efficiency crisis occurs. Table 1 shows four categories of hypothetical countries with four different statuses of legitimacy and effectiveness. Country A is a country with a high degree of state legitimacy and effectiveness. Countries like Sweden, Denmark, the USA, and Germany fall into this category. In category D (generally countries with a dictatorial system), the state maintains its security by using force. These countries have a low level of legitimacy and effectiveness. Countries like Syria and Guinea fall into this category. Intermediate modes also exist among countries. For example, in the 1920s, the state of Germany and Austria was not recognized as legitimate by most of the population, but it was effective to a large extent (group C countries). Some countries are legitimate by the majority of the country's population but have low effectiveness (group B countries). For example, we can refer to Cuba during the post-communist revolution.

From the point of view (Merelman, 1966), legitimacy is the government's capacity to create authority. (Lipset, 1958) and (Merelman, 1966) are complements of Weber's view. A number of social science scholars believe that the fall of dictatorial regimes depends on their inability to protect their legitimacy in the minds of their subordinates. From this point of view, the only important issue is not the people's belief in the legitimacy of the state, but the state must continuously protect the legitimacy of its power and its decisions for the people. Political legitimacy seeks to justify political authority; This means how the dominant power should convince people to follow the rules (Williams, 2016).

(Weber, 1984) says: "All states are established by resorting to force." The use of power and the use of force are necessary to create a state. Of course, force can gain political power, but it does not maintain it. It is the willingness of the subordinates to obey the dominant power that maintains the state. After gaining power, it should be made legitimate so that power becomes the authority and subordinates obey it (Schaar, 1984).

Weber considers the state as the exclusive and legitimate right to use force in a specific territory. From the point of view of (Weber, 1984), politics is an attempt to divide power or influence the distribution of power, both among states and groups present in a state. He also considers the state to be the domination of humans over humans, which is protected by the use of legitimate or presumed legitimate violence. The secret of the state's survival is the obedience of subordinates to the ruler's rule. (North et al., 2013) The Weberian state (the legitimate right to use violence) is not considered a policy that countries can easily achieve, but it is the result of a historical process. Therefore, achieving this political system is not an easy task for some countries.

If we consider power as the ability to use other people to achieve our goals, it is not only related to the ability, resources, and capacities of people; but also, people should be willing to do this. This issue means that it does not matter how many subordinates the dominant power has with what level of education or physical ability and skills; To advance its goals and policies, the dominant power needs people who consider its power as legitimate and are willing to follow its orders. Incentives or punishments cannot create desire in people. The factor that creates this desire in people is the normative status of the power holder and the normative considerations of subordinates to create a commitment to him. The normative situation is defined through the characteristics of a legitimate state; That is, 1- it should be legally valid, 2- it should be justified based on the norms and common beliefs of society, and 3- society should show its satisfaction with power through its actions. If the normative status of the state is suitable among the people of society and is considered legitimate from their point of view, then people will follow the policies of the state and will implement the policies. In this regard, (Kant, 1996) says:

> *For a unilateral will (and a bilateral but still particular will is also unilateral) cannot put everyone under an obligation that is in itself contingent; this requires a will that is omnilateral, that is united not contingently but a priori and therefore necessarily, and because of this is the only will that is lawgiving.*

According to (Kant, 1996), unilateral will cannot affect everyone with a commitment. If this will be multilateral, then this will can be a lawmaker. Kant (1996) expresses the importance of the legislator's legitimacy and his acceptability from the sight of his subordinates for legislation.

(Signé, 2017) for the failure of policies in implementation, puts forward 4 major reasons: ambiguity in policy goals and tools, asymmetry of information between policy implementers and designers, financing and resources, politics and conflicts. As mentioned in the fourth point, political power and competition of different groups can sometimes lead to the failure of policies. Problem diagnosis and problem solutions are determined according to the institutional history and the opinions of the interested groups. Differences in views cause conflict and conflict. For conflict to occur, there must be 3 conditions: interdependence of actors, incompatibility of goals and zero-sum element in actors' interactions (Dahrendorf, 1958). Also, policy conflicts will occur when the goals of each policy are related to the interests of more than one group and the groups have different opinions about that policy (Signé, 2017). If these conflicts exist and they are not resolved with the help of a legitimate and legal institution in the society (which can find the main problem of the society and use the appropriate tools and policies to solve it), there will definitely be severe power struggles or it will face the failure of policies. This issue is also valid for environmental policy. Policy failure will reduce electoral support and legitimacy. For this reason, there is a need for a state (with the cooperation and support of the majority of the society and elites and paying attention to their demands) to make policy and implement it (Hibbing & Theiss-Morse, 2002).

Reus-Smit (2007) considers the crisis of legitimacy as the inability of actors to achieve their goals, or the low capacity of institutions to employ behavior in accordance with norms. In fact, the crisis of legitimacy is a crisis in the power of an actor or an institution. Inadequate legitimacy or a deficit of legitimacy destroys power and leaves power unprotected. Strong legitimacy creates power for the government and not just protects its survival.

Omotola (2012) by examining popular uprisings in North Africa, concluded that legitimacy crisis will cause popular uprisings. A state is legitimate when its authority and power come from the will of the people, protects the lives and property of the people well, respects the rule of law, is accountable to the people and meets the human security needs of the people. Having these features, a state can maintain its social base and remain legitimate. Decreasing legitimacy causes dissatisfaction, and if it continues, it can lead to popular uprisings against the state. The reason for many uprisings against autocratic states is the crisis of legitimacy (Omotola, 2012). Carment and Samy (2011) consider the lack of legitimacy as the cause of instability in the Middle East and North Africa (MENA) countries.

In short, in this section, some basic points about the relationship between state legitimacy and power were stated. States must be recognized as legitimate by the people who rule them. This legitimacy is not naturally given to any dominant power. The dominant power must act to gain legitimacy with mechanisms that are appropriate to its values, competing groups, and the general public. As mentioned earlier, from the point of view of (Weber, 1984), there are three ways of tradition, charisma, and law to gain legitimacy. For today's modern state systems, the law is the most important way to generate legitimacy. In this chapter, we have taken into consideration the legitimacy of power through legal mechanisms. The recognition of the legitimacy of the state by the people is a necessary condition for the creation of effectiveness, order, and stability by states in every country. If the legitimacy of the state is low among the people, states will face problems in implementing their policies. In this section, it was said that the willingness of people to go along with the policies and goals of states is a fundamental issue. If people do not agree with these policies, even if it is the best possible policy and decision, they will fail in implementation. This failure is due to the state's legitimacy crisis. This obstacle to the implementation of the policy of the policymaker is a factor for creating institutional inertia. Institutional inertia here is an obstacle that is created through the lack of legitimacy of the state from the sight of the people. If the dominant power does not represent the values of different groups in society, it will fail in implementing policies and achieving its goals.

3 Sources of Institutional Inertia in Climate Change

Institutional inertia can be interpreted to "stickiness" and considered the resistance of institutions to change.[1] Institutions are not plastic that can be easily manipulated into any desired shape (Pierson, 2004). Institutions show significant resistance and inertia to change. The existence of institutional inertia causes a lag in the response of the political system and the dominant power to issues and problems. The greater the inertia of a political system, the less capable that political system will be in solving the problems ahead.

The issue of climate change is one of the major and fundamental issues of societies. Due to the emergence of global warming, polar ice melting, and extreme climate change, there is a high need for quick global coordinated action. In the meantime, some countries do not accompany the international community in this direction due to internal or international problems, or if they want to, they cannot. One of the reasons for this lack of cooperation or incomplete cooperation is the existence of institutional inertia (mainly political inertia) in these countries. This issue is discussed in this section.

In a general classification, new institutionalism is divided into three strands: rational choice institutionalism, historical institutionalism, and sociological institutionalism. From the point of view of rational choice institutionalists, formal and informal institutions are the rational output of what actors want from them. In this case, individual benefits are maximized, transaction costs are reduced, and collective

[1] To read more about the concepts of inertia, institutional inertia, and sources of institutional inertia refer to Chapters "Inertia: Resistance and Endurance" and "An Introduction to Institutional Inertia: Concepts, Types and Causes" of this book.

action problems are minimized. From the point of view of historical institutionalists, formal and informal institutions and norms are similar to rational choice institutionalists' point of view, with the difference that they do not consider them independent of actors. In the framework of this view, it is the institutions and political structures that shape people's behavior, attitudes, and motives, and in the form of political models, institutions are produced or reproduced. In sociological institutionalism, institutions are known as a set of cultural artifacts namely norms, values, routines, and scripts. In this view, the socialization force of these institutions tells people which behavior is legitimate or appropriate. As a result, people's choices and preferences will be closely related to institutions. In the strand of rational choice, institutional inertia can be resolved by satisfying private interests. While in the other two strands, collective action in line with public interests can help in solving institutional inertia. Regardless of the differences between the three strands of new institutionalism, from the point of view of new institutionalists, five important mechanisms create institutional inertia in climate change issues: Costs, uncertainty, path dependence, power, and legitimacy (Munck af Rosenschöld et al., 2014).

In the discussion of climate change, two types of costs are important: *free riding costs* and *transaction costs*. The free rider problem is one of the main obstacles to coordinated global action to solve climate change problems. A large number of economic agents are not motivated to solve the problems of climate change in a scattered, personal and rational way. This problem is a major obstacle to collective action with many participants. In addition to the high number of people and countries involved in the issue of climate change, the result of the cooperation is determined in the long term and mainly in an intergenerational way, and the cost of people or countries in the form of improving living conditions and things like this is returned to people. These issues increase the desire of people to not cooperate and expect to benefit from the cost and efforts of others. If the number of people or countries participating in dealing with climate change is less than optimal, effective action will not be taken in this regard. The *transaction cost* also occurs due to the inefficiencies of societies in solving conflicts between themselves. Since the measures to deal with the problems of climate change show their effects in the long term and the agents do not pay the costs, in the same way, the issue of costs can be a big and main obstacle in solving this problem and providing the cost of this public good.

According to some new institutionalists, climate change effects are not accurately and rationally predictable. Uncertainty in shocks and turning points and change makes system discontinuities fundamentally unpredictable and subsequently cannot be modeled. This uncertainty about how the system behaves, along with the fact that tackling climate change is a global public good (possibility of free riding) and on a large scale, causes less desire to invest in this field; Because the result of investment in related technologies can be seen with a long delay and the profit of the investment is not clear. This structural uncertainty creates and strengthens institutional inertia.

Path dependence in social systems is related to the output of self-reinforcing or positive feedback processes. This mechanism is the inability of the system to change the choices and decisions made in the past. Path dependence is related to both formal and informal institutions. For example, many countries are in a trap of old and polluting technologies based on fossil energy, and changing this situation requires political and technological support; but this support is not there due to previous investments, benefits, and cost of change. According to (Burch, 2011), the set of technologies, worldviews, bureaucracy, and artifacts indicate that "inertia is inherent in practices, habits, and institutional arrangements". For informal institutions, the habit of people using a certain technology or energy can be an example. In this case, people resist change.[2]

One of the important and influential factors on climate change is the power structure and the forces with interests in power. Power at both the national and international levels is effective in influencing policies related to climate change. In cooperation at the international level to solve this problem, the national interests of a country may not be provided in the implementation of international environmental agreements. With the formation of nation-states and respecting the issue of national sovereignty, international cooperation in this field becomes difficult. On the other hand, governments take actions that affect their international behavior in order to gain legitimacy inside the country. Eckersley (2007) considers the unilateralist behavior of the United States of America and the insufficient commitment of some developing countries such as China to erode the legitimacy of the Kyoto Protocol. He believes that this behavior by some countries reduces the effectiveness of environmental agreements. Teehankee (2016) also considers the mobilization of nationalism to gain legitimacy by political regimes as an effective factor on domestic and foreign policy. Also, at the national level, the conflict and struggle between generations and the time-consuming nature of environmental policies make the approval and implementation of these policies more difficult. In fact, in order to legislate and adopt appropriate environmental policies, we need the legitimacy of the ruling power to reach a desirable level. On the other hand, parties and political groups are classically less active in the field of climate change, and long-term interests may be sacrificed in the competition between parties; Because the effects of environmental policies are seen much later than the time spent and planning to solve environmental problems. From Blühdorn's (2020) point of view, once democratic norms and procedures were necessary for social and environmental changes, but now they are the obstacles to these changes. This obstacle can be seen as a result of political inertia against changes. In this chapter we have focused on power at the national level. The dominant power in all countries should be able to make policies effectively and its policies should be implemented by the members of the society. As mentioned earlier, the issue of the legitimacy of power is effective in its effectiveness and efficiency.

Legitimacy of the environmental policy-maker is another mechanism to justify the reasons for the weak performance of the institutions in helping to solve the problem of climate change. "It is these institutions that determine which actions are appropriate and acceptable, which policies should be abolished and which policies should be maintained" (Munck af Rosenschöld et al., 2014).

---

[2]To read more about the inertia in informal institutions refer to Chapter "The Roots of Cognitive Inertia: An Introduction to Institutional Changes" of this book.

The occurrence of institutional inertia due to the lack of legitimacy can be done in two ways; the state resists making changes, or people oppose the state's decisions and prevent them from being implemented. In the first case, the delegitimizing of new ideas by the use of power tools by those in power is one of the factors that create institutional inertia. Since the power holders have the power to determine legitimate or illegitimate things through legislation and the like, they prevent or encourage institutional changes by using the mechanism of legitimacy. By using this tool in international or national climate change policies, powerful actors legitimize policies that are in line with their own interests and those of their interest groups. This action is carried out by various tools in the hands of the dominant power such as the legislative assembly, state decisions and orders, media, and political groups. With this tool, they can establish the three conditions of legitimacy (legality, justification, and public consent), and implement their decision. We describe this process with an example:

Suppose a group of environmental activists in an oil country proposes an "energy transition" policy. This policy is a proposal to the state to replace the use of renewable energy to produce electricity instead of fossil energy. But the state opposes this policy due to its interests and its supporting groups, so tries to prevent this institutional change by using the tools in its hand. This supposed state, using the media, insinuates to society that this is not for the good of the society. With the use of renewable energy, production efficiency in the country will decrease and many people will be unemployed. Also, a lot of money should be spent on investing in new energy sources; The lower capacity of solar power plants compared to gas power plants causes a reduction in electricity production and thus blackouts. By using this tool in society, the state questions the legitimacy of the new proposal. It may even approve a plan to deal with these things by proposing to the parliament. The dominant power can create an obstacle in front of the changes and strengthen the institutional inertia with the mentioned tools.

In the second case, people stand against the implementation of the government's decisions due to the lack of legitimacy of the ruling power. This issue was explained in detail earlier in the second section. In this chapter, we examine this state of the relationship between legitimacy and power. To better understand the problem, consider the following example:

Suppose a government plans to make a large investment in new energy to improve the quality of the environment. In order to finance this action, it wants to increase the tax on fossil energy consumption and receive a heavy loan from the World Bank. But different political groups and people are against this decision for various reasons. Parties A, B and C, as powerful parties in the parliament, declare their opposition to the approval of this plan. Suppose in a democratic country, party A is supported by oil companies, party B is against imposing more tax pressure on the people, and party C is a conservative party and against cooperation with the World Bank and other international organizations. Also suppose that, according to polls, the people are also against this plan because of the previous decisions and policies of the government and the increase in taxes. The consumption culture of society currently has the desire to consume more fossil energy. With the mentioned assumptions, most of the parties and people will be against the implementation of this policy. People's opposition reduces the possibility of the current president getting votes in the next elections. In addition, the next state may cancel these decisions. These are the reasons for strengthening the institutional inertia in front of this plan. Having said that, this policy cannot gain the necessary legal validity, social justification and people's satisfaction and be considered legitimate. This state should first negotiate with the interested groups and bring the people with them through awareness and education using the media and other tools. A concrete example of this is the United States of America joining the Paris Agreement during Obama's presidency, withdrawing during Trump's presidency, and rejoining during Biden's presidency. The legitimacy of non-democratic governments is far worse from the point of view of the people under control and it is more difficult to bring them together.

Non-democratic governments mainly face some degree of crisis of legitimacy, or lack of legitimacy. In addition to not having the support of the people to implement policies, these governments must spend resources to gain legitimacy or show it. In such governments, resources are used for such things as internal and external propaganda of the government, the army, suppression of protesting people, patronage and control of civil disobedience. Also, under the rule of such governments, new investments will not be made and the existing funds tend to leave the country. In this case, there will be no resources to invest in new environmental technologies, and basically, there will be no ability and desire for environmental policy and importance to it. Also, these governments have low legitimacy in the international community and have fewer international allies. This issue will cause the lack of cooperation of these countries in coordinated international actions. These issues indicate the institutional inertia caused by the crisis of legitimacy in non-democratic countries.

In the issue of climate change, local governments are at the forefront of environmental governance and policymaking. It is after this that the governments together can plan and cooperate for a collective action to deal with climate change.

Considering that environmental governance is a public good; For this purpose, democratic governments should inform society about its importance. This issue is important from the point of view that governments must first attract the opinion of the people. Also, in order to institutionalize or reproduce institutions related to climate change, governments must convince the society and legitimize their decisions and policies. Since the effects of environmental policies are mostly long-term, those in power need to accompany and interact with the people to implement policies. In fact, it is the legitimacy, the executive guarantee of these decisions from the eyes of the people. If the people do not agree with these policies and do not understand their necessity well, they may take action to oppose the policies and stop them after a few years of their implementation, or they may refuse to accompany the state in their implementation. In addition, because these policies are a public good and the cost of their implementation is financed from people's taxes, it can lead to the fall of the state implementing it if the people do not interact. As a result, local governments should first legitimize their environmental programs and policies and apply them after establishing legitimacy.

4 Institutions and Environment

In recent years, many studies have been conducted on the relationship between institutional quality and environmental quality. Egbetokun and Ogundipe (2016) show how institutions (a combination of rights, laws and decision-making procedures) influence environmental change (Fig. 2). Institutions affect governance. Governance also affects environmental changes. This issue creates interactions between governance, human security and environmental change. It has been shown in Egbetokun and Ogundipe (2016) and Afroozeh (2022) that the improvement of institutional quality leads to the reduction of environmental degradation. This, in turn, makes us reach the return point of the environmental Kuznets curve sooner. This issue means that the improvement of the institutional quality leads to the improvement of the technology and development level of the countries.

In addition, the deterioration of the quality of the environment leads to a decrease in social welfare. Samadi et al. (2019) showed that low institutional quality reduces the quality of the environment and, as a result, reduces social well-being (Fig. 3).

Figures 2 and 3 show the importance of institutional quality in governance, environmental quality, human security, and social welfare. If the institutional quality is low, all four mentioned items are threatened. For this reason, positive institutional changes should be on the agenda. If there is resistance to positive institutional changes, this resistance prevents countries from improving their environmental performance. Investigating the effect of mechanisms that create institutional inertia in climate change issues becomes important here. State legitimacy crisis (as a proxy variable for institutional quality) can weaken environmental performance. The crisis of the legitimacy of the state strengthens the institutional inertia.

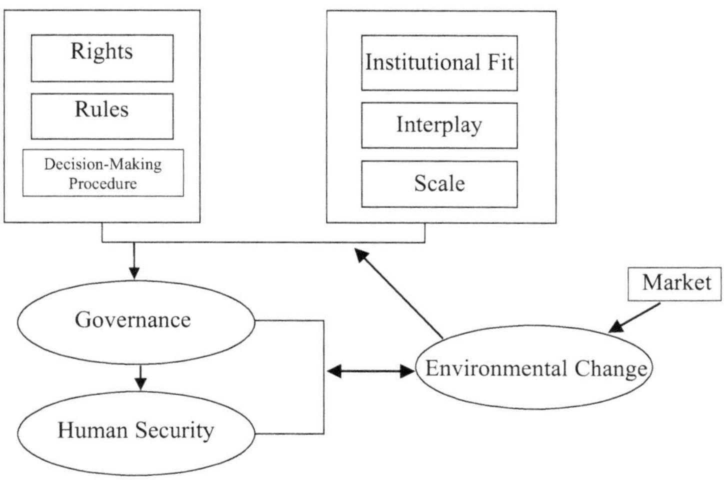

Fig. 2 The relationship between quality of institutions and environmental quality. (Source: Egbetokun and Ogundipe (2016))

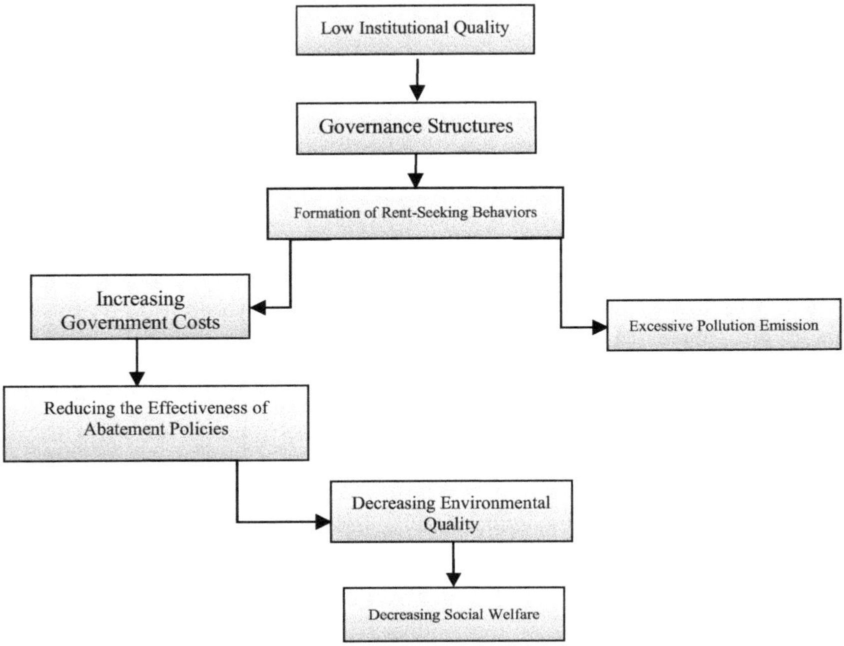

Fig. 3 The effect of low institutional quality on environmental quality and social welfare. (Source: Samadi et al. (2019))

5 Empirical Relationship Between State Legitimacy and Environmental Performance

State legitimacy index (SLI) considers the representation and openness of the state and its relationship with the citizens. This index looks at the level of people's trust in state organizations and processes. If people do not trust state organizations and processes, they react through massive public demonstrations, persistent civil disobedience, or armed rebellions. SLI is a tool to evaluate these conditions. Although the SLI does not necessarily judge the state of governance in democratic or non-democratic political systems; Rather, the validity of elections where they are held (such as flawed or sanctioned elections), takes into account the nature of political transitions and non-democratic systems.SLI, assesses the openness of government, particularly the openness of ruling elites to transparency, accountability, and political representation, or vice versa, levels of corruption, profiteering, and the marginalization, harassment, or exclusion of opposition groups. The SLI considers the ability of a state to perform basic functions such as the ability to collect taxes. This index is provided by "Fund for Peace". It is published annually since 2006. The legitimacy score of governments is graded from 0 (the highest level of legitimacy) to 10 (the lowest level of legitimacy). SLI is the only indicator that measures the legitimacy of states (Taft et al., 2022).

The *environmental performance index* (EPI) is an index to evaluate environmental sustainability. Using 40 environmental indicators in 11 categories of environmental problems, this index examines the performance of countries in the field of environment and climate change. Also, this index ranks climate change performance, environmental health, and ecosystem vitality in 180 countries. This index shows how close or far countries are from the goals related to a sustainable environment. Also, EPI provides a complete and comprehensive view of the state of the environmental performance of almost all countries. According to these explanations and comprehensiveness of EPI, this index has been used in the present study to examine the state of environmental governance of countries.

5.1 *Statistical Analysis*

To answer the question of whether there is a relationship between the degree of legitimacy of a state (as a factor in creating institutional inertia) and its environmental performance, we turn to statistics. In this sub-section, we want to examine the existence of a possible relationship between SLI and EPI. For a better understanding, the statistics of two categories of countries have been used (the first countries at the top and the second countries at the bottom of the state legitimacy table). In Sect. 5.1.3, the 10-year environmental performance of the countries has been analyzed. This type of classification of countries makes the status of the relationship SLI and EPI better understood.

5.1.1 Countries With the Highest Level of State Legitimacy

In Table 2, the status of 30 countries with the highest level of SLI is given along with the EPI of these countries in 2022. In 2022, 21 of these 30 countries (70 percent) are among the first 30 countries, in the highest category of the EPI. This issue can indicate the effect of the government's legitimacy on environmental governance and better implementation of these policies. The global average EPI in 2022, was 43.1; While the score for the 30 countries with the highest SLI was 59.25 (37% EPI above the global average). Also among these top 30 countries, only Uruguay with EPI = 37.4 is lower than the global average. Based on this, it can be concluded that there is probably a positive relationship between the degree of legitimacy of governments and their environmental performance. Also, the high level of legitimacy of the government can help to improve the environmental performance.

Figure 4 and Table 2 show well the relationship between EPI and SLI for the 30 countries with the highest level of legitimacy. The trend line of the graph also shows that the lower the SLI (higher legitimacy), the better the environmental performance in this category of countries.

Table 2 SLI and EPI of 30 countries with the highest SLI in 2022

Country	SLI	EPI
Japan	0.2	57.2
Netherlands	0.3	62.6
Luxembourg	0.3	72.3
Switzerland	0.3	65.9
Denmark	0.3	77.9
Norway	0.3	59.3
Finland	0.3	76.5
Uruguay	0.4	37.4
Germany	0.4	62.4
Australia	0.4	60.1
Canada	0.4	50
Iceland	0.4	62.8
New Zealand	0.5	56.7
Austria	0.6	66.5
Sweden	0.6	72.7
Ireland	0.6	57.4
Portugal	0.8	50.4
Belgium	0.9	58.2
France	1.1	62.5
Costa Rica	1.2	46.3
Estonia	1.2	61.4
Barbados	1.3	53.2
Lithuania	1.3	55.9
Slovenia	1.7	67.3
Latvia	2.1	61.1
Mauritius	2.1	44.8
Italy	2.3	57.7
Croatia	2.4	60.2
Botswana	2.5	54
South Korea	2.7	46.9

Source: Author's own table Based on (Taft et al., 2022; Wolf et al., 2022)

Five countries Norway, New Zealand, Finland, Sweden, and Denmark have the highest 16-year SLI average. In Table 3, SLI changes for these five countries are shown from 2007 to 2022. Based on Fig. 5 and Table 3, it can be seen that the degree of state legitimacy in these five countries has improved to a high extent.

In Table 4, the rate of change in EPI of these five countries is given over the 10 years ending in 2022. The EPI has improved in the last 10 years in Sweden, Denmark, Finland, and Norway, and only in New Zealand, it has decreased by 0.4. However, New Zealand in this period has always been among the countries with the best environmental performance. These statistics also confirm the positive effect of state legitimacy on the environmental performance of countries.

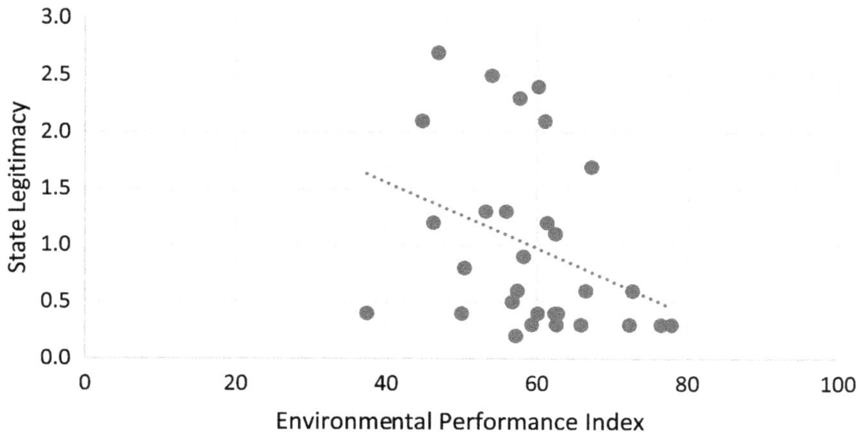

Fig. 4 SLI and EPI of 30 countries with the highest SLI in 2022. (Source: Author's own figure Based on (Taft et al., 2022; Wolf et al., 2022))

Table 3 SLI of Five countries with the most average of SLI in 2007–2022

	Norway	New Zeland	Finland	Sweden	Denmark
2007	1.0	1.1	0.9	1.0	1.0
2008	1.0	1.1	0.9	1.0	1.0
2009	1.0	1.1	0.9	1.0	1.3
2010	0.8	1.0	0.7	0.8	1.1
2011	1.0	1.1	1.0	0.9	1.2
2012	0.8	0.8	0.8	0.8	0.8
2013	0.5	0.5	1.0	0.5	1.0
2014	0.5	0.5	0.8	0.8	0.8
2015	0.4	0.5	0.5	1.0	0.5
2016	0.5	0.6	0.6	1.0	0.6
2017	0.8	0.9	0.9	1.0	0.9
2018	0.6	0.6	0.9	0.8	0.9
2019	0.6	0.6	0.9	0.8	0.9
2020	0.5	0.5	0.6	0.5	0.6
2021	0.5	0.5	0.5	0.5	0.5
2022	0.3	0.5	0.3	0.6	0.3

Source: Author's own table Based on Fragile States Index Annual Report (2007–2022)

5.1.2 Countries With the Lowest Level of State Legitimacy

In this sub-section, SLI and EPI statistics are analyzed for 30 countries that had the lowest level of legitimacy of the state in 2022. EPI for Syria, Yemen, North Korea, South Sudan, Somalia, Libya, and Guinea-Bissau were not available in 2022. Therefore, the average EPI for the other 23 countries in 2022 was 36.46, which

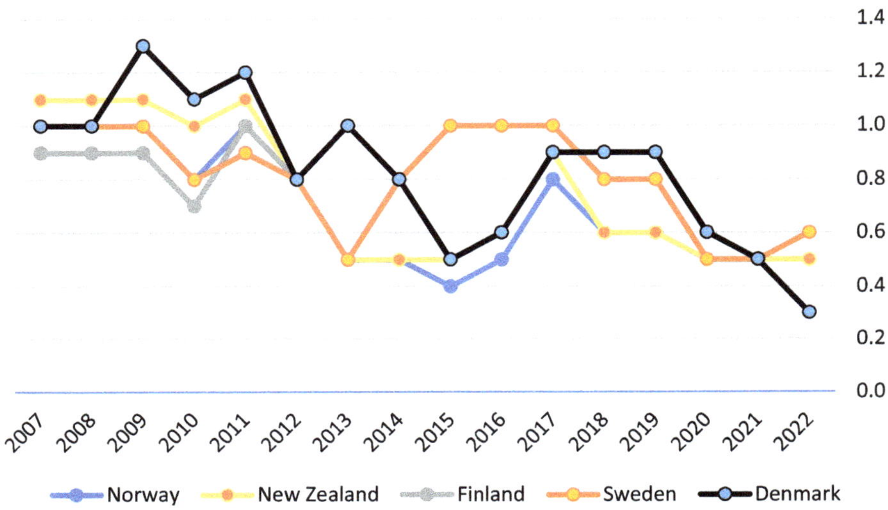

Fig. 5 SLI of five countries with the most average of SLI in 2007–2022. (Source: Author's own figure Based on Fragile States Index Annual Report (2007–2022))

Table 4 EPI 10-Year Change of five countries with most average of SLI in 2007–2022

Country	EPI score (2022)	EPI 10-year change
Denmark	77.9	+14.9
Norway	59.3	+5.8
Sweden	72.7	+15.8
Finland	76.5	+21.0
New Zeeland	56.7	−0.4

Source: Author's own table Based on Wolf et al., 2022

is lower than the global average EPI for this year, 43.1. Only four countries (Zimbabwe, Equatorial Guinea, Belarus, and Venezuela) had a better environmental performance than the global average. EPI in these countries has changed by −0.7, +15.2, +3.5, and + 0.2 respectively in the last 10 years. In the meantime, except in Guinea-Bissau, there has been no significant change in environmental performance. This statistic also strengthens the possibility of accepting the hypothesis of the positive effect of state legitimacy on environmental performance. For a better understanding of the explanations, these statistics are shown in Table 5 and Fig. 6.

Due to the unavailability of EPI data in 2022 for the countries of Syria, Yemen, North Korea, South Sudan, Somalia, Libya, and Guinea-Bissau, Fig. 6 was drawn using the data of 23 other countries. As it is clear from Fig. 6, in the category of countries with low state legitimacy, the environmental performance is mostly weak. The trend line in this graph shows that countries move towards higher EPI as the number of SLI decreases (more legitimacy), but no noticeable changes are observed. This point can also be another reason for the positive effect of improving state legitimacy on environmental performance

Table 5 SLI and EPI of 30 countries with the lowest SLI in 2022

Country	SLI	EPI
Cambodia	8.8	30.1
Zimbabwe	8.9	46.2
Nicaragua	8.9	37.7
Guinea Bissau	9.0	N/A
Laos	9.0	30.7
Myanmar	9.1	19.4
Congo Republic	9.1	40.1
Azerbaijan	9.1	38.6
Central African Republic	9.2	44.9
Afghanistan	9.2	43.6
Uzbekistan	9.2	38.2
Congo Democratic Republic	9.3	36.9
Sudan	9.3	27.6
Iran	9.3	34.5
Tajikistan	9.3	37.1
Belarus	9.3	48.5
Chad	9.4	28.1
Burundi	9.4	30.5
Libya	9.4	N/A
Somalia	9.5	N/A
South Sudan	9.6	N/A
Eritrea	9.6	31.7
Venezuela	9.6	46.4
Haiti	9.8	26.1
Equatorial Guinea	9.8	44.8
Turkmenistan	9.8	37
Yemen	9.9	N/A
North Korea	9.9	N/A
Syria	10.0	N/A
Guinea	10.0	31.6

Source: Author's own table Based on (Taft et al., 2022; Wolf et al., 2022)

According to the analysis of SLI, for all countries, the state of five countries North Korea, Guinea, Equatorial Guinea, Sudan, and Somalia in the period from 2007 to 2022, on average, had the lowest level of legitimacy among the countries of the world. The status of SLI in these countries is shown in Table 6 and Fig. 7.

Table 7 shows the 10-year EPI changes for the three countries of Sudan, Equatorial Guinea, and Guinea. This index is not available for Somalia and North Korea. EPI did not change much in Sudan and Guinea, but it improved a lot in Equatorial Guinea. Equatorial Guinea has reached the global average by improving its environmental performance, but Sudan and Guinea are still among the weak countries.

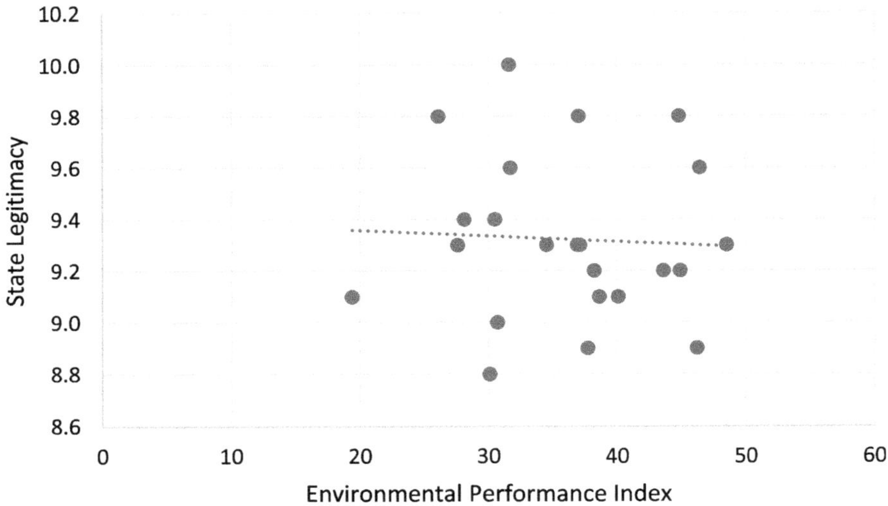

Fig. 6 SLI and EPI of 23 countries with the lowest SLI in 2022. (Source: Author's own figure Based on (Taft et al., 2022; Wolf et al., 2022))

Table 6 SLI of Five countries with the least average of SLI in 2007–2022

	Somalia	Sudan	Equatorial Guinea	Guinea	North Korea
2007	10.0	10.0	9.4	9.6	9.8
2008	10.0	10.0	9.4	9.7	9.8
2009	10.0	9.8	9.4	9.8	9.8
2010	10.0	9.9	9.6	9.8	9.9
2011	9.8	9.4	9.6	9.4	9.9
2012	9.9	9.5	9.4	9.5	9.9
2013	9.5	9.6	9.6	9.8	9.8
2014	9.1	9.3	9.7	9.9	9.9
2015	9.3	9.6	9.8	9.9	10.0
2016	9.5	9.8	9.9	9.8	10.0
2017	9.3	9.8	9.8	9.6	10.0
2018	9.1	9.7	9.8	9.7	10.0
2019	9.0	9.8	9.8	9.8	10.0
2020	8.9	9.3	9.8	9.9	9.9
2021	9.2	8.8	9.8	10.0	9.9
2022	9.5	9.3	9.8	10.0	9.9

Source: Author's own table Based on Fragile States Index Annual Report (2007–2022)

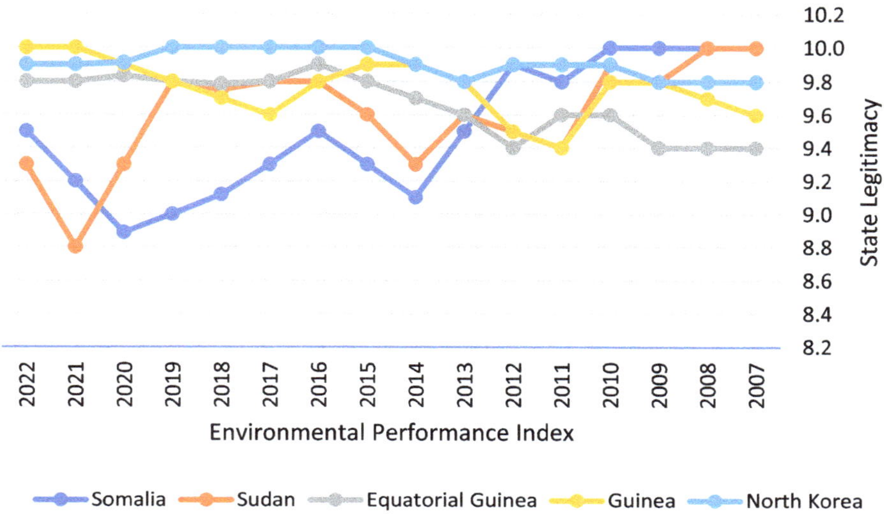

Fig. 7 SLI of 5 countries with the least average SLI in 2007–2022. (Source: Author's own figure Based on Fragile States Index Annual Report (2007–2022))

Table 7 EPI 10-Year Change of Five countries with the least average of SLI in 2007–2022

Country	EPI score	EPI 10-year change
Somalia	N/A	N/A
Sudan	27.6	+ 1.7
Equatorial Guinea	44.8	+15.3
Guinea	31.6	+0.2
North Korea	N/A	N/A

Source: Author's own table Based on (Wolf et al., 2022)

5.1.3 The Best and Worst Change in Environmental Performance in the Last 10 years

In Sects. 5.1.1 and 5.1.2, we analyzed the countries according to SLI and their EPI and we concluded that higher state legitimacy is likely to lead to better environmental performance. In this section, we examine the state of SLI in countries that have had the most positive and negative changes in EPI.

In Table 8, SLI and its changes for the countries with the most positive 10-year EPI changes are given. It is obvious that the negative change of SLI means improvement and its positive change means the deterioration of the state legitimacy. According to Table 8, state legitimacy has decreased in only 4 of the 15 countries that have had the best environmental performance over the last 10 years (United Kingdom, Equatorial Guinea, Kuwait, and Djibouti); this situation has not changed in one country (United Arab Emirates), but it has improved in the rest of the countries. These points also indicate the positive effect of improving the state's legitimacy on environmental performance.

Table 8 EPI and SLI in 2022 for countries with the most EPI 10-year change

Country	EPI 10-year change	EPI (2022)	SLI 10 year change	SLI (2022)
Malta	25.40	75.20	−0.8	3.2
Afghanistan	23.90	43.60	−0.3	9.2
United Kingdom	23.0	77.70	+1.4	3.3
Finland	21.0	76.5	−0.5	0.3
Trinidad and Tobago	19.0	47.80	−2.9	3.0
Croatia	17.2	60.20	−1.8	2.4
Namibia	16.40	50.90	−1.3	3.1
United Arab Emirates	15.90	52.40	0	6.4
Sweden	15.80	72.70	−0.2	0.6
Equatorial Guinea	15.30	44.80	+0.4	9.8
Kuwait	15.20	42.40	+0.6	7.1
Denmark	14.90	77.90	−0.5	0.3
Luxembourg	13.50	72.30	−1.9	0.3
Djibouti	12.90	47.50	+1.0	8.5
Barbados	12.7	53.2	−2.3	1.3

Source: Author's own table Based on (Taft et al., 2022; Wolf et al., 2022)

Table 9 shows the statistics of 10-year changes in SLI for 15 countries that had the most negative changes in EPI in the last 10 years. Among the 15 countries that have had the greatest decline in environmental performance, only in two countries, Burundi and Eritrea, SLI has decreased and in the rest, it has increased. These countries are among the average and weak countries in terms of state legitimacy. Since countries in Table 9 are in the initial stages of development, at this stage, with greater economic growth, the amount of pollution emission increases and the environmental performance becomes weaker (i.e. the environmental Kuznets hypothesis). According to this issue, the reason for the decrease in environmental performance and the increase in the state legitimacy in this group of countries can be justified.

5.2 *Empirical Relationship Between EPI and SLI*

The purpose of this subsection is to investigate the empirical relationship between EPI and SLI using econometric modeling. In the empirical literature, no study was found that directly examines the relationship between government legitimacy and environmental performance. The purpose of regression estimation in the present study is only to investigating the existence of a possible relationship between SLI and EPI. For this reason, a simple bivariate regression model was used. Our question in this section is: Does state legitimacy, as a factor creating institutional inertia, affect environmental performance?

Table 9 EPI and SLI in 2022 for countries with the least EPI 10-year change

Country	EPI 10-year change	EPI (2022)	SLI 10-year change	SLI (2022)
Burundi	−13.0	30.5	1.1	9.4
Nepal	−10.3	28.3	−1.9	6.1
Vanuatu	−9.2	36.9	N/A	N/A
Côte d'Ivoire	−8.20	32.80	−1.8	7.8
Suriname	−8.00	45.90	−2.9	3.5
Bhutan	−7.90	42.50	−3.5	2.8
Philippines	−7.50	28.90	−0.8	7.1
Samoa	−7.40	36.40	−1.6	4.4
Zambia	−6.90	38.40	−0.8	7.2
Ghana	−6.10	27.70	−1.6	3.2
Nigeria	−6.10	28.30	−0.6	8.5
Guyana	−6.10	38.50	−2.0	4.5
Paraguay	−6.00	40.90	−0.9	6.7
Micronesia	−5.90	37.40	−1.9	4.4
Eritrea	−5.50	31.70	1.2	9.6

Source: Author's own table Based on (Taft et al., 2022; Wolf et al., 2022)

(Dkhili, 2018) '(Mavragani et al., 2016) and (Abduqayumov et al., 2020) are among the studies in which the relationship between institutional quality and environmental performance has been investigated. Due to the use of two other studies of unrelated variables and far from the purpose of this chapter, we use the model used in (Mavragani et al., 2016). In this paper, the effect of per capita gross domestic product (GDPc) in terms of US dollars, open market index (OMI), and six indicators of the quality of good governance on the environmental performance index have been used.

The OMI is calculated and published by the International Chamber of Commerce. This index measures 4 main issues: trade openness ratio, trade policy status, foreign direct investment openness, and trade-enabling infrastructure. This index was last published in 2017 for 75 countries.

Using the model introduced by (Mavragani et al., 2016) and replacing SLI with the World Bank's governance indicators as a proxy variable for institutional quality, we will examine the factors affecting EPI.

The regression model used is in the form of Eq. 1:

$$\mathrm{EPI_i} = \beta_0 + \beta_1 \mathrm{GDP_{C_i}} + \beta_2\, \mathrm{OMI_i} + \beta_3 \mathrm{SLI_i} + \in_i \tag{1}$$

In this sub-section, using the data of the 2022 EPI and SLI for 30 countries with the highest level of legitimacy, using the ordinary least squares method, the relationship between EPI and SLI, GDPc, and OMI was estimated. The exclusion of five countries, Botswana, Croatia, Mauritius, Costa Rica, and Barbados, was due to the lack of data for the market openness index of these countries. The estimated function is as eq. 2:

$$\mathrm{EPI_i} = 40.161 + 0.0000784\ \mathrm{GDPC_i} + 4.197\mathrm{OMI_i} - 0.806\mathrm{SLI_i} \tag{2}$$

The amount of R^2 for this estimate, was equal to 0.19. The results of this estimation show that EPI has a negative relationship with the SLI ($\beta_3 = -0.806$). The Durbin-Watson (D.W.) statistic for this equation is 2.08 and there is no autocorrelation. This result means a direct relationship between EPI and SLI. Therefore, environmental performance in countries with high legitimacy also improves as state legitimacy increases.

Now, to better understand the direct relationship between EPI and SLI for different categories, we estimate the $y_i = \alpha_i + \mu_i x + \epsilon_i$ regression model. In this regression function, y is the dependent variable (EPI) and x is the independent variable (SLI).

For the first case, we use data on SLI and EPI of the 30 countries with the highest levels of state legitimacy in 2022. The regression equation in this case is written as equation:

$$y_i = \alpha_1 + \mu_1 x_i + \epsilon_i \tag{3}$$

In the second case, since EPI data is not available for 7 countries out of 30 countries with the lowest level of legitimacy, the data of 23 countries and eq. 4 have been used.

$$y_i = \alpha_2 + \mu_2 x_i + \epsilon_i \tag{4}$$

For the third case, we used the data from 30 countries with the highest and 23 countries with the lowest level of state legitimacy. The regression equation is given in eq. 5.

$$y_i = \alpha_3 + \mu_3 x_i + \epsilon_i \tag{5}$$

In the fourth case, the data of 29 countries in 2022 that have had the most positive or negative EPI changes in the last 10 years (Tables 7 and 8) have been used. The data of Vanuatu has been excluded from the estimation due to the unavailability of the SLI (Eq. 6).

$$y_i = \alpha_4 + \mu_4 x_i + \epsilon_i \tag{6}$$

In the last case, the eq. 7 has been estimated using data from 171 countries for which SLI and EPI data are available in 2022.

$$y_i = \alpha_5 + \mu_5 x_i + \epsilon_i \tag{7}$$

The estimation results of models 3 to 7 are given in Table 10.

Coefficient μ_i has been negative in all cases. Because in the SLI, a lower number indicates greater legitimacy, the negative coefficient SLI shows the positive relationship between state legitimacy and environmental performance; The point that was stated in the analysis of the raw categorized data is also confirmed by estimating

Table 10 Results of estimation of models 3 to 7 in 2022

Equation	α_i	μ_i	t-statistic	F	R^2	Std.Error	Prob.	D.W.
$y = \alpha_1 + \mu_1 x$	63.23	−3.99	−1.922	3.69	0.11	2.07	0.0647	1.89
$y = \alpha_2 + \mu_2 x$ [a]	47.75	−1.25	−0.24	0.058	0.002	5.162	0.8110	1.33
$y = \alpha_3 + \mu_3 x$	62.11	−2.8	−10.31	106.36	0.67	0.271	0.00	2.13
$y = \alpha_4 + \mu_4 x$	62.78	−2.78	−4.27	14.65	0.63	0.65	0.002	2.42
$y = \alpha_5 + \mu_5 x$	60.018	−3.053	−12.32	151.8	0.47	0.247	0.00	1.90

Source: Author's own table

[a]For the group of countries with low legitimacy, the explanatory power of the model is almost zero and it faces the problem of autocorrelation

the regression model in different cases. These results indicate that higher legitimacy of state will improve environmental performance and lower legitimacy will lead to weakening of environmental performance. Considering that the low legitimacy of the state can be a mechanism causing institutional inertia, it can be said that institutional inertia has an opposite relationship with environmental performance. This means that the higher the institutional inertia (less state legitimacy), the weaker the environmental performance and vice versa. Determination coefficient R^2 for the category of countries with low legitimacy is near zero. This issue shows that legitimacy does not affect environmental performance in countries with low legitimacy. However, the coefficients show that with the increase in the legitimacy of the state in these countries, the environmental performance will improve. Since these countries generally lack a state with democratic and modern standards, environmental issues are not important to them.

6 Conclusion

The legitimacy of power, due to power relations, party interests, societal values , and laws, affects the performance of governments and the ability to implement their policies. In case of illegitimacy, most governments will face an efficiency crisis in the short term and almost all of them in the long term. This issue is due to the non-cooperation of other political groups and society with the policies and goals of that government. The situation is the same with the issues of climate change. If a state or a dominant power does not have legal validity, is not in harmony with the values and norms of the subordinate society, and its decisions are not accompanied by the consent of the society, it does not have legitimacy; As a result, it is difficult to deal with climate change and improve environmental performance. This problem is caused by the institutional inertia caused by the lack of legitimacy. As shown by the analysis of statistics in different countries, the crisis of legitimacy creates an obstacle in the way for countries to improve their environmental performance by creating institutional cohesion. Environmental decisions and policies are a public good with a very long and permanent supply period. If the society and the groups in power are not with the environmental policies, the governments will face the failure of the policy. The reason for this failure can be due to the legitimacy crisis of the state and as a result, the legitimacy of the decisions and policies of that government.

From the statistical data and regression results of Sect. 5, it is clear that the countries in which governments have less legitimacy have a worse situation in environmental performance. Of course, this issue is better seen in countries with a higher level of legitimacy. This could indicate that we need a threshold level of legitimacy for legitimacy to affect EPI. Legitimacy is not a given issue. Also, once a power or policy is recognized as legitimate by society, it does not mean its permanent legitimacy, rather governments should always prove their legitimacy and their policies to the nation and protect it. By comparing statistics SLI and EPI It is clear that at the same time as the state of state legitimacy has improved, their environmental performance has also improved (for example, see Tables 3 and 4).

In this chapter, we sought to find an answer to the question of whether the legitimacy of the state, as a mechanism that creates institutional inertia, affects the performance of countries in dealing with climate change or not. For this reason, we introduced the concept of state legitimacy first. Experimental results showed that the degree of state legitimacy has a direct effect on environmental performance (Table 10). In the literature of institutionalism, the legitimacy of the state as one of the effective factors in the efficiency of governance has been less discussed. The purpose of this chapter of the book is to show the importance of this issue for further studies in this field. The effect of legitimacy on environmental performance and its effect on climate change was also brought up as an example of the importance of state legitimacy. This chapter is the first research to find the relationship between state legitimacy and environmental performance.

In general, states and societies should strive to reach a common understanding of power in order to define their acceptable governance system. The issue of the legitimacy of power and, as a result, trust in the position and the owner of the position of power is one of the issues that many countries are still facing. However, this issue is not only a problem for less developed, dictatorial, and poor countries; Rather, the power structure in developed countries and democracies must always protect their legitimacy and increase it so as not to face the problem of policy failure and lack of efficiency as a result of lack of legitimacy. The legitimacy crisis hinders the optimal performance of governments by creating institutional inertia. This inertia comes from both the people and the state and political parties. In the issue of climate change, the legitimacy of the state has been less addressed. It is necessary to conduct more studies on the issue of the legitimacy of power, both at the domestic level of countries and at the international level, and for international organizations and conventions.

References

Abduqayumov, S., Arshed, N., & Bukhari, S. (2020). Economic impact of institutional quality on environmental performance in post-soviet countries. *Transition Studies Review, 27*(2), 13–24.

Afroozeh, S. (2022). *Evaluating environmental Kuznets Curve with technological, environmental and institutional switching: Application of optimal control theory.* Thesis submitted Shiraz University.

Beetham, D. (2013). *The legitimation of power*. Bloomsbury Publishing.

Blühdorn, I. (2020). The legitimation crisis of democracy: emancipatory politics, the environmental state and the glass ceiling to socio-ecological transformation. *Environmental Politics, 29*(1), 38–57.

Burch, S. (2011). Sustainable development paths: Investigating the roots of local policy responses to climate change. *Sustainable Development, 19*(3), 176–188. https://doi.org/10.1002/sd.435

Carment, D., & Samy, Y. (2011). *The social underpinnings of the current unrest in North Africa and the middle east*. Canadian Defence & Foreign Affairs Institute.

Connelly, S., Richardson, T., & Miles, T. (2006). Situated legitimacy: Deliberative arenas and the new rural governance. *Journal of Rural Studies, 22*(3), 267–277. https://doi.org/10.1016/j.jrurstud.2005.11.008

Connolly, W. (1984). *Legitimacy and the state*. New York University Press.

Dahrendorf, R. (1958). Toward a theory of social conflict. *Journal of Conflict Resolution, 2*(2), 170–183.

Dkhili, H. (2018). Environmental performance and institutions quality: evidence from developed and developing countries. *Marketing and Management of Innovations, 3*, 333–344. https://doi.org/10.21272/mmi.2018.3-30

Eckersley, R. (2007). Ambushed: The Kyoto Protocol, the Bush administration's climate policy and the erosion of legitimacy. *International Politics, 44*, 306–324.

Egbetokun, S. O., & Ogundipe, A. (2016). Attaining EKC in Africa: Why institutions really matter. Africa: Why institutions really matter (September 1, 2016). *Research Journal of Applied Science*, (Forthcoming).

Habermas, J. (1979). *Communication and the evolution of society*. Beacon Press.

Habermas, J. (1998). Between facts and norms: An author's reflections. *Denv UL Rev, 76*, 937.

Hibbing, J. R., & Theiss-Morse, E. (2002). *Stealth democracy: Americans' beliefs about how government should work*. Cambridge University Press.

Kant, I. (1996). The metaphysics of morals. In M. Gregor (Ed.), *Information ethics: Privacy, property, and power*. Cambridge University Press. https://doi.org/10.1163/9789004458970_011

Lipset, S. M. (1958). A sociologist looks at history. *Pacific Sociological Review, 1*(1), 13–17.

Lipset, S. M. (1984). Social conflict, legitimacy, and democracy. In W. Connolly (Ed.), *Legitimacy and the state* (pp. 88–103). New York University Press.

Luhmann, N. (1969). *Legitimation durch Verfahren* [Legitimation through procedure]. Luchterhand.

Mavragani, A., Nikolaou, I. E., & Tsagarakis, K. P. (2016). Open economy, institutional quality, and environmental performance: A macroeconomic approach. *Sustainability (Switzerland), 8*(7), 601. https://doi.org/10.3390/su8070601

Merelman, R. M. (1966). Learning and legitimacy1. *Merican Political Science Review, 60*(3), 548–561.

Munck af Rosenschöld, J., Rozema, J. G., & Frye-Levine, L. A. (2014). Institutional inertia and climate change: A review of the new institutionalist literature. *Wiley Interdisciplinary Reviews: Climate Change, 5*(5), 639–648. https://doi.org/10.1002/wcc.292

North, D. C., Wallis, J. J., Webb, S. B., & Weingast, B. R. (2013). *In the shadow of violence: Politics, economics, and the problems of development*. Cambridge University Press.

Omotola, J. S. (2012). Legitimacy crisis and 'popular uprisings' in North Africa. *Strategic Analysis, 36*(5), 713–719.

Pierson, P. (2004). *Politics in time: History, institutions, and social analysis*. Princeton University Press.
Reus-Smit, C. (2007). International crises of legitimacy. *International politics, 44*, 157–174.
Rousseau, J. J. (1978). *On the social contract*, ed (trans. J. R. M. Roger D. Masters (ed.)). St. Martin's Press.
Samadi, A. H., Zibaei, M., Ghaderi, J., & Bahlouli, P. (2019). Optimal environmental policy, Uncertainty and institutional quality: The case of Iran. *The Economic Research(Sustainbale Growth and Development), 19*(1), 53–82.
Schaar, J. H. (1984). Legitimacy in the modern state. In W. Connolly (Ed.), *Legitimacy and the state* (pp. 104–133). New York University Press.
Schmitter, P. C. (2001). *What is there to legitimize in the European Union... and how might this be accomplished?* (p. 20). Institut für Höhere Studien (IHS).
Signé, L. (2017). *Policy implementation – A synthesis of the study of policy implementation and the causes of policy failure* (pp. 9–26). OCP Policy Center.
Taft, P., Blyth, H., & Wilson, W. (2022). *Fragile states index annual report 2022*. https://fragilestatesindex.org/wp-content/uploads/2022/01/fsi2019-report-updated.pdf
Teehankee, J. C. (2016). Duterte's resurgent nationalism in The Philippines: a discursive institutionalist analysis. *Journal of Current Southeast Asian Affairs, 35*(3), 69–89.
Weber, M. (1968). *Economy and society*. University of California Press.
Weber, M. (1984). Legitimacy, politics and the state. In W. Connolly (Ed.), *Legitimacy and the state* (pp. 32–62). New York University Press.
Wheeler, B. R. (2001). Law and legitimacy in the work of Jürgen Habermas and Carl Schmitt. *Ethics & International Affairs, 15*(1), 173–183.
Williams, M. S. (2016). Reasons to obey: "Multiple modernities" and constructions of political legitimacy. In *East Asian perspectives on political legitimacy: Bridging the empirical-normative divide* (pp. 25–54). Cambridge University Press. https://doi.org/10.1017/9781316466896.003
Wolf, M. J., Emerson, J. W., Esty, D. C., de Sherbinin, A., & Wendling, Z. A. (2022). *Environmental Performance Index*. Yale Center for Environmental Law & Policy.

Part V
Innovation and Entrepreneurship

Early Entrepreneurship Entry and Institutional Rigidities in Emerging Market Economies: Evidence from the Global Entrepreneurship Monitor

Kameliia Petrova and Agnitra RoyChoudhury

1 Introduction

Emerging market economies (EME) have slowly taken a leading role in the global economy over the past few decades. The fast growth and successful economic development of the BRICS[1] countries, among others, have attracted the attention of the investment, academic, and political world. EME are typically characterized with low to moderate GDP per capita, high GDP growth rates, dynamic consumer markets, increased competition levels, underdeveloped financial markets, predominance of state-owned enterprises, and policies for active reduction of trade barriers and participation in global trade and financial market integration. The industrial development of EME is focused on mostly labor-intensive sectors such as heavy manufacturing, large-scale equipment, and heavy machinery.

This chapter investigates how institutional rigidities affect early entrepreneurship entry in emerging market economies. The empirical analysis is based on a multilevel logit model estimation. The measure of nascent entrepreneurship is taken from the Global Entrepreneurship Monitor Adult Population Surveys. Macroeconomic controls are obtained from the World Bank World Development Indicators, and institutional rigidity indices are acquired from the Economic Freedom of the World data set. The results indicate that better functioning capital markets, relaxed trade barriers have a positive effect on nascent entrepreneurs. The effect of administrative

[1] China, India, Brazil, Indonesia, and South Africa.

K. Petrova (✉)
Department of Economics and Finance, SUNY Plattsburgh, Plattsburgh, NY, USA
e-mail: kpetr001@plattsburgh.edu

A. RoyChoudhury
Department of Economics, Auburn University at Montgomery, Montgomery, AL, USA
e-mail: achoudhu@aum.edu

N. Faghih, A. H. Samadi (eds.), *Institutional Inertia*, Contributions to Economics,
https://doi.org/10.1007/978-3-031-51175-2_13

requirements and bureaucracy on the propensity to become a nascent entrepreneur is insignificant. This could be due to entrepreneurs in emerging market economies operating in the informal sector to avoid dealing with regulations. Higher prevalence of state ownership positively affects the propensity to become a nascent entrepreneur likely because when associated with state-owned enterprises, new companies will be able to easily compensate for losses.

This chapter contributes to the literature on entrepreneurship entry and institutions in several ways. First, the focus is on early-stage entrepreneurship, or the propensity to become a nascent entrepreneur, which is different than looking at all entrepreneurs in general. Established businesses have more resources, financial and social, and experience to weather market shocks. Second, the study looks at a set of several institutional rigidities tailored specifically for EME. Previous studies focused predominantly on labor market rigidities, and in a few cases on individual rigidities. Third, a mixed level model is employed that allows the inclusion of both macro and micro level factors.

The rest of the chapter is structured as follows. Section 2 provides literature review of institutional rigidities in emerging markets and discusses their relationship to entrepreneurship. We discuss studies on institutional inertia and how it affects the economy in general. Next, the effect of institutional rigidities is narrowed down to emerging economies. Finally, we introduce entrepreneurship, entrepreneurial ecosystems, and discuss their interaction with market institutions. Section 2 also presents the theory behind our analysis, and develops the hypotheses being tested in the chapter. Section 3 describes the datasets used in the study. Section 4 goes over the empirical model and estimation, and Sect. 5 presents the estimation results. We present policy implications and concluding remarks in Sect. 6.

2 Literature Review and Hypotheses Development

2.1 Institutions

North (1990) defines institutions as the 'rules of the game' that serve as the backbone of economic transactions. Well-established and properly functioning institutions lessen transaction costs (North, 1994; Williamson, 2000). While institutions governing social, political, and cultural interactions are predominantly informal in nature (Hodgson, 2006; Powell & DiMaggio, 1991; Scott, 1995), this chapter focusses on formal institutions, defined as legal and judicial constructs. A change in formal institutions involves changing the existing laws, rules, and regulations. The more comprehensive notion of institutional field, viewed as a mix of institutions, has been introduced in the entrepreneurship literature (Bourdieu, 2005; Garud et al., 2007; Kalantaridis & Fletcher, 2012; Powell, 2007). A change in institutional fields may simply be a new arrangement of existing institutions.

It has been established that the most important reason behind the differences in economic development among countries is the difference in the effectiveness of economic institutions (Acemoglu et al., 2005; North, 1990; Rodrik et al., 2004). Underdeveloped institutions may reduce the net capital inflows and FDI into the country (Baek & Yang, 2010; Javorcik & Wei, 2009); have a negative impact on the level of innovation (Lin et al., 2010; Silve & Plekhanov, 2015; Tebaldi & Elmslie, 2013), and the development of the financial system (Pasali, 2013). Finally, Goes (2015) found that developing countries and emerging markets will gain more than developed countries from improving their institutions.

2.2 Institutional Inertia and Entrepreneurship

Most studies on the relationship between institutions and entrepreneurship concentrate on how institutions and institutional frameworks support or obstruct entrepreneurial activities and the creation of new ventures. It has been documented that country-level formal and informal institutional characteristics affect the level and type of entrepreneurship (Busenitz et al., 2000; Estrin et al., 2013; Harbi & Anderson, 2010; Muralidharan & Pathak, 2017; Nyström, 2008; Sobel, 2008; Spencer & Gómez, 2004; Stenholm et al., 2013; Stephen et al., 2005), the allocation of entrepreneurial effort (Bowen & De Clercq, 2008; Urbano & Alvarez, 2014), formal and informal entrepreneurship (Dau & Cuervo-Cazurra, 2014), and opportunity and necessity entrepreneurship (Angulo-Guerrero et al., 2017; Aparicio et al., 2016; Fuentelsaz et al., 2015; Samadi, 2018; Sambharya & Musteen, 2014; Simón-Moya et al., 2014). This one-sided approach is mainly because institutions are considered exogenous and stable social constructs that are resistant to change (Bjørnskov & Foss, 2016; Kalantaridis & Fletcher, 2012). While the theoretical underpinning is still deficient, some studies have established that institutions do in fact change over time. Some studies have documented entrepreneurial actions that bring transformation at both the regional and national levels (Baez & Abolafia, 2002; Fuentelsaz et al., 2015; Kalantaridis & Fletcher, 2012; Kuchař, 2016; Petrova, 2021; Yu, 2001). Thus, the literature may benefit from exploring a "bidirectional" relationship between institutions and entrepreneurs (Henrekson & Sanandaji, 2011; Samadi, 2018, 2019; Smallbone & Welter, 2012).

Institutional change is directly related to institutional embeddedness and institutional entrepreneurship. The former, also referred to as the "paradox of an embedded agency," is an attribute of institutions reflected in the influence that entrepreneurs exercise over the formation and development of institutions and institutional frameworks (Granovetter, 1992; Seo & Creed, 2002; Sewell, 1992). The latter, a notion developed by DiMaggio (1988), describes the actions of entrepreneurs who seek to bring changes to the institutional framework for personal gain, thus moving the discourse in the direction of acknowledging the role of entrepreneurs as leaders of change (Dorado, 2005; Garud et al., 2007; Leca et al., 2008). Still, some authors caution that the role of entrepreneurs in transforming institutions may be overstated (Bika, 2012; McCarthy, 2012; Smallbone & Welter, 2012), and that institutions change when the socio-economic, cultural, and political factors work together to create an environment for adjustment (Kalantaridis & Fletcher, 2012). Furthermore, Bika (2012) and Dorado (2005) argue that entrepreneurs' action directed towards bringing institutional changes may not always be fully intentional.

Probably the most studied type of institutional rigidities[2] are labor market rigidities. See Fu et al. (2018) for a detailed overview of studies on labor market rigidity and entrepreneurial activities using the GEM Data. This is mainly because of the availability and popularity of the World Bank's Ease of Doing Business dataset on employment rigidity and labor market regulations. We do not analyze labor market rigidities because the World Bank's methodology has come under scrutiny in recent years.

2.3 *Emerging Market Economies*

EME have taken a major position in the global economy, accounting for 34% of the world's nominal GDP and almost 50% on the basis of purchasing power in the 2010–2022 period (Duttagupta & Pazarbasioglu, 2021; Marquis & Raynard, 2015). The fast economic development of China, India, Brazil, Indonesia, and South Africa among others over the past fifty years has drawn the attention of the investment world (Marquis & Raynard, 2015). Financial Companies such as FTSE Russell,[3] MSCI,[4] and S&P Dow Jones[5] all have their own lists of emerging markets. Marqus and Raynard show that there is a consensus on which countries are included in the EME lists. While there is no officially recognized definition of what constitutes an EME, the International Monetary Fund World Economic Outlook (IMF, 2022) provides the most systematic classification. Countries are divided into "advanced" and "emerging market and developing" based on "per capita income, exports of diversified goods and services, and greater integration into the global financial system" (Duttagupta & Pazarbasioglu, 2021). Among the "emerging market and developing" countries, a subgroup of "emerging market and middle-income" economies is designated based on higher incomes. EME are identified from GDP per capita, population, share of exports in global trade, the share of a country's external debt in the global external debt, whether the country is included in global indices such as FTSE, MSCI, and S&P Dow Jones, and the frequency and amount of

[2]To read more about the concepts of inertia, institutional inertia, and sources of institutional inertia refer to Chapters "Inertia: Resistance and Endurance" and "An Introduction to Institutional Inertia: Concepts, Types and Causes" of this book.

[3]FTSE Russell EME classification, September 2022, https://research.ftserussell.com/products/downloads/FTSE-Country-Classification-Update-2022.pdf

[4]MSCI EME classification, August 2022, https://www.msci.com/documents/1296102/1330218/MSCI-Country-Classification-Standard-cfs-en.pdf

[5]S&P Dow Jones Indices' 2021 Country Classification Consultation, https://www.spglobal.com/spdji/en/documents/indexnews/announcements/20210803-1431359/1431359_spdji2021countryclassificationconsultation8-3-2021.pdf

international bonds issued. See IMF (2022) and Duttagupta and Pazarbasioglu (2021) for a detailed description of the ranking and classification. The IMF World Outlook identifies the following countries as EME: Argentina, Brazil, Chile, China, Colombia, Egypt, Hungary, India, Indonesia, Iran, Malaysia, Mexico, the Philippines, Poland, Russia, Saudi Arabia, South Africa, Thailand, Turkey, and the United Arab Emirates.

2.4 Hypotheses Development

EME, typically between developed and developing countries, are characterized with low to moderate GDP per capita, sustained high GDP growth rates, dynamic consumer markets, increased competition levels, and policies for active reduction of trade barriers and participation in global trade and financial market integration (Arnold & Quelch, 1998; Duttagupta & Pazarbasioglu, 2021; Hoskisson et al., 2000). In contrast, developed economies experience high GDP per capita with low GDP growth rate, predominantly service-oriented industries, low trade barriers, and very little to no government involvement at the enterprise level. On the opposite side, developing economies exhibit low GDP per capita with varied, but often low, GDP growth rates, high poverty and unemployment levels, and often high trade barriers. EME have crossed the stage of development typical for developing economies where stringent bureaucracy, rigid labor-market, business, and credit regulations prevent enterprise development, stifle entrepreneurship, and inhibit investment (Marquis & Raynard, 2015). Further differences involve the type of industries that predominantly form in EME: heavy manufacturing, large-scale equipment and heavy machinery; mostly labor-intensive sectors (Marquis & Raynard, 2015; Murrell & Wang, 1993; Sit & Liu, 2000). In addition to fast industrialization, EME have experienced an increased integration into the global economy. The main channel for promoting economic development is by borrowing advanced technologies, methodological practices, and organizational structures from the developed world, and adapt them successfully to the EME's needs. Thus, the openness of EME to FDI (Herrera-Echeverri et al., 2014; Paul & Jadhav, 2019) and international trade is essential for successful growth and development (Gurvich, 2016; Iwasaki & Suganuma, 2015).

Hypothesis 1: Decreased tariffs in EME positively affects the propensity to become a nascent entrepreneur.

Another important characteristic of EME is the insufficiently developed and volatile capital markets with low levels of market liquidity, the presence of high inflation driven by the strong growth in productivity, and an unstable currency (Marquis & Raynard, 2015). La Porta et al. (2002) found that many EME experience a lack of internal financial market development, coupled with a heavily regulated baking system. Since EME have less access to external capital, debt or equity (Gregory, 2019), entrepreneurs, in their pursuit for external resources, may often rely on alternative non-price mechanism capitalizing on relationships with banking and government agents (Khanna & Yafeh, 2007; Morck et al., 2005). Access to the financial system allows entrepreneurs to obtain capital (Straub, 2005). Access to venture capital promotes innovation entrepreneurship (Gu & Qian, 2019). The availability of microfinancing institutions stimulates the creation of new ventures (Newman et al., 2017). Herrera-Echeverri et al. (2014) found that the availability of investment has a highly significant positive impact on business development in EME. Financial controls in EME are associated with a decline in entrepreneurship (Gregory, 2019), while Omri (2020) has established the existence of a positive effect of financial development on formal entrepreneurship and a negative impact on an informal entrepreneurship. Lack of properly functioning financial institutions forces businesses and entrepreneurs to operate in an environment with high levels of risk and uncertainty (Aidis, 2005; Luthans & Ibrayeva, 2006; Manolova et al., 2008). This, in turn, promotes opportunism (Hiatt & Sine, 2014; Peng & Heath, 1996; Tracey & Phillips, 2011) and resourcefulness (Gurvich, 2016), and decreases the opportunity costs of producing in the informal sector (Berdiev & Saunoris, 2018).

Hypothesis 2: Better-functioning capital markets in EME positively affects the propensity to become a nascent entrepreneur.

One of the most distinctive attributes of EME is the predominance of state-owned enterprises (SOE), which removes a significant part of the economy from participating in market-driven processes, decreasing market efficiency and competitiveness (Douma et al., 2006; Gurvich, 2016; Musacchio & Lazzarini, 2014; Ralston et al., 2006). In 2013, the proportion of SOE among the Forbes Global 2000 in China, India, and Indonesia was above 50%, for Russia, the proportion was 39%, and 19% for Brazil (Kowalski et al., 2013). In 2018, SOEs represented 26% of the MSCI Emerging Markets Index (Zhou, 2019). Europe, Middle East, and Africa (EMEA) and Asia have a much larger share of companies owned and controlled by the state than Latin America (LA). In 2021, the SOE represented 40% of MSCI Emerging Markets Index in LA, 24% in EMEA, and 19% in Asia (Mendoza & Harris, 2021). SOE and companies linked to them are usually compensated for their losses, which further exacerbates the inefficiencies (Gurvich, 2016). This leads to what Gurvich refers to as "policy of industrial paternalism" that promotes economically unsound companies and, to some extent, industries, undermining the public administration structures. Thus, one can reasonably expect that higher prevalence of SOE will increase the propensity to become a nascent entrepreneur because new companies associated with SOE will be able to avoid dealing with competitors or incurring losses because of being subsidized for the losses.

Hypothesis 3: Higher prevalence of SOE in EME positively affects the propensity to become a nascent entrepreneur.

EME have less developed administrative and legislative infrastructures, which is directly correlated with the lack of transparency, corporate governance accountability, and protection of intellectual property rights (Marquis et al., 2011; Marquis & Qian, 2014). Further, due to certain socio-demographic characteristics and historical trends, EME experience political tensions and instability, which negatively affects the access to resources and information (Hiatt & Sine, 2014). Protection of property rights is considered crucial among all economic institutions for successful economic development (Acemoglu & Johnson, 2005). Insufficient protection of property rights disincentivizes businesses to continue investing and grow because successful and profitable companies are more valuable and attractive for expropriation by the government. This is directly related to the rise of the shadow or informal economy where businesses can operate unaffected. It has been documented that the shadow economy accounts for approximately 30–35% of the GDP in EME, which much higher than the corresponding number of 10–15% for developed economies (Hassan & Schneider, 2016; Kelmanson et al., 2019; Schneider, 2015). Gurvich (2016) reports that the actual adherence to property rights is more important than their formal definition citing Keefer's (Keefer, 2007) example of China in the 1980s. The government's focus to guarantee individual property rights brought unprecedented economic growth, while at the same time no formal definition was established. Therefore, it is possible that a lack of property rights protection may incentivize individuals to become nascent entrepreneurs, who operate in a shadow economy without having to deal with bureaucratic rules and regulations.

Hypothesis 4: Lack of protection of property rights in EME positively affects the propensity to become a nascent entrepreneur.

While regulations play a significant role in any economy, Djankov et al. (2002) observed that they are not instituted due to necessity. The authors found that more and stricter regulations do not improve the outcome for consumers. At the same time, more regulations result in corruption, bribes, bureaucracy, inefficiencies, and decreased competition. Strict regulations related to formal business registration forces entrepreneurs to engage in underground activities (Berdiev & Saunoris, 2018; De Soto, 1989). Favoritism practiced by government officials is designed to protect private interests and safeguard the officials' own positions (Gurvich, 2016). An alternative explanation is that regulations are meant to serve as barriers to entry instituted to protect the "old" players from newcomers (Acemoglu, 2008). In return, they will share their profits with the government official. Corruption undermines the effectiveness of institutions and has fiscal consequences when entrepreneurs move to the informal sector to escape corrupt public agents (Aidis, 2017; Buehn & Schneider, 2012; Friedman et al., 2000; Torgler & Schneider, 2009). Berdiev and Saunoris (2018) argue that corruption 'distorts' the marginal benefits and marginal costs of businesses that function in the formal economy and forces business owners to make a decision on whether they may be better off in the informal economy instead. Williams and Nadin (2011) found evidence that entrepreneurs respond to corruption and the external costs it imposes by moving from the formal to the informal sector, but also as a form of a "resistance" act. In addition, corruption interferes with public funds distributions (Mauro, 1998) and competition by granting public projects to corrupt contractors (Buehn & Schneider, 2012; Torgler & Schneider, 2009). The external cost incurred by the necessity to bribe public agents is linked to the rise of the informal sector in Ukraine (Williams & Round, 2007), Pakistan (Williams et al.,

2016; Williams & Shahid, 2016), and Russia (Shleifer, 1997). Thus, nascent entrepreneurs experience significant barriers to entry unless they are able to successfully adapt to the environment. Businesses react by moving to the shadow economy as an alternative to the formal economy (Berdiev & Saunoris, 2018; Hindriks et al., 1999; Johnson et al., 2000).

Hypothesis 5: Stricter administrative regulations, higher bureaucracy costs, and bribes and favoritism in EME decrease the propensity to become a nascent entrepreneur.

3 Data

We use data from several different sources. The individual-level data on entrepreneurship comes from the GEM APS (Reynolds, 2007). The GEM is a cross-country survey initiated in 1999 with 10 countries that expanded consequently to 116 countries currently involved. The GEM APS looks at the role of the individual in entrepreneurial setting using harmonized socio-demographic characteristics, as well as entrepreneurial motivation, aspirations, attitudes, and activities. The survey is based on nationally representative samples of a minimum of 2000 adults (18–64 years old) in every country. Macroeconomic controls are obtained from the World Bank World Development Indicators (WDI, 2022), while institutional rigidity indices are acquired from the Economic Freedom of the World (FI, 2017) data set. There are 473,999 observations included in the sample from 2001 to 2017. The list of countries participating in the sample includes Argentina, Brazil, Chile, China, Colombia, Egypt, Greece, Hungary, India, Indonesia, Iran, Malaysia, Mexico, Peru, Poland, Russia, South Africa, Thailand, Turkey, and UAE. Detailed variable descriptions are presented in Table 1.

3.1 Dependent Variable

The dependent variable in our model is a binary variable that equals one if the individual is a nascent entrepreneur and zero otherwise. According to the GEM APS, nascent entrepreneurs are defined based on the following criteria – people: (i) who consider themselves involved in business, (ii) who participated in activities directed towards creating of a new business during the past 12 months, (iii) who expect to own or co-own the business, and (iv) whose business has not paid salaries, wages, or made any other payments to the owners for more than three months (Reynolds et al., 2005). The three-month criterion is important because it separates start-ups who have achieved some initial success from those that have not yet proven their economic viability. The dependent variable is equal to zero if the respondent is not involved in a start-up, a young or an established business. The control group

Table 1 Variables description and sources

Variable	Description and source
	Source: General Entrepreneurship Monitor Adult Population Survey (http://www.gemconsortium.org/)
Nascent entrepreneur	A binary variable equal to one if the respondent is a nascent entrepreneur defined is someone actively involved in setting up a business they will own or co-own; this business has not paid salaries, wages, or any other payments to the owners for more than three months. The variable is equal to zero is the respondent has no involvement in a start-up, a young or an established business.
Gender	Gender is recorded as male or female.
Workforce status	Workforce status is recorded on six categories: full/full or part-time, part-time only, retired or disabled, homemaker, student, not working (other).
Education	Educational attainment with four categories: no education, some secondary education completed, secondary degree, post-secondary degree, and graduate degree.
Income	Household or personal income recorded in three categories: lowest 33rd percentile, middle 33rd percentile, and upper 33rd percentile. .
Fear of failure	Binary variable that equals one if the respondent believes that fear of failure would prevent the start-up from being created, and zero otherwise.
Skills and knowledge	Binary variable that equals one is the respondent believes that they have skills and ability for the start-up, and zero otherwise
TEA Rate– total early-stage entrepreneurial activity	Percentage of 18–64 population who are either a nascent entrepreneur or owner-manager of a new business.
	Source: World Development Indicators World Bank Database (http://data.worldbank.org/indicator)
GDP per capita	Gross domestic product divided by midyear population. GDP is the sum of gross value added by all resident producers in the economy plus any product taxes and minus any subsidies not included in the value of the products. It is calculated without making deductions for depreciation of fabricated assets or for depletion and degradation of natural resources. (In current U.S. dollars)
Life expectancy	Total life expectancy at birth (in years) – indicates the number of years a newborn infant would live if prevailing patterns of mortality at the time of its birth were to stay the same throughout its life.
Unemployment rate	Total unemployment as percentage of the total labor force (modeled ILO estimate). Unemployment refers to the share of the labor force that is without work but available for and seeking employment.
Total adolescent fertility rate	Births per 1000 women ages 15–19
FDI net inflows	Foreign direct investment, net inflows (BoP, current US$). Refers to direct investment equity flows in the economy. It is the sum of equity capital, reinvestment of earnings, and other capital. Ownership of 10% or more of the ordinary shares of

(continued)

Table 1 (continued)

Variable	Description and source
	voting stock is the criterion for determining the existence of a direct investment relationship.
	Source: Economic Freedom of the World Indicators (http://www.freetheworld.com/)
State ownership of assets	Degree to which the state owns and controls capital (including land) in the industrial, agricultural, and service sectors. It does not measure the extent of government revenue and expenditure as a share of total output. Countries with greater government ownership of assets get lower scores.
Property rights protection	Property rights, including over financial assets, are poorly defined and not protected by law (= 1) or are clearly defined and well protected by law (= 7)
Tariffs	Has three components: (i) *revenues from trade taxes (% of trade sector)* – lower ratings are given as the average tax rate on international trade increases. Countries with no specific taxes on international trade earn a perfect 10; (ii) *mean tariff rate* – a rating of 10 is given to countries that do not impose tariffs, and as the mean tariff rate increases, countries are assigned lower ratings. The rating decline toward zero as the mean tariff rate approaches 50%; and (iii) *standard deviation of tariff rates* – a rating of 10 is given to countries that impose a uniform tariff. As the standard deviation of tariff rates increases toward 25%, ratings decline toward zero.
Capital and people movement control	Has three components: (i) *foreign ownership/investment restrictions* – based on the answers to the following two questions "How prevalent is foreign ownership of companies in your country? 1 = Very rare, 7 = Highly prevalent" and "How restrictive are regulations in your country relating to international capital flows? 1 = Highly restrictive, 7 = Not restrictive at all"; (ii) *capital controls* – the IMF reports on up to 13 types of international capital controls. The zero-to-10 rating is the percentage of capital controls not levied as a share of the total number of capital controls listed, multiplied by 10; and (iii) *freedom of foreigners to visit* – measures the percentage of countries for which a country requires a visa from foreign visitors, and reflects the freedom of foreigners to travel to this country for tourist and short-term business purposes. Zero-to-10 ratings are assigned.
Credit market regulations	Has three components: (i) *ownership of banks* – countries with larger shares of privately held deposits received higher ratings; (ii) *private sector credit* – greater government borrowing indicates more central planning and results in lower ratings, calculated as the government fiscal deficit as a share of gross saving. Higher ratings are given as the deficit gets smaller relative to gross saving; and (iii) *interest rate controls/negative real interest rates* – Countries with interest rates determined by the market, stable monetary policy, and reasonable real-deposit and lending-rate spreads received higher ratings. Zero-to-10 ratings are assigned.

(continued)

Table 1 (continued)

Variable	Description and source
Administrative requirements	Based on the Global Competitiveness Report question: "Complying with administrative requirements (permits, regulations, reporting) issued by the government in your country is (1 = burdensome, 7 = not burdensome)".
Bureaucracy costs	Measures "[t]he risk that normal business operations become more costly due to the regulatory environment. This includes regulatory compliance and bureaucratic inefficiency and/or opacity. Regulatory burdens vary across sectors so scoring should give greater weight to sectors contributing the most to the economy". The raw scores range, roughly, from 0 to 7, with higher values indicating greater risk.
Bribes and favoritism	Based on the Global Competitiveness Report questions: (1) "In your industry, how commonly would you estimate that firms make undocumented extra payments or bribes connected with the following: A – Import and export permits; B – Connection to public utilities (e.g., telephone or electricity); C – Annual tax payments; D – Awarding of public contracts (investment projects); E – Getting favorable judicial decisions. Common (= 1), Never occur (= 7)". (2) "Do illegal payments aimed at influencing government policies, laws or regulations have an impact on companies in your country? 1 = Yes, significant negative impact, 7 = No, no impact at all". (3) "To what extent do government officials in your country show favoritism to well-connected firms and individuals. when deciding upon policies and contracts? 1 = Always show favouritism, 7 = Never show favouritism"

represents people with no personal engagement in owning or managing a business. This allows us to analyze the extensive margin for people to enter into entrepreneurship.

3.2 Independent Variables

The institutional rigidity indices include state ownership of assets, property rights protection, tariffs, trade barriers, capital and people movement control, credit market regulations, administrative requirements, bureaucracy costs, and bribes and favoritism. A full description of the rigidity indices is provided in Table 1. The average values for the various institutional rigidity indices are presented Table 2. We treat our institutional rigidity quality indices as institutional inertia due to a lack of variations of such indices within a country across multiple time periods. We illustrate this using a series of line-graphs in Fig. 1 by plotting the eight institutional rigidity indices for every country in our sample across 17 years. The graph shows

Table 2 Country-level rigidities and entrepreneurial activities

Country	State ownership	Property rights protection	Inflation	Tariffs	Trade barriers	Capital & people movement control	Credit market regulations	Admin requirements	Bureaucracy	Bribes and favoritism	TEA macro	Nascent entrepr.
Argentina	7.65	3.56	5.73	6.33	5.21	2.73	6.77	2.16	5.05	6.38	0.15	0.11
Brazil	7.43	5.28	8.74	7.24	5.98	4.70	6.43	1.47	4.53	6.32	0.16	0.04
Chile	8.32	6.86	9.38	9.45	7.51	6.28	9.03	4.39	7.61	8.37	0.21	0.14
China	4.22	5.94	9.52	8.07	6.34	0.86	7.02	5.05	4.17	3.56	0.15	0.06
Colombia	8.27	4.14	9.29	7.74	5.87	4.75	9.08	3.02	7.47	5.83	0.21	0.13
Egypt	4.58	5.10	7.08	4.94	5.08	4.46	4.72	3.70	2.56	2.39	0.10	0.06
Greece	7.73	5.50	9.53	8.36	7.42	6.65	7.92	2.37	5.46	7.19	0.07	0.03
Hungary	7.53	5.41	9.11	8.05	7.60	7.32	8.90	2.76	6.91	8.79	0.07	0.03
India	7.00	5.16	8.85	6.01	5.23	0.68	6.66	4.59	3.44	5.81	0.10	0.06
Indonesia	7.52	5.56	8.76	8.04	5.31	4.14	8.11	4.88	4.68	5.87	0.17	0.06
Iran	4.09	5.07	8.14	4.07	4.06	1.68	4.61	3.32	1.42	5.90	0.13	0.07
Malaysia	5.00	6.09	9.52	7.07	7.29	4.59	9.53	6.21	9.31	4.34	0.07	0.04
Mexico	7.57	5.09	9.14	7.40	7.15	4.64	8.77	2.91	6.53	4.92	0.13	0.11
Peru	8.85	4.50	9.38	8.79	6.45	9.26	8.85	2.46	6.70	6.44	0.27	0.24
Poland	7.49	5.09	9.55	8.23	7.27	4.61	8.35	2.89	7.67	7.57	0.09	0.04
Russia	4.96	4.12	8.35	5.18	5.4	4.58	7.86	2.86	5.42	3.37	0.05	0.02
South Africa	7.86	7.12	8.89	7.16	5.92	3.22	9.38	3.23	4.08	7.16	0.08	0.05
Thailand	7.16	4.59	9.56	7.12	6.76	2.31	9.21	4.15	7.88	3.34	0.19	0.08
Turkey	7.28	5.42	8.42	6.05	6.92	5.46	7.88	3.93	6.38	4.40	0.10	0.07
United Arab Emirates	4.31	7.30	9.07	8.62	8.13	6.73	7.89	6.39	6.46	7.26	0.08	0.05

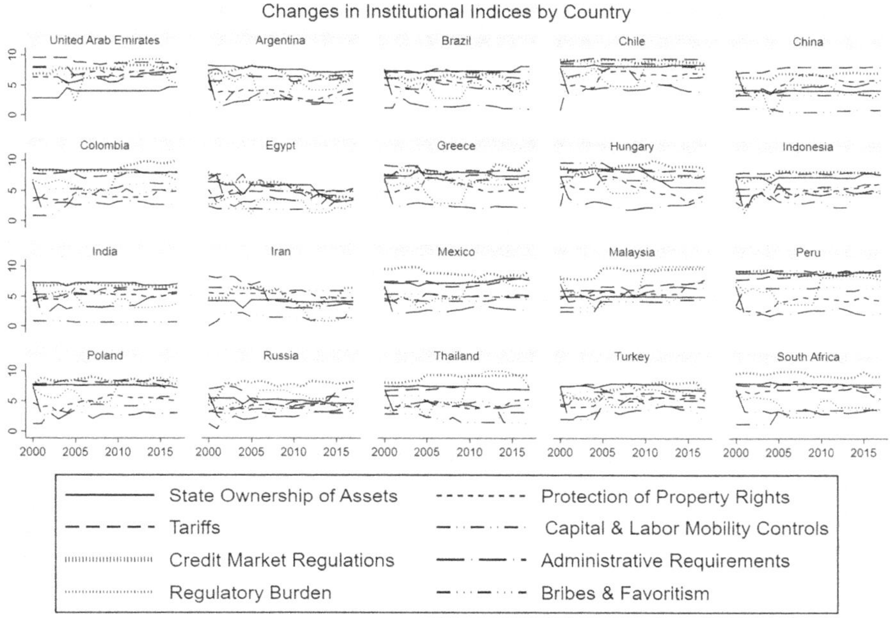

Fig. 1 Changes in institutional indices by county. (Authors' own figure)

that the indices do not vary within a nation across time, supporting our assertion that these metrics display characteristics of institutional inertia. There are differences in the levels across institutional indices across countries. For example, the value for the index monitoring state-ownership of assets in year 2000 varies from a low of 2.82 for United Arab Emirates to a high of 8.87 for Peru. However, there is very little variation in this index for each nation across time. The index varies from 2.82–4.69 and 8.87–9.04 between 2000 and 2017 for United Arab Emirates and Peru respectively.

3.3 Control Variables

We use two sets of control variables: individual-level controls that correlate with the individual's predisposition to become an entrepreneur, and macro-level controls that relate to the overall economic environment in the country. The individual level controls obtained from the GEM APS include age, gender, education, workforce status and household income. Following (Fu et al., 2018), we include two additional variables, fear of failure and entrepreneurial knowledge and skills; two binary variables that indicate whether individuals perceive that fear of failure may prevent them from creating the start-up, and whether they have the entrepreneurial skills and knowledge for the start-up process.

The macro-level controls include GDP per capita, life expectancy, unemployment rate, average adolescent fertility rate, and Foreign Direct Investment (FDI) net inflows. Previous studies have shown that individuals' involvement in entrepreneurship is highly correlated with the country's overall economic wellbeing as measured by the GDP per capita and life expectancy, as well as government policies and social climate, (Acs & Amorós, 2008; Autio & Fu, 2015; Galindo & Méndez, 2014; Jeon, 2018; Levie & Autio, 2011). We include the country's adolescent fertility rate instead of population growth (Fu et al., 2018) because emerging market economies, and developing countries in general, with the exception of Sub-Saharan Africa, have reportedly experienced an unprecedented decline in fertility rates over the past decade as well as some puzzling trends (Klasen, 2019; Vollset et al., 2020). We use adolescent fertility rate instead of total fertility rate to capture differential human capital investments for adolescent girls, which would have long term labor market effects due to having children early. The decline is faster than what would be predicted by the corresponding national levels of income growth, and hence correlated with rising female employment (Jayachandran, 2021). To capture the latter effect, we interact fertility rates and unemployment. The FDI net inflows control for the increasing attractiveness of emerging economies to foreign investors (Bhasin & Garg, 2020; Contractor et al., 2021; Paul & Jadhav, 2019) and intensified integration into the global economy (Marquis & Raynard, 2015). We also control for the prevalence of total early-stage entrepreneurial activities in a country (TEA), which studies have found to have an effect on the individual level entrepreneurial engagement (Bird & Wennberg, 2014; Fu et al., 2018).

3.4 Descriptive Statistics

Table 2 presents country-level rigidity indices and entrepreneurial activities. The last two columns of the table show the TEA and nascent entrepreneurship across the countries in the sample. The highest level of nascent entrepreneurship is observed among countries in Latin America: Peru (24%), Chile (14%), Columbia (13%) and Argentina and Mexico (11%). The lowest level of nascent entrepreneurship is observed in Russia (2%), Greece and Hungary (3%), and Brazil, Poland, and Malaysia (4%). The countries with the highest TEA are Peru (27%), Chile and Columbia (21%), and Thailand (19%). Russia (5%), Greece and Hungary (7%), and the UEA (8%) are the countries with the lowest TEA. While Chile, Columbia, and Peru have both the highest levels of nascent entrepreneurship and the highest TEA, Russia, Greece, and Hungary have both the lowest levels of nascent entrepreneurship and the lowest TEA.

The country-level rigidity data shows that Latin American countries have the lowest level of state ownership of assets, but also the lowest level of property rights protection. There are some exceptions, such as Chile, for example, which has both low level of assets state ownership and high level of property rights protection. China, Egypt, Iran, Russia, and the UAE have the highest level of state ownership of assets. The most restrictive tariffs and trade barriers are observed in Egypt, India, Iran, and Russia, while the highest control of movement of capital and people is observed in China, India, and Iran. The strictest credit market and regulations and administrative requirements are reported in Egypt and Iran, and Brazil and Argentina respectively. The countries with the highest level of bureaucracy are Poland, Malaysia, and Thailand. Finally, the highest level of bribes and favoritism are detected in Egypt, Russia, and Thailand. Overall, there are few countries, with consistent rigidity levels. For example, Chile has low rigidities across all indices except for bureaucracy and at the same time high levels of nascent entrepreneurship and TEA. Iran and Russia, on the other hand, have high levels of rigidities and low levels of nascent entrepreneurship and TEA. However, the rest of the countries in the sample fall somewhere in between these two groups. For example, Columbia and Peru, two of the countries with the highest level of nascent entrepreneurship and TEA, report low level of state ownership of assesses, but at the same time high rigidity levels.

Table 3 provides descriptive statistics for the variables used in the study. As mentioned above, there is a good amount of variation in both the level of nascent entrepreneurship and the TEA across countries. Among the macro variables, the average GDP per capita, before the logarithmic transformation, varies from $1460 for India to $39,320 for the UAE. Life expectancy at birth in the overall sample varies from 53 to 81 years, with an average of 74 years. The highest average life expectancy is observed in Greece and Chile (80), while South Africa has the lowest (59). The average Net FDI, before the logarithmic transformation, varies from 2.4 billion U.S. dollars for Greece to 200 billion U.S. dollars for China. The average unemployment rate across countries varies from 0.8% for Thailand to 26% for South Africa, with an average of 8.63% for the whole sample. The average total adolescent fertility rate in the sample is 44 births per 1000 women between 15 and 19 years old. The highest average over time of the total adolescent fertility rate is observed in Colombia, 74 births, and the lowest in China, 8 birth per 1000 women between 15 and 19 years old.

Table 3 presents descriptive statistics for the individual-level variables for the overall sample, while Table 4 presents the descriptive statistics separately for the nascent entrepreneurs and control group. While only 27% of the nascent entrepreneurs believe that fear of failure would prevent their start-up from being created, the corresponding statistics for the control group is 40%. Among the nascent entrepreneurs, 84% believe that they have skills and ability for the start-up process, only 51% among the control share the same sentiment. The percentage of respondents in the middle 33rd percentile of the household income is approximately the same for both the nascent entrepreneurs and the control group, 31% vs. 33%. However, the percentage of respondents in the top 33rd percentile of the household income for the nascent entrepreneurs' group is 43% vs. 34% for the control group. The percentage of females in the study that are nascent entrepreneurs is 42% vs 50% for the control group. The average age across the two groups is very similar, 36 vs 38 years old. There is, however, a distinctive difference between the workforce status for the two groups. Among the nascent entrepreneurs 76% hold full-time and full-time or part-time jobs, while the corresponding number among the control group

Table 3 Descriptive statistics: GEM, N = 473,999

	Mean	Std. Dev.	Min	Max
Nascent entrepreneur[a]	0.08	(0.27)	0	1
TEA rate	0.14	(0.07)	0.02	0.4
GDP per capita (logarithm)	8.97	(0.69)	6.11	10.64
Life expectancy	74	(4.98)	53.44	81.39
Net FDI (logarithm)	23.36	(1.27)	18.56	26.4
Unemployment rate	8.63	(6.18)	.25	33.29
Total adolescent fertility rate	44.39	(22.88)	6.55	84.82
State ownership of assets	7.02	(1.49)	3.08	9.07
Property rights protection	5.44	(1.13)	2.45	8.2
Tariffs	7.41	(1.35)	4.07	9.48
Trade barriers	6.37	(1.19)	2.43	9.08
Capital & ppl movement control	4.44	(2.12)	0.63	9.49
Credit market regulations	7.97	(1.44)	2.9	10
Administrative requirements	3.55	(1.30)	1.05	7.25
Bureaucracy costs	5.79	(2.20)	0.89	10
Bribes & favoritism	5.93	(1.73)	1.18	9.6
Fear of failure[a]	0.39	(0.49)	0	1
Skills & knowledge[a]	0.53	(0.50)	0	1
HH Income – mid 33%[a]	0.33	(0.47)	0	1
HH Income – top 33%[a]	0.34	(0.47)	0	1
Gender (female)[a]	0.49	(0.50)	0	1
Age[a]	38.01	(12.75)	18	64
Workforce status[a]				
Full/full or part time	0.59	(0.49)	0	1
Part time only	0.06	(0.25)	0	1
Retired/disabled	0.06	(0.24)	0	1
Homemaker	0.12	(0.32)	0	1
Student	0.06	(0.33)	0	1
Other non-working	0.01	(0.24)	0	1
Education[a]	2.93	(1.07)	1	5

[a]*Individual-level covariates*

is 57%. The percentage of nascent entrepreneurs with post-secondary or graduate degrees is 40%, 33% and 7% respectively. In the control group, 30% hold post-secondary or graduate degrees, 25% and 5% respectively.

Finally, Table 5 displays the correlation matrix.

Table 4 Descriptive statistics: Nascent entrepreneurs vs Control group

	Nascent	Entrepr.	Control	Group
	N =	38,405	N =	435,594
	Mean	SD	Mean	SD
Fear of failure	0.27	(0.44)	0.4	(0.49)
Skills & knowledge	0.84	(0.36)	0.51	(0.50)
HH Income – mid 33%	0.31	(0.46)	0.33	(0.47)
HH Income – top 33%	0.43	(0.49)	0.34	(0.47)
Gender (female)	0.42	(0.49)	0.5	(0.50)
Age	36.3	(11.27)	38.16	(12.86)
Workforce status				
Full/full or part time	0.76	(0.43)	0.57	(0.49)
Part time only	0.07	(0.26)	0.06	(0.24)
Retired/disabled	0.01	(0.12)	0.06	(0.25)
Homemaker	0.05	(0.23)	0.13	(0.34)
Student	0.03	(0.16)	0.06	(0.24)
Other non-working	0.08	(0.26)	0.11	(0.31)
Education				
No education	0.07	(0.26)	0.12	(0.32)
Some secondary education	0.17	(0.38)	0.22	(0.41)
Secondary degree	0.36	(0.48)	0.36	(0.48)
Post-secondary degree	0.33	(0.47)	0.25	(0.44)
Graduate degree	0.07	(0.26)	0.05	(0.22)

4 Empirical Model and Estimation

4.1 Empirical Model

The empirical analysis is based on estimating a random-intercept multilevel regression model. The GEM APS is hierarchical, or nested, in structure, with individuals nested within their country of residence. Such data lends itself to the application of mixed level modeling (Hoffman, 1997; Hoffman et al., 2000; Hoffman & Gavin, 1998). The random-intercept model is considered a special case of the basic multilevel model. We specify the following multilevel model where individual *i* is nested, or clustered, within their country of residence *j* (Antonakis et al., 2021; Raudenbush & Bryk, 2002):

$$y_{ij} = \beta_{0j} + \beta_{1j} X_{ij} + \varepsilon_{ij}$$

$$\beta_{0j} = \gamma_{00} + \gamma_{01} Z_j + u_{0j}$$

$$\beta_{1j} = \gamma_{10} + u_{1j}$$

Table 5 Correlation matrix

Variables	(1)	(2)	(3)	(4)	(5)	(6)	(7)	(8)	(9)	(11)	(12)	(13)	(14)	(15)	(16)	(17)	(18)	(19)	(20)	(21)	(22)	(23)	(24)	(25)
(1) Nascent entrepreneur*	1.00																							
(2) TEA rate	0.16	1.00																						
(3) GDP per capita (logarithm)	–0.01	–0.11	1.00																					
(4) Life expectancy	0.05	0.33	0.50	1.00																				
(5) Net FDI (logarithm)	–0.02	0.14	–0.02	0.12	1.00																			
(6) Unemployment rate	–0.04	–0.31	0.04	–0.47	–0.46	1.00																		
(7) Average fertility rate (logarithm)	0.08	0.45	–0.17	–0.26	–0.14	0.21	1.00																	
(8) State ownership of assets	0.09	0.38	0.06	0.02	–0.24	0.20	0.56	1.00																
(9) Property rights protection	–0.02	–0.14	0.28	–0.14	0.05	0.17	–0.20	–0.03	1.00															
(10) Tariffs	0.07	0.38	0.29	0.34	0.11	–0.11	0.01	0.47	0.36	1.00														
(11) Trade barriers	0.01	–0.04	0.41	0.30	–0.01	–0.12	–0.20	0.24	0.30	0.54	1.00													
(12) Capital & ppl movement control	0.07	0.16	0.50	0.37	–0.25	–0.06	0.15	0.49	0.12	0.47	0.42	1.00												
(13) Credit market regulations	0.06	0.14	0.19	–0.01	–0.16	0.05	0.14	0.49	0.17	0.57	0.46	0.37	1.00											
(14) Administrative requirements	–0.01	–0.08	–0.06	0.06	0.10	–0.33	–0.49	–0.41	0.41	0.15	0.18	–0.19	0.20	1.00										
(15) Bureaucracy costs	0.06	0.25	0.36	0.40	–0.05	–0.26	0.00	0.36	–0.02	0.49	0.52	0.42	0.64	0.18	1.00									
(16) Bribes & favoritism	0.04	0.09	0.33	0.07	–0.25	0.31	0.17	0.53	0.34	0.50	0.24	0.43	0.23	–0.20	0.11	1.00								
(17) Fear of failure*	–0.07	–0.05	0.05	0.05	–0.02	–0.01	–0.09	–0.03	–0.03	–0.00	0.01	–0.00	–0.01	–0.01	0.01	–0.02	1.00							

(18) Skills & knowledge*	0.19	0.13	0.01	0.08	–0.06	–0.02	0.11	0.12	–0.01	0.05	0.01	0.10	–0.01	–0.05	0.01	0.08	–0.15	1.00						
(19) HH Income – mid 33%*	–0.01	–0.01	–0.02	0.00	–0.02	0.01	0.01	0.02	–0.04	–0.00	0.01	–0.01	0.01	–0.02	–0.01	–0.00	0.01	–0.00	1.00					
(20) HH Income – top 33%*	0.05	0.01	0.07	0.02	–0.01	0.00	–0.02	0.00	0.04	0.04	0.04	0.01	0.03	0.04	0.06	0.04	–0.04	0.08	–0.51	1.00				
(21) Gender*	–0.04	0.03	–0.02	–0.01	0.02	0.01	0.03	0.04	–0.02	0.03	–0.02	–0.01	0.02	–0.04	0.00	0.02	0.07	–0.12	0.01	–0.08	1.00			
(22) Age*	–0.04	–0.02	0.05	0.06	0.01	–0.02	–0.06	0.02	–0.02	0.04	0.05	0.03	0.03	–0.01	0.06	–0.00	0.04	–0.02	–0.02	–0.02	0.02	1.00		
(23) Workforce status*	–0.09	–0.07	–0.05	–0.15	–0.11	0.19	0.09	0.04	0.02	–0.09	–0.05	–0.04	–0.01	–0.07	–0.08	0.05	0.02	–0.15	–0.00	–0.12	0.21	–0.13	1.00	
(24) Education*	0.07	–0.03	0.10	0.12	–0.07	–0.04	–0.12	–0.06	0.02	0.03	0.05	0.06	0.04	0.09	0.05	0.04	–0.02	0.11	–0.01	0.27	–0.05	–0.18	–0.12	1.00

*Individual-level covariates

We are interested in how individual level characteristics affect the individual level outcomes while taking into consideration the nested structure of the data. The first equation above is referred to as Level 1 equation, and it indicates that the expected value of the individual propensity to become a nascent entrepreneur depends on the set of observed individual-level characteristics X in a linear manner. X in our model is age, gender, education, workforce status and household income. The second and third equations are referred to as Level 2 equations, and they specify that the linear relationship described by the Level 1 equation varies among countries, so that each country has a unique intercept, β_{0j}, and a unique slope, β_{1j}, in the Level 1 equation. The individual-level error term, ε_{ij}, is the classical regression error term (Wooldridge, 2013). The γ_{00} and γ_{10} coefficients in the Level 2 equations are the mean values of the slope and intercept, respectively, across all countries, while the country-level residuals, u_{0j} and u_{1j}, determine how the slope and intercept vary among countries. The γ_{01} coefficient is the slope of the country-level characteristics, Z. Z in our model is the set of rigidity indices, GDP per capita, life expectancy, unemployment rate, average fertility rate, and FDI net inflows. The country-level residuals, u, are uncorrelated over countries, the individual-level residuals, ε, are uncorrelated across individuals, and ε and u, are uncorrelated with each other.

The Level 1 and 2 equations put together will result in

$$y_{ij} = \gamma_{00} + \gamma_{01} Z_j + \gamma_{10} X_{ij} + X_{ij} u_{1j} + u_{0j} + \varepsilon_{ij},$$

where the first three components have coefficients, γ, to be estimated, or they form the fixed part of the model (Antonakis et al., 2021). In a random-intercept model, u_{1j} is zero because the model assumes that β_{1j} does not vary across countries. Thus, the random-intercept mixed level model becomes:

$$y_{ij} = \gamma_{00} + \gamma_{01} Z_j + \gamma_{10} X_{ij} + u_{0j} + \varepsilon_{ij},$$

The last two parts, u_{0j} and ε_{ij}, form the random part of the model. The u_{0j} component, or the random intercept, represents the unobserved heterogeneity at the country level. The random-effects model assumption that X_{ij} and u_{0j} are uncorrelated requires that we control for all relevant country-level macro-economic variables. The random-effect model, as opposed to the fixed-effects model, is appropriate because we are interested in generalizing the results for the population of all emerging market economies and not for the specific group of countries in the sample (Antonakis et al., 2021; Rabe-Hesketh & Skrondal, 2022).

4.2 *Estimation, Regression Diagnostics and Robustness Checks*

We use a multilevel logit model to estimate the propensity to become a nascent entrepreneur and include the average marginal effects for all independent variables. The likelihood-ratio test for the variance components was performed to determine whether a mixed model is necessary, or a simpler linear model would suffice. The likelihood ratio test suggests that the logistic mixed model regressions perform better compared to a linear regression model.

An important characteristic of random effect models is the estimation of the so called intraclass correlation, ρ, which is calculated as the variance of u_{0j} divided by the total variance of $u_{0j} + \varepsilon_{ij}$ (Rabe-Hesketh & Skrondal, 2022). The intraclass correlation is the proportion of the variance explained by the clustering in the population, or by the countries in our case (Hox, 2010). Since our model has covariates, we have conditional or residual intraclass correlation. For latent-response dependent variables, the dependence among the propensity to become a nascent entrepreneur among individuals within the same country of residence is calculated in a slightly different manner, but bears the same interpretation (Rabe-Hesketh & Skrondal, 2022, p. 344). We further report several measures of the marginal association of the reported propensity at the median fixed part of the model using the ***xtrho*** command provided by Stata (Rodríguez & Elo, 2003).

We perform additional robustness checks. First, in addition to using the multilevel logit model to estimate the propensity to become a nascent entrepreneur, we also employed the linear probability model estimation. The results are very similar. Second, we compute the variance inflation factors (VIFs) to check for multicollinearity. The VIFs determines whether the variance has been inflated by the correlation among the individual variables. As a rule of thumb, VIFs greater than 10 indicate that multicollinearity is present.

5 Estimation Results and Discussion

The main results of the empirical analysis are displayed in Table 6. We report the odds-ratio first (all odd number columns), followed by the average marginal effect (all even number columns). The regressors are separated into three panels: institutional rigidity indexes (testing each hypothesis), macroeconomic controls affecting propensity to become a nascent entrepreneur, and individual characteristics. Column (1) shows that removal of tariffs significantly increases the propensity of an individual to become a nascent entrepreneur. The marginal effect, reported in Column (2), suggests that reducing tariffs can increase the probability of becoming a nascent entrepreneur by 1.2%, holding other independent variables constant. Better functioning credit markets increase the odds of becoming a nascent entrepreneur, with an average increase in the probability of 0.6% at the margin. This is also visible by

Table 6 Empirical results – odd ratios in shaded, margins in white columns

	Variables	H(1)	Margins	H(2)	Margins	H(3)	Margins	H(4)	Margins	H(5i)	Margins	H(5ii)	Margins	H(5iii)	Margins	(15)	(16)	(17)
Rigidity Indicators	Tariffs	1.184*** (0.023)	0.012*** (0.002)															
	Credit market regulations			1.104*** (0.012)	0.006*** (0.001)													
	State ownership of assets					0.926*** (0.017)	– 0.005*** (0.001)											
	Property rights protection							0.991 (0.011)	0.001 (0.001)									
	Administrative requirements									0.983 (0.015)	0.001 (0.001)							
	Bureaucracy costs											1.014*** (0.005)	0.001*** (0.000)					
	Bribes & favoritism													1.002 (0.012)	0.000 (0.001)			
	Capital & ppl movement control															1.066*** (0.010)	0.004*** (0.001)	
Macro-economic Controls	TEA	1.050*** (0.002)	0.003*** (0.000)	1.050*** (0.002)	0.003*** (0.000)	1.050*** (0.002)	0.003*** (0.000)	1.050*** (0.002)	0.003*** (0.000)	1.050*** (0.002)	0.003*** (0.000)	1.050*** (0.002)	0.003*** (0.000)	1.052*** (0.002)	0.003*** (0.000)	1.052*** (0.002)	0.003*** (0.000)	
	GDP per capita (logarithm)	0.923*** (0.026)	– 0.006*** (0.002)	0.947*** (0.027)	–0.004* (0.002)	0.911*** (0.026)	– 0.006*** (0.002)	0.917*** (0.026)	– 0.006*** (0.000)	0.919*** (0.026)	– 0.006*** (0.002)	0.899*** (0.026)	– 0.007*** (0.002)	0.915*** (0.026)	– 0.006*** (0.002)	0.948*** (0.027)	–0.004* (0.002)	
	Life expectancy	0.970*** (0.006)	– 0.002*** (0.000)	0.975*** (0.006)	– 0.002*** (0.000)	0.971*** (0.006)	– 0.002*** (0.000)	0.976*** (0.006)	– 0.002*** (0.000)	0.977*** (0.006)	– 0.002*** (0.000)	0.975*** (0.006)	– 0.002*** (0.000)	0.977*** (0.007)	– 0.002*** (0.000)	0.968*** (0.006)	– 0.002*** (0.000)	
	Net FDI (logarithm)	1.024*** (0.013)	0.002* (0.001)	1.021*** (0.012)	0.001* (0.001)	1.040*** (0.013)	0.002*** (0.001)	1.040*** (0.013)	0.003*** (0.001)	1.042*** (0.013)	0.003*** (0.001)	1.040*** (0.013)	0.002*** (0.001)	1.038*** (0.013)	0.002*** (0.001)	1.046*** (0.013)	0.003*** (0.001)	
	Unemployment rate	1.002 (0.005)	– 0.001*** (0.000)	0.990* (0.005)	– 0.001*** (0.000)	0.998 (0.005)	– 0.001*** (0.000)	1.000 (0.005)	– 0.001*** (0.000)	1.000 (0.005)	– 0.001*** (0.000)	1.000 (0.005)	– 0.001*** (0.000)	1.001 (0.005)	– 0.001*** (0.000)	1.010* (0.005)	0.000 (0.000)	
	Total adolescent fertility rate	1.004*** (0.002)	0.000 (0.000)	0.998 (0.002)	0.000 (0.000)	0.998 (0.002)	– 0.000** (0.000)	1.000 (0.002)	–0.000* (0.000)	0.999 (0.002)	–0.000* (0.000)	1.000** (0.000)	–0.000* (0.000)	1.000 (0.002)	–0.000* (0.000)	1.001 (0.005)	–0.000 (0.000)	
	Unemp. Rate X Fertility Rate	1.000*** (0.000)		1.000 (0.000)		0.999 (0.000)		1.000** (0.000)		1.000** (0.000)		1.000 (0.002)		1.000** (0.000)		1.000*** (0.000)		
	Fear of failure																	

Individual-level variables		0.781*** (0.010)	– 0.017*** (0.001)	0.780*** (0.010)	– 0.016*** (0.001)	0.782*** (0.010)	– 0.015*** (0.001)	0.781*** (0.010)	– 0.016*** (0.001)	0.782*** (0.010)	– 0.016*** (0.001)	0.781*** (0.010)	– 0.016*** (0.001)	0.781*** (0.010)	– 0.016*** (0.001)	0.781*** (0.010)	– 0.016*** (0.001)	
	Skills & knowledge	3.914*** (0.058)	0.082*** (0.006)	3.906*** (0.058)	0.077*** (0.005)	3.900*** (0.058)	0.076*** (0.006)	3.903*** (0.058)	0.076*** (0.005)	3.901*** (0.058)	0.076*** (0.005)	3.904*** (0.058)	0.076*** (0.005)	3.902* (0.058)	0.076*** (0.005)	3.900*** (0.058)	0.076*** (0.005)	
	HH income – mid 33rd percentile	1.002 (0.015)	0.000 (0.001)	1.005 (0.015)	0.000 (0.001)	1.004 (0.015)	0.000 (0.001)	1.000 (0.015)	0.000 (0.001)	1.000 (0.015)	0.000 (0.001)	1.000 (0.015)	0.000 (0.001)	1.001 (0.015)	0.000 (0.001)	1.001 (0.015)	0.000 (0.000)	
	HH income – top 33rd percentile	1.173*** (0.017)	0.011*** (0.001)	1.177*** (0.018)	0.011*** (0.001)	1.179*** (0.018)	0.011*** (0.001)	1.172*** (0.017)	0.010*** (0.001)	1.173*** (0.017)	0.010*** (0.001)	1.169*** (0.017)	0.010*** (0.001)	1.172*** (0.017)	0.010*** (0.001)	1.176*** (0.018)	0.011*** (0.001)	
	Gender (female)	0.948*** (0.011)	– 0.004*** (0.001)	0.949*** (0.011)	– 0.004*** (0.001)	0.949*** (0.011)	– 0.003*** (0.001)	0.949*** (0.011)	– 0.003*** (0.001)	0.949*** (0.011)	– 0.003*** (0.001)	0.949*** (0.011)	– 0.003*** (0.001)	0.949*** (0.011)	– 0.003*** (0.001)	0.949*** (0.011)	– 0.003*** (0.001)	
	Age	0.988*** (0.001)	– 0.001*** (0.000)	0.988*** (0.001)	– 0.001*** (0.000)	0.988*** (0.001)	– 0.001*** (0.000)	0.988*** (0.001)	– 0.001*** (0.000)	0.988*** (0.001)	– 0.001*** (0.000)	0.988*** (0.001)	– 0.001*** (0.000)	0.988*** (0.001)	– 0.001*** (0.000)	0.988*** (0.001)	– 0.001*** (0.000)	
	Constant (Constant SE) Wald Chi^2 Level 2 variance SE (Level2 vari- ance SE) Intraclass corre- lation Marginal proba- bility Joint probabil- ity Odds ratio Pearson's r Yule's Q	0.076 (0.037) 16,723 0.142 (0.047) 0.041 0.058 0.004 1.150 0.008 0.070		0.082 (0.040) 16,729 0.120 (0.040) 0.035 0.054 0.003 1.126 0.006 0.059		0.410 (0.228) 16,656 0.195 (0.068) 0.056 0.054 0.003 1.210 0.011 0.095		0.148 (0.072) 16,644 0.136 (0.046) 0.040 0.054 0.003 1.143 0.007 0.067		0.132 (0.064) 16,646 0.133 (0.045) 0.039 0.054 0.003 1.140 0.007 0.065		0.169 (0.082) 16,653 0.133 (0.045) 0.039 0.054 0.003 1.141 0.007 0.066		0.136 (0.072) 16,645 0.133 (0.045) 0.039 0.054 0.003 1.13 0.006 0.060		0.110 (0.053) 16,692 0.121 (0.040) 0.035 0.054 0.003 1.13 0.006 0.060		

***Significant at the 1% level, **5% level, *10% level. Standard errors in parentheses

looking at the results for capital and labor controls. Free capital and labor movements increase the likelihood of nascent entrepreneurship by 0.4% at the margin.

Decreased state ownership of assets lowers the probability of nascent entrepreneurship by 0.5%. As suggested in our hypothesis, operating in collaboration with state-owned enterprises might allow nascent entrepreneurs to remain in business despite incurring heavy losses. It is common in countries with large proportion of state-owned companies to subsidize loss making industries to maintain the full employment levels. In that sense, high prevalence of state ownership of assets acts as a safety-net for nascent entrepreneurs to weather market downturns.

We do not find any statistically significant relationship between nascent entrepreneurship and protection of property rights. This might be related to the nature of constructing this index. The index includes two opposing factors in the classification: how well property rights are defined, and how strongly they are protected. The literature suggests that the actual adherence to strict property rights is a stronger predictor of nascent entrepreneurship rather than how property rights are defined. We cannot disentangle these two effects from our index, making it difficult to establish which factor is more dominant. Alternatively, it is possible that property rights are not a big determinant of nascent entrepreneurship in emerging economies since most of them tend to operate in the informal sector of the economy.

While higher bureaucratic costs of doing business increase the likelihood of being a nascent entrepreneur, cumbersome administrative requirements do not statistically influence the odds of becoming a nascent entrepreneur in an emerging economy. This might suggest that nascent entrepreneurs in emerging economies figure out how to operate around administrative requirements to suit their operations. Higher bureaucracy reduces the chance of an incumbent entrepreneur facing increased competition through newcomers. This suggests that bureaucracy might behave as a barrier to entry to markets, rewarding current nascent entrepreneurs that succeeded in operating a business despite the red tape. Interestingly, we do not find any significant relationship between bribes and favoritism and nascent entrepreneurship.

The results for macroeconomic indicators and individual characteristics are very similar across different specifications. The TEA rate prevalent in a country increases nascent entrepreneurship amongst individuals. Specifically, our results suggest that for every point increase in the TEA score of a nation, the marginal probability of engaging in nascent entrepreneurship increases by 0.3%. This is not surprising because the TEA score for a country reflects the entrepreneurial environment present within that nation. Foreign direct investment is another factor that statistically increases nascent entrepreneurship. Increases in FDI increase the odds of becoming a nascent entrepreneur through better investment opportunities and improved credit options. Alternatively, higher FDI flows into a country reflects the attractiveness of an emerging market to foreign investors. Increased GDP per capita and higher life expectancy reduce the odds of becoming a nascent entrepreneur. Finally, unemployment and total adolescent fertility does not significantly influence the odds of nascent entrepreneurship. The statistical significance changes across specifications, and marginal estimates are close to zero in magnitude.

Contrary to our macroeconomic variables, most individual characteristics statistically influence the odds of becoming a nascent entrepreneur. A higher skill level and being from the top one-third household income threshold increases the odds of being a nascent entrepreneur. The average marginal effect of the individual saying that they possess the skill and knowledge required to become an entrepreneur increases the likelihood of being one by approximately 8%. Belonging to a household in the top one-third income distribution increases the likelihood of nascent entrepreneurship by 1% at the margin. Fear of failure significantly reduces the odds of being a nascent entrepreneur. Finally, women and older people are less likely to become nascent entrepreneurs, even though the marginal effect is less than 0.5% in each case. We have further controlled for individual education and labor market status. Adding these controls do not change our estimates. The results are omitted from Table 6 for brevity purposes but are available from authors upon request.

Table 6 also reports the results from xtrho and the intraclass correlation estimation. The intraclass correlation coefficient tells us the proportion of variation in the outcome variable (being a nascent entrepreneur) due to similarities in individuals from the same nation. Intraclass correlation coefficient ranges between 4% and 6%. This suggests that clustering the analysis at the nation level explains very little variation in the differences of nascent entrepreneurship within different countries. The magnitude of the ICC is very stable across different institutional indexes. The marginal probability of an individual, with an observed propensity at the sample median, being a nascent entrepreneur is approximately 5.4%. This marginal probability stays stable across the use of all institutional rigidity indices.

6 Conclusion and Policy Implications

Our study seeks to investigate how different types of institutional rigidities affect early-stage entrepreneurship, or nascent entrepreneurship, in emerging economies. We used a series of different datasets to capture both individual and macroeconomic factors to disentangle the association of institutional rigidities. We look at 7 different kinds of institutional rigidities to conduct our analysis: tariffs on free trade, credit and capital market regulations, protection of property rights, state ownership of assets, administrative burden, bureaucratic costs, bribes and favoritism.

Nascent entrepreneurship in emerging economies is often driven by different factors such as economic survival and ease of doing business in the informal marketplace. Our study finds evidence that removal of tariffs, well-functioning credit markets, and higher bureaucratic costs increase the likelihood of individuals participating in nascent entrepreneurship. A higher GDP per capita is associated with lower nascent entrepreneurship, highlighting that engaging such form of entrepreneurship in emerging economies may be driven by poor economic circumstances. Removal of tariffs makes it easier for individuals to access imports and sell their goods in an international market. Well-functioning credit markets and free capital movements can improve access to business opportunities for nascent entrepreneurs. We see a similar association between higher FDI and nascent entrepreneurship.

This chapter also finds that less state ownership of assets is associated with lower probability of nascent entrepreneurship. This might be due to entrepreneurs working in an economy with high state ownership of assets are less likely to be driven out of business during negative market shocks. Most nascent entrepreneurs are small business owners with few employees. These types of firms have a greater likelihood of surviving when functioning alongside state owned companies. This increased probability of survival can in turn incentivize people to become nascent entrepreneurs. Conversely, we do not find any statistical relationship between protection of private property, administrative requirements and bribes and favoritism, and likelihood of becoming a nascent entrepreneur. The lack of a significant relationship between protection of private property and nascent entrepreneurship may be explained by the manner of creating the index that was used in our study. Individuals operating as nascent entrepreneurs in emerging economies likely have the skill to navigate bureaucracy, explaining the null result on administrative requirements, and bribes and favoritism. The average marginal effect of the various rigidity indices across our different specifications on the probability of engaging in nascent entrepreneurship is approximately 5.4%.

Our results on the importance of individual characteristics on nascent entrepreneurship is supported by other studies. Individuals with more skill, education, and lack of fear for failure are more likely to report being nascent entrepreneurs. Women, retired individuals, students, and homemakers are less likely to be involved in nascent entrepreneurship. Furthermore, the likelihood of becoming a nascent entrepreneur decreases monotonically as one gets older. We can explain this using the human capital model. Older individuals have less time to recoup the initial investments needed to engage in nascent entrepreneurship. Furthermore, risk aversion is higher for older individuals and females.

This chapter suggests that countries seeking to incentivize entrepreneurship can use public policies to promote nascent entrepreneurships. Policies that remove tariffs, promote private ownership of banks, properly regulated credit markets, free capital and labor movement can help facilitate nascent entrepreneurship. Finally, we find that privatizing assets in emerging market economies can have an unintended consequence of reducing nascent entrepreneurship. Privatization can improve efficiency in firms but may force many small business owners out of business if they are tied to loss-making state-owned enterprises. The decision needs to be evaluated by comparing the gain from increased efficiencies through market operations and welfare loss due to failing small businesses tied to state owned enterprises. Policymakers can maintain the incentive for individuals in emerging economies to participate in nascent entrepreneurship by stating that they will compensate nascent entrepreneurs that lose their business due to closure of loss-making state companies. However, this safety net will be phased out eventually as more of the economy becomes privatized. This policy might help reduce the welfare loss while maintaining the gains from increased efficiency in production.

Acknowledgements This work received support from the Institute for Humane Studies under grant no. IHS016651. We would like to thank our research assistant, Haily Dang, who helped compile the studies used in the literature review.

References

Acemoglu, D. (2008). Oligarchic versus democratic societies. *Journal of the European Economic Association, 6*(1), 1–44. https://doi.org/10.1162/JEEA.2008.6.1.1

Acemoglu, D., & Johnson, S. (2005). Unbundling institutions. *Journal of Political Economy, 113*(5), 949–995. https://doi.org/10.1086/432166

Acemoglu, D., Johnson, S., & Robinson, J. (2005). Institutions as the fundamental cause of long-run growth. In P. Aghion & S. N. Durlauf (Eds.), *Handbook of economic growth* (pp. 385–472). Elsevier.

Acs, Z. J., & Amorós, J. E. (2008). Entrepreneurship and competitiveness dynamics in Latin America. *Small Business Economics, 31*(3), 305–322. https://doi.org/10.1007/s11187-008-9133-y

Aidis, R. (2005). Institutional barriers to small- and medium-sized enterprise operations in transition countries. *Small Business Economics, 25*(4), 305–317. https://doi.org/10.1007/s11187-003-6463-7

Aidis, R. (2017). Staying in the family: The impact of institutions and mental models on entrepreneurship development in post-soviet transition countries. In A. Sauka & A. Chepurenko (Eds.), *Entrepreneurship in transition economies* (pp. 15–32). Springer. https://doi.org/10.1007/978-3-319-57342-7_2

Angulo-Guerrero, M. J., Pérez-Moreno, S., & Abad-Guerrero, I. M. (2017). How economic freedom affects opportunity and necessity entrepreneurship in the OECD countries. *Journal of Business Research, 73*, 30–37. https://doi.org/10.1016/j.jbusres.2016.11.017

Antonakis, J., Bastardoz, N., & Rönkkö, M. (2021). On ignoring the random effects assumption in multilevel models: Review, critique, and recommendations. *Organizational Research Methods, 24*(2), 443–483. https://doi.org/10.1177/1094428119877457

Aparicio, S., Urbano, D., & Audretsch, D. (2016). Institutional factors, opportunity entrepreneurship and economic growth: Panel data evidence. *Technological Forecasting and Social Change, 102*, 45–61. https://doi.org/10.1016/j.techfore.2015.04.006

Arnold, D. J., & Quelch, J. A. (1998). New strategies in emerging markets. *Sloan Management Review, 40*(1), 7–20.

Autio, E., & Fu, K. (2015). Economic and political institutions and entry into formal and informal entrepreneurship. *Asia Pacific Journal of Management, 32*(1), 67–94. https://doi.org/10.1007/s10490-014-9381-0

Baek, S., & Yang, D. (2010). Institutional quality, capital flight and capital flows. *Korean Economic Review, 26*(1), 121–155.

Baez, B., & Abolafia, M. Y. (2002). Bureaucratic entrepreneurship and institutional change: A sense-making approach. *Journal of Public Administration Research and Theory, 12*(4), 525–552. https://doi.org/10.1093/oxfordjournals.jpart.a003546

Berdiev, A. N., & Saunoris, J. W. (2018). Corruption and entrepreneurship: Cross-country evidence from formal and informal sectors: Corruption and entrepreneurship. *Southern Economic Journal, 84*(3), 831–848. https://doi.org/10.1002/soej.12250

Bhasin, N., & Garg, S. (2020). Impact of institutional environment on inward FDI: A case of select emerging market economies. *Global Business Review, 21*(5), 1279–1301. https://doi.org/10.1177/0972150919856989

Bika, Z. (2012). Entrepreneurial sons, patriarchy and the Colonels' experiment in Thessaly, rural Greece. *Entrepreneurship & Regional Development, 24*(3–4), 235–257. https://doi.org/10.1080/08985626.2012.670915

Bird, M., & Wennberg, K. (2014). Regional influences on the prevalence of family versus non-family start-ups. *Journal of Business Venturing, 29*(3), 421–436. https://doi.org/10.1016/j.jbusvent.2013.06.004

Bjørnskov, C., & Foss, N. J. (2016). Institutions, entrepreneurship, and economic growth: What do we know and what do we still need to know? *Academy of Management Perspectives, 30*(3), 292–315. https://doi.org/10.5465/amp.2015.0135

Bourdieu, P. (2005). *The social structures of the economy*. Polity.

Bowen, H. P., & De Clercq, D. (2008). Institutional context and the allocation of entrepreneurial effort. *Journal of International Business Studies, 39*(4), 747–767. https://doi.org/10.1057/palgrave.jibs.8400343

Buehn, A., & Schneider, F. (2012). Corruption and the shadow economy: Like oil and vinegar, like water and fire? *International Tax and Public Finance, 19*(1), 172–194. https://doi.org/10.1007/s10797-011-9175-y

Busenitz, L. W., Gómez, C., & Spencer, J. W. (2000). Country institutional profiles: Unlocking entrepreneurial phenomena. *Academy of Management Journal, 43*(5), 994–1003. https://doi.org/10.5465/1556423

Contractor, F. J., Nuruzzaman, N., Dangol, R., & Raghunath, S. (2021). How FDI inflows to emerging markets are influenced by country regulatory factors: An exploratory study. *Journal of International Management, 27*(1), 100834. https://doi.org/10.1016/j.intman.2021.100834

Dau, L. A., & Cuervo-Cazurra, A. (2014). To formalize or not to formalize: Entrepreneurship and pro-market institutions. *Journal of Business Venturing, 29*(5), 668–686. https://doi.org/10.1016/j.jbusvent.2014.05.002

De Soto, H. (1989). *The other path: The invisible revolution in the Third World* (1st ed.). Harper & Row.

DiMaggio, P. (1988). Interest and agency in institutional theory. In L. G. Zucker (Ed.), *Research on institutional patterns: Environment and culture*. Ballinger Publishing Co.

Djankov, S., La Porta, R., Lopez-de-Silanes, F., & Shleifer, A. (2002). The regulation of entry. *The Quarterly Journal of Economics, 117*(1), 1–37. https://doi.org/10.1162/003355302753399436

Dorado, S. (2005). Institutional entrepreneurship, partaking, and convening. *Organization Studies, 26*(3), 385–414. https://doi.org/10.1177/0170840605050873

Douma, S., George, R., & Kabir, R. (2006). Foreign and domestic ownership, business groups, and firm performance: Evidence from a large emerging market. *Strategic Management Journal, 27*(7), 637–657. https://doi.org/10.1002/smj.535

Duttagupta, R., & Pazarbasioglu, C. (2021). *Miles to go: The future of emerging markets* [Finance and Development]. https://www.imf.org/external/pubs/ft/fandd/2021/06/pdf/the-future-of-emerging-markets-duttagupta-and-pazarbasioglu.pdf

Estrin, S., Korosteleva, J., & Mickiewicz, T. (2013). Which institutions encourage entrepreneurial growth aspirations? *Journal of Business Venturing, 28*(4), 564–580. https://doi.org/10.1016/j.jbusvent.2012.05.001

FI. (2017). *Economic Freedom of The World Data*. Fraser Institute.

Friedman, E., Johnson, S., Kaufmann, D., & Zoido-Lobaton, P. (2000). Dodging the grabbing hand: The determinants of unofficial activity in 69 countries. *Journal of Public Economics, 76*(3), 459–493. https://doi.org/10.1016/S0047-2727(99)00093-6

Fu, K., Larsson, A.-S., & Wennberg, K. (2018). Habitual entrepreneurs in the making: How labour market rigidity and employment affects entrepreneurial re-entry. *Small Business Economics, 51*(2), 465–482. https://doi.org/10.1007/s11187-018-0011-y

Fuentelsaz, L., González, C., Maícas, J. P., & Montero, J. (2015). How different formal institutions affect opportunity and necessity entrepreneurship. *BRQ Business Research Quarterly, 18*(4), 246–258. https://doi.org/10.1016/j.brq.2015.02.001

Galindo, M.-Á., & Méndez, M. T. (2014). Entrepreneurship, economic growth, and innovation: Are feedback effects at work? *Journal of Business Research, 67*(5), 825–829. https://doi.org/10.1016/j.jbusres.2013.11.052
Garud, R., Hardy, C., & Maguire, S. (2007). Institutional entrepreneurship as embedded agency: An introduction to the Special Issue. *Organization Studies, 28*(7), 957–969. https://doi.org/10.1177/0170840607078958
Goes, C. (2015). *Institutions and growth: A GMM/IV panel VAR approach* (IMF Working Paper WP/15/174). International Monetary Fund.
Granovetter, M. (1992). Economic institutions as social constructions: A framework for analysis. *Acta Sociologica, 35*(1), 3–11. https://doi.org/10.1177/000169939203500101
Gregory, R. P. (2019). Financial openness and entrepreneurship. *Research in International Business and Finance, 48*, 48–58. https://doi.org/10.1016/j.ribaf.2018.12.006
Gu, W., & Qian, X. (2019). Does venture capital foster entrepreneurship in an emerging market? *Journal of Business Research, 101*, 803–810. https://doi.org/10.1016/j.jbusres.2018.12.011
Gurvich, E. (2016). Institutional constraints and economic development. *Russian Journal of Economics, 2*(4), 349–374. https://doi.org/10.1016/j.ruje.2016.11.002
Harbi, S. E., & Anderson, A. R. (2010). Institutions and the shaping of different forms of entrepreneurship. *The Journal of Socio-Economics, 39*(3), 436–444. https://doi.org/10.1016/j.socec.2010.02.011
Hassan, M., & Schneider, F. (2016). Size and development of the shadow economies of 157 worldwide countries: Updated and new measures from 1999 to 2013. *Journal of Global Economics, 04*(03). https://doi.org/10.4172/2375-4389.1000218
Henrekson, M., & Sanandaji, T. (2011). The interaction of entrepreneurship and institutions. *Journal of Institutional Economics, 7*(1), 47–75. https://doi.org/10.1017/S1744137410000342
Herrera-Echeverri, H., Haar, J., & Estévez-Bretón, J. B. (2014). Foreign direct investment, institutional quality, economic freedom and entrepreneurship in emerging markets. *Journal of Business Research, 67*(9), 1921–1932. https://doi.org/10.1016/j.jbusres.2013.11.020
Hiatt, S. R., & Sine, W. D. (2014). Clear and present danger: Planning and new venture survival amid political and civil violence: Clear and present danger. *Strategic Management Journal, 35*(5), 773–785. https://doi.org/10.1002/smj.2113
Hindriks, J., Keen, M., & Muthoo, A. (1999). Corruption, extortion and evasion. *Journal of Public Economics, 74*(3), 395–430. https://doi.org/10.1016/S0047-2727(99)00030-4
Hodgson, G. (2006). What are institutions? *Journal of Economic Issues, 40*(1), 1–25. https://doi.org/10.1080/00213624.2006.11506879
Hoffman, D. A. (1997). An overview of the logic and rationale of hierarchical linear models. *Journal of Management, 23*(6), 723–744. https://doi.org/10.1177/014920639702300602
Hoffman, D. A., & Gavin, M. B. (1998). Centering decisions in hierarchical linear models: Implications for research in organizations. *Journal of Management, 24*(5), 623–641. https://doi.org/10.1177/014920639802400504
Hoffman, D. A., Griffin, M. A., & Gavin, M. B. (2000). The application of hierarchical linear modeling to organizational research. In K. J. Klein & S. W. J. Kozlowski (Eds.), *Multilevel theory, research, and methods in organizations: Foundations, extensions, and new directions* (pp. 467–511). Jossey-Bass.
Hoskisson, R. E., Eden, L., Lau, C. M., & Wright, M. (2000). Strategy in emerging economies. *Academy of Management Journal, 43*(3), 249–267. https://doi.org/10.2307/1556394
Hox, J. J. (2010). *Multilevel analysis: Techniques and applications* (2nd ed.). Routledge, Taylor & Francis.
IMF. (2022). *World economic outlook: Managing divergent recoveries*. International Monetary Fund.
Iwasaki, I., & Suganuma, K. (2015). Foreign direct investment and regional economic development in Russia: An econometric assessment. *Economic Change and Restructuring, 48*(3–4), 209–255. https://doi.org/10.1007/s10644-015-9161-y

Javorcik, B. S., & Wei, S.-J. (2009). Corruption and cross-border investment in emerging markets: Firm-level evidence. *Journal of International Money and Finance, 28*(4), 605–624. https://doi.org/10.1016/j.jimonfin.2009.01.003
Jayachandran, S. (2021). Social norms as a barrier to women's employment in developing countries. *IMF Economic Review, 69*(3), 576–595. https://doi.org/10.1057/s41308-021-00140-w
Jeon, S. (2018). What influences entrepreneurial intentions? An empirical study using data from the Global Entrepreneurship Monitor. *Academy of Entrepreneurship Journal, 24*(3), 1–15.
Johnson, S., Kaufmann, D., McMillan, J., & Woodruff, C. (2000). Why do firms hide? Bribes and unofficial activity after communism. *Journal of Public Economics, 76*(3), 495–520. https://doi.org/10.1016/S0047-2727(99)00094-8
Kalantaridis, C., & Fletcher, D. (2012). Entrepreneurship and institutional change: A research agenda. *Entrepreneurship & Regional Development, 24*(3–4), 199–214. https://doi.org/10.1080/08985626.2012.670913
Keefer, P. (2007). Governance and economic growth. In L. A. Winters & S. Yusuf (Eds.), *Dancing with giants: China, India, and the global economy*. World Bank.
Kelmanson, K., Kirabaeva, L., Medina, B., Mircheva, B., & Weiss, J. (2019). *Explaining the shadow economy in Europe: Size, causes and policy options* (WP/19/278 Working Paper). International Monetary Fund.
Khanna, T., & Yafeh, Y. (2007). Business groups in emerging markets: Paragons or parasites? *Journal of Economic Literature, 45*(2), 331–372. https://doi.org/10.1257/jel.45.2.331
Klasen, S. (2019). What explains uneven female labor force participation levels and trends in developing countries? *The World Bank Research Observer, 34*(2), 161–197. https://doi.org/10.1093/wbro/lkz005
Kowalski, P., Buge, M., Sztajerowska, M., & Egeland, M. (2013). *State-owned enterprises: Trade effects and policy implications* (OECD Trade Policy Papers No. 147; OECD Trade Policy Papers, Vol. 147). OECD Publishing. https://doi.org/10.1787/5k4869ckqk7l-en
Kuchař, P. (2016). Entrepreneurship and institutional change: The case of surrogate motherhood. *Journal of Evolutionary Economics, 26*(2), 349–379. https://doi.org/10.1007/s00191-015-0433-5
La Porta, R., Lopez-De-Silanes, F., & Shleifer, A. (2002). Government ownership of banks. *The Journal of Finance, 57*(1), 265–301. https://doi.org/10.1111/1540-6261.00422
Leca, B., Battilana, J., & Boxenbaum, E. (2008). *Agency and institutions: A review of institutional entrepreneurship* (Working paper 08-096). Harvard Business School.
Levie, J., & Autio, E. (2011). Regulatory burden, rule of law, and entry of strategic entrepreneurs: An international panel study: Regulation, rule of law, and entrepreneurial entry. *Journal of Management Studies, 48*(6), 1392–1419. https://doi.org/10.1111/j.1467-6486.2010.01006.x
Lin, C., Lin, P., & Song, F. (2010). Property rights protection and corporate R&D: Evidence from China. *Journal of Development Economics, 93*(1), 49–62. https://doi.org/10.1016/j.jdeveco.2009.04.006
Luthans, F., & Ibrayeva, E. S. (2006). Entrepreneurial self-efficacy in Central Asian transition economies: Quantitative and qualitative analyses. *Journal of International Business Studies, 37*(1), 92–110. https://doi.org/10.1057/palgrave.jibs.8400173
Manolova, T. S., Eunni, R. V., & Gyoshev, B. S. (2008). Institutional environments for entrepreneurship: Evidence from emerging economies in Eastern Europe. *Entrepreneurship Theory and Practice, 32*(1), 203–218. https://doi.org/10.1111/j.1540-6520.2007.00222.x
Marquis, C., & Qian, C. (2014). Corporate social responsibility reporting in China: Symbol or substance? *Organization Science, 25*(1), 127–148. https://doi.org/10.1287/orsc.2013.0837
Marquis, C., & Raynard, M. (2015). Institutional strategies in emerging markets. *The Academy of Management Annals, 9*(1), 291–335. https://doi.org/10.1080/19416520.2015.1014661
Marquis, C., Zhang, J., & Zhou, Y. (2011). Regulatory uncertainty and corporate responses to environmental protection in China. *California Management Review, 54*(1), 39–63. https://doi.org/10.1525/cmr.2011.54.1.39

Mauro, P. (1998). Corruption and the composition of government expenditure. *Journal of Public Economics, 69*(2), 263–279. https://doi.org/10.1016/S0047-2727(98)00025-5

McCarthy, B. (2012). From fishing and factories to cultural tourism: The role of social entrepreneurs in the construction of a new institutional field. *Entrepreneurship & Regional Development, 24*(3–4), 259–282. https://doi.org/10.1080/08985626.2012.670916

Mendoza, R., & Harris, A. (2021, December 15). Ownership structures in emerging markets [MSCI ESG Research]. *Research and Insights/Global-Investing-Trends*. https://www.msci.com/research-and-insights/global-investing-trends/ownership-structures-in-emerging-markets

Morck, R., Wolfenzon, D., & Yeung, B. (2005). Corporate governance, economic entrenchment, and growth. *Journal of Economic Literature, 43*(3), 655–720. https://doi.org/10.1257/002205105774431252

Muralidharan, E., & Pathak, S. (2017). Informal institutions and international entrepreneurship. *International Business Review, 26*(2), 288–302. https://doi.org/10.1016/j.ibusrev.2016.07.006

Murrell, P., & Wang, Y. (1993). When privatization should be delayed: The effect of communist legacies on organizational and institutional reforms. *Journal of Comparative Economics, 17*(2), 385–406.

Musacchio, A., & Lazzarini, S. G. (2014). *Reinventing state capitalism: Leviathan in business, Brazil and beyond*. Harvard University Press.

Newman, A., Schwarz, S., Borgia, D. J., & Wei, W. (2017). The influence of formal and informal institutions on microcredit: Financial inclusion for micro-entrepreneurs by Lender type. In D. Cumming, Y. Dong, W. Hou, & B. Sen (Eds.), *Microfinance for entrepreneurial development* (pp. 23–52). Springer. https://doi.org/10.1007/978-3-319-62111-1_2

North, D. C. (1990). *Institutions, institutional change, and economic performance*. Cambridge University Press.

North, D. C. (1994). Economic performance through time. *The American Economic Review, 84*(3), 359–368.

Nyström, K. (2008). The institutions of economic freedom and entrepreneurship: Evidence from panel data. *Public Choice, 136*(3–4), 269–282. https://doi.org/10.1007/s11127-008-9295-9

Omri, A. (2020). Formal versus informal entrepreneurship in emerging economies: The roles of governance and the financial sector. *Journal of Business Research, 108*, 277–290. https://doi.org/10.1016/j.jbusres.2019.11.027

Pasali, S. (2013). *Where is the cheese? Synthesizing a giant literature on causes and consequences of financial sector development* (Policy Research Working Paper 6655). World Bank.

Paul, J., & Jadhav, P. (2019). Institutional determinants of foreign direct investment inflows: Evidence from emerging markets. *International Journal of Emerging Markets, 15*(2), 245–261. https://doi.org/10.1108/IJOEM-11-2018-0590

Peng, M. W., & Heath, P. S. (1996). The growth of the firm in planned economies in transition: Institutions, organizations, and strategic choice. *Academy of Management Review, 21*, 492–528.

Petrova, K. (2021). Entrepreneurship and institutional change in emerging markets. In N. Faghih & A. H. Samadi (Eds.), *Legal-economic institutions, entrepreneurship, and management. Contributions to management science*. Springer. https://doi.org/10.1007/978-3-030-60978-8_7

Powell, W. W. (2007). The new institutionalism. In J. R. Bailey & S. Clegg (Eds.), *International encyclopedia of organization studies*. SAGE.

Powell, W. W., & DiMaggio, P. (Eds.). (1991). *The New institutionalism in organizational analysis*. University of Chicago Press.

Rabe-Hesketh, S., & Skrondal, A. (2022). *Multilevel and longitudinal modeling using Stata* (4th ed.). Stata Press.

Ralston, D. A., Terpstra-Tong, J., Terpstra, R. H., Wang, X., & Egri, C. (2006). Today's state-owned enterprises of China: Are they dying dinosaurs or dynamic dynamos? *Strategic Management Journal, 27*(9), 825–843. https://doi.org/10.1002/smj.545

Raudenbush, S. W., & Bryk, A. S. (2002). *Hierarchical linear models: Applications and data analysis methods* (2nd ed.). SAGE.

Reynolds, P. (2007). *Global Entrepreneurship Monitor [GEM]: Adult population survey data set, 1998–2017: Version 6* (Version v6) [Data set]. ICPSR – Interuniversity Consortium for Political and Social Research. https://doi.org/10.3886/ICPSR20320.V6

Reynolds, P., Bosma, N., Autio, E., Hunt, S., De Bono, N., Servais, I., Lopez-Garcia, P., & Chin, N. (2005). Global Entrepreneurship Monitor: Data collection design and implementation 1998–2003. *Small Business Economics, 24*(3), 205–231. https://doi.org/10.1007/s11187-005-1980-1

Rodríguez, G., & Elo, I. (2003). Intra-class correlation in random-effects models for Binary Data. *The Stata Journal: Promoting Communications on Statistics and Stata, 3*(1), 32–46. https://doi.org/10.1177/1536867X0300300102

Rodrik, D., Subramanian, A., & Trebbi, F. (2004). Institutions rule: The primacy of institutions over geography and integration in economic development. *Journal of Economic Growth, 9*(2), 131–165. https://doi.org/10.1023/B:JOEG.0000031425.72248.85

Samadi, A. H. (2018). Institutions and entrepreneurship in MENA countries. In N. Faghih & M. R. Zali (Eds.), *Entrepreneurship ecosystem in the Middle East and North Africa (MENA)* (pp. 53–93). Springer. https://doi.org/10.1007/978-3-319-75913-5_3

Samadi, A. H. (2019). Institutions and entrepreneurship: Unidirectional or bidirectional causality? *Journal of Global Entrepreneurship Research, 9*(1), 3. https://doi.org/10.1186/s40497-018-0129-z

Sambharya, R., & Musteen, M. (2014). Institutional environment and entrepreneurship: An empirical study across countries. *Journal of International Entrepreneurship, 12*(4), 314–330. https://doi.org/10.1007/s10843-014-0137-1

Schneider, F. (2015). Size and development of the shadow economy of 31 European and 5 other OECD countries from 2003 to 2014: Different Developments? *Journal of Self-Governance and Management Economics, 3*(4), 7–29.

Scott, W. R. (1995). *Institutions and organizations*. SAGE.

Seo, M.-G., & Creed, W. E. D. (2002). Institutional contradictions, praxis, and institutional change: A dialectical perspective. *Academy of Management Review, 27*(2), 222–247. https://doi.org/10.5465/amr.2002.6588004

Sewell, W. H. (1992). A theory of structure: Duality, agency, and transformation. *American Journal of Sociology, 98*(1), 1–29. https://doi.org/10.1086/229967

Shleifer, A. (1997). Government in transition. *European Economic Review, 41*(3–5), 385–410. https://doi.org/10.1016/S0014-2921(97)00011-1

Silve, F., & Plekhanov, A. (2015). *Institutions, innovation and growth: Cross-country evidence* (EBRD Working Paper 117). SSRN.

Simón-Moya, V., Revuelto-Taboada, L., & Guerrero, R. F. (2014). Institutional and economic drivers of entrepreneurship: An international perspective. *Journal of Business Research, 67*(5), 715–721. https://doi.org/10.1016/j.jbusres.2013.11.033

Sit, V. F. S., & Liu, W. (2000). Restructuring and spatial change of China's auto industry under institutional reform and globalization. *Annals of the Association of American Geographers, 90*(4), 653–673. https://doi.org/10.1111/0004-5608.00216

Smallbone, D., & Welter, F. (2012). Entrepreneurship and institutional change in transition economies: The Commonwealth of Independent States, Central and Eastern Europe and China compared. *Entrepreneurship & Regional Development, 24*(3–4), 215–233. https://doi.org/10.1080/08985626.2012.670914

Sobel, R. S. (2008). Testing Baumol: Institutional quality and the productivity of entrepreneurship. *Journal of Business Venturing, 23*(6), 641–655. https://doi.org/10.1016/j.jbusvent.2008.01.004

Spencer, J. W., & Gómez, C. (2004). The relationship among national institutional structures, economic factors, and domestic entrepreneurial activity: A multicountry study. *Journal of Business Research, 57*(10), 1098–1107. https://doi.org/10.1016/S0148-2963(03)00040-7

Stenholm, P., Acs, Z., & Wuebker, R. (2013). Exploring country-level institutional arrangements on the rate and type of entrepreneurial activity. *Journal of Business Venturing, 28*(1), 176–193. https://doi.org/10.1016/j.jbusvent.2011.11.002

Stephen, F. H., Urbano, D., & van Hemmen, S. (2005). The impact of institutions on entrepreneurial activity. *Managerial and Decision Economics, 26*(7), 413–419. https://doi.org/10.1002/mde.1254

Straub, S. (2005). Informal sector: The credit market channel. *Journal of Development Economics, 78*(2), 299–321. https://doi.org/10.1016/j.jdeveco.2004.09.005

Tebaldi, E., & Elmslie, B. (2013). Does institutional quality impact innovation? Evidence from cross-country patent grant data. *Applied Economics, 45*(7), 887–900. https://doi.org/10.1080/00036846.2011.613777

Torgler, B., & Schneider, F. (2009). The impact of tax morale and institutional quality on the shadow economy. *Journal of Economic Psychology, 30*(2), 228–245. https://doi.org/10.1016/j.joep.2008.08.004

Tracey, P., & Phillips, N. (2011). Entrepreneurship in emerging markets: Strategies for new venture creation in uncertain institutional contexts. *Management International Review, 51*(1), 23–39. https://doi.org/10.1007/s11575-010-0066-8

Urbano, D., & Alvarez, C. (2014). Institutional dimensions and entrepreneurial activity: An international study. *Small Business Economics, 42*(4), 703–716. https://doi.org/10.1007/s11187-013-9523-7

Vollset, S. E., Goren, E., Yuan, C.-W., Cao, J., Smith, A. E., Hsiao, T., Bisignano, C., Azhar, G. S., Castro, E., Chalek, J., Dolgert, A. J., Frank, T., Fukutaki, K., Hay, S. I., Lozano, R., Mokdad, A. H., Nandakumar, V., Pierce, M., Pletcher, M., et al. (2020). Fertility, mortality, migration, and population scenarios for 195 countries and territories from 2017 to 2100: A forecasting analysis for the Global Burden of Disease Study. *The Lancet, 396*(10258), 1285–1306. https://doi.org/10.1016/S0140-6736(20)30677-2

Williams, C., & Nadin, S. (2011). Theorising the hidden enterprise culture: The nature of entrepreneurship in the shadow economy. *International Journal of Entrepreneurship and Small Business, 14*(3), 334. https://doi.org/10.1504/IJESB.2011.042757

Williams, C., & Round, J. (2007). Entrepreneurship and the informal economy: A study of Ukraine s hidden enterprise culture. *Journal of Developmental Entrepreneurship, 12*, 119–136.

Williams, C., & Shahid, M. S. (2016). Informal entrepreneurship and institutional theory: Explaining the varying degrees of (in)formalization of entrepreneurs in Pakistan. *Entrepreneurship & Regional Development, 28*(1–2), 1–25. https://doi.org/10.1080/08985626.2014.963889

Williams, C., Shahid, M. S., & Martínez, A. (2016). Determinants of the level of informality of informal micro-enterprises: Some evidence from the City of Lahore, Pakistan. *World Development, 84*, 312–325. https://doi.org/10.1016/j.worlddev.2015.09.003

Williamson, O. E. (2000). The new institutional economics: Taking stock, looking ahead. *Journal of Economic Literature, 38*(3), 595–613. https://doi.org/10.1257/jel.38.3.595

Wooldridge, J. M. (2013). *Introductory econometrics: A modern approach* (5th ed.). South-Western Cengage Learning.

World Development Indicators. (2022). World Bank. http://databank.worldbank.org

Yu, T. F.-L. (2001). An entrepreneurial perspective of institutional change. *Constitutional Political Economy, 12*(3), 217–236. https://doi.org/10.1023/A:1011607927754

Zhou, F. (2019, July 29). State-owned enterprises and emerging markets: What you need to know. *Capital Markets*. https://www.callan.com/blog-archive/em-soe/

Inertia, Innovation Failures, and Learning from Innovation Failures: Some Insights from MSEs in an Emerging Market Economy

Donard Games, Ares Albirru Amsal, Dessy Kurnia Sari, Rayna Kartika, and Dian Yuni Anggraini

1 Introduction

While small businesses have long been known as dominant business entities, especially in emerging market economies, most fail to transform their businesses into high-growth ones. This phenomenon has attracted many researchers (e.g., Tambunan, 2019; Laperche & Liu, 2013; Faghih et al., 2021). However, there has been limited research that examines why some micro and small-sized enterprises (MSEs) fail to innovate, or to be more precise, why some SMEs seem to experience inertia in most of their business while some others benefitted from their innovation experiences, including innovation failures. It is argued that MSEs' capability to interpret innovation failures and benefit from them can serve as a key differentiator for them to escape inertia despite lacking institutionalization in their organizations. This is mainly because, as Games and Rendi (2019) suggested, SMEs typically have no abundant resources and may see innovation as a costly and risky movement. As a result, they likely perceive innovation failures as representative of their aspirations of pursuing business growth.

In a broader sense, most of the MSEs in emerging market economies can be categorized as necessity-based entrepreneurs. Ninety-nine percent of Indonesia's businesses belong to this category. Fiqri and Yanuarta (2022) have proposed some valuable insights into the context of Indonesia's MSEs. For instance, they argue that most of these MSEs have never been able to expand their business scale. In their opinion, this is unsurprising as they are not designed for such business expansion.

This research received no specific grant from any funding agency in the public, commercial, or not-for-profit sectors. This work was supported by RIIM from the National Research and Innovation Agency of Indonesia (No: 31/IV/KS/06/2022).

D. Games (✉) · A. A. Amsal · D. K. Sari · R. Kartika · D. Y. Anggraini
Faculty of Economics and Business, Universitas Andalas, West Sumatra, Indonesia
e-mail: donardgames@eb.unand.ac.id

N. Faghih, A. H. Samadi (eds.), *Institutional Inertia*, Contributions to Economics,
https://doi.org/10.1007/978-3-031-51175-2_14

MSEs are characterized by a lack of separation between owners and business interests and the incapability to access funding and business partnership as they are trapped in their (dis)comfort zones. Usually, they are reluctant to innovate because innovation is not part of their business strategies if they have any. In other words, most of the MSEs in Indonesia have experienced inertia. The present study aims to examine inertia, innovation failures, and lessons that can be learned from innovation failures from the perspective of micro and small enterprises.

This study will contribute to the body of knowledge in the following manners. First, MSEs have long been known as the source of necessity-based entrepreneurs, especially in emerging market economies. The present study can provide some insights from MSEs on how they can survive inertia and innovation failures by learning from innovation failures. Previous research on innovation failures has shown that learning from innovation failures surprisingly provides the opportunity for future entrepreneurial success (Rhaiem & Amara, 2021; Laperche & Liu, 2013). Second, this study follows the suggestion from Forsman (2021) to investigate the failing factors from different cultural backgrounds. Forsman herself focuses on European countries. This study focuses on Indonesia as an emerging market economy and, more specifically, on West Sumatra, a province in Indonesia well known as a source of entrepreneurs in the country. West Sumatra, also known as the land of Minangkabau, is mostly populated by the Minangkabau ethnicity, who are mostly Muslims. It is also characterized as having a collectivist culture based on a matrilineal system. Such cultural characteristics are important because, as Dana et al. (2020) suggested, entrepreneurial activities and socio-cultural and ethnic contexts are inseparable. With this in mind, this study is expected to enhance our understanding of the topic at hand from such a unique cultural setting.

This study seeks to answer the following question: How do some MSEs in the designated provincial area (West Sumatra) perceive and experience innovation failures, and how do they learn their lessons from such innovation failures? It is expected that the lessons they learned from the innovation failures can reduce inertia and, at the same time, represent openness to change as the opposite of the state of inertia. As an emerging market economy that offers abundant business opportunities, Indonesia needs to create policies that support MSEs and entrepreneurship sectors to innovate. Regarding this, Games (2022) have emphasized the importance of avoiding the 'one-size-fits-all' approach' which may signify inertia in entrepreneurship and innovation policies. In short, the present study can contribute positively to MSEs and entrepreneurship policies by proposing key differentiators of MSEs that can potentially elevate their businesses.

It is expected that the present study can provide a greater understanding of SME inertia in the context of an emerging market economy from the lens of innovation failure. Learning from innovation failure in a collectivist culture such as Minangkabau in this study can also represent these people's capability to benefit from their social capital (Rhaiem & Amara, 2021). Learning from innovation failure may indicate the willingness to change that contradicts MSE inertia. The present study is expected to be able to explore the nature of MSE inertia and learning from innovation failure from a particular context of this study.

2 Literature Review

2.1 Inertia and Innovation Failures in MSEs

Inertia can be defined as resistance to all changes, including both incremental and radical (Tushman et al., 1985). This is unfortunate, considering that change has become the norm in responding to rapid and intense signs of progress in competition and technology. Godkin and Allcorn (2008) suggest that inertia can represent resistance against change. Also, Haag (2014) points out that inertia is an obstacle to accepting digital and business model innovation. Similarly, Sastry (1997) argues that inertia can be seen as an organizational inability to change. Inertia can also indicate an unwillingness to implement changes (Stål, 2015) regardless of environmental changes (Asano & Eto, 2007). In addition, Daviy and Shakina (2021) emphasize the importance of flexibility in implementing changes, particularly technological adoption, to reduce inertia. The present study departs from these definitions[1] and conceptualizes organizational[2] or institutional inertia[3] as an organization's unwillingness, incapability, and inflexibility to implement new strategies and changes as ways to innovate.

Any change in the core organizational structures needs a great deal of effort on the part of the firm to adjust its central processes and, consequently, causes a great risk of failures (Hannan & Freeman, 1984). In this sense, the absence of encouragement to implement innovation can naturally emerge as there is no guarantee that innovation can benefit the organization. Therefore, business owners need to be able to learn from innovation failures. In contrast to business failures, innovation failures do not necessarily lead to bankruptcy because the latter can be immediately followed by other innovations (Forsman, 2021). Boso et al. (2019) find that learning from failures heavily depends on understanding the learning process and entrepreneurial opportunities. Accordingly, entrepreneurs must update their knowledge by learning from past experiences to seek and benefit from business opportunities (Corbett, 2007).

Forsman (2021) has found some patterns regarding learning from innovation failures. These patterns include: *Passionate Innovators*-those who experience innovation failures because of overconfidence; *The Solo Innovators*-those who suffer from innovation failures because of a lack of market demand and business partnership; and *The Developer Innovators*-those who face innovation failures mainly because they perceive highly technological adoption but have no specific target for innovation implementation which in turns lead to the loss of momentum in the

[1]To read more about the concept of inertia, refer to Chapter "Inertia: Resistance and Endurance" of this book.

[2]To read more about the concept of Organizational inertia refer to Chapters "Internal Empowerment Dynamics of Organizational Inertia Management" and "Trade and Institutional Inertia" of this book.

[3]To read more about the concept of institutional inertia, and sources of institutional inertia refer to Chapter "An Introduction to Institutional Inertia: Concepts, Types and Causes" of this book.

marketplace. These patterns suggest that the sources of innovation failures may come from the internal organization (overconfidence), external factors (a lack of market demand and business partnership/external assistance), and mixed factors (business strategy and technological adoption). Concerning this, Games et al. (2021) found that both incremental and radical innovation can benefit MSEs. Consequently, business owners are required to make a prior judgment of their innovation activities, even if they are most likely beneficial.

Inertia may pose greater difficulties in the context of developing countries. Organizational inertia is a barrier to organizational change in developing countries (Daviy & Shakina, 2021). Inertia is distinct in emerging countries, and this should be taken into consideration by SMEs' policymakers, even in different environments (Indarti, 2017). Because of that, small businesses typically need to deal with more fundamental barriers, such as the absence of governance and formal legal status (Tambunan, 2019). Entrepreneurs from developing countries, who are likely to be informal entrepreneurs, face more difficulties running the business than their counterparts in developed countries (Bruton & Ahlstrom, 2003). In contrast, as suggested by Samadi (2019), the people in innovation-driven economies are motivated to establish a business on a voluntary basis rather than a mandatory choice. In brief, MSE inertia is typical in the context of emerging market economies. Therefore, it may be useful to predict whether or not the MSEs in such a context can transform themselves into high-growth businesses.

2.2 *Learning from Failures and MSEs*

People may learn more from their failures than their successes (McGrath, 1999). Learning from failures can benefit entrepreneurs in many ways, including the ability to identify new opportunities (Ucbasaran et al., 2010), organize new ventures (Cope, 2011), and increase the chances of success for future entrepreneurial activities (Yamakawa & Cardon, 2015). All of them signify the importance of learning. Likewise, Rhaiem and Amara (2021) argue that learning from failures can be revealed by examining the knowledge-based theory of the firm in question. The statement implies that firms can benefit from learning from failures by utilizing knowledge development and knowledge storage. This is why Rhaiem and Amara (2021) define learning from failures as an adaptation of the organization's knowledge informed by its past experience. As mentioned above, MSEs may not have sufficient resources to invest in knowledge (Tambunan, 2019). For this reason, MSEs may opt not to innovate. However, MSEs may have different viewpoints as they are now more aware of the importance of learning and knowledge (Games & Rendi, 2019) and are run by younger entrepreneurs who are open to changes (Games et al., 2021). In short, MSEs have the opportunity to transform themselves, for they may have particular characteristics that support their organizations.

3 Research Methodology

The present study uses a qualitative approach by interviewing twenty-five MSE owners in West Sumatra, Indonesia. As mentioned above, the research question in this study focuses on how MSE owners perceive and experience innovation failures and how they can benefit from such innovation failures. Therefore, the MSEs, in this sense, are assumed to be capable of innovating but, for some reason, are not fully committed to doing so. Of the 25 interviewees (12 females, 13 males), 12 ran their businesses in food and beverage (4 females; 8 males), seven in handicraft business (2 females; 5 males), and six in Muslim fashion (6 females). The majority of the participants were aged between 25 and 35 years old (16 interviewees) and had a bachelor's degree (13 interviewees). Interviews were conducted from May to July 2022. Each interview took approximately 30 min to complete. Two criteria were set as to how the interviewees were selected. First, the interviewees must have experienced an innovation failure in the context of MSEs. As suggested by Rhaiem and Amara (2021), innovation failures can be divided into two groups: those who experience technical failures that terminate the initiative during the development stage and those who experience commercial failures that end the initiative after the innovation is launched in the target market. All of the interviewees fall into the second category. Second, the interviewees made an informed decision to participate in this research. Interestingly, none of them refused to sharing their failures stories and identities. All of them mentioned that they experienced innovation failures, but they have taken some lessons from these experiences and they have tried to benefit from mistakes in the past.

As for the data analysis, this study uses thematic analysis. It followed the steps of conducting a thematic analysis of entrepreneurial fear of failures proposed by Cacciotti et al. (2016). In this case, we analyzed the collected data from the interviewees by reading them closely and classifying them into three groups: inertia, innovation failures, and learning from innovation failures. The data were then arranged according to the organizing themes (sources of inertia, innovation failures narrative, and learning from failures). Afterward, the results of the interviewees' perceptions and experiences interviewees were compared. In addition, this study followed the suggestions of Miles et al. (2014) and Forsman (2021), who introduced three coding systems: descriptive, process, and emotion. While descriptive coding reduces the data, the process coding tells the action in the data, and the emotion coding recalls the emotions experienced by the interviewees (MSE owners). Such a classification enables us to see the patterns of the data. Finally, frameworks and propositions were derived from the study.

4 Findings and Discussion

Table 1 shows that the interviewees' reasoning for experiencing inertia is mostly related to their incapability to innovate and shortage of business strategy. While inertia may be caused by the unwillingness to innovate, this is not the case encountered by the interviewees in this study. All of them confirmed that they to some extent have learnt that they have made some mistakes. For example, Nowizar (male, 30 yo) says:

> *I am motivated enough to innovate. But, I made a wrong judgment about the customer trend. A coffee shop is not only about the taste of the coffee but also good customer service. This is a good business, but perhaps I forgot that I should anticipate more changes for this kind of business in the long run.*

This study found a strong link between inertia and innovation failures. For instance, passionate entrepreneurs (those who show overconfidence), as suggested by

Table 1 Themes of the present study

	Basic themes (examples)	Organizing themes	Global themes
Inertia	"I am too dependent on my supplier." "I did not upgrade my competence in this business." "I thought planning as rigid and ideal" "I expect markets are the same"	Business as usual Entrepreneurial competence Consumer trend	A lack of business strategy Incapability to innovate A lack of business strategy
Innovation failures and learning from innovation failures	"I chose the wrong business." "I presume that my clothes will be highly demanded." ("know the market first, and make sure products are needed.") "I was too passionate, but sometimes I lost my passion for business changes. (connecting with those who are highly motivated in doing business) "I focused so heavily on tools that I forgot the customer services." (customer first; experience the failures and reflect on them) "I underestimate control even though the standardized product is our strength." "Failure is part of destiny. My duty is to survive difficulties and hopefully it pleases God. My task is to keep trying."	A lack of market demand Market knowledge and market validation Passion Customer satisfaction A lack of quality control Spirituality as a foundation for learning	Solo innovators Passionate innovators Developer innovators Autonomy-motivated entrepreneurs

Source: The authors

Forsman (2021), may overestimate their business ideas. I found this in several interviewees. They seem to think it is unnecessary to have a deeper knowledge of their selected businesses. Yanti (female, 25 yo) says, *"I thought cakes were good business, quick cash, but I found myself at a loss in this simple business"*.

Both incapability to innovate and a lack of business strategy contribute negatively to innovation implementation. Dian (female, 29 yo) says:

> *I was too passionate, but sometimes I lost my passion for business changes. It is too complicated sometimes like I consider many business opportunities, but when I selected one, I got distracted, I lost my focus.*

Rina (female, 27 yo) says:

> *I am too dependent on my supplier. For 3 years, I have never thought of any alternatives. Now, I realize it is important for my business to create my own fashion brand. I can do that.*

According to the patterns of innovation failures proposed by Forsman (2021), the present study found that the majority of the interviewees are categorized as Solo Innovators (overconfidence) and Developer Innovators (too dependent on technological adoption). Interestingly, those who experienced such situations also suffered from inertia. It seems that innovation failures lead to inertia, and inertia leads to innovation failures in particular, if inertia occurs because of inflexibility in business strategy and innovation. As stated by Rina (female, 27 yo), she previously could not fully express herself when she was too dependent on suppliers. Once she can find alternatives, she can find more flexible ways to innovate. In addition, the Solo Innovators (overconfidence) made them excessively complacent. Complacency leads to overconfidence as they view their current situation as the best they can do. Inertia and innovation failures put together may lead to both innovation failures and entrepreneurial failures. However, it is to their credit that all the interviewees have reflected on their experiences and learned their lessons. For example, most interviewees have construed market knowledge and competency as factors that can pave the way to success. A study by Rhaiem and Amara (2021) suggests that there is a link between learning from innovation failure and innovation. This means that innovation failure as a result of inertia or vice versa can temporarily occur, but there is a way to enhance innovation from the way they learn from failures.

Additionally, most interviewees mentioned about COVID-19 pandemic and post-pandemic crises. However, instead of blaming the pandemic for the inertia and innovation failures they experience, they now seem to positively force themselves to create significant changes in their business after inertia and failure experiences. This is in line with Yamakawa and Cardon (2015), who argue that entrepreneurs blame external factors for their entrepreneurial failures. Mira (28 yo, a Muslim fashion designer) describes it best:

> *For such a long time I believe that technology is only a tool. I heavily focus on tools; I forgot the customer services are more important, too. This pandemic has made me put digital technology first, but this is not true, right? My customers need good customer service. I need to make them feel special.*

The results of the interviews show a new possible source of innovation failure: a lack of control due to misplaced autonomy-motivated innovators. Most interviewees implemented a vertical structure organization or centralization. However, they did so against their will; they had to choose such an option because they could not set up formal business organizations and knowledgeable human resources. Most importantly, most interviewees admitted that they did not have someone (among their employees) whom they could trust. As stated by Sukri (male, 34 yo):

> *When I was younger, I highly trusted one of my employees. I let him do the managing and controlling, which was a big mistake. He betrayed me. Now, I have to do everything by myself. This is not good, but I have to.*

A study by Games et al. (2021) points out that MSEs in West Sumatra province are characterized by a lack of written or formal organizational structure. After all, such a preference for a centralized system can equip owners with the ability to control their businesses fully. Interestingly, a centralized, top-down approach seemed to have improved the MSE innovation effectiveness. The present study has given us some new perspectives on this issue. First, most interviewees seem to have taken the wrong direction regarding autonomy or control in their organizations. They began their businesses by providing autonomy, which, unfortunately, did not work. To tackle this, they acted as the center of everything in their organizations, which practically inhibited their business growth. They did so because they did not have individuals they could trust to run their businesses. As a result, these MSEs faced difficulties and failed to break the chains of both inertia and innovation failures.

Lastly, it is interesting to see that some interviewees mentioned spirituality as a way to boost their willingness and confidence to learn from failures. Burhan (male, 34yo) says:

> *I have failed many times. From selling clothes to selling this coconut based handicraft. Failure is a part of destiny. My duty is to survive the difficulties and hopefully it pleases God. My task is to keep trying. God willing, there must be a way. . . .*

The inclusion of spirituality as such is not new. Neubert et al. (2017) found the link between spiritual capital and SME innovation. In this sense, spiritual capital is seen as a set of resources that emerge from religion and are able to be used in entrepreneurial activities (Berger & Redding, 2011). Learning from failures can benefit MSEs if they possess capabilities to benefit from their resources, that is, spirituality. All interviewees are Muslims and live in West Sumatra, a province in Indonesia that has long been known as a source of both pious entrepreneurs in Indonesia. Such a cultural depiction likely influenced the mindset of some of the business owners in this study.

The findings of this study lead us to identify the following research frameworks (Fig. 1):

The present study offers some propositions as follows:

P1. Organizational inertia and innovation may be inseparable. Inertia can cause innovation failures or vice versa.

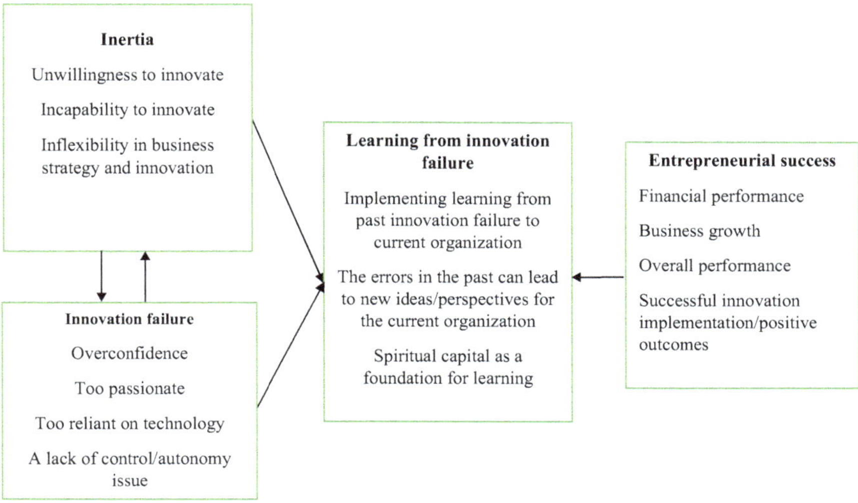

Fig. 1 Proposed framework resulting from the study. (Source: The authors)

P2. Institutional inertia and innovation failures may lead to entrepreneurial failures. However, implementing the learning from failures principle can lead to success.

P3. While most MSEs may encounter difficulties in becoming a real organization due to their inability to instill institutionalization in their organizations, the business owners can play a greater role in reflecting on their inertia and innovation failures. Therefore, only those who failed or experienced inertia and did not blame external factors for its emergence can fully benefit from failures. In the long run, it is expected that this practice will make the MSEs real organizations.

P4. Learning from innovation failures and inertia can be effectively implemented if MSEs have capable human resources whom the owners can trust. The present study discloses a situation in which the owners could not put their ideas into action as they did not have at least someone capable and trustworthy to control the organizations.

P5. Learning from innovation failures can overcome inertia if MSE owners fully utilize their resources, including spiritual capital. The MSE owners may construe hardship and failure as trials from God, which may help as an opener for learning from innovation failures.

5 Conclusion

MSEs may not be predominantly designed for business growth but they can still pave the way to success. Answering the research question of this study allows us to identify a key differentiator between typical MSEs and MSEs with business growth. The main differing factor is their ability to learn from failures, which, in turn, can be used to overcome inertia. All interviewees in this study indicate their preferences to escape inertia, although they may not fully understand how to do it. This study views inertia as an organization's unwillingness, incapability, and inflexibility in adopting and implementing innovation. In this study, the interviewees show willingness and flexibility because of their size and business owners. However, they are often incapable of innovating due to the absence of business strategies. This means that their inertia is not because of their lack of commitment, but it is caused by their poor business strategies. Therefore, their inertia and innovation failures can be seen as temporary; they can even serve as a turning point to succeed if they can learn from their past experiences. It is also worth noting that the present study provides some insights from the interviewees, reinforcing the idea that innovation may emerge due to a lack of control resulting from misled autonomy-motivated innovators. Most MSEs are a one-man or one-woman show in their organization. Consequently, they must take full control of their organizations or established organizations that embrace formal organizational structures. Either one needs at least one trustworthy employee to help the owners run the organizations. Most of the interviewees in this study lack this. Interestingly, the interviewees also refer to spirituality as a foundation for learning from failures. Spiritual capital may be seen as a source of resilience. In a broader sense, the present study reinforces the importance of learning from failures in the effort to reduce inertia from MSEs, which often lack institutionalization in their organizations.

Regarding managerial implications, the MSEs in this study show their resilience from inertia and failures to innovate by reflecting on the situations and learning from them. They also reflect on how inertia caused by the incapability to innovate can be solved by evaluating the cause of innovation failures in the past. The issue of autonomy innovators in this study captures the essence of learning from failures. It is found that autonomy and capability to innovate are closely linked. Policymakers may underestimate MSEs as the latter characteristically represent the necessity-based entrepreneurs who typically do not pursue business growth. However, due to the nature of most of the young business owners in this study, it is safe to say that the interviewees have had an openness to change and some familiarity with technologies. What they did not possess was the time to renew their commitment to reflect on their inertia and failures as a way to elevate their businesses. Also, they lacked trustworthy workers and managers.

Policymakers in small businesses can promote collaborative culture in which the MSE owners and workers/managers can be matched up. In the past, such matchings were designed for well-established business organizations. The online job market can be helpful, but offline events are preferable considering the issue of trustworthiness involving the knowledgeable-type managers/workers. In addition, policymakers can focus on business strategies for MSEs. Such a focus is important as the interviewees are merely confused with their stagnant situations. MSE incubation-like models can be implemented, particularly a one-on-one business consultation with experts.

Moreover, it is highly recommended that MSEs or larger organizations with MSE backgrounds sit together and discuss inertia and innovation failures from their perspectives. Success stories are encouraging; failure stories can also be useful in connecting the MSEs with realities and increasing eagerness to learn from failures. In addition, more incentives and attention can be devoted to those who have failed but tried their best to bounce back. Hence, MSE directories should also include MSE failure experiences along with solutions to overcome the problems.

This study applies a qualitative approach. As such, it is not designed to generalize its findings but offers more in-depth perspectives and patterns from the MSE owners. Future research may use propositions proposed in this study as the foundation of their research. They can also examine learning from innovation as a possible key differentiator for MSEs, enabling them to transform MSEs into high-growth businesses or opportunity-based entrepreneurships. More specifically, further research can focus on how both inertia and innovation failures play their roles in wider contexts by comparing cases in two different countries, in specific cultures, or startup phases, such as technology-based startups. On the whole, these MSEs may likely face institutional issues because they have limited resources. However, the MSEs that can learn from inertia and innovation failures and benefit from their resources, including spirituality, can expect better outcomes in the near future.

References

Asano, A., & Eto, T. (2007). Organisational inertia in Japanese institutions. *Journal of Asian Economics, 18*(6), 915–933.

Berger, P. L., & Redding, G. (2011). *The hidden form of capital: Spiritual influences in societal progress*. Anthem Press.

Boso, N., Adeleye, I., Donbesuur, F., & Gyensare, M. (2019). Do entrepreneurs always benefit from business failure experience? *Journal of Business Research, 98*, 370–379.

Bruton, G. D., & Ahlstrom, D. (2003). An institutional view of China's venture capital industry: Explaining the differences between China and the West. *Journal of Business Venturing, 18*(2), 233–259.

Cacciotti, G., Hayton, J. C., Mitchell, J. R., & Giazitzoglu, A. (2016). A reconceptualization of fear of failure in entrepreneurship. *Journal of Business Venturing, 31*(3), 302–325.

Cope, J. (2011). Entrepreneurial learning from failure: An interpretative phenomenological analysis. *Journal of Business Venturing, 26*(6), 604–623.

Corbett, A. C. (2007). Learning asymmetries and the discovery of entrepreneurial opportunities. *Journal of Business Venturing, 22*(1), 97–118.

Dana, L. P., Gurau, C., Light, I., & Muhammad, N. (2020). Family, community, and ethnic capital as entrepreneurial resources: Toward an integrated model. *Journal of Small Business Management, 58*(5), 1003–1029.

Daviy, A., & Shakina, E. (2021). Excess momentum or excess inertia: Do companies adopt technologies at the right time?☆,☆☆,★,★★. *European Research on Management and Business Economics, 27*(3), 100174.

Faghih, N., Bonyadi, E., & Sarreshtehdari, L. (2021). Comparison of the entrepreneurial motivation in different economic groups. *Journal of Global Entrepreneurship Research, 11*, 29–39. https://doi.org/10.1007/s40497-021-00268-z

Fiqri, H., & Yanuarta, R. (2022). The effect of financial literacy and education level on the profitability of micro and small enterprises in Indonesia. *Financial Management Studies, 2*(1), 57–66.

Forsman, H. (2021). Innovation failure in SMEs: A narrative approach to understand failed innovations and failed innovators. *International Journal of Innovation Management, 25*(09), 2150104.
Games, D. (2022). Innovating Indonesia: Strategic paths to be adopted from neighbouring countries. In *Context-based entrepreneurship* (pp. 95–105). Springer.
Games, D., & Rendi, R. P. (2019). The effects of knowledge management and risk taking on SME financial performance in creative industries in an emerging market: The mediating effect of innovation outcomes. *Journal of Global Entrepreneurship Research, 9*(1), 1–14.
Games, D., Soutar, G., & Sneddon, J. (2021). Personal values and SME innovation in a Muslim ethnic group in Indonesia. *Journal of Entrepreneurship in Emerging Economies, 13*(5), 1012–1032.
Godkin, L., & Allcorn, S. (2008). Overcoming organizational inertia: A tripartite model for achieving strategic organizational change. *The Journal of Applied Business and Economics, 8*(1), 82.
Haag, S. (2014). Organizational inertia as barrier to Firms' IT adoption – Multidimensional scale development and validation. Publications of Darmstadt Technical University, Institute for Business Studies (BWL) 82763, Darmstadt Technical University, Department of Business Administration, Economics and Law, Institute for Business Studies (BWL). Twentieth Americas Conference on Information Systems, Savannah, 2014.
Hannan, M. T., & Freeman, J. (1984). Structural inertia and organizational change. *American Sociological Review, 49*, 149–164.
Indarti, N. (2017). Impacts of external knowledge and interaction on innovation capability among Indonesian SMEs. *International Journal of Business Innovation and Research, 13*(4), 430–450.
Laperche, B., & Liu, Z. (2013). SMEs and knowledge-capital formation in innovation networks: A review of literature. *Journal of Innovation and Entrepreneurship, 2*(1), 1–16.
McGrath, R. G. (1999). Falling forward: Real options reasoning and entrepreneurial failure. *Academy of Management Review, 24*(1), 13–30.
Miles, M. B., Huberman, A. M., & Saldaña, J. (2014). *Qualitative data analysis. A methods sourcebook* (3rd ed.). Sage Publications.
Neubert, M. J., Bradley, S. W., Ardianti, R., & Simiyu, E. M. (2017). The role of spiritual capital in innovation and performance: Evidence from developing economies. *Entrepreneurship Theory and Practice, 41*(4), 621–640.
Rhaiem, K., & Amara, N. (2021). Learning from innovation failures: A systematic review of the literature and research agenda. *Review of Managerial Science, 15*(2), 189–234.
Samadi, A. H. (2019). Institutions and entrepreneurship: Unidirectional or bidirectional causality? *Journal of Global Entrepreneurhip Research, 9*, 3.
Sastry, M. A. (1997). Problems and paradoxes in a model of punctuated organizational change. *Administrative Science Quarterly, 42*, 237–275.
Stål, H. I. (2015). Inertia and change related to sustainability–an institutional approach. *Journal of Cleaner Production, 99*, 354–365.
Tambunan, T. (2019). Recent evidence of the development of micro, small and medium enterprises in Indonesia. *Journal of Global Entrepreneurship Research, 9*(1), 1–15.
Tushman, M. L., Virany, B., & Romanelli, E. (1985). Executive succession, strategic reorientations, and organization evolution: The minicomputer industry as a case in point. *Technology in Society, 7*(2–3), 297–313.
Ucbasaran, D., Westhead, P., Wright, M., & Flores, M. (2010). The nature of entrepreneurial experience, business failure and comparative optimism. *Journal of Business Venturing, 25*(6), 541–555.
Yamakawa, Y., & Cardon, M. S. (2015). Causal ascriptions and perceived learning from entrepreneurial failure. *Small Business Economics, 44*(4), 797–820.

Index

N. Faghih, A. H. Samadi (eds.), *Institutional Inertia*, Contributions to Economics,
https://doi.org/10.1007/978-3-031-51175-2

www.ingramcontent.com/pod-product-compliance
Ingram Content Group UK Ltd.
Pitfield, Milton Keynes, MK11 3LW, UK
UKHW022226051026
15624UKWH00002B/372
* 9 7 8 3 0 3 1 5 1 1 7 4 5 *